GUIDE TO
LITERARY AGENTS
2017

includes a one-year online subscription to **Guide to Literary Agents** on

Where & How to Sell What You Write

THE ULTIMATE MARKET RESEARCH TOOL FOR WRITERS

To register your *Guide to Literary Agents 2017* book and **start your one-year online subscription to listings related to literary agents**, scratch off the block below to reveal your activation code, then go to www.WritersMarket.com. Find the box that says "Purchased a Deluxe Edition?" then click on "Activate Your Account" and enter the activation code. It's that easy!

GLA-U37AL484

UPDATED MARKET LISTINGS FOR YOUR INTEREST AREA
EASY-TO-USE SEARCHABLE DATABASE • RECORD-KEEPING TOOLS
PROFESSIONAL TIPS & ADVICE • INDUSTRY NEWS

Your purchase of *Guide to Literary Agents* gives you access to updated listings related to literary agents (valid through 12/31/17). For just $9.99, you can upgrade your subscription and get access to listings from all of our best-selling Market Books. Visit **www.WritersMarket.com** for more information.

WritersMarket.com
Where & How to Sell What You Write

Activate your WritersMarket.com subscription to get instant access to:

- **UPDATED LISTINGS FOR AGENTS AND AGENCIES:** Find additional listings that didn't make it into the book, updated contact information, and more. WritersMarket.com provides the most comprehensive database of verified agents available anywhere.

- **EASY-TO-USE SEARCHABLE DATABASE:** Looking for a specific agent or agency? Just type in its name. Or widen your prospects with the Advanced Search. You can also search for listings that have been recently updated!

- **PERSONALIZED TOOLS:** Store your best-bet agent leads, and use our popular recording-keeping tools to track your queries. Plus, get new and updated agent listings, query reminders, and more every time you log in!

- **PROFESSIONAL TIPS & ADVICE:** From pay-rate charts to sample query letters, and from how-to articles to Q&As with literary agents, we have the resources writers need.

YOU'LL GET ALL OF THIS WITH YOUR INCLUDED SUBSCRIPTION TO

WritersMarket.com
Where & How to Sell What You Write

GLA17

◀ 26TH ANNUAL EDITION ▶

GUIDE TO LITERARY AGENTS

2017

Chuck Sambuchino, Editor

WRITER'S DIGEST
BOOKS

WritersDigest.com
Cincinnati, Ohio

Guide to Literary Agents 2017. Copyright © 2016 F+W Media. Published by Writer's Digest Books, an imprint of F+W, 10151 Carver Road, Suite 200, Blue Ash, Ohio 45242. Printed and bound in the United States of America. All rights reserved. No part of this book may be reproduced in any form or by any electronic or mechanical means, including information storage and retrieval systems, without permission in writing from the publisher, except by a reviewer, who may quote brief passages in a review.

Publisher: Phil Sexton

Writer's Market website: www.writersmarket.com
Writer's Digest website: www.writersdigest.com

Distributed in Canada by Fraser Direct
100 Armstrong Avenue
Georgetown, Ontario, Canada L7G 5S4
Tel: (905) 877-4411

Distributed in the U.K. and Europe by F+W: A Content & E-Commerce Company
Brunel House, Newton Abbot, Devon, TQ12 4PU, England
Tel: (+44) 1626-323200, Fax: (+44) 1626-323319
E-mail: postmaster@davidandcharles.co.uk

Library of Congress Catalog Number 31-20772
ISSN: 1078-6945
ISBN-13: 978-1-4403-4776-4
ISBN-10: 1-4403-4776-X

Attention Booksellers: This is an annual directory of F+W Media.
Return deadline for this edition is December 31, 2017.

Edited by: Chuck Sambuchino
Designed by: Claudean Wheeler
Production coordinated by: Debbie Thomas

CONTENTS

FROM THE EDITOR

A wonderful part of my job is helping writers answer their questions. And one of the most important questions any writer has regarding submissions is why an agent may stop considering their work. In other words: *What makes an agent say no? What makes an agent stop reading?* I sought answers to these questions in this edition of the *Guide to Literary Agents* with a new "Agents Evaluate First Pages" article—an incredible chance to read how four agents judge and analyze writers' unpublished first manuscript pages in real time. I hope you find the article as informative and eye-opening as I did.

Agents are still as hungry as ever for excellent manuscripts and book ideas, so if you want to find a helpful and enthusiastic advocate, you've come to the right place. Welcome to the 26th edition of *GLA*. As always, we have plenty of great instruction in these pages to help you get published: spotlights on new agents actively building their lists, query letter examples, synopsis writing tips, lists of writers conferences, and much more. Inside this resource is your future agent. Now start researching and find that perfect match.

Please stay in touch with me through my blog—www.guidetoliteraryagents.com/blog—or on Twitter (@chucksambuchino) and continue to pass along feedback and success stories. Until we next meet, good luck on your writing journey. (And don't forget to access your free webinar download at www.writersmarket.com/gla17-webinar.)

Chuck Sambuchino
Editor, *Guide to Literary Agents/Children's Writer's & Illustrator's Market*
Author, *Get a Literary Agent* (2015); *Create Your Writer Platform* (2012)

HOW TO USE
GUIDE TO LITERARY AGENTS

//

Searching for a literary agent can be overwhelming, whether you've just finished your first book or you have several publishing credits on your résumé. More than likely, you're eager to start pursuing agents and anxious to see your name on the spine of a book. But before you go directly to the listings in this book, take time to familiarize yourself with the way agents work and how you should approach them. By doing so, you will be more prepared for your search and, ultimately save yourself effort and unnecessary grief.

READ THE ARTICLES

This book begins with feature articles organized into three sections: **Getting Started**, **Contacting Agents**, and **Perspectives**. These articles explain how to prepare for representation, offer strategies for contacting agents, and provide perspectives on the author/agent relationship. You may want to start by reading through each one and then refer back to relevant articles during each stage of your search.

Because there are many ways to make that initial contact with an agent, we've also provided a section called. These personal accounts from agents and published authors offer information and inspiration for any writer hoping to find representation.

DECIDE WHAT YOU'RE LOOKING FOR

A literary agent will present your work directly to editors or producers. It's the agent's job to get her client's work published or sold, and to negotiate a fair contract. In the **Literary Agents** section, we list each agent's contact information and explain both what type of work the agency represents and how to submit your work for consideration.

For face-to-face contact, many writers prefer to meet agents at **Conferences**. By doing so, writers can assess an agent's personality, attend workshops, and have the chance to get more feedback on their work than they get by mailing submissions and waiting for a response. The Conferences section lists conferences agents and/or editors attend. In many cases, private consultations are available, and agents attend with the hope of finding new clients to represent.

UTILIZE THE EXTRAS

Aside from the articles and listings, this book offers a section of **Resources**. If you come across a term with which you aren't familiar, check out the Resources section for a quick explanation. Also, note the gray tabs along the edge of each page. The tabs identify each section so they are easier to flip to as you conduct your search.

Finally—and perhaps most importantly—are the **Indexes** in the back of the book. These can serve as an incredibly helpful way to start your search because they categorize the listings according to different criteria. For example, you can look for literary agents according to their specialties (fiction/nonfiction genres).

LISTING POLICY AND COMPLAINT PROCEDURE

Listings in *Guide to Literary Agents* are compiled from detailed questionnaires and information provided by agents. The industry is volatile, and agencies change frequently. We rely on our readers for information about their dealings with agents, as well as changes in policies or fees that differ from what has been reported to the editor of this book. Write to us (*Guide to Literary Agents*, F+W, 10151 Carver Road, Suite 200, Cincinnati, OH 45242) or e-mail us (literaryagent@fwcommunity.com) if you have new information, questions, or problems dealing with the agencies listed.

Listings are published free of charge and are not advertisements. Although the information is as accurate as possible, the listings are not endorsed or guaranteed by the editor or publisher of *Guide to Literary Agents*. If you feel you have not been treated fairly by an agent or representative listed in *Guide to Literary Agents*, we advise you to take the following steps:

- First try to contact the agency. Sometimes one letter or e-mail can clear up the matter. Politely relate your concern.
- Document all your correspondence with the agency. When you write to us with a complaint, provide the name of your manuscript, the date of your first contact with the agency, and the nature of your subsequent correspondence.
- We will keep your letter on file and attempt to contact the agency. The number, frequency, and severity of complaints will be considered when we decide whether or not to delete an agency's listing from the next edition.
- *Guide to Literary Agents* reserves the right to exclude any agency for any reason.

FREQUENTLY ASKED QUESTIONS

1. **WHY DO YOU INCLUDE AGENTS WHO ARE NOT SEEKING NEW CLIENTS?** Some agents ask that their listings indicate they are currently closed to new clients. We include them so writers know the agents exist and know not to contact them at this time.

2. **WHY ARE SOME AGENTS NOT LISTED?** Some agents may not have responded to our requests for information. We have taken others out of the book after we received complaints about them.

3. **DO I NEED MORE THAN ONE AGENT IF I WRITE IN DIFFERENT GENRES?** It depends. If you have written in one genre and want to switch to a new style of writing, ask your agent if she is willing to represent you in your new endeavor. Occasionally, an agent may feel she has no knowledge of a certain genre and will recommend an appropriate agent to her client. Regardless, you should always talk to your agent about any potential career move.

4. **WHY DON'T YOU LIST MORE FOREIGN AGENTS?** Most American agents have relationships with foreign co-agents in other countries. It is more common for an American agent to work with a co-agent to sell a client's book abroad than for a writer to work directly with a foreign agent. If you decide to query a foreign agent, make sure they represent American writers (if you're American). Some may request to receive submissions only from Canadians, for example, or from United Kingdom residents.

5. **DO AGENTS EVER CONTACT A SELF-PUBLISHED WRITER?** If a self-published author attracts the attention of the media, or if his book sells extremely well, an agent might approach the author in hopes of representing him.

6. **WHY WON'T THE AGENT I QUERIED RETURN MY MATERIAL?** An agent may not answer your query or return your manuscript for several reasons. Perhaps you did not include a self-addressed, stamped envelope (SASE). Many agents will discard a submission without a SASE. Or the agent may have moved. To avoid using expired addresses, use the most current edition of *Guide to Literary Agents* or access the information online at www.writersmarket.com. Another possibility is that the agent is swamped with submissions. An agent can be overwhelmed with queries, especially if the agent recently has spoken at a conference or has been featured in an article or book. Also, some agents specify in their listings that they never return materials of any kind.

WHAT AN AGENT DOES

The scoop on day-to-day responsibilities.

A writer's job is to write. A literary agent's job is to find publishers for her clients' books. Because publishing houses receive more and more unsolicited manuscripts each year, securing an agent is becoming increasingly necessary. But finding an eager and reputable agent can be a difficult task. Even the most patient writer can become frustrated or disillusioned. As a writer seeking agent representation, you should prepare yourself before starting your search. Learn when to approach agents, as well as what to expect from an author/agent relationship. Beyond selling manuscripts, an agent must keep track of the ever-changing industry, writers' royalty statements, fluctuating market trends—and the list goes on.

So you face the question: Do I need an agent? The answer, much more often than not, is yes.

WHAT CAN AN AGENT DO FOR YOU?

For starters, today's competitive marketplace can be difficult to break into, especially for unpublished writers. Many larger publishing houses will only look at manuscripts from agents—and rightfully so, as they would be inundated with unsatisfactory writing if they did not. In fact, approximately 80 percent of books published by the five major houses are acquired through agents.

But an agent's job isn't just getting your book through a publisher's door. The following describes the various jobs agents do for their clients, many of which would be difficult for a writer to do without outside help.

Agents know editors' tastes and needs

An agent possesses information on a complex web of publishing houses and a multitude of editors to ensure her clients' manuscripts are placed in the right hands. This knowledge is gathered through relationships she cultivates with acquisitions editors—the people who decide which books to present to their publisher for possible publication. Through her industry connections, an agent becomes aware of the specializations of publishing houses and their imprints, knowing that one publisher wants only contemporary romances while another is interested solely in nonfiction books about the military. By networking with editors, an agent also learns more specialized information—which editor is looking for a crafty Agatha Christie–style mystery for the fall catalog, for example.

Agents track changes in publishing

Being attentive to constant market changes and shifting trends is another major requirement of an agent. An agent understands what it may mean for clients when publisher A merges with publisher B and when an editor from house C moves to house D. Or what it means when readers—and therefore editors—are no longer interested in westerns but can't get their hands on enough suspense novels.

Agents get your work read faster

Although it may seem like an extra step to send your work to an agent instead of directly to a publishing house, the truth is that an agent can prevent you from wasting months sending manuscripts that end up in the wrong place or buried in someone's slush pile. Editors rely on agents to save them time as well. With little time to sift through the hundreds of unsolicited submissions arriving weekly in the mail, an editor is naturally going to prefer a work that has already been approved by a qualified reader (i.e., the agent) who knows the editor's preferences. For this reason, many of the larger publishers accept agented submissions only.

Agents understand contracts

When publishers write contracts, they are primarily interested in their own bottom line rather than the best interests of the author. Writers unfamiliar with contractual language may find themselves bound to a publisher with whom they no longer want to work. Or they may find themselves tied to a publisher who prevents them from getting royalties on their first book until subsequent books are written. Agents use their experiences and knowledge to negotiate a contract that benefits the writer while still respecting the publisher's needs. After all, more money for the author will almost always mean more money for the agent—another reason they're on your side.

Agents negotiate—and exploit—subsidiary rights

Beyond publication, a savvy agent keeps in mind other opportunities for your manuscript. If your agent believes your book also will be successful as an audio book, a Book-of-the-Month-Club selection, or even a blockbuster movie, she will take these options into consideration when shopping your manuscript. These additional opportunities for writers are called subsidiary rights. Part of an agent's job is to keep track of the strengths and weaknesses of different publishers' subsidiary rights offices to determine the deposition of these rights regarding your work. After contracts are negotiated, agents will seek additional moneymaking opportunities for the rights they kept for their clients.

Agents get escalators

An escalator is a bonus an agent can negotiate as part of the book contract. It is commonly given when a book appears on a bestseller list or if a client appears on a popular television show. For example, a publisher might give a writer a $30,000 bonus if he is picked for a book club. Both the agent and the editor know such media attention will sell more books, and the agent negotiates an escalator to ensure the writer benefits from this increase in sales.

Agents track payments

Because an agent receives payment only when the publisher pays the writer, it's in the agent's best interest to make sure the writer is paid on schedule. Some publishing houses are notorious for late payments. Having an agent distances you from any conflict regarding payment and allows you to spend time writing instead of making phone calls.

Agents are advocates

Besides standing up for your right to be paid on time, agents can ensure your book gets a better cover design, more attention from the publisher's marketing department, or other benefits you may not know to ask for during the publishing process. An agent also can provide advice during each step of the way, as well as guidance about your long-term writing career.

Are you ready for an agent?

Now that you know what an agent is capable of, ask yourself if you and your work are at a stage where you need an agent. Look at the to-do lists for fiction and nonfiction writers in this article and judge how prepared you are for contacting an agent. Have you spent enough time researching or polishing your manuscript? Does your nonfiction book proposal include everything it should? Is your novel completely finished? Sending an agent an incomplete project not only wastes your time but also may turn off the agent in the process. Is the work thoroughly revised? If you've finished your project, set it aside for a few weeks, then examine it again with fresh eyes. Give your novel or proposal to critique group partners ("beta readers") for feedback. Join up with peers in your community or a writing site online.

BEFORE YOU SUBMIT YOUR FICTION BOOK

1. Finish your novel manuscript or short story collection. An agent can do nothing for fiction without a finished product. Never query with an incomplete novel.
2. Revise your manuscript. Seek critiques from other writers or an independent editor to ensure your work is as polished as possible.
3. Proofread. Don't ruin a potential relationship with an agent by submitting work that contains typos or poor grammar.
4. Publish short stories or novel excerpts in literary journals, which will prove to prospective agents that editors see quality in your writing.
5. Research to find the agents of writers whose works you admire or are similar to yours.
6. Use the Internet and resources like *Guide to Literary Agents* to construct a list of agents who are open to new writers and looking for your category of fiction. (Jump to the listings sections of this book to start now.)
7. Rank your list according to the agents most suitable for you and your work.
8. Write your novel synopsis.
9. Write your query letter. As an agent's first impression of you, this brief letter should be polished and to the point.
10. Educate yourself about the business of agents so you will be prepared to act on any offer. This guide is a great place to start.

Moreover, your work may not be appropriate for an agent. Most agents do not represent poetry, magazine articles, short stories, or material suitable for academic or small presses; the agent's commission does not justify spending time submitting these types of works. Those agents who do take on such material generally represent authors on larger projects first and then adopt the smaller items as a favor to the client.

If you believe your work is ready to be placed with an agent, make sure you're personally ready to be represented. In other words, consider the direction in which your writing career is headed. Besides skillful writers, agencies want clients with the ability to produce more than one book. Most agents say they're looking to represent careers, not books.

WHEN DON'T YOU NEED AN AGENT?

Although there are many reasons to work with an agent, some authors can benefit from submitting their own work directly to book publishers. For example, if your project focuses on a very specific area, you may want to work with a small or specialized press. These houses usually are open to receiving material directly from writers. Small presses

BEFORE YOU SUBMIT YOUR NONFICTION BOOK

1. Formulate a concrete idea for your book. Sketch a brief outline, making sure you'll have enough material for a book-length manuscript.
2. Research works on similar topics to understand the competition and determine how your book is unique.
3. Write sample chapters. This will help you estimate how much time you'll need to complete the work and determine whether or not your writing will need editorial help. You will also need to include a few sample chapters in the proposal itself.
4. Publish completed chapters in journals and/or magazines. This validates your work to agents and provides writing samples for later in the process.
5. Polish your nonfiction book proposal so you can refer to it while drafting a query letter—and to be prepared when agents contact you.
6. Brainstorm three to four subject categories that best describe your material.
7. Use the Internet and resources like *Guide to Literary Agents* to construct a list of agents who are open to new writers and looking for your category of nonfiction.
8. Rank your list. Research agent websites and narrow your list further, according to your preferences.
9. Write your query. Give an agent an excellent first impression by professionally and succinctly describing your premise and your experience.
10. Educate yourself about the business of agents so you can act on any offer.

often can give more attention to writers than large houses can, providing editorial help, marketing expertise, and other advice. Academic books or specialized nonfiction books (such as a book about the history of Rhode Island) are good bets for unagented writers.

Beware, though, as you will now be responsible for reviewing and negotiating all parts of your contract and payment. If you choose this path, it's wise to use a lawyer or entertainment attorney to review all contracts. Lawyers who specialize in intellectual property can help writers with contract negotiations. Instead of earning a commission on resulting book sales, lawyers are paid only for their time.

And, of course, some people prefer working independently instead of relying on others. If you're one of these people, it's probably better to submit your own work instead of potentially butting heads with an agent. Let's say you manage to sign with one of the few literary agents who represents short story collections. If the collection gets shopped around to publishers for several months and no one bites, your agent may suggest retooling the work into a novel. Agents suggest changes—some bigger than others—and not all writers think their work is malleable. It's all a matter of what you're writing and how you feel about it.

ASSESSING CREDIBILITY

Check out agents before you query.

//

Many people wouldn't buy a used car without at least checking the odometer, and savvy shoppers would consult the blue books, take a test drive, and even ask for a mechanic's opinion. Much like the savvy car shopper, you want to obtain the best possible agent for your writing, so you should research the business of agents before sending out query letters. Understanding how agents operate will help you find an agent appropriate for your work, as well as alert you about the types of agents to avoid.

Many writers take for granted that any agent who expresses interest in their work is trustworthy. They'll sign a contract before asking any questions and simply hope everything will turn out all right. We often receive complaints from writers regarding agents *after* they have lost money or have work bound by contract to an ineffective agent. If writers put the same amount of effort into researching agents as they did writing their full manuscripts, they would save themselves unnecessary grief.

The best way to educate yourself is to read all you can about agents and other authors. Organizations such as the Association of Authors' Representatives (AAR; www.aar-online.org), the National Writers Union (NWU; www.nwu.org), American Society of Journalists and Authors (ASJA; www.asja.org) and Poets & Writers, Inc. (www.pw.org), all have informational material on finding and working with an agent.

The magazine *Publishers Weekly* (www.publishersweekly.com) covers publishing news affecting agents and others in the publishing industry. The Publishers Lunch newsletter (www.publishersmarketplace.com) comes free via e-mail every workday and offers news on agents and editors, job postings, recent book sales, and more.

Even the Internet has a wide range of sites where you can learn basic information about preparing for your initial contact, as well as specific details on individual agents. You can also find online forums and listservs, which keep authors connected and allow them to share experiences they've had with different editors and agents. Keep in mind, however, that not everything printed on the Web is fact; you may come across the site of a writer who is bitter because an agent rejected his manuscript. Your best bet is to use the Internet to supplement your other research.

Once you've established what your resources are, it's time to see which agents meet your criteria. Below are some of the key items to pay attention to when researching agents.

LEVEL OF EXPERIENCE

Through your research, you will discover the need to be wary of some agents. Anybody can go to the neighborhood copy center and order business cards that say "literary agent," but that title doesn't mean she can sell your book. She may lack the proper connections with others in the publishing industry, and an agent's reputation with editors can be a major strength or weakness.

Agents who have been in the business awhile have a large number of contacts and carry the most clout with editors. They know the ins and outs of the industry and are often able to take more calculated risks. However, veteran agents can be too busy to take on new clients or might not have the time to help develop an author. Newer agents, on the other hand, may be hungrier, as well as more open to unpublished writers. They probably have a smaller client list and are able to invest the effort to make your book a success.

If it's a new agent without a track record, be aware that you're taking more of a risk signing with her than with a more established agent. However, even a new agent should not be new to publishing. Many agents were editors before they were agents, or they worked at an agency as an assistant. This experience is crucial for making contacts in the publishing industry, and learning about rights and contracts. The majority of listings in this book explain how long the agent has been in business, as well as what she did before becoming an agent. You could also ask the agent to name a few editors off the top of her head who she thinks may be interested in your work and why they sprang to mind. Has she sold to them before? Do they publish books in your genre?

If an agent has no contacts in the business, she has no more clout than you do. Without publishing prowess, she's just an expensive mailing service. Anyone can make photocopies, slide them into an envelope, and address them to "Editor." Unfortunately, without a contact name and a familiar return address on the envelope, or a phone call from a trusted colleague letting an editor know a wonderful submission is on its way, your work will land in the slush pile with all the other submissions that don't have representation. You can do your own mailings with higher priority than such an agent could.

PAST SALES

Agents should be willing to discuss their recent sales with you: how many, what type of books, and to what publishers. Keep in mind, though, that some agents consider this in-

WARNING SIGNS

- Excessive typos or poor grammar in an agent's correspondence.

- A form letter accepting you as a client and praising generic things about your book that could apply to any book. A good agent doesn't take on a new client very often, so when she does, it's a special occasion that warrants a personal note or phone call.

- Unprofessional contracts that ask you for money up front, contain clauses you haven't discussed, or are covered with amateur clip-art or silly borders.

- Rudeness when you inquire about any points you're unsure of. Don't employ any business partner who doesn't treat you with respect.

- Pressure, by way of threats, bullying, or bribes. A good agent is not desperate to represent more clients. She invites worthy authors but leaves the final decision up to them.

- Promises of publication. No agent can guarantee you a sale. Not even the top agents sell everything they choose to represent. They can only send your work to the most appropriate places, have it read with priority, and negotiate you a better contract if a sale does happen.

- A print-on-demand book contract or any contract offering you no advance. You can sell your own book to an e-publisher any time you wish without an agent's help. An agent should pursue traditional publishing routes with respectable advances.

- Reading fees from $25–$500 or more. The fee is usually nonrefundable, but sometimes agents agree to refund the money if they take on a writer as a client, or if they sell the writer's manuscript. Keep in mind, however, that payment of a reading fee does not ensure representation.

- No literary agents who charge reading fees are listed in this book. It's too risky of an option for writers, plus non-fee-charging agents have a stronger incentive to sell your work. After all, they don't make a dime until they make a sale. If you find that a literary agent listed in this book charges a reading fee, please contact the editor at literaryagent@fwcommunity.com.

formation confidential. If an agent does give you a list of recent sales, you can call the publishers' contracts department to ensure the sale was actually made by that agent. While it's true that even top agents are not able to sell every book they represent, an inexperienced agent who proposes too many inappropriate submissions will quickly lose her standing with editors.

You can also find out details of recent sales on your own. Nearly all of the listings in this book offer the titles and authors of books with which the agent has worked. Some of them also note to which publishing house the book was sold. Again, you can call the publisher and affirm the sale. If you don't have the publisher's information, simply go to your local library or bookstore to see if they carry the book. Consider checking to see if it's available on websites like Amazon.com, too. You may want to be wary of the agent if her books are nowhere to be found or are only available through the publisher's website. Distribution is a crucial component to getting published, and you want to make sure the agent has worked with competent publishers.

TYPES OF FEES

Becoming knowledgeable about the different types of fees agents may charge is vital to conducting effective research. Most agents make their living from the commissions they receive after selling their clients' books, and these are the agents we've listed. Be sure to ask about any expenses you don't understand so you have a clear grasp of what you're paying for. Described here are some types of fees you may encounter in your research.

Office fees

Occasionally, an agent will charge for the cost of photocopies, postage, and long-distance phone calls made on your behalf. This is acceptable, so long as she keeps an itemized account of the expenses and you've agreed on a ceiling cost. The agent should only ask for office expenses after agreeing to represent the writer. These expenses should be discussed up front, and the writer should receive a statement accounting for them. This money is sometimes returned to the author upon sale of the manuscript. Be wary if there is an upfront fee amounting to hundreds of dollars, which is excessive.

Reading fees

Agencies that charge reading fees often do so to cover the cost of additional readers or the time spent reading that could have been spent selling. Agents also claim that charging reading fees cuts down on the number of submissions they receive. This practice can save the agent time and may allow her to consider each manuscript more extensively. Whether such promises are kept depends upon the honesty of the agency. You may pay a fee and never receive a response from the agent, or you may pay someone who never submits your manuscript to publishers.

Officially, the Association of Authors' Representatives' (AAR) Canon of Ethics prohibits members from directly or indirectly charging a reading fee, and the Writers Guild of America (WGA) does not allow WGA signatory agencies to charge a reading fee to WGA members, as stated in the WGA's Artists' Manager Basic Agreement. A signatory may charge you a fee if you are not a member, but most signatory agencies do not charge a reading fee as an across-the-board policy.

Critique fees

Sometimes a manuscript will interest an agent, but the agent will point out areas requiring further development and offer to critique it for an additional fee. Like reading fees, payment of a critique fee does not ensure representation. When deciding if you will benefit from having someone critique your manuscript, keep in mind that the quality and quantity of comments varies from agent to agent. The critique's usefulness will depend on the agent's knowledge of the market. Also be aware that agents who spend a significant portion of their time commenting on manuscripts will have less time to actively market work they already represent.

In other cases, the agent may suggest an editor who understands your subject matter or genre, and has some experience getting manuscripts into shape. Occasionally, if your story is exceptional, or your ideas and credentials are marketable but your writing needs help, you will work with a ghostwriter or co-author who will share a percentage of your commission, or work with you at an agreed-upon cost per hour.

An agent may refer you to editors she knows, or you may choose an editor in your area. Many editors do freelance work and would be happy to help you with your writing project. Of course, before entering into an agreement, make sure you know what you'll be getting for your money. Ask the editor for writing samples, references or critiques he's done in the past. Make sure you feel comfortable working with him before you give him your business.

An honest agent will not make any money for referring you to an editor. We strongly advise writers not to use critiquing services offered through an agency. Instead, try hiring a freelance editor or joining a writer's group until your work is ready to be submitted to agents who don't charge fees.

HOW TO WRITE A SYNOPSIS

6 tips to compose your novel summary.

by Chuck Sambuchino

I've never met a single person who liked writing a synopsis. Seriously—not one. But still, synopses are a necessary part of the submission process (until some brave publishing pro outlaws them), so I wanted to share tips and guidelines regarding how to compose one.

A synopsis is a *summary* of your book. Literary agents and editors may ask to see one if you're writing an adult novel, a memoir, or a kids novel (young adult, middle-grade). The purpose of a synopsis request is for the agent or editor to evaluate what happens in the three acts of your story and decide if the characters, plot, and conflict warrant a complete read of your manuscript. And if you haven't guessed yet, these summaries can be pretty tough to write.

SYNOPSIS GUIDELINES

Here are some guidelines that will help you understand the basics of synopsis writing, no matter what your novel or memoir is about:

1. REVEAL EVERYTHING MAJOR THAT HAPPENS IN YOUR BOOK, EVEN THE ENDING.
Heck, revealing the story's ending is a synopsis's defining unique characteristic. You shouldn't find a story's ending in a query or in-person pitch, but it does leak out in a synopsis. On this note, know that a synopsis is designed to explain *everything major* that happens, not to tease—so avoid language such as "Krista walks around a corner into a big surprise." Don't say "surprise," but rather just tell us what happens. This touches upon a bigger point. The most common failure of a synopsis is that it confuses the reader. Have no language in your page that is vague and undefined that could lead to multiple interpretations. One of the fundamental purposes of a synopsis is to show your book's narrative arc, and how your story possesses rising action, the three-act structure, and a satisfying ending.

2. MAKE YOUR SYNOPSIS ONE PAGE, SINGLE-SPACED. There is always some disagreement on length. This stems from the fact that synopses used to trend longer (four, six, or even eight pages). But over the last five years, agents have requested shorter and shorter synopses—with most agents finally settling on one or two pages, total. If you write yours as one page, single-spaced, it's the same length as two pages, double-spaced—and either are acceptable. There will be the occasional agent who requests something strange, such as a "five-page synopsis on beige paper that smells of cinnamon!" But if you turn in a solid one-page work, you'll be just fine across the board. In my opinion, it's the gold standard.

3. TAKE MORE CARE AND TIME IF YOU'RE WRITING GENRE FICTION. Synopses are especially difficult to compose if you're writing character-driven (i.e., literary) fiction, because there may not be a whole lot of plot in the book. Agents and editors understand this, and put little (or no) weight into a synopsis for literary or character-driven stories. However, if you're writing genre fiction—specifically categories like romance, fantasy, thriller, mystery, horror, or science fiction—agents will quickly want to look over your characters and plot points to make sure your book has a clear beginning, middle, and end, as well as some unique aspects they haven't seen before in a story. So if you're getting ready to submit a genre story, don't blow through your synopsis; it's important.

4. FEEL FREE TO BE DRY, BUT DON'T STEP OUT OF THE NARRATIVE. When you write your prose (and even the pitch in your query letter), there is importance in using style and voice in the writing. A synopsis, thankfully, not only can be dry, but probably *should* be dry. The synopsis has to explain everything that happens in a very small amount of space. So if you find yourself using short sentences like "John shoots Bill and then sits down to contemplate suicide," don't worry. This is normal. Lean, clean language is great. Use active verbs and always strive for clarity. And lastly, do not step out of the narrative. Agents do not want to read things such as "And at the climax of the story," "In a rousing scene," or "In a flashback."

5. CAPITALIZE CHARACTER NAMES WHEN CHARACTERS ARE INTRODUCED. Whenever a new character is introduced, make sure to CAPITALIZE them in the first mention and then use normal text throughout. This helps a literary agent immediately recognize each important name. On this subject, avoid naming too many characters, and try to set a limit of five, with no more than six total. I know this may sound tough, but it's doable. It forces you to excise smaller characters and subplots from your summary—actually strengthening your novel synopsis along the way. Sometimes writers fall in love with a minor character or joke or setting, and insist on squeezing in mentions of these elements into the synopsis, even though they are not a piece of the larger plot. These mistakes will water down your summary, and also cause the synopsis to be more than one page.

6. USE THIRD-PERSON, PRESENT-TENSE. The exception of this is memoir. While you can write your memoir synopsis in third person, it's probably a better idea to write it in first person. "Feeling stifled: I enlist in the Army that very day."

Every agent has a different opinion of the synopsis. Some agents openly state in interviews that they're well aware of how difficult a synopsis is to write, and they put little consideration into them. But we must presume that most or all of the agents who do not openly speak out against synopses put some weight into them, and that's why it's important for you to treat this step with care.

A poor synopsis will confuse the reader, and during the pitching process, confusion equals death. A poor synopsis will also reveal big problems in your story, such as strange plot points, how ridiculous acts of God get the main character out of tight situations, or how your romance actually ends in a divorce (a major category no-no).

CHUCK SAMBUCHINO (www.chucksambuchino.com, @chucksambuchino) edits *Guide to Literary Agents* (www.guidetoliteraryagents.com/blog) as well as *Children's Writer's & Illustrator's Market*. His humor books include *How to Survive a Garden Gnome Attack* (film rights optioned by Sony) and *When Clowns Attack: A Survival Guide* (Sept. 2015, Ten Speed Press). Chuck's other writing guides include *Formatting & Submitting Your Manuscript (3rd. Ed.)*, *Create Your Writer Platform*, and *Get a Literary Agent*. Besides that, he is a husband, guitarist, father, dog owner, and cookie addict.

NONFICTION BOOK PROPOSALS

Pitch your nonfiction with confidence.

....

by Chuck Sambuchino

A *book proposal* is a business plan that explains the details of a nonfiction book. Because your project is not complete during the pitching stages, the proposal acts as a blueprint and diagram for what the finished product will look like, as well as exactly how you will promote it when the product is in the marketplace.

Better yet, think about it like this: If you wanted to open a new restaurant and needed a bank loan, you would have to make a case to the bank as to why your business will succeed and generate revenue. A book proposal acts in much the same way. You must prove to a publisher that your book idea is a proven means to generate revenue—showing that customers will buy your worthwhile and unique product, and you have the means to draw in prospective customers.

"There are several factors that can help a book proposal's prospects: great writing, great platform, or great information, and ideally all three," says Ted Weinstein, founder of Ted Weinstein Literary. "For narrative works, the writing should be gorgeous, not just functional. For practical works, the information should be insightful, comprehensive, and preferably new. And for any work of nonfiction, of course, the author's platform is enormously important."

If you're writing a work of fiction (novel, screenplay, picture book) or memoir, the first all-important step is to simply *finish* the work, because agents and editors will consider it for publication based primarily on how good the writing is. On the other hand, when you have a nonfiction project of any kind, you do *not* need to finish the book to sell it. In fact, even if you're feeling ambitious and knock out the entire text, finishing the book will not help you sell it because all an editor really needs to see are several sample chapters that adequately portray what the rest of the book will be like.

THE STRUCTURE OF A BOOK PROPOSAL

A book proposal is made up of several key sections that flesh out the book, its markets, and information about the author. All of these important sections seek to answer one of the three main questions that every proposal must answer:

1. What is the book, and why is it timely and unique?
2. What is its place in the market?
3. Why are you the best person to write and market it?

Every book proposal has several sections that allow the author to explain more about their book. Though you can sometimes vary the order of the sections, here are the major elements (and suggested order) that should be addressed before you pitch a nonfiction book to a literary agent.

TITLE PAGE. Keep it simple. Put your title and subtitle in the middle, centered—and put your personal contact information at the bottom right.

TABLE OF CONTENTS (WITH PAGE NUMBERS). A nonfiction book proposal has several sections, and can run many pages, so this is where you explain everything the agent can find in the proposal, in case they want to jump around immediately to peruse different sections at different times.

OVERVIEW. This section gets its name because it's designed to be an overview of the entire proposal to come. It's something of a "greatest hits" of the proposal, where you discuss the concept and content, the evidence of need for this new resource in the market, and your platform. Overviews typically run up to three double-spaced pages, and immediately make the case as to why this book is worthwhile for consideration and timely for readers *now*. Another way to think about this section is by imagining it as an extended query letter, because it serves the same purpose. If an agent likes your overview, they will review the rest of the document to delve deeper into both you and your ideas. The overview is arguably the most important part of the proposal. "Your overview is the sizzle in your nonfiction book proposal," says agent Michael Larsen of Larsen/Pomada Literary Agents. "If it doesn't sell you and your book, agents and editors won't check the bones (the outline of your book) or try the steak (your sample chapter)."

FORMAT. This section explains how the book will be formatted. Remember that your finished, completed product does not physically exist, and all nonfiction books look different from one another in terms of appearance. So spell out exactly what it will look like. What is the physical size of the book? What is your estimated word count when everything is said and done? How long after the contract is signed will you be able to submit the finished product? Will there be sidebars, boxed quotes, or interactive elements? Will there be photos, illustrations, or other art? (If so, who will be responsible for collecting this art?)

SPINOFFS (OPTIONAL). Some nonfiction projects lend themselves to things like sequels, spinoffs, subsidiary rights possibilities, and more. For example, when I pitched my political humor book for dog lovers, *Red Dog / Blue Dog*, this is the section where I mentioned the possibility of a tear-off calendar if the book succeeded, as well as a possible sequel, *Red Cat / Blue Cat*. Unlike other sections of a proposal, this one is optional, as some ideas will *not* lend to more variations.

CHAPTER LIST. While you will only be turning over a few completed, polished chapters, agents still want to know exactly what will be in the rest of the book. So list out all your chapter concepts, with a paragraph or so on the content of each. This section is important, as it shows that, although the book is not complete, the author has a clear path forward in terms of the exact content that will fill all the pages.

SAMPLE CHAPTERS. Although you do not have to finish the book before pitching nonfiction, you do have to complete up to four book chapters as an appropriate sample. The goal is to write chapters that you believe give a great representation as to what the book is about. Typical sample chapters include the book's first chapter, and the others from different sections of the book. Your goal is to make these chapters represent what the final product will be like in both appearance and content. So if the book is going to be funny, your sample chapters better be humorous. If the book will be infused with art and illustrations, gather what images you can to insert in the pages. The sample chapters are the one place in a proposal where the author can step out of "business mode" and into "writer mode"—focusing on things like voice, humor, style, and more.

TARGET AUDIENCES. You've probably heard before that "a book for everyone is a book for no one," so target your work to small, core, focused audience groups. This section is your chance to prove an *evidence of need*. Or, as agent Mollie Glick of Foundry Literary + Media says, "You want an original idea—but not too original."

For example, when I was listing audiences for my book, *How to Survive a Garden Gnome Attack*, they were (1) garden gnome enthusiasts, (2) gardeners, (3) survival guide parody lovers, and (4) humor book lovers. Note how I resisted the urge to say "Everyone everywhere loves a laugh, so I basically see the entire human population snatching this bad boy up at bookstores."

When I was pitching a book on historical theaters around the country, my audiences were (1) theater lovers, (2) historical preservationists in the regions where featured theaters are located, (3) nostalgia lovers, and (4) architecture buffs and enthusiasts. Again, the audiences were concise and focused. I proved I had done my

AN AGENT EXPLAINS 3 COMMON BOOK PROPOSAL PROBLEMS

1. LACK OF A STORY ARC. Many failed nonfiction proposals are mere surveys of a subject. The books that sell have strong characters who are engaged in some project that eventually is resolved. Don't do a book about slime mold. Do a book about the Slime Mold Guy who solved the mystery of slime mold.

2. SKIMPINESS. I like big fat proposals. Writers worry too much about how much reading editors have to do and they self-defeatingly try to keep proposals short. Busy editors are not the problem. A great proposal will hook a reader within a few pages and keep that reader spellbound until the last page no matter how long. Short, skimpy proposals often quit before they can get me, or an editor, truly immersed and engaged. You aren't just informing us about your book, you are recruiting us into joining you on what is going to be a long and expensive expedition. If crazy, fire-eyed Christopher Columbus wants me to join him on his trip to the "Here Be Monsters" part of the ocean, I'd like to inspect his ships very, very carefully before I set sail. Editors are scared to buy books because they are so often wrong. Thoroughness builds confidence.

3. EXTRAPOLATION. Many proposals say, in effect, "I don't know all that much about this subject, but give me a six-figure contract and I will go and find out everything there is to know." I understand the problem writers face: How are they supposed to master a subject until after they've done the travels, interviews, and research? Nevertheless, unless you are already an established writer, you can't simply promise to master your subject. Book contracts go to those who have already mastered a subject. If you haven't mastered your subject but you really think you deserve a book contract, try to get a magazine assignment so that you can do at least some of the necessary research, funded by the magazine. But if you're just winging it, I probably can't help you unless you have a superb platform.

Sidebar courtesy of literary agent Russell Galen (Scovil Galen Ghosh Literary Agency).

research and honed in on the exact pockets of people who would pay money for what I was proposing.

And once you identify these audiences, you must *quantify* them. If you want to write a book about the history of the arcade game Donkey Kong, a logical target audience would be "Individuals who currently play Donkey Kong"—but you must quantify the audience, because an agent has no idea if that audience size is 1,000 or 500,000. So tell them what it really is—and explain how you came to find that true number. You can find these quantifying numbers by seeing where such audiences get their news. For example, if www.donkeykong news.com has a newsletter reach of 12,000 individuals, that is a proven number you can use.

If the official Donkey Kong Twitter account has 134,000 followers, that will help you, as well. If *Classic Games Magazine* has a circulation of 52,000, that number can help you, too. "Use round, accurate numbers in your proposal," Larsen says. "If a number isn't round, qualify it by writing nearly, almost, or more than (not over). Provide sources for statistics if asked."

COMPARATIVE TITLES. This is where you list any and all books that are similar to yours in the marketplace. What you're aiming for is showing that many books that have similarities to your title exist and have healthy sales, but no one book accomplishes everything yours will do. If you can show that, you've made an argument that your book is unique (and therefore worthwhile), and also that people have shown a history of buying such a book (and therefore the book is even more worthwhile). You're essentially trying to say "Books exist on Subject A and books exist on Subject B, but no book exists on Subject AB, which is exactly what my book, [*Title*], will do."

You can find comparative titles by searching through the appropriate bookshelf in Barnes & Noble or any local bookstore, as well as by scouring Amazon. Once you have your list, it's your time to write them all down—laying out details such as the publisher, title, year, and any signs of solid sales (such as awards or a good Amazon sales ranking). After you explain a book's specifics, you should quickly say why your book is different from it. At the same time, don't trash competing books. Because your book shares some similarity to it, you don't want your own work to come under fire.

MARKETING / WRITER PLATFORM. This massively important section details all the many avenues you have in place to market the work to the audiences you've already identified. This section will list out your social media channels, contacts in the media, personal marketing abilities, public speaking engagements, and much more. This section is of the utmost importance, as an agent needs to be assured you can currently market your book to thousands of possible buyers, if not more. Otherwise, the agent may stop reading the proposal. "Develop a significant following before you go out with your nonfiction book. If you build it, publishers will come," says agent Jeffery McGraw of The August Agency. "How visible are you to the world? That's what determines your level of platform. Someone with real platform is the 'go to' person in their area of expertise. If you don't make yourself known to the world as the expert in your field, then how will [members of the media] know to reach out to you? Get out there. Make as many connections as you possibly can."

AUTHOR BIO / CREDENTIALS. Now is your chance to explain what makes you qualified to write the content in this book. Tell the agent things such as your degrees, memberships, endorsements, and more. Anything that qualifies you to write this book but is not technically considered "platform" should go in this section.

CRAFTING A QUERY

How to write a great letter that gets agents' attention.

....

by Kara Gebhart Uhl

So you've written a book. And now you want an agent. If you're new to publishing, you probably assume that the next step is to send your finished, fabulous book out to agents, right? Wrong. Agents don't want your finished, fabulous book. In fact, they probably don't even want *part* of your finished, fabulous book—at least, not yet. First, they want your query.

A query is a short, professional way of introducing yourself to an agent. If you're frustrated by the idea of this step, imagine yourself at a cocktail party. Upon meeting someone new, you don't greet them with a boisterous hug and kiss and, in three minutes, reveal your entire life story including the fact that you were late to the party because of some gastrointestinal problems. Rather, you extend your hand. You state your name. You comment on the hors d'oeuvres, the weather, the lovely shade of someone's dress. Perhaps, after this introduction, the person you're talking to politely excuses himself. Or, perhaps, you become best of friends. It's basic etiquette, formality, professionalism—it's simply how it's done.

Agents receive hundreds of submissions every month. Often they read these submissions on their own time—evenings, weekends, on their lunch break. Given the number of writers submitting, and the number of agents reading, it would simply be impossible for agents to ask for and read entire book manuscripts off the bat. Instead, a query is a quick way for you to, first and foremost, pitch your book. But it's also a way to pitch yourself. If an agent is intrigued by your query, she may ask for a partial (say, the first three chapters of your manuscript). Or she may ask for the entire thing.

As troublesome as it may first seem, try not to be frustrated by this process. Because, honestly, a query is a really great way to help speed up what is already a monumentally slow-paced industry. Have you ever seen pictures of slush piles—those piles of unread queries on many well-known agents' desks? Imagine the size of those slush piles if they held full manuscripts instead of one-page query letters. Thinking of it this way, query letters begin to make more sense.

Here we share with you the basics of a query, including its three parts and a detailed list of dos and don'ts.

PART I: THE INTRODUCTION

Whether you're submitting a 100-word picture book or a 90,000-word novel, you must be able to sum up the most basic aspects of it in one sentence. Agents are busy. And they constantly receive submissions for types of work they don't represent. So upfront they need to know that, after reading your first paragraph, the rest of your query is going to be worth their time.

An opening sentence designed to "hook" an agent is fine—if it's good and if it works. But this is the time to tune your right brain down and your left brain up—agents desire professionalism and queries that are short and to the point. Remember the cocktail party and always err on the side of formality. Tell the agent, in as few words as possible, what you've written, including the title, genre, and length.

In the intro, you also must try to connect with the agent. Simply sending one hundred identical query letters out to "Dear Agent" won't get you published. Instead, your letter should be addressed not only to a specific agency, but to a specific agent within that agency. (And double, triple, quadruple check that the agent's name is spelled correctly.) In addition, you need to let the agent know why you chose her specifically. A good author-agent relationship is like a good marriage. It's important that both sides invest the time to find a good fit that meets their needs. So how do you connect with an agent you don't know personally? Research.

1. Make a connection based on a book the agent already represents.

Most agencies have websites that list who and what they represent. Research those sites. Find a book similar to yours and explain that, because such-and-such book has a similar theme or tone or whatever, you think your book would be a great fit. In addition, many agents will list specific genres/categories they're looking for, either on their websites or in interviews. If your book is a match, state that.

2. Make a connection based on an interview you read.

Search agents' names online and read any and all interviews they've given. Perhaps they mentioned a love for X and your book is all about X. Perhaps they mentioned that they're looking for Y and your book is all about Y. Mention the specific interview. Prove that you've invested as much time researching them as they're about to spend researching you.

3. Make a connection based on a conference you both attended.

Was the agent you're querying the keynote speaker at a writing conference you were recently at? If so, mention it, and comment on an aspect of his speech you liked. Even better, did you meet the agent in person? Mention it, and if there's something you can say to jog her memory about the meeting, say it. Better yet, did the agent specifically ask you to send your manuscript? Mention it.

Finally, if you're being referred to a particular agent by an author the agent represents—that's your opening sentence. That referral is guaranteed to get your query placed at the top of the stack.

PART II: THE PITCH

Here's where you really get to sell your book—but in only three to ten sentences. Consider a book's jacket flap and its role in convincing readers to plunk down $24.95 to buy what's in between those flaps. Like a jacket flap, you need to hook an agent in the confines of very limited space. What makes your story interesting and unique? Is your story about a woman going through a mid-life crisis? Fine, but there are hundreds of stories about women going through mid-life crises. Is your story about a woman who, because of a mid-life crisis, leaves her life and family behind to spend three months in India? Again, fine, but this story, too, already exists—in many forms. Is your story about a woman who, because of a mid-life crisis, leaves her life and family behind to spend three months in India, falls in love with someone new while there, and starts a new life—and family? And then has to deal with everything she left behind upon her return? *Now* you have a hook.

Practice your pitch. Read it out loud, not only to family and friends, but to people willing to give you honest, intelligent criticism. If you belong to a writing group, workshop your pitch. Share it with members of an online writing forum. Know anyone in the publishing industry? Share it with them. Many writers spend years writing their books. We're not talking about querying magazines here; we're talking about querying an agent who could become a lifelong partner. Spend time on your pitch. Perfect it. Turn it into jacket-flap material so detailed, exciting, and clear that it would be near impossible to read your pitch and not want to read more. Use active verbs. Write your pitch, put it aside for a week, then look at it again. Don't send a query simply because you finished a book. Send a query because you finished your pitch and are ready to take the next steps.

PART III: THE BIO

If you write fiction for adults or children, unless you're a household name or you've recently been a guest on some very big TV or radio shows, an agent is much more interested in your pitch than in who you are. If you write nonfiction, who you are—more specifically, your platform and publicity—is much more important. Regardless, these are key elements that must be present in every bio:

1. Publishing credits

If you're submitting fiction, focus on your fiction credits—previously published works and short stories. That said, if you're submitting fiction and all your previously published work is nonfiction—articles, essays, etc.—that's still fine and good to mention. Don't be overly long about it. Mention your publications in bigger magazines or well-known literary journals. If you've never had anything published, don't say you lack official credits. Simply skip this altogether and thank the agent for his time.

2. Contests and awards

If you've won many, focus on the most impressive ones and those that most directly relate to your work. Don't mention contests you entered and weren't named in. Also, feel free to leave titles and years out of it. If you took first place at the Delaware Writers Conference for your fiction manuscript, that's good enough. Mentioning details isn't necessary.

3. MFAs

If you've earned or are working toward a Master of Fine Arts in writing, say so and state the program. Don't mention English degrees or online writing courses.

4. Large, recognized writing organizations

Agents don't want to hear about your book club and the fact that there's always great food, or the small critique group you meet with once a week. And they really don't want to hear about the online writing forum you belong to. But if you're a member of something like the Romance Writers of America (RWA), the Mystery Writers of America (MWA), the Society of Children's Book Writers and Illustrators (SCBWI), the Society of Professional Journalists (SPJ), the American Medical Writers, etc., say so. This shows you're serious about what you do and you're involved in groups that can aid with publicity and networking.

5. Platform and publicity

If you write nonfiction, who you are and how you're going to help sell the book once it's published become very important. Why are you the best person to write it and what do you have now—public speaking engagements, an active website or blog, substantial cred in your industry—that will help you sell this book?

Finally, be cordial. Thank the agent for taking the time to read your query and consider your manuscript. Ask if you may send more, in the format she desires (partial, full, etc.).

DOS AND DON'TS FOR QUERYING AGENTS

DO:

- Keep the tone professional.
- Query a specific agent at a specific agency.
- Proofread. Double-check the spelling of the agency and the agent's name.
- Keep the query concise, limiting the overall length to one page (single-spaced, twelve-point type in a commonly used font).
- Focus on the plot, not your bio, when pitching fiction.
- Pitch agents who represent the type of material you write.
- Check an agency's submission guidelines to see how to query—for example, via e-mail or mail—and whether or not to include a SASE.
- Keep pitching, despite rejections.

DON'T:

- Include personal info not directly related to the book. For example, stating that you're a parent to three children doesn't make you more qualified than someone else to write a children's book.
- Say how long it took you to write your manuscript. Some best-selling books took ten years to write—others, six weeks. An agent doesn't care how long it took—an agent only cares if it's good. Same thing goes with drafts—an agent doesn't care how many drafts it took you to reach the final product.
- Mention that this is your first novel or, worse, the first thing you've ever written aside from grocery lists. If you have no other publishing credits, don't advertise that fact. Don't mention it at all.
- State that your book has been edited by peers or professionals. Agents expect manuscripts to be edited, no matter how the editing was done.
- Bring up scripts or film adaptations—you're querying an agent about publishing a book, not making a movie.
- Mention any previous rejections.
- State that the story is copyrighted with the U.S. Copyright Office or that you own all rights. Of course you own all rights. You wrote it.
- Rave about how much your family and friends loved it. What matters is that the agent loves it.
- Send flowers or anything else except a self-addressed stamped envelope (and only if the SASE is required), if sending through snail mail.
- Follow up with a phone call. After the appropriate time has passed (many agencies say how long it will take to receive a response), follow up in the manner you queried—via e-mail or mail.

Think of the time you spent writing your book. Unfortunately, you can't send your book to an agent for a first impression. Your query *is* that first impression. Give it the time it deserves. Keep it professional. Keep it formal. Let it be a firm handshake—not a sloppy kiss. Let it be a first meeting that evolves into a lifelong relationship—not a rejection slip. But expect those slips. Just like you don't become best friends with everyone you meet at a cocktail party, you can't expect every agent you pitch to sign you. Be patient. Keep pitching. And in the meantime, start writing that next book.

KARA GEBHART UHL, formerly managing editor at *Writer's Digest* magazine, now freelance writes and edits in Fort Thomas, Kentucky. She also blogs about parenting at www.pleiadesbee. com. Her essays have appeared on The Huffington Post, *The New York Times'* Well Family blog, and *TIME: Healthland.* Her parenting essay, "Apologies to the Parents I Judged Four Years Ago" was named one of *TIME's* "Top 10 Opinions of 2012."

❶ SAMPLE QUERY 1: LITERARY FICTION
Agent's Comments: Jeff Kleinman (Folio Literary Management)

From: Garth Stein
To: Jeff Kleinman
Subject: Query: "The Art of Racing in the Rain" ❶

Dear Mr. Kleinman:

❷ Saturday night I was participating in a fundraiser for the King County Library System out here in the Pacific Northwest, and I met your client Layne Maheu. He spoke very highly of you and suggested that I contact you.

❸ I am a Seattle writer with two published novels. I have recently completed my third novel, *The Art of Racing in the Rain*, and I find myself in a difficult situation: My new book is narrated by a dog, and my current agent ❹ told me that he cannot (or will not) sell it for that very reason. Thus, I am seeking new representation.

❺ *The Art of Racing in the Rain* is the story of Denny Swift, a race car driver who faces profound obstacles in his life, and ultimately overcomes them by applying the same techniques that have made him successful on the track. His story is narrated by his "philosopher dog," Enzo, who, having a nearly human soul (and an obsession with opposable thumbs), believes he will return as a man in his next lifetime.

❻ My last novel, *How Evan Broke His Head and Other Secrets*, won a 2006 Pacific Northwest Booksellers Association Book Award, and since the award ceremony a year ago, I have given many readings, workshops and lectures promoting the book. When time has permitted, I've read the first chapter from *The Art of Racing in the Rain*. Audience members have been universally enthusiastic and vocal in their response, and the first question asked is always: "When can I buy the book about the dog?" Also very positive.

❼ I'm inserting, below, a short synopsis of *The Art of Racing in the Rain*, and my biography. Please let me know if the novel interests you; I would be happy to send you the manuscript.

Sincerely,
Garth Stein

❶ Putting the word "Query" and the title of the book on the subject line of an e-mail often keeps your e-mail from falling into the spam folder. ❷ One of the best ways of starting out correspondence is figuring out your connection to the agent. ❸ The author has some kind of track record. Who's the publisher, though? Were these both self-published novels, or were there reputable publishers involved? (I'll read on, and hope I find out.) ❹ This seems promising, but also know this kind of approach can backfire, because we agents tend to be like sheep—what one doesn't like, the rest of us are wary of, too (or, conversely, what one likes, we all like). But in this case getting in the "two published novels" early is definitely helpful. ❺ The third paragraph is the key pitch paragraph and Garth gives a great description of the book—he sums it up, gives us a feel for what we're going to get. This is the most important part of your letter. ❻ Obviously it's nice to see the author's winning awards. Also good: The author's not afraid of promoting the book. ❼ The end is simple and easy—it doesn't speak of desperation, or doubt, or anything other than polite willingness to help.

② SAMPLE QUERY 2: YOUNG ADULT
Agent's Comments: Ted Malawer (Upstart Crow Literary)

Dear Mr. Malawer:

I would like you to represent my 65,000-word contemporary teen novel *My Big Nose & Other Natural Disasters.*

① Seventeen-year-old Jory Michaels wakes up on the first day of summer vacation with her same old big nose, no passion in her life (in the creative sense of the word), and all signs still pointing to her dying a virgin. Plus, her mother is busy roasting a chicken for Day #6 of the Dinner For Breakfast Diet.

② In spite of her driving record (it was an accident!), Jory gets a job delivering flowers and cakes to Reno's casinos and wedding chapels. She also comes up with a new summer goal: saving for a life-altering nose job. She and her new nose will attract a fabulous boyfriend. Nothing like the shameless flirt Tyler Briggs, or Tom who's always nice but never calls. Maybe she'll find someone kind of like Gideon at the Jewel Café, except better looking and not quite so different. Jory survives various summer disasters like doing yoga after sampling Mom's Cabbage Soup Diet, Enforced Mother Bonding With Crazy Nose Obsessed Daughter Night, and discovering Tyler's big secret. But will she learn to accept herself and maybe even find her passion, in the creative (AND romantic!) sense of the word?

③ I have written for *APPLESEEDS, Confetti, Hopscotch, Story Friends, Wee Ones Magazine,* the *Deseret News, Children's Playmate* and Blooming Tree Press' *Summer Shorts* anthology. I won the Utah Arts Council prize for *Not-A-Dr. Logan's Divorce Book.* My novels *Jungle Crossing* and *Going Native!* each won first prize in the League of Utah Writers contest. I currently serve as an SCBWI Regional Advisor.

④ I submitted *My Big Nose & Other Natural Disasters* to Krista Marino at Delacorte because she requested it during our critique at the summer SCBWI conference (no response yet).

Thank you for your time and attention. I look forward to hearing from you.

Sincerely,
Sydney Salter Husseman

① With hundreds and hundreds of queries each month, it's tough to stand out. Sydney, however, did just that. First, she has a great title that totally made me laugh. Second, she sets up her main character's dilemma in a succinct and interesting way. In one simple paragraph, I have a great idea of who Jory is and what her life is about—the interesting tidbits about her mother help show the novel's sense of humor, too. **②** Sydney's largest paragraph sets up the plot and the conflict, and introduces some exciting potential love interests and misadventures that I was excited to read about. Again, Sydney really shows off her fantastic sense of humor, and she leaves me hanging with a question that I needed an answer to. **③** She has writing experience and has completed other manuscripts that were prize-worthy. Her SCBWI involvement—while not a necessity—shows me that she has an understanding of and an interest in the children's publishing world. **④** The fact that an editor requested the manuscript is always a good sign. That I knew Krista personally and highly valued her opinion was, as Sydney's main character Jory would say, "The icing on the cake."

③ SAMPLE QUERY 3: NONFICTION (SELF-HELP)
Agent's Comments: Michelle Wolfson (Wolfson Literary Agency)

Dear Ms. Wolfson:

❶ Have you ever wanted to know the best day of the week to buy groceries or go out to dinner? Have you ever wondered about the best time of day to send an e-mail or ask for a raise? What about the best time of day to schedule a surgery or a haircut? What's the best day of the week to avoid lines at the Louvre? What's the best day of the month to make an offer on a house? What's the best time of day to ask someone out on a date? ❷

My book, *Buy Ketchup in May and Fly at Noon: A Guide to the Best Time to Buy This, Do That, and Go There*, has the answers to these questions and hundreds more.

❸ As a long-time print journalist, I've been privy to readership surveys that show people can't get enough of newspaper and magazine stories about the best time to buy or do things. This book puts several hundreds of questions and answers in one place—a succinct, large-print reference book that readers will feel like they need to own. Why? Because it will save them time and money, and it will give them valuable information about issues related to health, education, travel, the workplace and more. In short, it will make them smarter, so they can make better decisions. ❹

Best of all, the information in this book is relevant to anyone, whether they live in Virginia or the Virgin Islands, Portland, Oregon, or Portland, Maine. In fact, much of the book will find an audience in Europe and Australia.

❺ I've worked as a journalist since 1984. In 1999, the Virginia Press Association created an award for the best news writing portfolio in the state—the closest thing Virginia had to a reporter-of-the-year award. I won it that year and then again in 2000. During the summer of 2007, I left newspapering to pursue book projects and long-form journalism.

❻ I saw your name on a list of top literary agents for self-help books, and I read on your website that you're interested in books that offer practical advice. *Buy Ketchup in May and Fly at Noon* offers plenty of that. Please let me know if you'd like to read my proposal.

Sincerely,
Mark Di Vincenzo

❶ I tend to prefer it when authors jump right into the heart of their book, the exception being if we've met at a conference or have some other personal connection. Mark chose clever questions for the opening of the query. All of those questions are, in fact, relevant to my life, with groceries, dinner, e-mail and a raise—and yet I don't have a definitive answer to them. ❷ He gets a little more offbeat and unusual with questions regarding surgery, the Louvre, buying a house and dating. This shows a quirkier side to the book and also the range of topics it is going to cover, so I know right away there is going to be a mix of useful and quirky information on a broad range of topics. ❸ By starting with "As a long-time print journalist," Mark immediately establishes his credibility for writing on this topic. ❹ This helps show that there is a market for this book, and establishes the need for such a book. ❺ Mark's bio paragraph offers a lot of good information. ❻ It's nice when I feel like an author has sought me out specifically and thinks we would be a good fit.

④ SAMPLE QUERY 4: WOMEN'S FICTION
Agent's Comments: Elisabeth Weed (Weed Literary)

Dear Ms. Weed:

① Natalie Miller had a plan. She had a goddamn plan. Top of her class at Dartmouth. Even better at Yale Law. Youngest aide ever to the powerful Senator Claire Dupris. Higher, faster, stronger. This? Was all part of the plan. True, she was so busy ascending the political ladder that she rarely had time to sniff around her mediocre relationship with Ned, who fit the three Bs to the max: basic, blond and boring, and she definitely didn't have time to mourn her mangled relationship with Jake, her budding rock star ex-boyfriend.

The lump in her right breast that Ned discovers during brain-numbingly bland morning sex? That? Was most definitely not part of the plan. And Stage IIIA breast cancer? Never once had Natalie jotted this down on her to-do list for conquering the world. When her (tiny-penised) boyfriend has the audacity to dump her on the day after her diagnosis, Natalie's entire world dissolves into a tornado of upheaval, and she's left with nothing but her diary to her ex-boyfriends, her mornings lingering over "The Price is Right," her burnt-out stubs of pot that carry her past the chemo pain, and finally, the weight of her life choices—the ones in which she might drown if she doesn't find a buoy.

② *The Department of Lost and Found* is a story of hope, of resolve, of digging deeper than you thought possible until you find the strength not to crumble, and ultimately, of making your own luck, even when you've been dealt an unsteady hand.

③ I'm a freelance writer and have contributed to, among others, *American Baby, American Way, Arthritis Today, Bride's, Cooking Light, Fitness, Glamour, InStyle Weddings, Men's Edge, Men's Fitness, Men's Health, Parenting, Parents, Prevention, Redbook, Self, Shape, Sly, Stuff, USA Weekend, Weight Watchers, Woman's Day, Women's Health*, and ivillage.com, msn.com and women.com. I also ghostwrote *The Knot Book of Wedding Flowers.*

If you are interested, I'd love to send you the completed manuscript. Thanks so much! Looking forward to speaking with you soon.

Allison Winn Scotch

① The opening sentence reads like great jacket copy, and I immediately know who our protagonist is and what the conflict for her will be. (And it's funny, without being silly.) **②** The third paragraph tells me where this book will land: upmarket women's fiction. (A great place to be these days!) **③** This paragraph highlights impressive credentials. While being able to write nonfiction does not necessarily translate over to fiction, it shows me that she is someone worth paying more attention to. And her magazine contacts will help when it comes time to promote the book.

⑤ SAMPLE QUERY 5: MAINSTREAM/COMEDIC FICTION
Agent's Comments: Michelle Brower (Folio Literary Management)

Dear Michelle Brower:

❶ "I spent two days in a cage at the SPCA until my parents finally came to pick me up. The stigma of bringing your undead son home to live with you can wreak havoc on your social status, so I can't exactly blame my parents for not rushing out to claim me. But one more day and I would have been donated to a research facility."

Andy Warner is a zombie.

After reanimating from a car accident that killed his wife, Andy is resented by his parents, abandoned by his friends, and vilified by society. Seeking comfort and camaraderie in Undead Anonymous, a support group for zombies, Andy finds kindred souls in Rita, a recent suicide who has a taste for consuming formaldehyde in cosmetic products, and Jerry, a 21-year-old car crash victim with an artistic flair for Renaissance pornography.

❷ With the help of his new friends and a rogue zombie named Ray, Andy embarks on a journey of personal freedom and self-discovery that will take him from his own casket to the SPCA to a media-driven, class-action lawsuit for the civil rights of all zombies. And along the way, he'll even devour a few Breathers.

Breathers is a contemporary dark comedy about life, or undeath, through the eyes of an ordinary zombie. In addition to *Breathers*, I've written three other novels and more than four dozen short stories—a dozen of which have appeared in small press publications. Currently, I'm working on my fifth novel, also a dark comedy, about fate.

Enclosed is a two-page synopsis and the first chapter of *Breathers*, with additional sample chapters or the entire manuscript available upon request. I appreciate your time and interest in considering my query and I look forward to your response.

Sincerely,
Scott G. Browne

❶ What really draws me to this query is the fact that it has exactly what I'm looking for in my commercial fiction—story and style. Scott includes a brief quote from the book that manages to capture his sense of humor as an author and his uniquely relatable main character (hard to do with someone who's recently reanimated). I think this is a great example of how query letters can break the rules and still stand out in the slush pile. I normally don't like quotes as the first line, because I don't have a context for them, but this quote both sets up the main concept of the book *and* gives me a sense of the character's voice. This method won't necessarily work for most fiction, but it absolutely is successful here. ❷ The letter quickly conveys that this is an unusual book about zombies, and being a fan of zombie literature, I'm aware that it seems to be taking things in a new direction. I also appreciate how Scott conveys the main conflict of his plot and his supporting cast of characters—we know there is an issue for Andy beyond coming back to life as a zombie, and that provides momentum for the story.

QUERY LETTER FAQS

Here are answers to 18 of the most tricky and confusing query questions around.

by Chuck Sambuchino

Readers and aspiring writers often find querying literary agents to be intimidating and terrifying. Here are some important questions and answers to consider as you craft your query letter.

When contacting agents, the query process isn't as simple as, "Just keep e-mailing until something good happens." There are ins, outs, strange situations, unclear scenarios, and plenty of what-have-you's that block the road to signing with a rep. In short, there are plenty of murky waters out there in the realm of submissions. Luckily, writers have plenty of questions to ask. Here are some of the most interesting (and important) questions and answers regarding protocol during the query process.

When should you query? When is your project *ready*?

There is no definitive answer, but here's what I suggest. Get outside criticism of the material from "beta readers"—peers who can give you feedback that is both honest and helpful. These beta readers (usually members of a critique group) will give you feedback. You do not want major concerns, such as, "It starts too slow" or "This character is not likeable." Address these problems through revisions. After rewriting, give it to more beta readers. If they come back with no major concerns, the book is ready, or at least very close.

How should you start your query? Should you begin with a paragraph from the book?

I would not include a paragraph from the book nor would I write the letter in the "voice" of one your characters—those are gimmicks. If you choose, you can just jump right into the pitch—there's nothing wrong with that. But what I recommend is laying out the details of your book in one easy sentence: "I have a completed seventy-thousand-word thriller titled *Dead Cat Bounce*." I suggest this because jumping into a pitch can be jarring and confusing. Think about it. If you started reading an e-mail and the first sentence was simply "Billy has a problem," you don't know if Billy is an adult or a child, or if he is being held captive by terrorists versus being nervous because his turtle is missing. In other words, the agent doesn't know whether to laugh or be worried. He's confused. And when an agent gets confused, he may just stop reading.

Can you query multiple agents at the same agency?

Generally, no. A rejection from one literary agent usually means a rejection from the entire agency. If you query one agent and she thinks the work isn't right for her but still has promise, she will pass it on to fellow agents in the office who can review it themselves.

Should you mention that the query is a simultaneous submission?

You certainly can, but you don't have to. If you say it's exclusive, they'll understand no other eyes are on the material. If you say nothing, they will assume multiple agents must be considering it right now. However, some literary agents will specifically request in their guidelines to be informed if it's a simultaneous submission.

Even if an agent doesn't request It, should you Include a few sample pages with your query letter?

This is up to you. When including sample pages, though, remember to paste the pages below the query letter. Do not attach them in a document. Also, do not include much—perhaps one to five pages. Most people asking this question probably have more faith in their opening pages than in their query. That's understandable, but keep in mind that while including sample pages may help with an occasional agent who checks out your writing, it doesn't solve the major problem of your query being substandard. Keep working on the query until you have faith in it, regardless of whether you sneak in unsolicited pages or not.

Can your query be more than one page long?

The rise of e-queries removed the dreaded page break, so now it's easy to have your query go over one page. This does not necessarily mean it's a wise move. Going a few sentences over one page is likely harmless, but you don't need a query that trends long. Lengthy letters are a sign of a rambling pitch, which will probably get you rejected. Edit and trim your pitch down as need be. Find beta readers or a freelance query editor to give you ideas and notes. Remember that a succinct letter is preferred, and oftentimes more effective. An exception to this, however, is querying for nonfiction books. Nonfiction queries have to be heavy on author platform, and those notes (with proper names of publications and organizations and websites, etc.) can get long. Feel free to go several sentences over one page if you have to list out platform and marketing notes, as long as the pitch itself is not the item making your letter too long.

How do you follow up with an agent who hasn't responded to your submission?

This is a complicated question, and I'll try to address its many parts.

First, check the agency website for updates and her latest formal guidelines. She may have gone on leave, or she may have switched agencies. She may also have submission guidelines that state how she only responds to submissions if interested. So keep in mind there might be a very good reason as to why you shouldn't follow up or rather why you shouldn't follow up right now.

However, let's say an agent responds to submissions "within three months" and it's been three and a half months with no reply. A few weeks have passed since the "deadline," so now it's time to nicely follow up. All you do is paste your original query into a new e-mail and send it to the agent with a note above the query that says, "Dear [agent], I sent my query below to you [length of time] ago and haven't heard anything. I'm afraid my original note got lost in a spam filter, so I am pasting it below in the hopes that you are still reviewing queries and open to new clients. Thank you for considering my submission. Sincerely, [name]." That's it. Be polite and simply resubmit. If an agent makes it sound like he does indeed respond to submissions but doesn't have a time frame for his reply, I say follow up after three months.

But before you send that follow up, make sure you are not to blame for getting no reply. Perhaps your previous e-mail had an attachment when the agent warned, "No attachments." Perhaps your previous e-mail did not put "Query" in the subject line even though the agent requested just that. Or perhaps your previous e-mail misspelled the agent's e-mail address and the query truly got lost in cyberspace. In other words, double-check everything. If you send that follow up and the agent still doesn't reply, it's probably time to move on.

How many query rejections would necessitate a major overhaul of the query?

Submit no more than twelve queries to start. If only zero or one respond with requests for more, then you've got a problem. Go back to the drawing board and overhaul the query before the next wave of eight to twelve submissions. Doing this ensures that you can try to identify where you're going wrong in your submission.

Should you mention that you've self-published books in the past?

In my opinion, you don't have to. If you self-published a few e-books that went nowhere, you don't have to list every one and their disappointing sales numbers. The release of those books should not affect your new novel that you're submitting to agents.

However, if your self-published projects experienced healthy sales (3,000-plus print books, 10,000-plus e-books), mention it. Only talk about your self-published projects if they will help your case. Otherwise, just leave them out of the conversation and focus on the new project at hand.

Should you mention your age in a query? Do agents have a bias against older writers and teenagers?

I'm not sure any good can come from mentioning your age in a query. Usually the people who ask this question are either younger than twenty or older than seventy. Some literary agents may be hesitant to sign older writers because reps are looking for career clients, not simply individuals with one memoir/book to sell. If you're older, write multiple books to convince an agent that you have several projects in you, and do not mention your age in the query to be safe.

Should you mention in the query that your work is copyrighted and/or has had book editing?

No. All work is copyrighted the moment you write it down in any medium, so saying something that is obvious only comes off as amateurish. On the same note, all work should be edited, so saying that the work is edited (even by a professional editor) also comes off as amateurish.

Is it better to send a query over snail mail or e-mail?

If you have a choice, do not send a snail mail query. They're more of a hassle to physically produce, and they cost money to send. Ninety percent (or more) of queries are sent over e-mail for two very good reasons. E-mail is quicker, in terms of sending submissions and agents' response time, and it's free. Keep in mind that almost all agents have personal, detailed submission guidelines in which they say exactly what they want to receive in a submission and how they want to receive it. So you will almost always not have a choice in how to send materials. Send the agent what they asked for, exactly how they asked for it.

What happens when you're writing a book that doesn't easily fall into one specific genre? How do you handle that problem in a query letter?

Know that you have to bite the bullet and call it *something*. Even if you end up calling it a "middle grade adventure with supernatural elements," then you're at least calling it something. Writers really get into a pickle when they start their pitches with an intro such as, "It's a sci-fi western humorous fantastical suspense romance, set in steampunk Britain … with erotic werewolf transvestite protagonists." Fundamentally, it must be something, so pick its core genre and just call it that—otherwise your query might not even get read. I'm not a huge fan of writers comparing their work to other projects (saying, "It's X meets Z"—that type of thing), but said strategy—comparing your book to others in the marketplace—is most useful for those authors who have a hard time describing the plot and tone of their tale.

If you're writing a memoir, do you pitch it like a novel (i.e., with a completed manuscript ready) or like a nonfiction book (i.e., with a completed book proposal and a few sample chapters finished)?

I'd say eighty percent of agents review memoir like they would a novel. If interested, they ask for the full book and consider it mostly by how well it's written. I have met several agents, however, who want to see a nonfiction book proposal—either with some sample chapters, or sometimes in addition to the whole book. So to answer the question, you can choose to write only the manuscript, and go from there. Or you can choose to complete a proposal, as well, so you have as many weapons as possible as you move forward. (In my opinion, a writer who has both a complete memoir manuscript and nonfiction book proposal seems like a professional who is ahead of the curve and wise to platform matters—and, naturally, people in publishing are often attracted to writers who are ahead of the curve and/or can help sell more books.)

If you're pitching a novel, should the topics of marketing and writer platform be addressed in the query?

Concerning query letters for novels, the pitch is what's paramount, and any mention of marketing or platform is just gravy. If you have some promotional credentials, these skills will definitely be beneficial in selling more books when your title is released. But a decent platform will not get a mediocre novel published. Feel free to list worthwhile, impressive notes about your platform and marketing skills, but don't let them cloud your writing. Remember, the three most crucial elements to a novel selling are *the writing, the writing, the writing*.

Do you need to query conservative agents for a conservative book? A liberal agent for a liberal book?

I asked a few agents this question and some said they were willing to take on any political slant if the book was well written and the author had a great writer platform. A few agents, on the other hand, said they needed to be on the same page politically with the author for a political/religious book, and would only take on books they agreed with. Bottom line: Some will be open-minded; some won't. Look for reps who have taken on books similar to yours, and feel free to query other agents, too. The worst any agent can say is no.

If you're writing a series, does an agent want you to say that in the query?

The old mentality for this was no, you should not discuss a series in the query, and instead just pitch one book and let any discussion naturally progress to the topic of more books, if the agent so inquires. However, I've overheard more and more literary agents say that they do want to know if your book is the potential start of the series. So, the correct answer, it appears, depends on who you ask. In circumstances like these, I recommend crafting an answer to cover all bases: "This book could either be a standalone project or the start of a series." When worded like this, you disclose the series potential, but don't make it sound like you're saying, "I want a five-book deal or NOTHING." You'll sound like an easy-to-work-with writing professional and leave all options open.

Can you query an agent for a short story collection?

I'd say ninety-five percent of agents do not accept short story collection queries. The reason? Collections just don't sell well. If you have a collection of short stories, you can do a few different things. You can repurpose some or all of the stories into a novel, which is easier to sell. You can write a new book—a novel—and sell that *first* to establish a reader base. That way, you can have a base that will purchase your next project—the collection—ensuring the publisher makes money on your short stories. Or you can query the few agents who do take collections and hope for the best. If you choose this third route, I suggest you get some of the stories published to help the project gain some momentum. A platform and/or media contacts would help your case, as well.

PITCH AGENTS THROUGH TWITTER

Agents love online pitch parties.

by Lisa Katzenberger

The publishing industry has embraced Twitter with open arms, and it's time for you to join the party. If you're an aspiring writer looking to secure an agent, Twitter is absolutely the easiest, quickest, and most impactful way to connect with the gatekeepers of the publishing industry.

Twitter is not just for tech-savvy professionals, young adults, extroverts, or folks with too much to say. It's a free, easy-to-use communication platform accessible to—and welcoming of—everyone. And while Twitter is a viable tool for getting a literary agent, that doesn't mean it can't also be fun.

The key to a successful Twitter experience is who you follow; in other words, whose status updates you will be able to read in your Twitter feed. To get started, create your profile and Twitter handle, and then determine who to follow. Start with your favorite writers, and then search for agents, editors, publishing houses, and bookstores. The publishing industry is very active on Twitter, and you can learn so much just by reading the posts of those you follow. The great thing about Twitter is that you don't actually have to post anything to reap the benefits. At first you can just sit back and read what others have to say.

HOW TO USE TWITTER TO PITCH YOUR BOOK

Once you're comfortable with the basics of Twitter, it's time to use it to your advantage. The *pitch party* is an emerging trend on Twitter that can prove a valuable strategy for snagging an agent's attention. During a pitch party, writers pitch their completed, submission-ready, unpublished manuscript to an agent within a specified time frame. They create 140-character pitches of their manuscripts and post them to Twitter with a hashtag to make them searchable. A group of invited agents and editors attend the party (i.e., read the hashtagged Twitter feed) and review as many pitches as they can. If an agent enjoys your pitch, she will like (or "heart") your tweet by clicking the heart icon. This is an invitation for the writer to submit a query or manuscript to the agent—she is interested in your story and wants to know more!

While the pitch party is an up-and-coming method for securing representation, it already boasts its share of success stories. If you're ready to join them, follow these simple steps.

1. Craft your Twitter pitch.

A stellar pitch requires a few key ingredients. Here is a great formula I came across (on Twitter, of course):

> When [Main Character] encounters [Obstacle], he/she must [Reaction] or else [Stakes.] #MG #PitMad

Aside from the actual pitch, you also need to include the name of the pitch party, which in this example is "#PitMad." (The hashtag symbol is used to group posts together. In this example, adding the "#PitMad" hashtag would group your pitch with other writers' pitches for this particular party.) You should also include the genre or category, such as #HF for historical fiction or #MG for middle-grade. (Lists of genre shortcut names are typically provided with the contest rules online.) You must convey your pitch in 140 characters, which includes spaces, punctuation, and the content of the hashtags. Think about what you can abbreviate without sacrificing proper grammar.

"Focus on what makes your story readable—mainly stakes," says agent Heather Flaherty of The Bent Agency (@HeddaFlaherty). "If the plot stakes are high, they need to be in the pitch. If the emotional (character development) stakes are high, that needs to go in. Think about what in your story keeps people turning the page, and make sure that gets in the pitch."

If you've dreaded whittling down your story to a 250-word synopsis—much less a 140-character pitch—fear not. I personally think that crafting a Twitter pitch is easier. First, if you cannot summarize the essence of your story in one sentence, it might simply not be ready to submit—so keep writing and revising. I'm not saying you will come up with a perfect pitch on your first attempt; it absolutely takes time and practice. But pitch writing is an important exercise to ensure your story is clear and complete.

Author Brenda Drake (@brendadrake), who runs the #PitMad pitch party, believes that pitch parties can be an opportunity for writers to test the attractiveness of their hooks and pitches. "Sometimes it's successful, sometimes not, but it's great practice," Drake says. "It teaches a writer how to focus on the main plot and how to pitch it."

Just as you would for your manuscript, enlist some beta readers or critique partners to help you refine your tweet before you send it out. Also, because Twitter doesn't like spam any more than you do, it will not let you tweet the same text twice in a row. To get around this rule, you can tweet different pitches (as the rules of the party allow), or change the placement of the hashtag.

2. Plan ahead.

While I'm sure we all wish we could devote the entire day to writing and tweeting, we writers often have other responsibilities like day jobs, school, or children to keep us busy. The good news is that you do not have to be active on Twitter the day of the party in order to participate. Many free scheduling tools, such as TweetDeck and Hootsuite, allow you to write your tweets in advance and set specific times to post them.

3. Grab an agent's attention.

Agents who participate in parties scan through hundreds of tweets in a row, and they are looking for something to jump out and grab their attention. Thao Le (@ThaoLe8) of Sandra Dijkstra & Associates Literary Agency, offers her advice on building a great pitch: "I want to know what the conflict is! Too often people are vague in their pitches, and it comes off as cliché or generic. Know what your hook is, and present it concisely."

Bear in mind that the agent isn't just considering your pitch party tweet; she's also looking at your Twitter presence as a whole. "What also grabs me is the person's Twitter picture and profile," Flaherty says. "Can I see that they've thought through how they wish to be seen by the industry and the world? Have they considered their profile pic or just thrown something random up from last year's barbecue?"

4. Follow the rules.

Even though it's a party, you're still making a business pitch. "Read the rules carefully for each pitch party—they can be different," Le says. "Follow those rules for the best results. Be polite. Be professional."

Be sure to check the pitch party website for specific instructions. For example, pitch parties often start and end at specific times, and some limit the number of times you can post your pitch within that time frame. To prevent the feed from becoming too cluttered, many parties ask that you not retweet any pitch party posts (in which you share someone else's post on your own feed).

Make sure you do not like or heart someone else's pitch—let the agents do that! Also, be prepared to get a few likes from well-meaning strangers who enjoy your topic. These likes from strangers are encouraging, but don't really help you in the pitch party and should be ignored.

5. Submit requested materials.

So an agent expressed interest in your work and has asked you to submit your manuscript—congratulations! Each agent has his own submission process. If an agent likes your tweet, it is your responsibility to go to his website, research the agency guidelines, and then follow him. Sometimes an agent will tweet a tip about additional information

With their extremely busy schedules and overflowing slush piles of queries, many agents still choose to join Twitter pitch parties. Agent Thao Le of Sandra Dijkstra Literary Agency finds that writers who are active on Twitter are typically more industry savvy. "They've done their research, and they know how to pitch in 140 characters or less," she says. "Also, they usually have mentors and/or critique partners, so I know that their work is polished. Twitter pitch party participants tend to be an active part of the writing community, which is great because the relationships they build will support them later down the road ([in soliciting] blurbs and reviews, or generating buzz), and social media is so important to readers today."

Heather Flaherty of The Bent Agency thinks Twitter is having an impact on the writing community: "I feel we're getting to know authors more through Twitter, and bonds are made as we're considering their queries. If the Twitter parties do anything for querying, I think and hope they're teaching writers how to create a dynamic, pithy, and perfectly brief pitch, and that this skill will transfer into their queries."

you should provide with your submission. For example, he may ask you to include the name of the pitch party in the subject of your e-mail.

SUCCESS STORIES

Rena Olsen, author of *The Girl Before*, secured her agent, Sharon Pelletier of Dystel & Goderich Literary Management, through the #PitMad pitch party. Pelletier actually liked a pitch from Olsen:

> Clara raised them as her own daughters. She didn't know her husband kidnapped them to be sold to the highest bidder. #PitMad

"Sharon tweeted on the day of #PitMad that if she favorited the tweet, you should send the query and manuscript," Olsen says. "I thought she couldn't possibly want the full [manuscript] right away, so I went on the agency website to double-check her submission guidelines and followed those. The same day, she e-mailed back and requested the full manuscript. #PitMad was September 9, I sent the initial request in the wee hours of the morning on September 10, and her request came at a more reasonable hour later on September 10."

Now, things don't always happen this quickly. Remember that getting published is a process that requires lots of patience. Pitch parties are just one avenue to agent representation. Olsen emphasizes: "My biggest advice is to not stress if you don't get requests from a Twitter pitch contest. I did many where I got only a couple of favorites, and several more

---

PARTY HOPPING

Twitter is an evolving tool that changes over time. Keep in mind that what is true today might be slightly different a few months down the road. Here is a list of popular Twitter pitch parties, with more popping up all the time:

- #DVPit (marginalized and diverse voices) www.bethphelan.com/dvpit
- #PBPitch (picture books) no website
- #PitMad (open to all kinds of books, but usually novels) www.brenda-drake.com/pitmad/
- #AdPit (adult and new adult novels) www.heidinorrod.webs.com/
- #PitchMAS (general and open) www.pitchmas.blogspot.com/
- #PitMatch (general and open) www.manuscriptwishlist.com
- #PitchCB (special for pitching the agency Curtis Brown): www.curtisbrowncreative.co.uk/blog/pitchcb
- #SFFPit (science fiction and fantasy): www.dankoboldt.com/sffpit

---

where I got none at all. It's a wonderful opportunity, and obviously it can turn out really well, but it's not the only path."

Le has a success story, too: "I discovered the amazingly talented Jessie Sima via #PitMad last June. She tweeted the most darling picture of a baby unicorn in a clamshell with the caption 'Kelp always thought he was a narwhal. Turns out he was wrong. He's a unicorn. KELP, THE NOT-QUITE NARWHAL #PitMad #pb.' I immediately fell head-over-heels in love and requested her full picture book. We went on to sell that picture book, *Not Quite Narwhal*, to Simon and Schuster, with publication coming in spring 2017."

Any opportunity to pitch your work to agents is worth looking into—from sending a query letter to meeting them in person at a writers conference. Pitch parties are a hot and growing opportunity, so engage with agents on Twitter right now and give yourself another avenue to find a rep who loves your work.

LISA KATZENBERGER (www.lisakatzenberger.com) is an Illinois-based freelance writer.

AGENTS EVALUATE FIRST PAGES

Learn why agents stop reading your work.

by Carly Watters, Kirsten Carleton, MacKenzie Fraser-Bub, and Kate McKean

Writing a compelling first page is difficult. No matter what genre or category you write in, combining the right degree of action, description, dialogue, and voice is a delicate balancing act. Agents and editors want to get pulled in on page 1. And when they don't, writers wonder: Where did I go wrong? At what point did the agent give up?

So to help you understand exactly what goes through an agent's mind, we've asked four literary agents to participate in a brand-new *GLA* "First Page Evaluation," which documents exactly when an agent stops reading your submission and why. Here you'll find nine real, unpublished first pages of manuscripts accompanied with notes from four literary agents. (The authors of these pages are anonymous and have given their consent to be included in this article.) Pay attention to where and why the agents stopped to issue a rejection—or where they didn't stop—and note the advice they have to share. But before we begin, meet the four participating literary agents:

MACKENZIE FRASER-BUB is the founder of Fraser-Bub Literary (www.fraserbubliterary. com). Fraser-Bub began her career at the Crown Publishing Group, a division of Penguin Random House. She's a veteran of the Columbia Publishing Course, having taught and worked there. She also spent several years at Simon and Schuster (Touchstone Books), in one of the industry's finest marketing departments, before becoming an agent at the venerable Trident Media Group. While at Trident, she quickly built a diverse list that included multiple *New York Times* and *USA Today* best-selling titles, including romance, new adult, women's fiction, and science fiction. The number ❶ on the following manuscript pages indicates where Fraser-Bub stopped reading.

CARLY WATTERS is a senior agent with P.S. Literary (www.psliterary.com). Watters began her publishing career in London at the Darley Anderson Literary, TV and Film Agency. She has a bachelor of arts degree in English literature from Queen's University and a master of arts degree in publishing studies from City University London. Since joining P.S. Literary in 2010, she has had great success launching new authors both domestically and abroad. Representing debut novels and bestsellers, Watters is drawn to emotional, well-paced fiction with a great voice and characters that readers can get invested in, as well as platform-driven nonfiction. The number ❷ on the following manuscript pages indicates where Watters stopped reading.

KIRSTEN CARLETON is a literary agent with Prospect Agency (www.prospectagency.com). Before joining Prospect in 2015, she learned the agenting ropes at Sobel Weber Associates and the Waxman Leavell Agency. Carleton fell in love with working with writers while getting her bachelor's degree in English with a creative writing concentration from Amherst College, and she cemented her fascination with publishing with a graduate certificate in publishing from the Columbia Publishing Course and internships at Charlesbridge and Liza Dawson Associates. The number ❸ on the following manuscript pages indicates where Carleton stopped reading.

KATE MCKEAN is a literary agent with Howard Morhaim Literary (www.morhaimliterary. com). McKean joined HMLA in 2006. She earned her master's degree in fiction writing at the University of Southern Mississippi and began her publishing career at the University Press of Florida. She is proud to work with *New York Times* best-selling authors in a wide variety of genres. In addition to working with clients, she is an adjunct professor at New York University. The number ❹ on the following manuscript pages indicates where McKean stopped reading.

While the manuscript pages below show agents' specific reasons for why they rejected a submission, they also reveal the extremely subjective nature of the business. After all, one agent could review a scene and say that it has "too much description," while another could be entranced by the same passage. Such subjective contradiction is nothing new, but it does prove that, when submitting fiction, memoir, or narrative nonfiction, you should cast a wide net and contact many agents. You never know which rep will completely fall in love with your storytelling, plot, and voice.

Also, it's important to note that just because an agent says no to one of the following submissions doesn't mean that the writer in question has written a poor book or is a poor writer. It simply means that the book fails to start in the right place, or that the submission doesn't pull the agent in with immediate story conflict or writing prowess.

Before we begin, remember that the numbers you see in each submission represent the exact point where the literary agent stopped reading and would issue a rejection. If agents' numbers appear at the bottom of the first page of the manuscript, this indicates that the agent read the entire first page.

1. URBAN FANTASY

If he hadn't known for sure that Hades was currently vacationing on an island somewhere in the South Pacific, he'd have bet every last cent of his family's dirty millions the bastard was behind this Texas heat wave.

Thanatos, formidable ancient Greek God of Death—known to his construction crew here as Zach Smith ❹—slammed the trailer door shut behind him and stomped to the back to crank up the window AC unit. He stood in front of the blower, letting the icy air infiltrate his soggy t-shirt and dry the sweat off his neck. Then he dropped his hard hat on the desk and sat down to check over the day's work orders, pondering where in the hell Bradford Construction found the idiots they called "skilled laborers." Days like these almost made him consider coming out of hiding to let his family kill him—something they'd intended to do for the last 150 years—just to be done with it. Almost.

A timid knock on the door interrupted his mental grumbling. "What?" he snapped.

"Boss," said the dust-covered, sunburned face that leaned in, "Mark says the PVC we got in this morning is one and a quarter, but it was s'posed to be one."

He pinched the bridge of his nose and took a deep cleansing breath. The strong, often-felt urge to toss a mortal out the nearest window was sometimes best resisted. "I'll take care of it." He sighed with the air of a martyr. "Tell him to start on the joists in the morning."

The door started to close then seemed to change its mind. Carlos' head appeared again. "And Thompson had to take off early. His old lady called. Something about a dog stuck in the dishwasher." ❷ ❸

> **1. FRASER-BUB:** (MacKenzie Fraser-Bub did not critique this submission.)
>
> **2. WATTERS:** This is a great example of a successful first page. The genre, setting, motive, and character were all set up with great pace. The intrigue of the fantasy elements juxtaposed with the real-life setting of the construction site was really accessible to readers and immediately draws you in.
>
> **3. CARLETON:** I liked this a lot and would read more. Strong writing with some snappy humor, engaging characterization through voice and dialogue, and we already know a bit of the premise and the stakes within the first few paragraphs.
>
> **4. MCKEAN:** I'm not in the market for stories surrounding Greek Gods. I see many in my query pile and they don't seem to capture my imagination.

2. MEMOIR

Whether you're a) flipping through books in Barnes & Noble while waiting for your mom to go to the bathroom, b) going through your friends bookshelf and looking at what kind of books he or she is into, or c) just opening this book and reading it because you feel like reading it, there's a question in your head: what's this book about? **②** Well, I have a tough time even calling it a book, but I guess it is "a written or printed work consisting of pages glued or sewn together along one side and bound in covers," so here we are. **③** This book is about a college student. Me, to be more specific. I'm a student at the University of Georgia, and as I've gone through my college career, I've written quite a bit. I'll write when I'm having a breakdown, I'll write when I have an epiphany, I'll write when I'm just feeling creative, and so on and so forth. Basically, I'm as emotional, psychotic, and lost as all of my peers, but I happen to write during all these phases, forever immortalizing my pituitary gland's erratic hormonal releases. **④**

When I recently went back and looked at this very large collection of things I have written over the past three years, I stopped and thought to myself, "Oh shit, I'm crazy!" At this point I would then begin the unhealthy process of going on social media and comparing myself to all of my peers who would be hanging out in bars or frolicking through patches of sunflowers, and meanwhile I'm over here huddled in a dark corner of my apartment contemplating why people are so mean to spiders and if God really exists. But then I looked at my own social media pages and all the pictures I've taken over my college career, and I realized I look exactly the same as my peers. By looking at the projection I put out of myself, you'd never know what was going on behind the scenes.

It was then that I really realized I'm no different than anyone else. Everyone is crazy, and no one shows what's really going on. **①**

1. FRASER-BUB: I'm intrigued by this. It does feels like it was written by a college student, and I like the tone.

2. WATTERS: This introduction felt really unnecessary. I thought this was a case of the writer not knowing where the story actually begins. Memoir needs to read like a novel. If someone has already bought this book they're going to know this information because they read the back cover copy.

3. CARLETON: The first sentence feels like a labored setup for a joke, and I'm put off by the attempt to chat with me before the narrator's done anything to make me care about her.

4. MCKEAN: This sounds like a journal, not a memoir with a narrative arc. It can be tempting to see a volume of writing and think it should go in a book, but readers want a story with a beginning, middle, and an end, not just a collection of thoughts.

3. PSYCHOLOGICAL THRILLER

With one hand on the steering wheel, Hailey Mantis used the other to rummage through her duffel bag. By the time she located the opaque cylinder of pills that her psychiatrist had prescribed she was panting like an animal in desperate need of water.

Get a grip. Get a grip. Hailey willed herself as she used her teeth to pry the medicine bottle open and then downed a few pills with a swig of Evian.

As Hailey merged onto the highway, her heartbeat continued to race. She exhaled in an attempt to slow her breathing but she knew this feeling all too well … it was the urge. ❷ ❸

If she took the East exit she would be home in time to eat dinner with her family but the urge beckoned her to veer onto the West exit and she obeyed.

Ten miles later Hailey arrived at her destination. Her pulse quickened as she slowed her Maserati to take in the surroundings. Drug peddlers occupied the street corners and plywood replaced shattered windows on the dilapidated houses.

She pressed a button to let her window down when she noticed a burly man who couldn't weigh any less than three hundred pounds approach her vehicle.

The man leaned over and the streetlights illuminated his diamond-encrusted necklace as he peered into Hailey's car. "I think you made a wrong turn Dorothy." A cigarette dangled between his thick lips as he spoke. "You're not in Kansas anymore."

Hailey's eyes met his and she smiled. *He's perfect! Oh dammit … I have Pilates with Angela tomorrow morning so I'll need to save my strength.* ❹ Without uttering a word, Hailey pressed the button once more and her window crept upward as she drove further down the street. ❶

1. FRASER-BUB: This is well paced and intriguing. There are some strong paranormal indicators—panting, racing heartbeat, the urge, the flashy car. Even though paranormal isn't usually my cup of tea, I would keep reading, as I like the style.

2. WATTERS: With a psychological thriller genre header, "the urge" sounded more horror-esque to me. I liked the rummaging for the pill bottle, but that was enough suspense for me. By this point I didn't want another teaser. This is a case of being too vague. I think it has all the right intentions, but it's missing the mark about how much to "show versus tell" and when to do it.

3. CARLETON: The writing is capable, but there's a hysterical tone that feels inauthentic to me, so by the time I get to "the urge," it seems melodramatic rather than ominous.

4. MCKEAN: The physical and visceral details here are very nice, but I wouldn't continue to read further. I would expect to know more of the why these things are happening here, not just the what of what's happening.

4. WOMEN'S FICTION

What color is your midlife crisis? ❸ Some mid-life crises manifest as boats, fast cars, or affairs. Mine came in the form of a fish camp. Sexy, huh? I really had no idea what I was getting into when I offered to buy old Max Johnson's dilapidated establishment, The Stinkin' Skunk Ape Fish Camp on the Santa Fe River. ❷ The site came complete with an eight-foot statue of North Florida's version of Bigfoot out by the road sign. I had been living in my old cracker house next door to the camp for about ten years. When Max's wife Charlene died, and Max had a stroke the following spring, it was obvious the place needed to be either rescued or torn down. I voted for the first option. Goofy as it seems, this sleepy fish camp is one of those old Florida places that are getting harder and harder to find, and I'd hate to see it get bought up by some developer who'd cut down all the two hundred-year-old live oaks, pave everything in sight, and charge a fortune for the hint of waterfront access. I want to keep it low-key and private. ❶

My name is Haint Blue, although Helena Blonichova is what it says on my birth certificate. I was born in Charleston, South Carolina, premature and albino. The nurses in the preemie ward took one look at me and said I looked like a "haint" and, since they weren't going to attempt Blonichova, they went with Blue. Haint blue is actually a narrow paint color spectrum in the periwinkle/gray hues intended to mimic water. Superstition has it that "haints," or ghosts can't pass over water, so if you painted your porch or trimmed your house in haint blue, you would avoid unwelcomed visitors from the spirit world. Not that I've been troubled by the spirit world mind you, but I'll give you only one guess as to what color I painted my meditation camp, just in case. ❹

1. FRASER-BUB: I do like the quirk factor, but this feels so rambling and conversational that I know an entire book written in this style isn't going to work for me.

2. WATTERS: The rhetorical questions I was willing to overlook, but the information dump here was too much for me. I would have liked a bit more nuance to make our character have a secret. Instead, we have a character spilling all her secrets and the reader isn't left with anything to wonder.

3. CARLETON: The story should tell itself rather than having the narrator try to chat with the reader. Rhetorical questions are almost always annoying, and often alienating. If I haven't had a midlife crisis, does that mean this book isn't for me?

4. MCKEAN: I read the whole selection because this is an area of Florida I know very well and love, but I felt lost in the second paragraph when we switch all the way back to the character's birth. Is this necessary in the second paragraph? Do we have to go back all the way through the character's life to get back to the narrative present?

5. ROMANCE

Kyle stood in the middle of his den looking at her curled up on the couch with her back to him. If she had turned around she would notice the look of complete disdain on his face, one side of his nose even snarling a little, involuntarily. She just lied there on the couch. **3** And these "episodes" seemed to be getting more and more frequent.

Why won't she do something about these migraines? Try something. Anything. She won't even let me try to help. He tried suggesting different treatments. But she was always so dismissive about anything he suggested. She made him feel so worthless.

The kids were at his parents. They were trying to give Kyle and his wife, Jacqueline, some time alone together. She, instead, used the day to bury her head under a pillow. They had the day to do whatever they wanted. But she just slept the whole day. No suggestion of going somewhere, no attempt at connecting, no sex, no housework, not even some conversation. She just stuck her head in a hole like an ostrich. **1**

At the very least she could use this time today to clean the house. Their house was small, a starter home. They had been there 11 years, and they still hadn't gone to the next level like Kyle had promised. Of course, Kyle wasn't exactly motivated to upgrade to a bigger house when Jacqueline couldn't even take care of herself and this one. He was always the one to clean. And half of the time he ended up being the one to cook, too. He actually wouldn't mind if he didn't feel so suckered into it. **2** **4**

Kyle continued to watch in disbelief as Jacqueline added another pillow over her head. *Fuck this*, Kyle thought to himself, completely exasperated. He threw his hands up in frustration and huffed audibly, then grabbed his keys and headed out.

1. FRASER-BUB: The wrong "lied" is a red flag as it indicates that this has not been edited at all. I also don't like either of these characters very much!.

2. WATTERS: I almost stopped at the beginning because I felt this was too heavily staged. Anything you have to force this much doesn't feel natural. But I glanced on a bit further and this was getting better; I like when the first page hints at characters' secrets. I stopped near the end because I found the text offensive. Even if it's the characters' opinion and not the author, you're alienating a female audience right away and for a romance novel that's your target market.

3. CARLETON: I'm willing to overlook the occasional typo or awkward phrase, but there's enough going on in this first paragraph that I'm skeptical about the author's command of language. After the errors, "lied" is the dealbreaker.

4. MCKEAN: There's a nice curious and mysterious mood already set up in these first paragraphs—this is clearly a family in crisis—but I couldn't connect with Kyle's. I would not spend 300+ pages with a character who lacks empathy.

6. MIDDLE-GRADE SCIENCE FICTION

As a recent graduate of the sixth grade, Michael Chapman knew a thing or two about how the world worked and felt more than qualified to say that this was the most boring summer in the history of the universe.

Michael was short for his age with straight blonde hair and ears that stuck out a little more than he would have liked. He lived with his father in a cabin on a river in the town of Beaver Creek, Alaska. Beavers were extinct, of course, and had been for centuries, but no one had bothered to change the name. In fact, no one on Earth had bothered to change much of anything in over three hundred years. It just took too much effort.

Beaver Creek was never an exciting place to live, but Michael didn't think it was too bad. There was great fishing right outside of his house, and his best friend, Tom Quinn, lived just down the road. Each summer the two of them would spend a month at Uncle Bunyan's Camp for Kids where they rode horses, practiced archery, and hiked in the mountains. While their town may not have had a zoo or a movie theater or enough kids for a baseball team, Michael didn't mind. It was his home, and he was happy.

But that was before this summer.

The trouble all started a month ago when the entire Quinn family disappeared. Mr. Quinn left a note on their front door that said they'd be vacationing in Borneo until August. Michael had no idea where Borneo was, but his father told him it was about as far from Alaska as somebody could get. This wasn't like them at all. Michael had known the Quinns his whole life, and they'd never even thought about traveling beyond Anchorage before. And Tom didn't even bother to say goodbye. **❶ ❷ ❸ ❹**

1. FRASER-BUB: I read to the end because this had some intriguing threads, but this is way too much information; I feel thoroughly confused about a lot of details, including: was it a boring summer, or did a family go missing?

2. WATTERS: I enjoyed this. It has the most crucial feature of middle grade fiction: voice. I liked that on the first page we were introduced to important information but it never felt like an "information dump" overload. We had a strong voice, interesting setting, and great sense of what the problem or conflict was going to be.

3. CARLETON: I enjoyed it. The first sentence has humor and personality, and I like the way the author slid the futuristic setting into the second paragraph. I think it could be clearer that the third paragraph is the way things used to be, not the way it is currently, but correcting the tense throughout would do the trick.

4. MCKEAN: I read the whole sample, but mainly to get to the part where the central problem of the novel is revealed. I was much less interested in what Tom and Michael normally did in the summer than what's different about this summer.

7. SOUTHERN FICTION

Round and round I went, pumping the whirlybird as fast as my four-year old legs could go, the windy motion tickling my eyelashes. I sang at the top of my lungs to my well-worn teddy, tucked in the front pocket of my pinafore. Teddy and I spent lots of time on the playground, so it weren't no big surprise that's where we was when Mama showed up to take me home. ❸ 'Course, when she and Matron Jones come walking across the yard that day, I didn't know the lady was my mama. Why, I didn't even know I had a mama. ❹

In the pictures made that year on the steps of the orphanage in Charleston, I was skinny as a beanpole with way too much hair. If them photographs had been in color, I bet my eyes was the first thing you'd seen, despite my wild head of red hair. I'd find out shortly they was Sullivan eyes. ❶

When the matron called to me real sweet-like to "come see who's here," I got a real bad feeling in my tummy. I doubled my grip on the handlebars, squeezed my eyes tight, and sang all the louder, "Me and my teddy bear, got one eye and got no hair."

When the two women got right up on me, and Matron Jones grabbed the seat to stop the spinning, my eyes popped open to a lady with rusty hair stuffed up under a hat. She was wearing a worm-colored suit, carrying a matching brown purse on the crook of her arm, and her gloved hands held on to each other for dear life and the lack of anything else to do. Without a doubt, that lady was my mama. Them eyes was a dead giveaway. ❷

1. FRASER-BUB: This four-year-old point of view doesn't work for me, and I feel like I'm being hit over the head with the very deliberate southern-ness of this, especially the dialect, which makes me cringe.

2. WATTERS: There were a few great lines that surprised me and kept me in suspense, so I read to the end. I was confused by what the time period was. I think that would have helped my understanding of this page more.

3. CARLETON: Child narrators in adult fiction are tricky, but this is just a bit too cutesy for my taste.

4. MCKEAN: As a Southerner, I'm well versed in Southern dialect. But I don't prefer to read it at this level. I believe a little goes a very, very long way in dialect. Too much can distract from otherwise nice prose.

8. YOUNG ADULT

The rafters stretch across the ceiling of the Zoo Chamber like honeycomb. I sit high in the metal branches, my legs thrown over one of the beams. It's a thirty meter drop into the sea of trees below. Not real trees, of course. The Zoo Chamber is filled with rubber trunks and plastic leaves, a fake forest that stretches beyond the horizon. I call it the horizon only because I have no better word. The so-called trees disappear where the curve of our ship takes a mighty turn. I haven't seen a real horizon since I was six. Normally I'm good at forgetting all of this isn't real, but today is different. Today I can't forget anything. I guess that's why they call it Remembrance Day. **1**

"Here it comes," Sybil whispers. My sister leans forward, as close as she can get to the glass wall that surrounds the Zoo Chamber.

Outside the glass, the moon slips from view.

Earth appears.

The colors always take me by surprise. Earth is color. A thousand shades of blue. A hundred tints of green. Ribbons of white, circling everything like a cage. It looks just like the pictures they used to show us in school, except for all the red light. That's new. The glow covers the planet like a second skin. If you watch carefully, you can almost see it pulse. I was born down there, somewhere in the green mountains of a country called the United Northern Republics. The red light is why I left. It's why we all left, while we still could.

Sybil holds up two fingers and closes an eye, extending her arm toward our old planet.

"What are you doing?"

"Picking a point."

I've had enough of this. **2 3 4**

> **1. FRASER-BUB:** I'm already exhausted. I need to feel immediately immersed in another world; the artificial forest is an interesting concept, but I want to be able to feel and see it, and I thought this description was needlessly convoluted.
> **2. WATTERS:** I read to the end. What I think this page did really well was set the scene, which is absolutely paramount in a fantasy novel's success.
> **3. CARLETON:** I read the full page and would read more, warily. I like the writing and the imagery, but the setup feels a bit familiar, especially the trope of the young adult story opening on an "Official Day" of some sort.
> **4. MCKEAN:** This does a great job of world-building and establishing mystery. I would keep reading to learn more about the story.

9. MAINSTREAM FICTION

Travis Montgomery knew he would rather bury her beneath the ground, then to let her walk this earth without him. Sweat from his palm slid down the grip of the revolver as he laid it on the nightstand. ❶ Thoughts of her began to fill him with sorrow. A melancholy so deep, he wished he was a praying man, a believer, so to speak. Because if he was, he would surely get down on his knees and beseech whatever God existed to keep her with him willingly. After all their years together, she wanted out. His fate hung in the balance as he waited for her to arrive. ❸ ❹

Cursing the Florida heat, he rose from the bed and began to pace. *It figured that there was no damn air conditioning in this dump.* His thin white cotton tee shirt was drenched with sweat. Stopping abruptly, he stared at his reflection in the large wood-framed mirror above the dresser. Streaks of grey, ❷ like silver thread ran through his dark brown hair. Managing a slight grin, he noted with approval the seamless skin on his face that encased deep set brown eyes. He had aged well. The tall, slim, but strong build contradicted the fifty-one years he carried with him. He rubbed his hands on the front of his jeans wiping the moisture from his hands. Picking up a small silver flask, he swallowed deep and mentally traced the burning sensation as the alcohol tumbled down his throat, traveling towards his navel. He clenched his jaw and heard the familiar click as his top and bottom teeth found each other. It was what he always did when he was on edge. A bad habit that he knew drove her crazy.

1. FRASER-BUB: This is so cliché that it does not bode well for a fresh story. I am very turned off by this character.

2. WATTERS: The first paragraph had a good start: creepy and ominous so I was waiting to see what happened next. Unfortunately, what happened next was a description of the character that felt cliché. Describing a character's looks in the mirror is not an advanced way of doing it.

3. CARLETON: Prose is too purple for my taste. This effort to flesh out the thought process of a violent misogynist also rubs me the wrong way—this might be a prologue from the point of view of a character who is quickly killed off, but if not, I'm not terribly interested in spending the rest of the book with him.

4. MCKEAN: I am not in the market for a book the hinges on domestic violence against women.

5 REASON QUERIES GET REJECTED

Don't make these query mistakes.

by Holly Jennings

In the summer of 2014, I set out on an epic quest: to draft a query letter that would not only garner the attention of literary agents, but would have them drooling over my book.

I spent every spare minute I had hunched over the computer, reading blog post after blog post on query-writing advice. At first, I could only find basic information about writing a three-part book summary for a query letter. This essentially boiled down to listing the character, conflict, and stakes of my novel. I wondered: Is that really all it took to impress an agent?

In a word: No.

Former agent Nathan Bransford once mentioned on his blog that he had received one hundred queries in a single holiday weekend. Of that one hundred, he requested material from two—which is a pretty abysmal rate for a hopeful author. Of course, some of those queries probably failed to follow the submission guidelines and were automatically rejected, and others probably weren't considered because they said nothing about the actual book. But a lot of queries do follow the agency's guidelines and faithfully follow the "character, conflict, and stakes" formula recommended by so many online resources. So of the dozens, if not hundreds, of queries that make it past the auto-reject stage, how can you make yours stand out from the slush pile?

Instead of sending you on the same virtual expedition I underwent, I'm going to share some commonly overlooked mistakes that can cripple your query letter—and your chances of securing representation. I'm no expert, but when I fixed these problems within my own query, something magical happened: I got requests.

Here's the breakdown. Between querying and pitching contests, I sent out fourteen letters. Six agents requested material, three passed, and five hadn't responded before I was offered representation.

That's a 42 percent request rate.

Wondering how you can achieve the same results? Examine your query letter for the following problems.

PROBLEM ONE:
YOU'RE NOT HOOKING THE AGENT FAST ENOUGH

When yours is one letter in a pile of a thousand queries, you don't have much time to grab an agent's attention. The hard truth is that most agents don't read every query all the way through. Frankly, they don't have time. Sometimes they skim. Sometimes they stop reading after the first few lines.

Pretend you only have one line to get the agent's attention. What is the most interesting thing you could say about your story or its main character?

Here are the opening lines to the query that landed me an agent:

> The warrior. It's a title twenty-year-old Kali Ling earned bringing men to their knees ... inside video games.

Is it perfect? No. But it does the job. It's short, simple, and ends in a twist. As the reader, you're left wondering: How is she bringing men to their knees inside video games? Is she literally inside a game? What's going on here? The only way anyone can find out—including the agent—is to continue reading the query.

With that first line, you need to catch the agent's attention—hook, line, and sinker. Here are some other ways to hook an agent within the first one to two sentences.

Include an unexpected twist:

> When Cate Benson was twelve, her sister died. Two hours after the funeral, they picked up Violet's replacement, and the family made it home in time for dinner and a game of cards.
> —*Falls the Shadow* by Stefanie Gaither

Include humor:

> You'd have to be drunk or crazy to hire Dahlia Moss as a detective, and her client was conveniently both.
> —*The Unfortunate Decisions of Dahlia Moss* by Max Wirestone, the New Adult Query Champion of the Query Kombat Contest 2014

Include something shocking:

> Shawn knows he's going to die on his eighteenth birthday.
> —Query #260 on QueryShark.com

Pull at the heartstrings:

> She had the talent, she had the drive, and she had the opportunity. Only one thing stood between Penelope Sparrow and the dance career of her dreams: her imperfect body.
> —*The Art of Falling* by Kathryn Craft

Remember to take your genre into consideration. A mysterious and unexpected detail might work well for science fiction, while a line with an emotional edge might bode better for contemporary fiction. Don't bore the agent with a bland opening line. Instead, toss the biggest bait you can into the querying ocean, and wait for an agent to bite.

PROBLEM TWO: YOUR CONCEPT ISN'T UNIQUE

Don't panic. This doesn't mean your book isn't unique enough. But your query letter summary paragraphs could probably use some work. The majority of queries agents receive are generic and boring, and don't describe the plot of the story. Instead, they contain trite phrases and clichés that could be used to describe every B-rated movie ever made. As Agent Moe Ferrara of BookEnds recently said on Twitter: "Authors! Don't be vague in your queries ('unfortunate events' or 'bad things happen to her'). Tell me what happened! I want plots!"

The key to having a memorable query is specifics, specifics, specifics. Here are two examples. (For the sake of simplicity, I've reduced these summaries to two sentences; yours will likely be longer.) The first example below is bland and generic. The second is specific and engaging.

> 1. Mandy loves scuba diving. But when someone mysterious starts killing those who love the water, she must uncover the killer's identity before it's too late.

> 2. Sixteen-year-old scuba diver Mandy lives for the water. But when a psychopath starts killing members of the local marina, she must uncover the murderer's identity before more than her tank runs out of oxygen.

Calling the killer a "psychopath" is much more chilling than saying "someone mysterious." And "before her tank runs out of oxygen" is much more distinct than "before it's too late." See how the specific details add more emotion, create concrete imagery, and make the story memorable?

Look at every line of your query and ask yourself: Could this line apply to other queries from other authors? If so, can you describe the plot, the characters, and other summary components in a way that applies to only your story?

As you revise your summary, avoid using these generic, overused phrases:

- "Things will never be the same again."
- "Things have changed forever."
- "Everyone will die if …"
- "… before time runs out."
- "Something unexpected happens."
- "All of a sudden …"

- "He is the chosen one."
- "It's the end of the world as she knows it."
- "She discovers she has superpowers!"
- "Someone mysterious starts at his school."
- "A stranger moves to town."

Your story is unique to you and only you. Make sure your individuality is reflected in your query paragraphs.

PROBLEM THREE: YOUR COMPARATIVE TITLES AREN'T UP TO PAR

A standard query letter should contain a few comparative titles that are similar to your own book. This helps the agent understand the tone and potential audience for your novel, while reassuring her that you understand the market you're writing in. Get your comp titles wrong and your query could be toast.

Agents are looking for a reason to say no. Don't make it easy for them by choosing poorly. Okay, if an agent was over-the-moon in love with your summary paragraphs, maybe they'd overlook this mistake. But if they're on the fence about requesting material, the wrong comp title can send you to Camp Rejection.

So how do you pick the right comp titles?

- Choose book titles within the upper-mid range of popularity. People who read the genre should be familiar with them, even if the general reading public is not.
- Make sure at least one of your titles was published in the last five years. Better yet, choose titles published in the last three years if you can.
- If applicable, try a mash-up of two titles that wouldn't naturally be paired together. Writing a comedy horror? Try: "It's Monster Island meets The Hangover."
- If you feel your writing is similar to another author's, mention that. (For example, "My book should appeal to fans of Author X.") Just make sure you don't compare yourself to Shakespeare or Mark Twain.

A FEW ADDITIONAL TIPS:

- Limit yourself to listing two to three titles. Including more makes you seem amateurish. Listing only one implies you don't know your genre or market.
- Strive for examples that match the tone of your novel. For example, if your writing is more upbeat and humorous, don't list a comp title with a dark and depressing tone.
- You can list movies, television shows, or comic books, but limit yourself to one nonbook title per query.
- Avoid listing mega-bestsellers like the Harry Potter or Twilight series books.

- Conversely, avoid listing superobscure titles that no one—not even an agent—has ever heard of.

PROBLEM FOUR: YOUR STAKES AREN'T HIGH ENOUGH

Stakes represent conflict and danger. They make the reader care about and root for your character. What happens if your protagonist wins? What happens if he loses?

Let's look at the stakes from my debut novel, *Arena*. The main character, Kali Ling, is stuck between becoming the first female captain to win a gaming tournament and honoring her fallen teammate by exposing the corruption within virtual sports.

If she exposes the corruption, she risks losing her spot as captain, and thousands of young girl gamers are counting on her to be the first woman to claim the title. But if she pursues becoming captain, then corruption in virtual sports lives on, and her friend will have died in vain.

Does she become a role model or a rebel? Notice how the plot presents no clear choice. Worst of all, what if she can't decide and accomplishes nothing? Or what if she picks one of the two options and fails miserably? OMG! The drama! Agents love this.

Even when superheroes have to save the entire world, their thoughts aren't about all of humanity. They think about those closest to them. Ironman thinks of Pepper Potts. Superman thinks of Lois Lane, Jimmy Olsen, and his parents. Neo thinks of Trinity. Thor thinks of Jane Foster and his newfound friends on Earth.

Stakes are defined by what is most important to your character and how she could lose it. So ask yourself: *What choices does my character make, and how will this affect her?*

PROBLEM FIVE: YOUR LETTER IS DEVOID OF VOICE

Ah, voice. This element is quite possibly the hardest thing to include in your query. But if your query is constructed properly and oozes with voice, chances are high that an agent will request your full manuscript.

Here's a perfect example of a voice-laden query:

> In fourteen-year-old Anne's opinion, there are two kinds of quests: the kind that lead to unicorns and lollipops, and the kind that get you and everyone you love killed, horribly and painfully (possibly by zombie sharks). She knows this because her budding magick abilities have accidentally entangled her in a quest, and so far she hasn't encountered any lollipops.
>
> She could opt out, but then, as per Paragraph 5 Subparagraph 3 of the Official Questing Regulations, she'd be exiled forever, and all of her friends would be tossed into a dungeon. She'd rather kiss a Steam Troll than let that happen …
>
> —*The Adventurer's Guide to Successful Escapes* by Wade Albert White, the Middle-Grade Query Champion of the Query Kombat Contest 2014

I'll be honest here: I don't even enjoy reading middle-grade fiction, but I need to read this novel now. And if you're wondering, White's book had multiple offers.

Notice how White names the prizes of the quest as "unicorns and lollipops." Maybe this isn't what you or I would want to find at the end of a quest, but these examples are completely in line with the tone of an middle-grade novel. And as adults, we know there are far worse things in life than kissing a troll, but from the perspective of a middle-grade girl? Ew, yuck.

Does voice really have that much impact on a query? Editor Jordan Wright of Jolly Fish Press had this to say on Twitter: "I know it's a good query when the synopsis alone convinces me the [manuscript] is worth reading. Great voice!"

Voice comes from knowing your point-of-view character intimately and funneling the world through their perspective. A ten-year-old boy wouldn't looks at things in the same way as an eighty-year-old woman. Use voice to your advantage in your query. Does your character have a favorite catchphrase? Put it in. Is he happy and optimistic, or does he have a dark, snarky sense of humor? His personality should be reflected in the words he chooses to describe his world.

This is *voice*.

If all the other parts of your query are solid, voice becomes the whipped cream on a hot fudge sundae. And you can never have too much whipped cream.

If you send your query out unedited, you allow an agent to find reasons to reject your work. Pay attention to these five common mistakes and aim for a 42 percent rate (or better!) for your work.

HOLLY JENNINGS writes from her home in Tecumseh, Ontario. Her short fiction has appeared in *Daily Science Fiction*, and *AE: The Canadian Science Fiction Review*, among others. *Arena*, her debut novel, released in April 2016. Described as *"Ready Player One* meets *The Hunger Games,"* it stars a female cyber-athlete inside a corrupt world of fame, venality, and gaming. Follow Jennings on Twitter: @HollyN_Jennings.

BETA TEST YOUR BOOK

Get feedback from readers before you submit.

by Amy Sue Nathan

Once you query an agent, there's no mulligan. Back when I started querying my first novel, I received targeted feedback from an agent who rejected the manuscript. She said the beginning chapters were too hard to follow—too many people, too much going on. That was something no one else had ever said to me. Then I realized that while this agent didn't give me the option to resubmit, she did give me something: a brand-new point of view on what I'd assumed were perfect-as-I-could-make-them pages. I changed the beginning, killing off darlings and reimagining a well-loved scene. With *that* opening I eventually found an agent who went on to sell the book.

So wouldn't it have been great if someone had given me that feedback before I had queried at all? Or at least hinted that something was amiss?

Yes. But I would have had to ask for it.

The truth is, I'd had years of feedback on my manuscript from writing partners when I polished my pages and then hit *Send*. I was finished. I was ready. I was wrong.

Agents don't look for reasons to say *no*; they look for reasons to say *yes*. That agent didn't have one, but in part thanks to her feedback, another one did.

So when you're ready to step on the query-go-round, take one final step back before you hit *Send*.

Yes, even though your manuscript is polished and proofread, even though others know your story almost as well as you do and you have a list of appropriate agents, a well-vetted query letter, maybe even a synopsis, stop and ask: Has anyone with fresh eyes, with no preconceived notions about your story, read the latest version of your book from start to finish with the specific and targeted task of offering the feedback you need in a timely manner?

Someone should.

That someone is a *beta reader*.

WHAT EXACTLY IS A BETA READER?

A beta reader will help ensure your story reads as you intend it to read to an agent, making sure it conveys what you intend to convey. A beta reader differs from a critique partner, where the label implies that work is shared. Also, critique partners often swap work *as* it is being written. With a beta reader, you share your *finished* novel. A beta reader is someone who will give you the feedback you ask for, someone who is willing and eager to read your work and provide the feedback you need, when you need it.

A beta reader isn't a proofreader (or shouldn't be, though catching a mistake is always welcome) or someone who believes you want to change your story or has her own "how abouts" in mind. A beta reader must believe in the story you have, and read to unearth any stumbling blocks to your getting an agent's attention—such as having too much commotion in an opening scene. When seeking an ideal beta reader, look for writing peers who are smart, critical, and honest.

WHO MAKES A GOOD BETA READER?

Anyone, but not everyone, can be a beta reader. Look for someone who has at least some of the following characteristics:

- reads published books in your genre
- writes in your genre
- has written thoughtful (not necessarily glowing) reviews or critiques online
- shares opinions about books, and other things, that you respect (even if you don't always agree)
- has time and enthusiasm (be wary of weary or very busy betas)
- has offered to help you prepare to query and submit (though this should not be the only criterion)
- has been a well-liked beta reader for a friend (just make sure she isn't worn out)

HOW MANY BETA READERS DO I NEED?

For each new project, I use two or three readers I know and feel I can trust, even if they haven't read for me before. When you're using readers for the first time, you might want to invite three or four, both to build your confidence in them as well as to help them feel less pressure by knowing you have "backup" readers. Although beta readers typically do this task as a generous favor (you're not hiring a professional), most readers are flattered by the request and take the task seriously, as they should. (In return, thank-yous in the form of a dinner out or a token gift are never a bad idea.)

WHERE DO I FIND BETA READERS?

I met a few of my beta readers during online workshops. I liked reading their work, admired their interaction with the other participants and the instructor, and liked the way they critiqued shared submissions. I clicked with their personalities and senses of humor. I have one beta reader who has been my friend for almost twenty-five years, and will say anything to me about my work. She remembers details of the story that I forget, and has a knack for making keen comparisons and observations. I find it helpful that she compares scenes in my manuscripts to scenes in movies we're both familiar with as a way to describe a reaction she'd like to have or an emotion she's experiencing.

You might find a beta reader among your friends and family who knows you well enough to do this. Just be careful it's not someone who will love whatever you do or, conversely, someone who will be critical just because she's been given a green light to tell you what she thinks.

Consider book clubs or writing groups you attend. Is there a member who often chimes in with thoughtful insights or asks questions that resonate? Online writer (or even reader) forums or Facebook groups are informal venues to become familiar with prospective betas, to gauge how they react to feedback and interact with others. If you don't belong to any such groups, consider joining some as you head toward the query stage with your manuscript.

Remember, you want honesty without attitude in a beta reader. If you don't like the way someone represents himself online or in person, pay attention. Even if this is someone noteworthy, it's not worth it.

WHAT DO I ASK A BETA READER TO DO (AND HOW DO I ASK)?

Being a beta reader is a big responsibility. You're not just asking this person to read your book, you're asking for a thoughtful critique of certain parts or aspects. This is where it's *your* job to be honest.

- Accompany your initial request with a start date and end date. Be kind but firm. If the potential beta reader can't fit in the reading and feedback when you need it, thank her for considering your request, but tell her you need to move forward. Make it clear it's okay for her to say no—no hard feelings, but maybe a rain check.
- Send a list of questions you'd like the betas to answer about the book. (More on that in the next section.) This will ensure you get the same areas of focused feedback from each reader and can compare their notes.
- Be sure the readers know they're making *suggestions* and that not all changes will be incorporated into the book. This eases the pressure on both them and you.
- Invite additional feedback outside of the areas you've highlighted in your questions.

- Ask for comments on what works well for the reader. This is about knowing what's *not* broken so you don't try to fix it. (And let's face it, positive feedback on some areas can also make negative feedback on others easier to swallow.)

HOW DO I MAKE SURE I GET THE FEEDBACK I NEED?

The best way to get what you need, and want, in any situation, is to ask for it. When preparing the aforementioned list of questions for your beta readers, be sure you're asking all the questions you want to know the answers to. Better yet, ask the questions you're *afraid* to know the answers to.

Here are some sample questions and prompts you can customize to spur your beta readers to action. You can request that these be addressed after each chapter, after reading the whole book, or both.

- What's one word to describe the main character after page one? After chapter one?
- On what page do you think you know what the story will be about? (Agents often read a few pages or a partial before asking for more. A strong opening is key.)
- Is there anything in chapter X that makes you particularly angry/sad/happy? (This question is helpful if there is an important scene in which you aim to evoke a certain reaction or emotion.)
- In the conflict between character A and character B, do you think the resolution took too long, or was too fast?
- What do you wish were different in chapter one? (I ask this question for every chapter, to get a sense of whether my readers' vision for the story is what I intend or hope it to be as the scenes unfold.)
- Note places where you were confused or had to reread.
- List scenes or lines that made you cringe/gasp/cry.
- List scenes or pages you skimmed. If you can pinpoint why, please do so.
- Share your favorite character/scene/chapter and why.

HOW DO I HANDLE THE FEEDBACK I GET (OR DON'T GET)?

Graciously. Someone just read your book and gave you the feedback you asked for, no matter what that happens to be. Thank your reader for her feedback and "dismiss" her from duty.

If a reader neglects to send the feedback she promised, a nudge is acceptable. Even two nudges. After that, it's likely that something "suddenly came up" or she didn't realize how much work this beta business would be. (You might assume she hated your book, but that's likely not the case, honest.)

Once you've received the feedback from all readers, compare notes, question by question and line by line. I print out pages and use my favorite pen to mark what makes sense to me, what resonates most strongly, and what doesn't resonate at all.

WHAT DO I DO WHEN FEEDBACK DOESN'T RESONATE, OR BETAS CLASH?

It happens all the time. Take time to let the comments sink in. Days. Weeks, even. I'll be honest, when I received that agent's feedback about the opening of my debut novel I scoffed at first. Rolled my eyes. Then I decided to take the seemingly ridiculous advice and see what would happen if I heeded it. You know the rest of the story.

Just as you wanted your beta reader to be honest with you, you must be honest with yourself. Is it just that you don't like what the beta reader said, or does it not mesh with your vision for your book? There's a difference.

While the feedback that prompted my final manuscript changes was from an agent, I believe I might have avoided some of my earliest rejections altogether if I had asked the right readers the right questions beforehand.

That being said, if there is feedback that really doesn't work for you, set it aside. When I offer feedback my final words are: "Take what you need and leave the rest."

If you find that your beta readers' comments contradict one another, and you're confused because nothing—or everything—seems reasonable (or ridiculous), approach one of your beta readers with questions about another reader's comments. This is not a bash-the-beta festival, but an attempt to get a little more help and another opinion. Again, ask for honesty. Does this other feedback make sense? How does this beta see her own feedback now, in light of what you've presented?

WILL MY BOOK EVER BE READY TO QUERY?

Yes! You've done the work. And then, you enlisted some help and did it all again. Maybe three times. Even four. You mean business and everyone knows it. It's time to query when your doubt (which never goes away) is laced with excitement, when you understand that hitting *Send* is not the end of your journey, but the beginning.

....

AMY SUE NATHAN is an author, writing instructor, freelance writer, and founder of www. WomensFictionWriters.com. Her latest novel, *The Good Neighbor*, was released in October 2015. Follow her on Twitter @AmySueNathan.

....

HOW NOT TO START YOUR NOVEL

Learn agents' chapter one pet peeves.

by Chuck Sambuchino

Ask literary agents what they're looking for in a first chapter and they'll all say the same thing: "Good writing that hooks me in." Agents appreciate the same elements of good writing that readers do. They want action; they want compelling characters and a reason to read on; they want to see your voice come through in the work and feel an immediate connection with your writing style.

Sure, the fact that agents look for great writing and a unique voice is nothing new. But, for as much as you know about what agents *want* to see in chapter one, what about all those things they *don't* want to see? Obvious mistakes such as grammatical errors and awkward writing aside, writers need to be conscious of first-chapter clichés and agent pet peeves—any of which can sink a manuscript and send a form rejection letter your way.

Have you ever begun a story with a character waking up from a dream? Or opened chapter one with a line of salacious dialogue? Both clichés! Chances are, you've started a story with a cliché or touched on a pet peeve (or many!) in your writing and you don't even know it—and nothing turns off an agent like what agent Cricket Freeman of The August Agency calls "nerve-gangling, major turn-off, ugly-as-sin, nails-on-the-blackboard pet peeves."

To help compile a grand list of these poisonous chapter one no-no's, plenty of established literary agents were more than happy to chime in and vent about everything that they can't stand to see in that all-important first chapter. Here's what they had to say.

DESCRIPTION

"I dislike endless 'laundry list' character descriptions. For example: 'She had eyes the color of a summer sky and long blonde hair that fell in ringlets past her shoulders. Her petite nose was the perfect size for her heart-shaped face. Her azure dress—with the empire waist and long, tight sleeves—sported tiny pearl buttons down the bodice and ivory lace

peeked out of the hem in front, blah, blah, blah.' Who cares! Work it into the story."
—**LAURIE MCLEAN,** *Fuse Literary*

VOICE AND POINT OF VIEW

"A pet peeve of mine is ragged, fuzzy point-of-view. How can a reader follow what's happening? I also dislike beginning with a killer's point of view. What reader would want to be in such an ugly place? I feel like a nasty voyeur."—**CRICKET FREEMAN,** *The August Agency*

"Avoid the opening line 'My name is …,' introducing the narrator to the reader so blatantly. There are far better ways in chapter one to establish an instant connection between narrator and reader."—**MICHELLE ANDELMAN,** *formerly of Regal Literary*

"I hate reading purple prose, taking the time to set up—to describe something so beautifully and that has nothing to do with the actual story. I also hate when an author starts something and then says '(the main character) would find out later.' I hate gratuitous sex and violence anywhere in the manuscript. If it is not crucial to the story then I don't want to see it in there, in any chapters."—**CHERRY WEINER,** *Cherry Weiner Literary*

"I recently read a manuscript when the second line was something like, 'Let me tell you this, Dear Reader …' What do *you* think of that?"—**SHEREE BYKOFSKY,** *Sheree Bykofsky Literary*

ACTION (OR LACK THEREOF)

"I don't really like first-day-of-school beginnings, or the 'From the beginning of time,' or 'Once upon a time' starts. Specifically, I dislike a chapter one where nothing happens."
—**JESSICA REGEL,** *Foundry Literary + Media*

" 'The Weather' is always a problem—the author feels he has to take time to set up the scene completely and tell us who the characters are. I like starting a story *in media res*."
—**ELIZABETH POMADA,** *Larsen/Pomada, Literary Agents*

"I want to feel as if I'm in the hands of a master storyteller, and starting a story with long, flowery, overly descriptive sentences (kind of like this one) makes the writer seem amateurish and the story contrived. Of course, an equally jarring beginning can be nearly as off-putting, and I hesitate to read on if I'm feeling disoriented by the fifth page. I enjoy when writers can find a good balance between exposition and mystery. Too much accounting always ruins the mystery of a novel, and the unknown is what propels us to read further. It is what keeps me up at night saying, 'Just one more chapter, then I'll sleep.' If everything is explained away in the first chapter, I'm probably putting the book down and going to sleep."—**PETER MILLER,** *Global Lion Management*

"Characters that are moving around doing little things, but essentially nothing. Washing dishes and thinking, staring out the window and thinking, tying shoes, thinking. Authors often do this to transmit information, but the result is action in a literal sense but no real energy in a narrative sense. The best rule of thumb is always to start the story where the story starts."—**DAN LAZAR,** *Writers House*

CLICHÉS AND FALSE BEGINNINGS

"I *hate* it when a book begins with an adventure that turns out to be a dream at the end of the chapter."—**MOLLIE GLICK,** *Creative Artists Agency*

"Anything cliché such as 'It was a dark and stormy night' will turn me off. I hate when a narrator or author addresses the reader (e.g., 'Gentle reader')."—**JENNIE DUNHAM,** *Dunham Literary*

"Sometimes a reasonably good writer will create an interesting character and describe him in a compelling way, but then he'll turn out to be some unimportant bit player. I also don't want to read about anyone sleeping, dreaming, waking up, or staring at anything. Other annoying, unoriginal things I see too often: some young person going home to a small town for a funeral, someone getting a phone call about a death, a description of a psycho lurking in the shadows or a terrorist planting a bomb."—**ELLEN PEPUS,** *Signature Literary Agency*

"I don't like it when the main character dies at the end of chapter one. Why did I just spend all this time with this character? I feel cheated."—**CRICKET FREEMAN,** *The August Agency*

"1) Squinting into the sunlight with a hangover in a crime novel. Good grief—been done a million times. 2) A sci-fi novel that spends the first two pages describing the strange landscape. 3) A trite statement ('Get with the program' or 'Houston, we have a problem' or 'You go girl' or 'Earth to Michael' or 'Are we all on the same page?'), said by a weenie sales guy, usually in the opening paragraph. 4) A rape scene in a Christian novel, especially in the first chapter. 5) 'Years later, Monica would look back and laugh ...' 6) 'The [adjective] [adjective] sun rose in the [adjective] [adjective] sky, shedding its [adjective] light across the [adjective] [adjective] [adjective] land.' "—**CHIP MACGREGOR,** *MacGregor Literary*

"A cheesy 'hook' drives me nuts. I know that they say 'Open with a hook!'—something to grab the reader. While that's true, there's a fine line between a hook that's intriguing and a hook that's just silly. An example of a silly hook would be opening with a line of overtly sexual dialogue. Or opening with a hook that's just too convoluted to be truly interesting."—**DAN LAZAR,** *Writers House*

"Here are things I can't stand: Cliché openings in fantasy novels can include an opening scene set in a battle (and my peeve is that I don't know any of the characters yet so why should I care about this battle) or with a pastoral scene where the protagonist is gathering herbs (I didn't realize how common this is). Opening chapters where a main protagonist is in the middle of a bodily function (jerking off, vomiting, peeing, or what have you) is usually a firm *no* right from the get-go. Gross. Long prologues that often don't have anything to do with the story. (So common in fantasy, again.) Opening scenes that are all dialogue without any context. I could probably go on ..."—**KRISTIN NELSON,** *Nelson Literary*

CHARACTERS AND BACKSTORY

"I don't like descriptions of the characters where writers make the characters seem too perfect. Heroines (and heroes) who are described physically as being unflawed come across as unrelatable and boring. No 'flowing, windswept golden locks'; no 'eyes as blue as the sky'; no 'willowy, perfect figures.' " —**LAURA BRADFORD,** *Bradford Literary Agency*

"Many writers express the character's backstory before they get to the plot. Good writers will go back and cut that stuff out and get right to the plot. The character's backstory stays with them—it's in their DNA—even after the cut. To paraphrase Bruno Bettelheim: The more the character in a fairy tale is described, the less the audience will identify with him ... The less the character is characterized and described, the more likely the reader is to identify with him." —**ADAM CHROMY,** *Movable Type Management*

"I'm really turned off when a writer feels the need to fill in all the backstory before starting the story; a story that opens on the protagonist's mental reflection of their situation is (usually) a red flag."—**STEPHANY EVANS,** *FinePrint Literary Management*

"One of the biggest problems I encounter is the 'information dump' in the first few pages, where the author is trying to tell us everything we supposedly need to know to understand the story. Getting to know characters in a story is like getting to know people in real life. You find out their personality and details of their life over time."—**RACHELLE GARDNER,** *Books & Such Literary*

OTHER PET PEEVES

"The most common opening is a grisly murder scene told from the killer's point of view. While this usually holds the reader's attention, the narrative drive often doesn't last once we get into the meat of the story. A catchy opening scene is great, but all too often it falls apart after the initial pages. I often refer people to the opening of *Rosemary's Baby* by Ira Levin, which is about nothing more than a young couple getting an apartment. It is masterfully written and yet it doesn't appear to be about anything sinister at all. And it keeps you reading." —IRENE GOODMAN, *Irene Goodman Literary*

"Things I dislike include: (1) Telling me what the weather's like in order to set atmosphere. OK, it was raining. It's *always* raining. (2) Not starting with action. I want to have a sense of dread quite quickly—and not from rain! (3) Sending me anything but the beginning of the book; if you tell me that it 'starts getting good' on page 35, then I will tell you to start the book on page 35, because if even you don't like the first 34, neither will I or any other reader." —JOSH GETZLER, *Hannigan Salky Getzler Agency*

"One of my biggest pet peeves is when writers try to stuff too much exposition into dialogue rather than trusting their abilities as storytellers to get information across. I'm talking stuff like the mom saying, 'Listen, Jimmy, I know you've missed your father ever since he died in that mysterious boating accident last year on the lake, but I'm telling you, you'll love this summer camp!' " —CHRIS RICHMAN, *Upstart Crow Literary*

"I hate to see a whiny character who's in the middle of a fight with one of their parents, slamming doors, rolling eyes, and displaying all sorts of other stereotypical behavior. I also tend to have a hard time bonding with characters who address the reader directly." —KELLY SONNACK, *Andrea Brown Literary Agency*

WHAT TO EXPECT AFTER YOU GET AN AGENT

Know what comes after you sign.

by Marie Lamba

//

Years ago, I didn't know much about agents, but what I did know, I liked. They represented the most talented writers. They got new writers' work in front of the right editors at the top publishing houses. They negotiated strong book deals and took care of those complex publishing contracts. Hey, that's all I needed to know, right?

Wrong.

When I actually got "the call," it came from Jennifer De Chiara of The Jennifer De Chiara Literary Agency, who encouraged me to ask her any questions I might have. That's when it hit me: I hadn't a clue of what to ask. I didn't know a thing about what to expect next.

Ten years and several books later, I'm still represented by Jennifer—and I'm also working as a literary agent at her agency, representing children's and adult fiction, and memoirs. I've learned a lot about what happens on both the author's and the agent's side of things. Here's what I wish I'd known right from the start.

OPENING UP COMMUNICATION

Online message boards are flooded with posts from writers who think they might have a problem with their literary agent. It's not because the world is flooded with terrible agents. It's because writers are often too afraid to tell their own agents when they have questions or concerns.

Hey, I totally get that. As nice as my agent is (and she is extremely nice and helpful), at the beginning of our journey together I wouldn't dare question anything she was doing or ask for any sort of change in our dealings with each other. I'd worked hard to land this agent. I didn't want to screw things up! Instead I just worried and stewed. Finally, though,

I "put on my big-girl panties" and started having direct conversations with my agent whenever I felt the need. As a result, our working relationship has only gotten stronger.

Be sure to start your own author-agent relationship on the right foot by developing great communication from the beginning. One of the very first things you should ask is how to get in touch. It's likely he'll prefer e-mail for most communications. But what if you need to talk on the phone at some point? I share my cell number with my clients but ask that, unless it's urgent, they shoot me an e-mail first so we can schedule a phone appointment.

If your agent shares his cell number with you, be respectful: Don't ever, unless it's extremely critical, call him outside of regular workday hours.

As you interact, you'll get a sense of your agent's style. Some agents are chatty, and you instantly feel comfortable talking with them. You'll quickly build a rapport, and over time you may even grow close. But no matter how friendly you become, remember that it's a professional relationship, so always check your personal drama at the door.

Other agents are more no-nonsense. Their phone calls will be short with little room for chitchat, their e-mails brief and to the point. If you know this, you'll know not to take it personally.

And remember, sometimes even a chatty agent is just too busy to chat. Early in my relationship with my own agent, she e-mailed me a one-word reply. It did answer my question, but I still wondered if I had made her mad. *Was she going to drop me?* We writers are all too capable of imagining all sorts of meanings between the lines. But if I'd had a better understanding of everything an agent does and how busy she really could be, that one-word reply wouldn't have fazed me.

UNDERSTANDING "AGENT TIME"

As writers, we essentially have one main job: Perfect our manuscript and send it to our agent. After that, we wait for him to read and respond to it. We check our e-mail incessantly. Oh, we try to keep our mind off of it, but still we obsess. Does the agent like it? Does it still need work? Can it be sent to editors now? A week passes. Then another. Then a month. We start to seriously freak out. What is taking so long? Don't we matter to our own agent?

Let's look at the flip side. Say you're my client, and your novel pings into my agency inbox. I acknowledge its receipt with a return e-mail (always confirm that your agent receives it). I log the novel into my queue, behind several others I've recently received from other clients. Then I head off to meetings with editors. Next I pitch another client's book, which can take several days. Then I dash off to a four-day conference where I meet with editors, do presentations, take author pitches, and then return to find my inbox filled with submissions from conference attendees—plus, a manuscript from *another* client. I finally block out some reading time and begin to review a client manuscript I received two weeks prior to yours. It's 400 pages long. I get interrupted by an offer from an editor on another project. Negotiating that deal involves contacting a number of other editors, plus the author, and preparing counteroffers. In between, I continue to read through that client manuscript, editing and inserting comments as I go.

You get the idea. Your agent is likely doing her best to get to your work as quickly as possible, all while taking care of the day-to-day business of repping and assisting authors.

If she has a Twitter feed or an appearance schedule posted online, you can get a glimpse of what's on her plate. Mind you, it's okay to check in after a few weeks for an update—something along the lines of, "Just checking to see whether you'd had a chance to give this a look yet, and wondering if you have an idea of when I might expect comments." (Good communication, right?) But don't continuously pester her with follow-up e-mails. She already knows your work is in the queue.

Still, waiting is never easy. Get busy writing your next manuscript—it'll help pass that time, plus advance your career. Do touch base with your agent, though, about at what stage she'd like to weigh in on your newest project. She'll likely want to offer a market and career perspective about it, and maybe even give you feedback on initial pages.

What if several months go by and you still haven't heard from your agent about that full manuscript? If you never get an answer to your inquiry, or your work remains unread for many months without a solid reason and no communication, then it's time to schedule a phone call and find out if there's anything going on that you should know about. You may discover there's an illness in the family or some other legit cause for the delay. What if there is no real reason? Then you need to have a frank discussion about what you can expect moving forward, and decide if this agent is the right fit for you.

Do keep in mind that if you are showering your agent with multiple completed projects, it's likely she'll work on only one of them at a time. Your other projects will then remain in the queue until she is able to circle back to them. She has many clients and must advance all of their careers.

SURVIVING SUBMISSION

Your manuscript will often need changes before it goes out on submission. Don't be discouraged or take it too personally. Editors now expect manuscripts to come to them as close to perfect as possible, and your agent is there to tell it to you straight.

If your agent is "highly editorial," expect plenty of comments and tracked edits to be sent your way. If not, then he'll probably let you know whether or not he deems your project ready for submission, but offer only a few comments as to why. Feel free to clarify any comments you don't quite understand, but then it's up to you to get the manuscript up to snuff on your own. Roll up your sleeves and do the best revision you possibly can before your agent sees it again.

Once a manuscript is ready for submission, I work with my client to shape the strongest synopsis and author bio possible, and then I take it from there. Your agent may do things slightly differently, but here's what I do: Using info I've put together through years of research and talking with editors, I create a list of editors to contact—ones who I know are looking for just this sort of project. I spend a lot of time perfecting my pitch, which succinctly captures the essence of the book. Then I get on the phone, calling each editor and delivering this pitch in a way that piques interest. Editors tell me they'd love to see it, and I e-mail the manuscript to them, along with the synopsis and bio.

I record where it was sent and when, and let my client know that the book has been submitted and who has it.

I always check back with each editor to make sure he received the manuscript. Then I wait. After a few weeks go by, if I haven't heard anything, I'll call these editors to see if they've had a chance to read it yet.

That, in essence, is the process. Before your manuscript goes out to editors, ask your agent what info he'll be sharing with you about submissions. Some agents provide details only if you ask. Otherwise they'll just let you know if anything significant happens—like an offer. So if you'd like to see every rejection and all comments from editors, let him know. If, however, you don't handle those well, tell him what level of info is right for you.

BUILDING TRUST

One important thing to remember at this stage is that you, the writer, must trust your agent. Don't demand to see her pitch and fix it for her. If you have truly informed suggestions about which editors you think would like your book, feel free to share them, but trust your agent to make the ultimate decision about who she contacts—this is her area of expertise.

Trust is also a sizeable part of what you hope will be the next stage of this process— negotiating a book contract. This, too, is the agent's area of expertise. Trust that he's negotiating the very best deal he can on your behalf. I should warn you, though—authors may feel really out of the loop during this stage. If a deal comes in, your agent will tell you about the initial basic deal points: which publisher is making the offer, and what advance and/or royalty rates have been offered. But after that the author shouldn't expect much more info until after the deal points are fully negotiated. It's just not practical timewise to be included in all the back-and-forth, and is not needed until things are firmed up.

When negotiations are complete, you'll see the final contract. If you have any questions about it, ask your agent, but understand that the time for haggling is over. Unless there is a huge deal breaker set in front of you, it's time to sign and celebrate.

KNOWING WHAT'S "NORMAL"

You can see how knowing what goes on behind the scenes can help you shape realistic expectations, and how good communication can help dispel insecurities and clear up misunderstandings. But what if you still have worries?

One common concern I've heard from writers is that their agent never sold their novel, even after submitting to a wide range of editors. These writers ask me if this means they have a bad agent. The answer is: Probably not. Sadly, having an agent doesn't truly guarantee that your book will sell. Every agent reps wonderful manuscripts that for whatever reason (or no real reason) never get sold. Sometimes the market isn't strong enough to support your type of book, or a recent deal on a similar book makes the timing bad. Publishing is subjective and not an exact science. All your agent can do is make a solid effort to shop your book. I'd be more worried if she'd barely sent it out before giving up completely (unless editor comments were particularly negative). That could signal someone who only wants a quick sale. You want someone fully invested in your success—and for not just that one book, but your whole career—and willing to work for you.

Another common concern? Writers worry that editors are taking a long time responding to their agent's submissions, and some editors don't answer at all. Does this mean they have a bad agent? A top agent doesn't guarantee a top response time, though a red-hot project with, say, a celebrity or A-list author might. Since the recession, there have been many cutbacks at publishing houses, which means editors don't have the support staff they need. Responses can take a day, a week, a month or several months, and some editors never respond at all. I think this often says more about the editor than the agent.

Now here's a situation I sometimes hear of that you definitely do need to worry about: when an agent doesn't like anything you send him, then stops answering your e-mails or returning calls. Unfortunately, in those cases the writer doesn't have an agent at all. An agent is someone who works with you and for you. If that's not happening, then it's time to look for new representation.

The author-agent relationship is a true partnership—a two-way street. So when you think you might spot signs of trouble, don't forget to first ask yourself whether you're being a good client. A good client is professional, personable, talented, prolific, has realistic expectations, and is positive and hard-working. And a bad client? Someone who is difficult, overly needy, reticent when it comes to revisions, never trusts the agent, and is otherwise unprofessional. You worked hard to become agented, so always make sure you are doing all you can to be someone your agent joyfully represents.

There are truly many components to an author-agent relationship, but I think what you need to remember most are those two important elements: communication and trust. Start off with these, and you'll build a strong partnership that will last for many years to come.

MARIE LAMBA (www.marielamba.com) is author of the young adult novels *What I Meant …*, *Over My Head*, and *Drawn*, and of the upcoming picture book *Green, Green*. She's also an associate literary agent at The Jennifer De Chiara Literary Agency (www.jdlit.com).

MYSTERY VS. CRIME VS. THRILLER

Define your genre and pitch the best agents.

by David Corbett

Every writer's job is to give the reader what she wants in a way she doesn't expect. (And it's wise to remember that every agent and editor is foremost a reader, too.)

One of the first things to consider when setting out, therefore, is what kinds of expectations your story creates, so you can go about gratifying readers in surprising ways. This is particularly true of writing in a genre, where conventions can seem ironclad—or all too often degrade into formula. And formula, by definition, surprises no one.

The suspense genres in particular have a number of seemingly hard-and-fast rules that a writer defies at his peril. And yet the most satisfying mysteries, thrillers, and crime stories find a way to create a new take on those rules to fashion something fresh, interesting, original. In other words, while you don't want to mistakenly pitch your cozy mystery to an agent who wants only high-octane thrillers, you also want to make sure that when you connect with that cozy-loving agent, she'll be jumping to sign you because *your* cozy stands out from the rest.

Here's a map to help you navigate subgenre subtleties.

MYSTERY

A crime is committed—almost always a murder—and the action of the story is the solution of that crime: determining who did it and why, and obtaining some form of justice. The best mystery stories often explore man's unique capacity for deceit—especially self-deceit—and demonstrate a humble respect for the limits of human understanding. This is usually considered the most cerebral (and least violent) of the suspense genres.

THEMATIC EMPHASIS: *How can we come to know the truth?* (By definition, a mystery is simply something that defies our usual understanding of the world.)

STRUCTURAL DISTINCTIONS: The basic plot elements of the mystery form are:

- the baffling crime

- the singularly motivated investigator
- the hidden killer
- the cover-up (often more important than the crime itself, as the cover-up is what conceals the killer)
- discovery and elimination of suspects (in which creating false suspects is often part of the killer's plan)
- evaluation of clues (sifting the true from the untrue)
- identification and apprehension of the killer

Additional Reader Expectations

THE HERO: Whether a cop, a private eye, a reporter, or an amateur sleuth, the hero must possess a strong will to see justice served, often embodied in a code (for example, Harry Bosch's "Everyone matters or no one matters" in the popular Michael Connelly series). He also often possesses not just a great mind but great empathy—a fascination not with crime, per se, but with human nature.

THE VILLAIN: The crime may be a hapless accident or an elaborately staged ritual; it's the *cover-up* that unifies all villains in the act of deceit. The attempt to escape justice, therefore, often best personifies the killer's malevolence. The mystery villain is often a great deceiver, or trickster, and succeeds because she knows how to get others to believe that what's false is true.

SETTING: Although mysteries can take place anywhere, they often thematically work well in tranquil settings—with the crime peeling back the mask of civility to reveal the more troubling reality beneath the surface.

REVEALS: Given its emphasis on determining the true from the untrue, the mystery genre has more reveals than any other—the more shocking and unexpected, the better.

Mystery Subgenres

COZY: One of the ironic strengths of this subgenre is the fact that, by creating a world in which violence is rare, a bloody act resonates far more viscerally than it would in a more urban or disordered setting.

Reader Expectations: A unique and engaging protagonist: Father Brown, Miss Marple, Kinsey Millhone. The crime should be clever, requiring ingenuity or even brilliance on the hero's part to solve. Secondary characters can be coarse, but never the hero—or the author. Justice triumphs in the end, and the world returns to its original tranquility.

HARD-BOILED: The hero is a cop or private investigator, tough and capable. The moral view is often that of hard-won experience in the service of innocence or decency. The hero tends to be more world-weary than bitter—but that ice can get slippery.

Reader Expectations: A strong hero who can "walk the mean streets but who is not himself mean," as Raymond Chandler once put it. A realistic portrayal of crime and its milieu, with detailed knowledge of criminal methods and investigative techniques. The style is often brisk and simple, reflecting the unpretentious nature of the hero, who is intelligent but not necessarily learned. Although the hero almost always sees that justice prevails, there is usually a bittersweet resolution. The streets remain mean; such is the human condition.

POLICE PROCEDURAL: A cousin to the hard-boiled subgenre, with the unit or precinct taking over for the lone cop.

Reader Expectations: Much like the hard-boiled detective story, but with a larger cast and special focus on police tactics, squad-room psychology, station-house politics, and the tensions between the police and politicians, the media, and the citizenry.

MEDICAL, SCIENTIFIC, OR FORENSIC MYSTERY: A refinement of the police procedural in which the protagonists—doctors, medical examiners, forensic pathologists, or other technical experts—use intelligence and expertise, not guns, as their weapons.

Reader Expectations: Similar to the police procedural, with extra emphasis on the physical details of analyzing unusual evidence.

LEGAL OR COURTROOM DRAMA: The crime is seen through the eyes of the lawyers who prosecute or defend the case.

Reader Expectations: A meticulous rendering of criminal court procedure and politics, along with how police and prosecutors work together (or don't).

CRIME

In this genre the focus is on the contest of wills between the lawman hero and the outlaw opponent, and their differing views of morality and the aspects of society they represent. The greatest crime stories deal with a moral accounting on the part of the hero for his entire life, or provide some new perspective on the tension between society and the individual.

THEMATIC EMPHASIS: *What is a just society?* The story world of the novel is out of balance, somewhere between a state of nature (where chaos prevails and those with money and/or guns wield power) and a police state (where paranoia prevails and the state monopolizes power). The hero hopes in some way to rectify that imbalance.

Other moral themes can include the challenge of decency, honor and integrity in a corrupt world; individual freedom versus law and order; and the tension between ambition and obligations to others.

STRUCTURAL DISTINCTIONS: There is seldom any "mystery" as to who the criminal is. Typically the story starts with a brilliant or daring crime, and then a cat-and-mouse game of wits and will ensues, with the tension created by the increasing intensity of the battle between the opponents. The underlying question is: *Will the cops prevail before the opponent stages his next crime?*

Given the similarity to war and action stories, crime novel prose often tends toward the naturalistic.

Additional Reader Expectations

THE HERO: Usually a tough and capable cop (or vigilante) who believes in the society she defends despite its flaws, the crime fiction hero is often seen as an outcast but is revealed to be the most morally engaged character in the story.

THE VILLAIN: Routinely a tough and brilliant criminal who considers the system rigged and society inherently flawed, he is often a kind of Luciferian rebel—the rogue individual *par excellence*—even if he commands a crew or organization.

SETTING: This genre gravitates toward urban locales, but suburban, rural, and even wilderness settings have all been used to great effect. Let the setting ground the moral theme.

REVERSALS: Just as the mystery genre, by focusing on the search for truth, obliges numerous reveals, the crime genre, by focusing on battle, obliges numerous reversals—with the hero and the villain trading knockout blows and suffering serious setbacks to their respective plans.

The Noir Subgenre

Here, the criminal, or someone who is morally compromised—perhaps even a cop—serves as hero. The moral calculus is usually Bad vs. Worse.

Generally, the "hero" finds himself in some sort of desperate situation, or is tempted into one by an opportunity he sees as his last, best chance at the brass ring. The lure of sex or money routinely leads to violence and often betrayal. If the hero is a cop, the reader is never quite sure whether he's going to solve a crime or commit one—or both.

Reader Expectations: The real allure is the psychology of temptation and desperation, the little guy trying not to drown. Readers expect plot twists, often based on the hero's inability to see what he's up against.

THRILLER

Where mystery stories represent the most cerebral of the three major suspense genres, and crime stories the most dramatic, thrillers are typically the most emotional, focusing on the fear, doubt, and dread of the hero as she faces some form of what Dean Koontz has deemed "terrible trouble." This genre is a hybrid of mystery and horror. However, the thriller also shares a literary lineage with the epic and myth. Monsters, terror, and peril prevail.

THEMATIC EMPHASIS: The dangerous world we live in, the vulnerability of the average person, and the inherent threat of the unknown.

STRUCTURAL DISTINCTIONS: The plot often proceeds along these lines:

- A devastating crime is about to be committed, or has been committed with the threat of an even worse one in the wings.
- The perpetrator is known, but his guilt is not absolutely certain—or the hero wishes not to accept the truth of his guilt. (The uncertainty enhances the suspense.)
- The hero is under constant attack as she tries to definitively prove the perpetrator's guilt and/or stop the next atrocity. (Note the difference from the mystery genre, where the villain typically remains hidden.)

Additional Reader Expectations

THE HERO: Given the relentless attack the villain inflicts, and the emphasis on terror and dread, the thriller hero must be vulnerable—not just physically but psychologically.

THE VILLAIN: In the best thrillers, the villain either targets the hero specifically from the outset or learns through the course of the story what his particular weaknesses and wants are, and targets them for ruthless attack.

SETTING: Whether as small as a cottage in the woods or as large as the planet, the world the hero seeks to protect represents everything she values. The stakes are ultimate.

Thriller Subgenres

EPIC THRILLER: This usually concerns the threat of some catastrophe affecting whole cities, communities, countries, and even the planet. The threat need not be total devastation—the assassination of a leader will do—but the *effect* of the action must be profound.

The villain can be a terrorist, a diabolical genius, or an ordinary person with a grudge and a unique capacity for damage.

Given the scope of the threat, the protagonist must possess the skills to defeat the villain, and thus is often a soldier, a spy, a trained assassin, a cop, or a civilian with a special skill set. The action is brisk, even nonstop, and the climax needs to be both thoroughly foreshadowed (we need to know the basic parameters of the threat all along, and the measures being taken to stop it) and unexpected (plot twists are not optional—they're required). This is a pull-out-all-the-stops genre.

Reader Expectations: A diabolical plot, a superbly capable and motivated nemesis, a hero with an impossible mission, breakneck pacing, and clever but credible plot twists.

PSYCHOLOGICAL THRILLER/SUSPENSE: Here the threat is still diabolical but more contained, even intimate—usually targeting the protagonist and/or his family—and the hero is often a relatively "ordinary" man, woman, or child. The pacing is a bit more deliberate, to reflect the ordinary person's difficulty understanding the exact nature of the threat—and the enemy—and then struggling to respond. The third act, however, moves briskly.

Reader Expectations: Emphasis is on the eerie over the sensational. Twists again are key, with chapters routinely ending in one disturbing revelation after another. Character is more important than pacing, but pacing can't be neglected. This subgenre demands an ability to reveal dread and panic without explosions or car chases.

SUPERNATURAL THRILLER: This subgenre is something of a hybrid, in that the nemesis presents an overwhelming threat—he might be Satan himself—and yet that threat is often focused on a single soul or a mere few, rather than the whole of mankind, at least within the story.

Reader Expectations: An amplification of the powers available to the villain, whether the threat posed is truly spiritual or merely psychological in nature. Also, obviously, a credibly rendered menace from the spirit realm.

Stumbling into a mystery, thriller, or crime story without understanding what agents, editors, and readers expect is a recipe for disaster. Know what they want—and then find a way to gratify that desire in ways they don't see coming. Your efforts will be rewarded with a resounding *yes*.

DAVID CORBETT (www.davidcorbett.com) is a regular contributor to *Writer's Digest* magazine and an in-demand writing instructor. His latest novel is *The Mercy of the Night* (2015).

CREATE GREAT CHARACTERS

15 ideas on how to bring characters to life.

....

by Elizabeth Sims

If you've ever finished reading a piece of fiction and thought, *I'm going to miss those people*, you've experienced true identification with the characters. This is one of the hallmarks of great fiction, and it doesn't happen by chance. (Please post a review wherever you hang out online.)

In creating compelling characters, the best authors work purposefully, and they don't waste time or words. Whether working in short form or long, they know how to sketch characters quickly and accurately, then add dimension in nimble strokes as they go. Difficult? It doesn't have to be. The hacks that follow can help you swiftly establish a character in a short story, and they also can make for economy and originality in longer fiction, particularly in your opening chapters, when it's crucial to draw readers in and make them care about your people right away.

1. TURN UP THE CONTRAST

As a university student, I learned how to make photographs using film, chemicals, paper, and time. When I was stumped as to how to improve a photograph, I would fiddle with the variables that affected contrast, knowing that sharper contrast often resulted in a more arresting picture.

It stands to reason: When something is viewed in contrast to another thing, it becomes keener, more vivid. In fiction, you can use countless aspects of character to differentiate and enhance: Holmes and Watson (temperament), Scrooge and Cratchit (morality), Romeo and Juliet (loyalty), HAL 9000 and Dave (humanity).

Here's how the romantic Watson sums up Holmes' heart: "He never spoke of the softer passions, save with a gibe and a sneer." Sir Arthur Conan Doyle took care to make the two men as different as possible, while uniting them through intellectual friendship.

Take risks! How about pairing a six-year-old genius with her demented grandpa? An Army drill instructor with a sleazy Mafia hood?

2. HOLD THEM HOSTAGE

Even small contrasts can be dramatic when amplified by *context*. In his well-loved Victorian novel *Tom Brown's School Days,* Thomas Hughes created characters who existed at their boys' school within a narrow range of age, race, privilege, values—and yet what a binful of personalities! In the pressure of a microcosm from which there is no escape, minor differences loom larger: a few inches of height, a few years of age, a propensity to follow, a propensity to lead, a weakness for pleasure, a disinclination toward responsibility.

Prompt your characters into memorable action by forcing them into close proximity. Think beyond a literal hostage situation (which itself can be a great choice): perhaps a pair of truck drivers who must share a sleeper cab on a long-haul trip, or a bartender who's being stalked by a regular customer.

3. DO SOME COSTUME DESIGN

While rewatching *The Birds* recently, I noticed that once Tippi Hedren gets to Bodega Bay, the character wears the same gorgeous green Edith Head suit through the rest of the movie (because she's stuck there without luggage). It reminded me of another Alfred Hitchcock classic, *North by Northwest*, wherein man-on-the-run Cary Grant remains in one exquisite gray suit.

A characterizing outfit is a great visual, you might think, *but how could that work on the page?* Consider Holden Caulfield's red hunting hat. There's symbolism there (alienation, perhaps; searching—or hunting), and after a point, mere mention of it plucks a little thread of emotion in the attentive reader.

In my novel, *Left Field*, one of my characters is the catcher on a women's softball team. To highlight her insecurity, I portrayed her as always wearing unnecessarily extreme safety gear: mask, chest protector, etc.

4. START WITH A NAME

In her bestselling Hunger Games trilogy, Suzanne Collins uses names to help distinguish many different characters while adding subtle meaning. For instance, Thresh is from the agricultural district. Cato (an homage to the Roman military figure and statesman Cato the Elder?) is a highly skilled warrior and leader.

If that seems too overt, try this: Instead of focusing on a character's primary identification, brainstorm a secondary trait that's hidden at first. A woman with a secret might be called Pearl, an alcoholic might be nicknamed Tip, and so forth. Be sparing with allegorical names—they can get tiresome in quantity, but their selective use can enrich your readers' experience.

5. SEND TRAITS TO WAR

William Shakespeare is terrific to study for character development in all grades of coarse and fine. He gives Macbeth, for instance, enough strength of character to be ruthlessly ambitious, but he also bestows him with a guilty conscience. Macbeth can't figure out how to have both a clean life and a triumphant one, so he blows everything and ends up annihilated.

Matching up contradictory traits within one character is story gold. To hit on something quickly, zero in on your character's key positive trait—valor, ingenuity, compassion— then write a short scene that reveals a fleck of the exact opposite. The warm, generous music teacher finds herself intensely envious of her star pupil, to the point of fantasizing about … sabotage at the upcoming recital?

6. SCAR TENDER FLESH

Everybody carries scars, both physical and psychological. Give one or two to your characters. The way a character deals with past pain can be deeply revealing: Is he a stoic? Or a wuss who will do anything to avoid more discomfort? A scar can represent a price paid for wisdom, or it can fuel a vengeful life.

It's easy to drop a scar into a character's life. In Flannery O'Connor's famously chilling short story "A Good Man Is Hard to Find," the Misfit clearly carries psychological scars having to do with whatever led him to murder his own father, and presumably more scars from his sub-sequent imprisonment. Captain Ahab's leg, missing down the gullet of the eponymous Moby Dick, fuels his monomaniacal—and doomed—drive to destroy the beast.

7. PUT IN A ROCK, THEN ADD A HARD PLACE.

The impossible choice serves as a lightning quick reveal of a character's true self. Usually we see this technique at the heart of a dramatic novel—William Styron's *Sophie's Choice*, for instance.

But the impossible choice can be used in a smaller, quicker way any time: The alcoholic nun must choose between a drink today and the confessional tomorrow; the little boy must choose which best friend to give his extra candy bar to; the army sentry must decide in a split second whether to shoot the apparently confused pregnant woman, who might be rushing forward with a bomb under her blouse instead of an unborn baby.

8. TAKE THEM TO THE BANK

Another brushstroke you can use to paint a character's true colors is the handling of money. In Thomas Wolfe's *You Can't Go Home Again*, the minor character of Nebraska Crane is introduced early. In the famous train scene, he's mobbed by his hometown's business leaders, who try to convince him to speculate on property, the value of which is surging.

When he resists, we understand the core of his character, and we gain a foreshadowing of what's to come:

> *"I already got me a farm out in Zebulon," he said, and, grinning—"It's paid fer, too! ... That's all I want. I couldn't use no more."*

You could write a character who does something as small as dropping pennies from his pocket because they're just too cumbersome to carry. Do we instantly know something about him without being told? You bet we do.

9. BESTOW A GIFT

In *The Mists of Avalon*, Marion Zimmer Bradley's 1983 blockbuster retelling of the Arthurian legend from the perspective of women, she distinguishes the character of Morgaine by giving her special powers: Morgaine might be considered a sorceress or a seer.

Although part of the deal is the supernatural power itself, the developmental part comes when the character becomes aware of the gift. How does she react? Furthermore, the gift keeps on giving (to you as the author *and* to your readers) by sustaining your story as the character encounters new and unexpected uses—and potential abuses—for her gifts.

One way to hack this one fast: Simply endow a character with intuition a shade better than anybody else's. Throughout the story, then, the reader will know to expect that character to sense things before others do, and react—or manipulate the situation—accordingly.

10. ALL IN A GURU.

The role of mentor is a powerful one, and can help you steer your protagonist in new directions without having to lay much groundwork. The gentle relationship between the lonely child Mary and the gardener Ben, depicted by Frances Hodgson Burnett in the perennial (pun intended) favorite *The Secret Garden*, is simple as can be, yet powerful. Same with Professor Dumbledore and Harry Potter in *The Sorcerer's Stone*.

The beauty of this one is that a guru or mentor can turn up suddenly and help your protagonist mature and develop when nothing else seems to work.

11. TOSS A NET

Throwing a net over a character is a way to give your readers instant insight into that play-er's self-control, courage, and competence (or lack thereof). George Saunders' protagonist in the blackly funny story "The Semplica Girl Diaries," for instance, is a family man who struggles in the net of his limited income and his family's expectations. Quickly enough, his struggles show that he's incapable of basic maturity. In fact, we perceive that he's a desperate loser, and damned in his quest to keep up with the richer folk by hyperextend-ing his credit, not to mention his credibility.

In your own work, try thwarting a character and see what happens. This thwarting can be large—divorce papers—or small—a traffic ticket. For instance, someone slapped with a speeding violation might lose his temper and launch an obscene tirade against the cop, thus making everything worse, while a different character in a similar situation would keep composed and carry on. These psychological responses are powerful indicators of character. Something as small as a shrug in the face of difficulty can speak volumes.

12. KNOW THEIR NUMBER

Even if you never discuss the birth order of your characters in your story, you can deepen their lives if you know how their place in their family has influenced their character. Most families have one kid—typically the youngest—who becomes the watcher: the one who figures out that Daddy is having an affair with Mrs. Thornside down the street before anybody else senses it. A younger child can observe an older one get in trouble, and learn how to fly under the radar and get away with a lot more.

Older children often learn bullying skills, naturally enough when the littler ones are so easy to push around. But they also can learn how to care for and nurture the small and the weak.

13. ENGINEER A TEMPTATION

In Homer's Greek epic *The Odyssey*, a gang of sexy temptresses called the Sirens loudly attempt to lure Ulysses and his ship to an inglorious end on the rocks. To foil them, he bids his men to plug their ears and then tie him to his ship's mast so he cannot himself steer them toward destruction. This is great drama that still scans well today, and that single scene has served to cement the character of Ulysses in millions of readers' minds and hearts.

Temptation works so well because we all can relate to it. From that package of cookies sitting alluringly in the cupboard to the Jaguar we cannot possibly afford, everybody has felt the pull of forbidden fruit, and wondered about the self-destructive impulses behind it. Arrange for your characters to be tempted, to yield, to resist, to feel the slings and arrows of self-sabotage, and to experience the consequences.

14. GIVE YOUR NARRATOR AN OPINION

Whether working in the first, second, or third person, you almost certainly have somebody doing bits of narration. Don't forget that your narrator has a point of view! Make use of it, as Alice Munro does in her story "Pictures of the Ice." A description of a female character in a photograph we see only this once:

> *Short fair hair combed around her face in a businesslike way, brown slacks, white sweatshirt, with the fairly large bumps of her breasts and stomach plain to see, she meets the camera head-on and doesn't seem worried about what it will make of her.*

We get it: She's not a knockout, and she's quite secure in herself. One sentence.

Your narrator, too, can notice telling details about your characters, and deliver the info just as decisively.

15. DIG DEEP

This last hack is one you can work on yourself as an author. When you find yourself stumped for character-development ideas, step back and get humble. Here's the key: If you operate on the theory that your characters are deeper than you'll ever discover, you can't go wrong.

Explore these three things about each of your main characters:

1. What does he *say* he wants?

2. What does he *think* he wants?

3. What does he *really* (subconsciously) want?

You'll discover endless possibilities, and if you've given the previous hacks a try, you'll be able to figure out your own new ones as you go.

ELIZABETH SIMS is a *Writer's Digest* contributing editor. She blogs on zestful writing and living at http://esimsauthor.blogspot.com.

4 QUESTIONS FOR 4 KIDLIT AGENTS

A quartet of agents talk kidlit submissions.

....

by Jessica Strawser

///

OUR 4 AGENTS

1. SARAH DAVIES The Greenhouse Literary Agency, www.greenhouseliterary.com

2. SARA MEGIBOW KT Literary, www.ktliterary.com

3. JOHN RUDOLPH Dystel & Goderich Literary Management, www.dystel.com

4. TINA WEXLER ICM Partners, www.icmtalent.com

1. What do you see as the most important difference between middle-grade (MG) and young adult (YA) books?

TINA WEXLER: "The most important difference is how the author shapes the elements of the story—the narrative voice, the way the subject matter is presented, the protagonist's evolution—for the intended readership, typically eight to twelve for MG and twelve-plus or fourteen-plus for YA. Everything falls out of that, in a sense."

SARA MEGIBOW: "The major conflict in a YA novel centers around the question of, *Who will I be when I grow up?* A YA novel is a coming-of-age story, whether the book is contemporary, fantastical, historical, dystopian, etc. In MG fiction, the major conflict is a bit different, as it's about firsts—first fight with parents, first questions of independence, first time friends are more important than family, etc.

"In addition, an important difference between MG and YA is the age of the protagonist(s). MG narrators are younger than YA narrators. I want to see MG protagonists at ten to thirteen years old and YA protagonists at fourteen to nineteen years old (generally)."

JOHN RUDOLPH: "For me, it's age of the protagonist … I know, that's totally arbitrary, but as MG keeps creeping into YA territory, other traditional markers like content and outward/inward perspective are starting to blur, so age seems like one clear and easy way to differentiate."

SARAH DAVIES: "MG fiction will revolve around a younger protagonist(s), which means the concerns and rites of passage will be preteen rather than older. But if we 'unpack' that difference, it will necessitate a different voice and character arc. It's not just baldly a question of characters' ages; for any age group, it's about a story that sees and explores the world through the lens of a particular stage in life. Teen fiction will inevitably have a touch more introspection and sophistication in the interpretation of relationships, the wider world and the self."

2. What makes standout writing for MG readers?

RUDOLPH "Showing [rather than telling], naturally, and sophistication of both vocabulary and sentence structure. I've been reading Harry Potter to my son lately, and I'm repeatedly blown away by [J.K.] Rowling's use of big words, virtually all of which can be understood in context without running to the dictionary. There's absolutely no need to dumb it down for MG!"

DAVIES: "In all fiction I look for a strong and unique hook, a voice that stands out and conveys the world and personalities of the characters, and an author's ability to craft that story so it becomes compelling on the page. With MG fiction, I'm also, of course, looking for a story with appeal and resonance to readers of that age, whether it be in the vein of classic, heartfelt fiction or a more adventurous and action-packed story."

MEGIBOW: "*Voice!* The most common mistake I see (by far) in MG submissions is writing that sounds too much like it's written by an adult for an adult. An authentic MG voice that matches the age, conflict, tone, and story makes for standout writing for MG readers."

WEXLER: "The strongest MG writing captures the experience of that particular age without being nostalgic; it feels lived and not remembered."

3. What do you want to see more of in young adult novel submissions?

DAVIES: "Unique ideas, diverse characters, and settings. I enjoy stories that make me think but also move me emotionally. I don't like being super-definite on genre—I'm just open to anything that feels fresh, vivid, and compelling."

WEXLER: "I'm always looking for stories with unreliable narrators, unconventional story structures, magical realism, and ambitious ideas fully realized. I'd love to see a sweeping, epic fantasy novel that is done and complete in one book—not a trilogy but a truly stand-alone epic fantasy.

MEGIBOW: "I'm always looking for more diversity—whether that's in fantasy YA or contemporary YA or historical YA or … anything. I'd like to see more protagonists of color, more religious diversity, cultural diversity, diversity of gender and sexual orientation, diversity of ability, socio-economic status, geography, etc. Diversity!"

RUDOLPH: "I would love to see more writers go Gonzo. Plots, characters, voice, whatever they can do to push the envelope in realistic or magical-realistic fiction. And humor—boy, would I love to find a funny YA."

4. What common story mistakes do you see in the MG and YA manuscripts you consider?

MEGIBOW: "Some common mistakes I see in MG and YA submissions include: incorrect voice (a narrator who sounds like an adult), data dump (too much telling, especially in the first thirty pages of the manuscript) and uneven dialogue (frequently too much or too stiff)."

RUDOLPH: "It's not so much mistakes as just the same tired clichés: dead parents, spunky redheaded heroines, superheroes in MG, dystopias in YA. But one thing I do see a lot is the opening chapter where everything is crammed in—plot, central problem, character, etc. I understand why writers do it, especially when submission guidelines ask for only a partial, but I'd much rather have a slower introduction and let the author's voice convince me that I want to read more. Or, to put it a different way, *show* us what you can do, don't *tell* us everything up front."

WEXLER: "The author has been too kind to the protagonist, where the worst thing that could happen isn't truly the worst, where bad things happen to the protagonist but never because the protagonist made a bad choice. Like a helicopter parent, the author is afraid to let the protagonist fail or fall. But fail and fall they must, or there is no story, no growth."

DAVIES: "Most commonly, I see ideas that are already out there in the marketplace and don't feel unique. I also see a lot of stiff writing where characters feel distant and unrelatable. Also, quite a bit of overwriting—by which I mean that the author is using tons of adjectives and adverbs in an attempt to convey emotion. Sometimes, less can be more, and spare writing can be very effective."

JESSICA STRAWSER (www.jessicastrawser.com) is the editor of *Writer's Digest* magazine. Her debut novel, *Almost Missed You,* comes out from St. Martin's Press in April 2017.

CREATE YOUR WRITER PLATFORM

8 quick tips on how to market and sell your books (and yourself).

by Chuck Sambuchino

The chatter about the importance of a writer platform builds each year. Having an effective platform has never been more important than right now. With so many books available and few publicists left to help promote, the burden now lies upon the author to make sure copies of their book fly off bookshelves. In other words, the pressure is on for writers to act as their own publicist and chief marketer, and very few can do this successfully.

Know that if you're writing nonfiction, a damn good idea won't cut it. You need to prove that people will buy your book by showing a comprehensive ability to market yourself through different channels such as social networking sites and traditional media.

WHAT IS PLATFORM?

Platform, simply put, is your visibility as an author. It's your personal ability to sell books right this instant. Better yet, I've always thought of platform like this: When you speak, who listens? In other words, when you have a something to say, what legitimate channels exist for you to release your message to audiences who will consider buying your books/services?

Platform will be your key to finding success as an author, especially if you're writing nonfiction. Platform is your personal ability to sell books through:

1. who you are
2. personal and professional connections you have
3. any media outlets (including personal blogs and social networks) that you can utilize to sell books

In my opinion, the following are the most frequent building blocks of a platform:

- a blog of impressive size
- a newsletter of impressive size

- article/column writing (or correspondent involvement) for the media—preferably for larger publications, radio, and TV shows
- contributions to successful websites, blogs, and periodicals helmed by others
- a track record of strong past book sales that ensures past readers will buy your future titles
- networking, and your ability to meet power players in your community and subject area
- public speaking appearances—especially national ones; the bigger the better
- an impressive social media presence (such as on Twitter or Facebook)
- membership in organizations that support the successes of their own
- recurring media appearances and interviews—in print, on the radio, on TV, or online
- personal contacts (organizational, media, celebrity, relatives) who can help you market at no cost to yourself, whether through blurbs, promotion, or other means.

Not all of these methods will be of interest/relevance to you. As you learn more about how to find success in each one, some will jump out at you as practical and feasible, while others will not. And to learn what constitutes "impressive size" in a platform plank, check out this article. www.tinyurl.com/8d2lmmj.

THE FUNDAMENTAL PRINCIPLES OF PLATFORM

1. It is in giving that we receive.

In my experience, this concept—*it is in giving that we receive*—is the fundamental rule of platform. Building a platform means that people follow your updates, listen to your words, respect and trust you, and, yes, will consider buying whatever it is you're selling. But they will only do that if they like you—and the way you get readers to like you is by legitimately helping them. Answer their questions. Give them stuff for free. Share sources of good, helpful information. Make them laugh and smile. Inform them and make their lives easier and/or better. Do what they cannot: cull together information or entertainment of value. Access people and places they want to learn more about. Help them achieve their goals. Enrich their lives. After they have seen the value you provide, they will want to stay in contact with you for more information. They begin to like you, and become a follower. And the more followers you have, the bigger your platform becomes.

2. You don't have to go it alone.

Creating a large and effective platform from scratch is, to say the least, a daunting task. But you don't have to swim out in the ocean alone; you can—and are encouraged to—work with others. There are many opportunities to latch on to bigger publications and groups in getting your words out. And when your own platform outlets—such as a blog—get large enough, they will be a popular source for others seeking to contribute guest content. You will find yourself constantly teaming with others on your way up, and even after you've found some success.

3. Platform is what you are *able* to do, not what you are *willing* to do.

I review nonfiction book proposals for writers, and in each of these proposals there is a marketing section. Whenever I start to read a marketing section and see bullet points such as "I am happy to go on a book tour" or "I believe that Fox News and MSNBC will be interested in this book because it is controversial," then I stop reading—because the proposal has a big problem. Understand this immediately: Your platform is not pie-in-the-sky thinking. It is not what you hope will happen sometime if you're lucky and all the stars align when your publicist works really hard. It's also not what you are *willing* to do, such as "be interviewed by the media" or "sign books at trade events." (Everyone is willing to do these things, so by mentioning them, you are making no case for your book because you're demonstrating no value.) The true distinction for writer platform is that it must be absolutely what you can make happen right now.

4. You can only learn so much about platform by instruction, which is why you should study what others do well and learn by example.

I don't know about you, but, personally, I learn from watching and doing better than I learn from reading. On that note, don't be afraid to study and mimic what others are doing. If you are looking for totally original ideas on how to blog and build your platform, I'll just tell you right now there likely are few or none left. So if you want to see what's working, go to the blogs and websites and Twitter feeds and newspaper columns of those you admire—then take a page from what they're doing. If you start to notice your favorite large blogs include all their social networking links at the top ("Find me on Twitter," "Find me on Facebook"), then guess what? Do the same. If people are getting large followings doing book reviews of young adult fantasy novels, why not do the same?

5. You must make yourself easy to contact.

I have no idea why people make themselves difficult to contact without a website and/or e-mail listed online. Besides "visibility," another way to think about platform is to examine your reach. And if your goal is reach, you do not want to limit people's abilities to find and contact you much if at all. You want people to contact you. You want other writers to e-mail from out of the blue. I love it when a member of the media finds my info online and writes me. I don't even mind it when a writer sends me an e-mail with a random question. I've made long-term friends that way—friends who have bought my book and

---

"PLATFORM" VS. "PUBLICITY"

Platform and publicity are interconnected yet very different. Platform is what you do before a book comes out to make sure that when it hits shelves, it doesn't stay there long. Publicity is an active effort to acquire media attention for a book that already exists. In other words, platform falls upon the author, whereas (hopefully) publicity will be handled by a publicist, either in-house or contracted for money.

Do something right now: Go to Amazon.com and find a book for sale that promises to teach you how to sell more books. Look at the comparable titles below it and start scrolling left to right using the arrows. (Do it now. I'll wait.) Tons of them, aren't there? It's because so many authors are looking for any way possible to promote their work, especially the many self-published writers out there. They've got a book out—and now they realize copies aren't selling. Apparently having your work online to buy at places like Amazon isn't enough to have success as a writer. That's why we must take the reins on our own platform and marketing.

As a last thought, perhaps consider it like this: Publicity is about asking and wanting: gimme gimme gimme. Platform is about giving first, then receiving because of what you've given and the goodwill it's earned you.

---

sung my praises to others. It's called networking—and networking starts by simply making yourself available, and taking the next step to encourage people with similar interests or questions to contact you.

6. Start small and start early.

A true writer platform is something that's built before your book comes out, so that when the book hits your hands, you will be above the masses for all to see. I won't lie—the beginning is hard. It's full of a lot of effort and not a whole lot of return. Fear not; this will pass. Building a platform is like building a structure—every brick helps. Every brick counts. Small steps are not bad. You must always be considering what an action has to offer and if it can lead to bigger and better things. "What frustrates most people is that they want to have platform now," says literary agent Roseanne Wells of the Marianne Strong Literary Agency. "It takes time and a lot of effort, and it builds on itself. You can always have more platform, but trying to sell a book before you have it will not help you."

7. Have a plan, but feel free to make tweaks.

At first, uncertainty will overwhelm you. What are you going to blog about? How should you present yourself when networking? Should your Twitter handle be your name or the title of your book/brand? All these important questions deserve careful

"PLATFORM" VS. "CREDENTIALS"

The most important question you will be asked as you try to get your nonfiction book published is: "Why are you the best person to write this book?" This question is two-fold, as it speaks to both your credentials and your platform. To be a successful author, you will need both, not just the former.

Your credentials encompass your education and experience to be considered as an expert in your category. For example, if you want to write a book called *How to Lose 10 Pounds in 10 Weeks*, then my first thought would be to wonder if you are a doctor or a dietician. If not, what position do you hold that would give you solid authority to speak on your subject and have others not question the advice you're presenting? Or maybe you want to write a book on how to sell real estate in a challenging market. To have the necessary gravitas to compose such a book, you would likely have to have worked as an agent for decades and excelled in your field—hopefully winning awards over the years and acting in leadership roles within the real estate agent community.

Would you buy a book on how to train a puppy from someone whose only credential was that they owned a dog? I wouldn't. I want to see accolades, leadership positions, endorsements, educational notes, and more. I need to make sure I'm learning from an expert before I stop questioning the text and take it as helpful fact.

All this—all your authority—comes from your credentials. That's why they're so necessary. But believe it or not, credentials are often easier to come by than platform.

Platform, as we now know, is your ability to sell books and market yourself to target audience(s). There are likely many dieticians out there who can teach people interesting ways to lower their weight. But a publishing company is not interested in the 90 percent of them who lack any platform. They want the 10 percent of experts who have the ability to reach readers. Publishing houses seek experts who possess websites, mailing lists, media contacts, a healthy number of Twitter followers, and a plan for how to grow their visibility.

It's where credentials meet platform—*that's* where book authors are born.

thought early on. The earlier you have a plan, the better off you will be in the long run—so don't just jump in blind. The more you can diagram and strategize at the beginning, the clearer your road will be.

As you step out and begin creating a writer platform, make sure to analyze how you're doing, then slowly transition so you're playing to your strengths and eliminating your weakest elements. No matter what you want to write about, no matter what platform elements you hone in on, don't ignore the importance of analysis and evolution in your journey. Take a look at what you're doing right and wrong to make sure you're not throwing good money after bad. And feel free to make all kinds of necessary tweaks and changes along the way to better your route.

8. Numbers matter—so quantify your platform.

If you don't include specific numbers or details, editors and agents will be forced to assume the element of platform is unimpressive, which is why you left out the crucial detail of its size/reach. Details are sexy; don't tease us. Try these right and wrong approaches below:

WRONG: "I am on Twitter and just love it."
CORRECT: "I have more than 10,000 followers on Twitter."

WRONG: "I do public speaking on this subject."
CORRECT: "I present to at least ten events a year—sometimes as a keynote. The largest events have up to 1,200 attendees."

WRONG: "I run a blog that has won awards from other friendly bloggers."
CORRECT: "My blog averages 75,000 page views each month and has grown at a rate of 8 percent each month over the past year."

Also, analyzing numbers will help you see what's working and not working in your platform plan—allowing you to make healthy changes and let the strategy evolve. Numbers reflect the success you're having, and it's up to you to figure out why you're having that success.

DEBUT AUTHORS TELL ALL

Learn how first-time authors got published.

....

compiled by Chuck Sambuchino

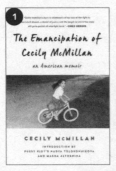
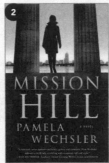
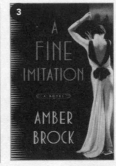
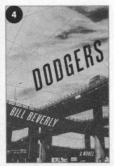

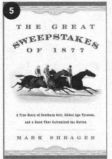

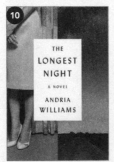

MEMOIR

❶ Cecily McMillan
WWW. JUSTICEFORCECILY.COM
The Emancipation of Cecily McMillan: An American Memoir (July 2016, Nation Books)

QUICK TAKE: "An American millennial coming-of-age story in search of the promise of democracy—a desperate attempt to make sense of identity, family, and duty in modern America." **WRITES FROM**: Atlanta **PRE-*EMANCIPATION***: In the spring of 2014, I was tried as the "Last Occupy Wall St. Defendant" for second-degree assault of an officer. In spite of public outcry, I was convicted and sentenced to three months in Rikers Island, New York's most notorious prison. When I was released, *The New York Times* featured my article, "What I Saw on Rikers Island, Cecily McMillan on Brutality and Humiliation on Rikers Island." **TIME FRAME**: I wrote the book from January 2015 to November 2015. **ENTER THE AGENT**: My closest friend and writing mentor, Maurice Isserman, had been trying to convince me to write a book since my days in Occupy Wall St., and when I got out of Rikers, I knew I had to expose what was going on in there. So he set up an introduction with the Sandra Dijkstra Literary Agency, who represents him, and it was a great fit. I was paired with agent Roz Foster and she's been the saving grace of this whole whirlwind of an experience. **WHAT I LEARNED**: Publishing is like its only little world, with its own (very coded!) language and everything. I had no idea how to write a book, no idea at all what goes into writing one. Someone ought to write a book called *What to Expect When Expecting a Book*. **PLATFORM**: I write regularly as a Huffington Post blogger, and will publish several articles on Rikers Island and on the state of America today (culturally and politically). I'll also be engaging the 160,000 people who lobbied for my freedom through a www.change.org petition and doing a thorough media run. **NEXT UP**: Something big, I hope—something that starts to reinvigorate a conversation about the responsibilities of Americans and reclamation of that term "patriotism" that seems to be degrading our values rather than inspiring our country to higher plane.

LEGAL THRILLER

❷ Pamela Wechsler
WWW. PAMELAWECHSLER.COM
Mission Hill (May 2016, Minotaur)

QUICK TAKE: "Boston's chief homicide prosecutor Abby Endicott—an indomitable, fashion-obsessed, adrenalin-addicted Brahmin with a lot of secrets, has to solve her most personal murder yet." **WRITES FROM**: Boston **PRE-*MISSION***: I was working as the on-set legal advisor for *The Judge*, a movie that was shot in Boston. In between takes, Billy Bob Thornton, who played the role of the prosecutor, suggested that I write the novel that has become *Mission Hill*. **TIME FRAME**: I gave myself one year to write and sell this book, and if it didn't work out I would go back to practicing law. I wrote the book in five months. It took another four months to get an agent, do the rewrites, and sign with a publisher. Luckily, I came in three months short of having to suit up and dig a briefcase out of the bottom of my closet. **ENTER THE AGENT**: I found my agent, Victoria Skurnick of Levine, Greenberg and Rostan, through a cold query. **WHAT I DID RIGHT**: I found a supportive community of writers, where I could workshop my pages, and get both feedback and fellowship. **I WISH I WOULD HAVE DONE DIFFERENT**: I would have taken classes and read more books and articles about fiction. **ADVICE FOR WRITERS**: "Writers write." My advice is that when you've finished a project, don't sit around waiting for a response—start something new. **NEXT UP**: *Mission Hill* is the first in a series of three. Currently, the second book is with my editor, and I'm working on the third. I've also been consulting on a couple of TV pilots, and if any of them gets picked up to series, I might move back to Los Angeles and join a writing staff.

HISTORICAL FICTION

③ Amber Brock
WWW.AMBERBROCK.NET
A Fine Imitation (May 2016, Crown)

QUICK TAKE: "Set in the glamorous 1920s, a privileged Manhattan socialite's restless life and the affair with a mysterious painter that upends her world, flashing back to her years at Vassar and the friendship that brought her to the brink of ruin." **WRITES FROM**: Atlanta **PRE-*IMITATION***: This is my fifth completed novel and my third historical novel. Though I queried some of those earlier novels (with varying levels of success), I knew from the time I started *A Fine Imitation* that it had the potential to be the one I broke in with. The others are keeping warm on my hard drive, but I needed the experience of writing them to be ready to write this one. There are never any wasted words, in my opinion. **TIME FRAME:** I did several weeks of preliminary research before diving in, including reading the 1922 edition of Emily Post's *Etiquette* and an art history textbook (both cover-to-cover). I wrote the first draft of this book in just under six weeks, though it was far from complete at that point! I picked it up again six months later, and revised until I felt it was ready to send to agents. Then I revised some more. **ENTER THE AGENT:** I queried my agent, Stefanie Lieberman of Janklow & Nesbit, about nine months from the time I started sending this novel to agents, after several revisions and a couple of near-misses. **WHAT I LEARNED:** Seeking publication has taught me patience and resilience. I've also picked up some serious research skills, because any level of success in this business requires that you know what you're doing. **WHAT I DID RIGHT**: I was patient, I worked hard, and I kept writing. Without hard work and patience, luck and timing don't make much of a difference. **PLATFORM**: I connect with other readers and writers on Goodreads and Twitter, and attend book festivals. **ADVICE FOR WRITERS**: The best thing I've done for my writing is working with a critique partner and some very opinionated beta readers. I've learned how to give and receive feedback. You also learn a great deal about your own work from reading others'. **NEXT UP**: The novel I'm working on now is set in the 1950s in New York City and Miami.

CRIME

④ Bill Beverly
WWW.DODGERSANOVEL.COM
Dodgers (April 2016, Crown)

QUICK TAKE: "When East, a shrewd young watchman for a Los Angeles drug house, finds himself out of a job, he takes the one opportunity he's given: pursue a bloody mission across the country, a land he's never seen." **WRITES FROM**: Hyattsville, Maryland **PRE-DODGERS**. I had studied writing at the University of Florida, then stayed on for the Ph.D. in American literature. Several of my short stories saw publication. **TIME FRAME**: I talked the story through to my wife in 2003. She said, "You should write that." She is wise about things, my wife. **ENTER THE AGENT**: I met Amy Williams, a partner at McCormick Literary, at a writers conference in 2013, and sent it to her. Amy passed the novel on to her co-agent, Alia Hanna Habib, and Alia signed me soon after. **BIGGEST SURPRISE**: How much I like the people I've met and worked with. I don't know why this would surprise me. They are people who love books. They're doing this because they love to read. **WHAT I DID RIGHT**: I managed to carve the whole story out of one tree. And at about the right moment, I took it to show to people who could help me. **I WISH I WOULD HAVE DONE DIFFERENT**: I would have developed a daily writing routine. I was originally skeptical that writing every day would help me. But it did. I wish I'd started earlier. **NEXT UP**: A new novel.

NONFICTION HISTORY

⑤ Mark Shrager
WWW.MARKBSHRAGER.COM
The Great Sweepstakes of 1877: A True Story of Southern Grit, Gilded Age Tycoons, and a Race That Galvanized the Nation (April 2016, Lyons Press)

QUICK TAKE: "In post-Reconstruction America, an iconic horse race brings together the two best thoroughbreds in the North and a near-legendary Southern horse, and captures the interest of the nation." **WRITES FROM:** Southern California **PRE-*SWEEPSTAKES*:** History and sports have always been interests. I first learned of the race while researching a long-ago article for a racing magazine. The information germinated in my subconscious for three or four decades until I realized that I could build an interesting book-length tale around the events. **TIME FRAME:** The heavy-duty research and writing took place over about three years. **ENTER THE AGENT:** I bought a copy of *Guide to Literary Agents* and sent off perhaps sixty queries. Then I watched the rejection letters begin pouring in. Finally, I received an e-mail from Greg Aunapu of the Salkind Literary Agency, indicating that he felt certain he could sell my book. **BIGGEST SURPRISE:** How much responsibility the author has beyond merely writing the book. I was expected to provide photos of my characters, arrange for a professional headshot photographer for the cover, and improve my platform with the public, among other tasks. **WHAT I DID RIGHT:** I kept working at it. The writing process sometimes became discouraging, but I refused to abandon my quirky characters and their phenomenal stories. **PLATFORM:** My "platform" consisted of over forty years of writing for racing magazines that most readers never see on a newsstand. I'm now seeking publicity for my book on TV via local horse racing channels, promoting myself in newspapers, and more. I send mailings to Civil War history groups, racing websites, and others with an interest either in the Reconstruction era or the Sport of Kings. **I WISH I WOULD HAVE DONE DIFFERENT:** I'd have started decades ago working to strengthen my platform. **ADVICE FOR WRITERS:** Once you've committed to a project, work on it every day. Avoid negative people, but share your story liberally with those who believe in you.

PICTURE BOOK

6 Julie Falatko
WWW.JULIEFALATKO.COM
Snappsy the Alligator (Did Not Ask to Be in This Book) (February 2016, Viking Books for Young Readers, illustrations by Tim Miller)

QUICK TAKE: "Snappsy the alligator is having an ordinary day until a pesky narrator steps in to spice up the story with slanderous claims." **WRITES FROM:** Maine **PRE-*SNAPPSY*:** I wrote a lot of stories that I pray no one will ever see. They were all part of the process. I did picture book reviews for the Brain Burps About Books podcast from 2011 to 2015, which allowed me to fuel my book reading habit while also talking into a cool-looking microphone. **TIME FRAME:** The idea for *Snappsy* came out of Picture Book Idea Month in November 2012. I had been diligently writing ideas all month, and the idea for this book inserted itself wholesale into my brain then. *Snappsy* is the only time a book has come to me all at once. **ENTER THE AGENT:** My agent is Danielle Smith of Red Fox Literary. When I read her blog it was easy to see that we had very similar taste in books. **WHAT I LEARNED:** There are so many people who work on making a book. There are dozens of people in marketing, publicity, media, and sales. It is boggling to think of how many people whose names I don't even know are talking about my book. **WHAT I DID RIGHT:** I took my time. I had heard that picture book authors should have three polished manuscripts before they start querying agents, and I spent two years writing and revising to get to those three manuscripts. **PLATFORM:** I got my name out through the Brain Burps About Books podcast, and I'm active on Twitter. So much of platform is building connections brick by brick. **ADVICE FOR WRITERS:** Write for you first. Write what you like. And keep at it. **NEXT UP:** A picture book from *Viking Children's: The Society for Underrepresented Animals*, illustrated by Charles Santoso, coming in 2017.

YOUNG ADULT

7 Jeff Garvin
WWW.JEFFGARVINBOOKS.COM
Symptoms of Being Human (February 2016, Harpercollins/Balzer & Bray)

QUICK TAKE: "16-year-old Riley Cavanaugh starts an anonymous blog about being gender fluid—fluctuating between feeling like a girl, a boy, or something in the middle—when an anonymous commenter threatens to out Riley to the world." **WRITES FROM:** Southern California **PRE-SYMPTOMS:** Before becoming a writer, I spent my time careening down U.S. highways in a rickety tour bus with my three-piece rock band, 7k. When the band broke up, I started writing. Fast-forward three years. My agent was shopping my first young adult manuscript when I sent her the opening chapters of a new story called *Symptoms of Being Human*. She told me she wanted to go out immediately with the partial manuscript. **TIME FRAME:** I was working full time when I wrote *Symptoms*, so I'd get up at four in the morning and write until I had to leave for work. All told, I think the first draft took about five months. **ENTER THE AGENT:** I met Rachel Ekstrom (of The Irene Goodman Literary Agency) at the Las Vegas Writers Conference in 2013. She's awesome. **WHAT I LEARNED:** Celebrate everything. So far, there's been no point when I've wiped my brow and said, "Well, that's over." It's one thing after another—in a wonderfully exciting and totally overwhelming way. So I've developed a policy: Celebrate Everything. **WHAT I DID RIGHT:** 1) I didn't write in a vacuum. I attended conferences, went to New York to meet my agent and fellow clients, and got into a small critique group of serious, ambitious writers. 2) I created a writing habit. Getting up at four in the morning sucked—but driving to work having already written for two hours was an unbeatable high. I stuck to it, every day, whether I was "inspired" or not. **ADVICE FOR WRITERS:** Play to your strengths. Set out to write something that allows you to showcase your best qualities as a writer—whether that's twisty plots, snappy dialogue, or a unique narrative voice. **NEXT UP:** My second book for Balzer + Bray/HarperCollins—a contemporary young adult novel set in Paris.

MIDDLE-GRADE FANTASY

8 Kathryn Tanquary
WWW.KATHRYNTANQUARY.COM
The Night Parade (January 2016, Sourcebooks)

QUICK TAKE: "A Tokyo girl stumbles into the spirit world with only three nights to break a deadly curse." **WRITES FROM:** Tokyo **PRE-PARADE:** I was writing a lot of very serious adult short stories in school and decided it would be a good challenge to try a novel. Also, I'd always been very interested in Japanese folklore. **TIME FRAME:** My initial research started a year before I sat down to write. That was a slow process of finding folklore texts and translating Japanese. I wrote the first draft over the course of nine months, then sat on it for two years. In the meantime I'd moved to Japan and started teaching students around my protagonist's age. All of those experiences were the foundation of my next revisions, and that's where the heart of the story really came to life. **ENTER THE AGENT:** My agent is the amazing Thao Le of the Sandra Dijkstra Agency. Like a lot of writers, I scoured the Internet and made a list of dream agents. **BIGGEST SURPRISE:** Even though you read the same words so many times that you start to get sick of them, you can still manage to forget the changes you've made. Sometimes I'd edit a phrase just to edit it back again in the next draft. The revision process changes a lot when you're getting all of these insightful notes from your agent and editor. **WHAT I DID RIGHT:** I finished the book! Once I completed the very first draft and got to write "The End" at the bottom of the page, somehow every word after that seemed a bit less scary. **I WISH I WOULD HAVE DONE DIFFERENT:** I would have tried to be more active on social media while I was in the process of revising and querying. There's a good camaraderie that builds from those shared experiences. **ADVICE FOR WRITERS:** Writing can be a hobby, but if you want to break into the industry and make it a career, then it also has to be a habit. Stretch those word muscles every day. **NEXT UP:** I'm working on a new series for middle grade and an unrelated fantasy novel for adult audiences.

SUSPENSE

⑨ Charlie Donlea
WWW.CHARLIEDONLEA.COM
Summit Lake (January 2016, Kensington)

QUICK TAKE: "Two women—one a dead law school student, the other an investigative reporter looking into her death—and the haunting bond that forms between them as secrets emerge in the quaint mountain town where the murder took place." **WRITES FROM**: Chicago **PRE-LAKE**: I wrote three full-length manuscripts before finally penning *Summit Lake*. God bless my agent, who stuck with me through the years of failure and rejection, and who encouraged me to keep writing when quitting was always an option. **TIME FRAME**: It took two full years to write *Summit Lake*. **ENTER THE AGENT:** My agent is the intelligent and patient Marlene Stringer of The Stringer Literary Agency. I found her on www.agentquery.com. **BIGGEST SURPRISE**: Discovering that so many folks inside my publishing house—whom I've never met and have never talked with—are pulling for me. From the production group to the art department, they have all worked so hard and have taken such good care of my story that I feel very blessed to have found them. **WHAT I DID RIGHT**: I decided never to give up. But before that, I quit. The rejections and self-doubt caused me one night to decide I'd had enough. Over the next week, though, I woke with an odd feeling of loss. I was no longer chasing my dream. Life is about the journey, not the destination. Maybe the same is true of writing. I would have been disappointed had I never broken through—there is no doubt about that. But not as disappointed as if, along the way, I'd given up. **I WISH I WOULD HAVE DONE DIFFERENT:** I wish I'd never read an article about how hard it is to get published. Or how you can only find an agent if you're published. If I could go back, I'd skip all the neg-head, downer garbage so many aspiring writers, myself included, seem to grovel in. Because if you fill your head with too much of the negative stuff, you start to believe it.

LITERARY HISTORICAL FICTION

⑩ Andria Williams
WWW.ANDRIAWILLIAMS.COM
The Longest Night (January 2016, Random House)

QUICK TAKE: "A young Army specialist and his wife have their lives intersect with the U.S.'s first and only fatal nuclear accident, which took place in Idaho, 1961." **WRITES FROM:** We are a military family, so that answer is always changing. Right now I'm in Colorado. **PRE-NIGHT**: This novel was the first thing I've ever published. I had gone to graduate school for creative writing, but then my husband went into the military and we had three children. But I had had this novel in my head for years, and I decided if I ever wanted to write it I just needed to make time. **TIME FRAME:** The first draft took me one year, start to finish, of setting my alarm clock at four in the morning and writing for two hours before my kids woke up. Revising the novel took another year. And, after all that, it sold in one day. **ENTER THE AGENT:** I found Sylvie Greenberg [of Fletcher & Company] the old-fashioned way—by browsing through *Guide to Literary Agents*. **WHAT I LEARNED**: It's helpful to locate newer agents at the agencies you're interested in. Newer agents tend to be building their client lists, and there's a greater chance they'll have room to take you on. **WHAT I DID RIGHT:** Before Sylvie signed me on, she wrote me a critique of my manuscript, and offered to re-read the manuscript if I made her requested changes. So I buckled down and did everything she suggested. When I sent back the manuscript back to her months later, she was happy with how it read. I think my willingness to make her suggested edits showed her that I was serious and got her attention. **WHAT I WISH I WOULD HAVE DONE DIFFERENT:** I would go back in time and give myself the confidence to have started writing sooner after having kids. I let myself be consumed by motherhood as if I didn't deserve to do what I'd trained for, career-wise. **PLATFORM:** I am slowly meeting other writers through a blog I keep called the Military Spouse Book Review, where I profile and promote writers from the military community. **ADVICE FOR WRITERS:** Everyone says this, but: Do. Not. Give. Up. **NEXT UP:** I'm working on another literary historical novel.

GRAPHIC NOVEL

 11 Ozge Samanci
WWW.OZGESAMANCI.COM
Dare to Disappoint (November 2015, Straus and Giroux / BYR)

QUICK TAKE: "Growing up on the Aegean Coast, Ozge is determined to hear her own voice over their voices and amid the religious and militaristic tensions of Turkey and the conflicts between secularism and fundamentalism." **WRITES FROM**: Chicago **PRE-*DARE*:** I worked as a comics artist for a weekly humor magazine, a monthly art magazine, and a monthly film magazine in Turkey. After I moved to the States in 2005. I started making my webcomic, *Ordinary Things*. **TIME FRAME:** Fifteen years ago, I drew about my own absurd childhood as anecdotes in a notebook. That is where it all began. Since then, I always wanted to share my growing-up story. I developed my webcomics with the aim of developing a graphic novel. **ENTER THE AGENT:** I e-mailed agents who represent graphic novels. Jason Yarn [of Jason Yarn Literary Agency] told me that he liked my images. He recommended for me to use the same aesthetic but tell a different story. Then I made another book proposal for *Dare to Disappoint* to Jason and he agreed to represent the book.

Within a month he sold the book to Farrar Straus and Giroux. **WHAT I LEARNED:** You get an agent, you think *Wow! I'm almost there.* You get a publisher, you think *Wow! I'm almost there.* I kept saying "Wow! I'm almost there" for five years. There were times that I thought this book would not make it. Telling a story that takes place in another culture and making it understandable without being didactic was a challenge. My editor Margaret Fergusson patiently worked with me to find ways to define the cultural information that may not have been accessible to international readers. **WHAT I DID RIGHT:** I was persistent, making my webcomic for years in order to develop an unconventional aesthetic to use in my graphic novel in the future and not giving up when my first book proposal was rejected. **PLATFORM:** I've gained a group of readers during last ten years while I have been doing *Ordinary Things*, my web drawings. I am active on social media—mainly on Tumblr. **ADVICE FOR WRITERS.** Be persistent. Finding a publisher may take years of preparation. **NEXT UP:** A new graphic novel.

HUMOROUS SCIENCE FICTION

12 Adam Rakunas
WWW.ADAMRAKUNAS.COM
Windswept (September 2015, Angry Robot)

QUICK TAKE: "Padma Mehta, a longtime labor organizer, has to save her neighborhood, her planet, and her sanity—all before Happy Hour." **WRITES FROM:** Santa Monica, California. **PRE-*WINDSWEPT*:** I had three stories published, and each one was a stepping-stone from the previous. The third sale, "Oh Give Me A Home," was the biggie. It got me my agent, but I'll get to that in a moment. **TIME FRAME:** All in all, it took a little over eight years to go from the first lines to the published book. **ENTER THE AGENT:** I spent nine months sending out queries to sixty-nine agents without much traction. In July of 2013, I was on a family vacation when I got an e-mail from an agent who had been closed to queries. He liked "Oh Give Me A Home," and did I have a novel? Why, yes, I did! I popped it off to him right away. That agent was Joshua Bilmes of JABberwocky. I now work with Sam Morgan, Joshua's Right Hand Of Doom, on *Windswept* and its sequel. **WHAT I LEARNED:** There is no such thing as a typical publishing experience. Publishers move at different paces, have their own procedures, do things their own way. I have to remember this when I hear my fellow writers tell stories, both positive and negative. The only thing that everyone agreed on: Keep writing. Don't stop writing. Even when you're up to your armpits in business, write. **WHAT I DID RIGHT:** I joined two good writing groups. They taught me how to make stories work, and they taught me how to take criticism without taking it personally. I would still be collecting rejection slips if it weren't for the Freeway Dragons and the Fictionados. **DO DIFFERENT NEXT TIME:** Picked myself off the floor earlier after those first crushing critiques. Moping is a terrible excuse for not getting any work done. **ADVICE FOR WRITERS**: If you don't find some joy in writing, stop. Life's too short to do something that doesn't bring you joy. **NEXT UP:** The sequel to *Windswept*. It was released early 2016.

NONFICTION SELF-HELP

 13 Jackson MacKenzie

WWW.PSYCHOPATHFREE.COM

Psychopath Free: Recovering from Emotionally Abusive Relationships with Narcissists, Sociopaths, and Other Toxic People (September 2015, Berkley/Penguin)

QUICK TAKE: "A hopeful guide for healing from abusive relationships with psychopaths, narcissists, and other manipulative people." **WRITES FROM**: Boston **PRE-BOOK**: The website I co-founded—www.psychopathfree.com—was growing fast. With millions of monthly page views, I wanted to take the next step in spreading awareness and giving back to the community that saved my life. I thought a book would be a great way to do this. **ENTER THE AGENT:** I wrote a young adult novel and got an agent, but I ended up backing out of the partnership due to creative differences. The whole experience left me feeling very sensitive to the publishing world. So when I wrote *Psychopath Free* a year later, I self-published it. I loved the process, but I certainly never expected the book to take off the way it did. With media inquiries, and people all over the world asking about translation rights, I was in way over my head. So instead of doing the smart thing (ask for help), I decided to write another book—a thriller. I queried Emmanuelle Morgen of Stonesong for it. She wrote back and asked to read all three of my books: the young adult novel, *Psychopath Free*, and the thriller. We spoke on the phone, and she offered representation. Given all of the overwhelming activity with *Psychopath Free*, we decided to find that one a home first. **WHAT I LEARNED**: To let go. When you self-publish, you have to do everything by yourself, which is really awesome for the creative stuff. But I became stressfully independent, if that's a thing. What I learned is that everyone in the publishing business loves books. Trusting them and being part of a team has lightened my heart so much. **WHAT I DID RIGHT**: Having knowledge about search engine optimization helped me promote and sell books. People always look at me weird when I tell them I majored in computer science and write books, but my technical background really helped to get the word out there. **PLATFORM**: The forum and Facebook page continue to grow faster than I can keep up with. **NEXT UP**: www.psychopathfree.com was receiving so many donations that we recently filed to become a non-profit organization for spreading abuse awareness. We got approved in May and we've already reached over two million people.

YOUNG ADULT

⑭ Dana Elmendorf
WWW.DANAELMENDORF.COM
South of Sunshine (April 2016, AW Teen)

QUICK TAKE: "A story about the complications of a lesbian teen falling in love in a small southern town filled with bigotry and religion, and what she's willing to risk to gain their acceptance." **WRITES FROM**: Carlsbad, California **PRE-*SUNSHINE***: Four horrible books that will never see the light of day are what led up to this book. After I attended an LGBT meeting at a Society of Children's Book Writers & Illustrators (SCBWI) conference, I went home thinking there is no way I could write a LGBT story, I had too many self doubts and fears. The more I tried to convince myself not to write the book, the more I knew I had to. With *South of Sunshine*, I had this personal passion to write an LGBT romance with a happy ending. The act of falling in love is universal, and a happy ending just makes the falling all the sweeter. **TIME FRAME**:It took me forty-five days to write the book and about six months of revisions before I started to query it. There are ten different drafts of the book with varying stages of revisions. **ENTER THE AGENT**: I found my agent, Lauren MacLeod with The Strothman Agency, the good old-fashioned way of sending out a query. She's pretty much the best thing ever. **WHAT I DID RIGHT**: Perseverance. Determination. Always willing to learn more and do more. Accepting criticism of my work and using it to better my craft. I kept moving forward despite all my self-doubts and inexperience. Continuing to believe in myself even though most of the time I didn't feel like I belonged. Connecting with other writers. I could go on and on. There isn't one particular thing I did right, but a collection of right things. Every writer must find their combination to success. **I WISH I WOULD HAVE DONE DIFFERENT**: I wish I would have found my network of writers sooner. Friends and family are a great support system, but they don't have the knowledge and skillset that writers have. My writing career really started to take shape once I found my village. **PLATFORM**: Originally I joined the social media groups to network with other writers. Over time it involved into my platform I have today (Facebook, Instagram, Twitter, Tumblr, Pinterest). But Twitter and Instagram are the websites I tend to gravitate toward the most. My goal is make it fun, unique, and different. **ADVICE FOR WRITERS**: Follow your gut. If it's telling you something isn't working in a story, it's not. There's no amount of makeup that will cover the blemishes of your story. No one is going to figure out how to solve the problem but you. And when your gut tells you you've nailed it, believe it. **NEXT UP**: I'm working on a young adult romantic comedy.

NEW AGENT SPOTLIGHTS

Learn about new reps seeking clients.

by Chuck Sambuchino and Hannah Haney

One of the most popular columns on my Guide to Literary Agents Blog is my "New Agent Alerts," a series where I spotlight new/newer literary reps who are open to queries and looking for clients right now.

Newer agents are golden opportunities for aspiring authors because they are actively building their client lists. They're hungry to sign new clients and start the ball rolling with submissions to editors and get books sold. Where an established agent with forty clients may have little to no time to consider new writers' work (let alone help them shape it), a newer agent may be willing to sign a promising writer whose work is not a guaranteed huge payday.

THE CONS AND PROS OF NEWER AGENTS

At writing conferences, a frequent question I get is "Is it OK to sign with a new agent?" The question comes about because people value experience and wonder about the skill of someone who's new to the scene. The concern is an interesting one, so let me try to list the downsides and upsides to choosing a rep who's in her first few years of agenting.

Possible cons

- They are less experienced in contract negotiations.
- They know fewer editors at this point than a rep who's been in business a while, meaning there is a smaller chance they can help you get published. This is a big, justified point—and writers' foremost concern.
- They are in a weaker position to demand a high advance for you.
- New agents come and some go. This means if your agent is in business for a year or two and doesn't find the success for which they hoped, they could bail on the biz altogether. That leaves you without a home. If you sign with an agent who's been in business for fourteen years, however, chances are they won't quit tomorrow.

Probable pros

- They are actively building their client lists—and that means they are anxious to sign new writers and lock in those first several sales.
- They are willing to give your work a longer look. They may be willing to work with you on a project to get it ready for submission, whereas a more established agent has lots of clients and no time—meaning they have no spare moments to help you with shaping your novel or proposal.
- With fewer clients under their wing, you will get more attention than you would with an established rep.
- If they've found their calling and don't seem like they're giving up anytime soon (and keep in mind, most do continue on as agents), you can have a decades-long relationship that pays off with lots of books.
- They have little going against them. An established agent once told me that a new agent is in a unique position because they have no duds under their belt. Their slates are clean.

HOW CAN YOU DECIDE FOR YOURSELF?

1. FIND OUT IF THE AGENT IS PART OF A LARGER AGENCY. Agents share contacts and resources. If your agent is the new girl at an agency with five people, those other four agents will help her (and you) with submissions. In other words, she's new, but not alone.

2. LEARN WHERE THE AGENT CAME FROM. Has she been an apprentice at the agency for two years? Was she an editor for seven years and just switched to agenting? If they already have a few years in publishing under their belt, they're not as green as you may think. Agents don't become agents overnight.

3. ASK WHERE SHE WILL SUBMIT THE WORK. This is a big one. If you fear the agent lacks proper contacts to move your work, ask straight out: "What editors do you see us submitting this book to, and have you sold to them before?" The question tests their plan for where to send the manuscript and get it in print.

4. ASK THE AGENT WHY SHE IS YOUR BEST OPTION. This is another straight-up question that gets right to the point. If she's new and has few (or no) sales at that point, she can't respond with "I sell tons of books and I make it rain cash money!! Dolla dolla bills, y'all!!!" She can't rely on her track record to entice you. So what's her sales pitch? Weigh her enthusiasm, her plan for the book, her promises of hard work and anything else she tells you. In the publishing business, you want communication and enthusiasm from agents (and editors). Both are invaluable. What's the point of signing with a huge agent when they don't return your e-mails and consider your book last on their list of priorities for the day?

5. IF YOU'RE NOT SOLD, YOU CAN ALWAYS SAY NO. It's as simple as that. Always query new/newer agents because, at the end of the day, receiving an offer of representation doesn't mean you're obligated to accept.

NEW AGENT SPOTLIGHTS

Peppered throughout this book's large number of agency listings are sporadic "New Agent Alert" sidebars. Look them over to see if these newer reps would be a good fit for your work. Always read personal information and submission guidelines carefully. Don't get rejected on a technicality because you submitted work incorrectly. Wherever possible, we have included a website address for their agency, as well as the Twitter handle for those reps that tweet.

Also please note that as of when this book went to press in fall 2016, all these agents were still active and looking for writers. That said, I cannot guarantee every one is still in their respective position when you read this, nor that they have kept their query inboxes open. I urge you to visit agency websites and double check before you query. (This is always a good idea in any case.) Good luck!

GLOSSARY OF INDUSTRY TERMS

Your guide to every need-to-know term.

#10 ENVELOPE. A standard, business-size envelope.

ACKNOWLEDGMENTS PAGE. The page of a book on which the author credits sources of assistance—both individuals and organizations.

ACQUISITIONS EDITOR. The person responsible for originating and/or acquiring new publishing projects.

ADAPTATION. The process of rewriting a composition (novel, story, film, article, play) into a form suitable for some other medium, such as TV or the stage.

ADVANCE. Money a publisher pays a writer prior to book publication, usually paid in installments, such as one-half upon signing the contract and one-half upon delivery of the complete, satisfactory manuscript. An advance is paid against the royalty money to be earned by the book. Agents take their percentage off the top of the advance as well as from the royalties earned.

ADVENTURE. A genre of fiction in which action is the key element, overshadowing characters, theme, and setting.

AUCTION. Publishers sometimes bid for the acquisition of a book manuscript with excellent sales prospects. The bids are for the amount of the author's advance, guaranteed dollar amounts, advertising and promotional expenses, royalty percentage, etc. Auctions are conducted by agents.

AUTHOR'S COPIES. An author usually receives about ten free copies of his hardcover book from the publisher; more from a paperback firm. He can obtain additional copies at a price that has been reduced by an author's discount (usually fifty percent of the retail price).

AUTOBIOGRAPHY. A book-length account of a person's entire life written by the subject himself.

BACKLIST. A publisher's list of books that were not published during the current season, but that are still in print.

BACKSTORY. The history of what has happened before the action in your story takes place, affecting a character's current behavior.

BIO. A sentence or brief paragraph about the writer; includes work, any publishing history, and educational experience.

BIOGRAPHY. An account of a person's life (or the lives of a family or close-knit group) written by someone other than the subject(s). The work is set within the historical framework (i.e., the unique economic, social, and political conditions) existing during the subject's life.

BLURB. The copy on paperback book covers or hardcover book dust jackets, either promoting the book and the author or featuring testimonials from book reviewers or well-known people in the book's field. Also called flap copy or jacket copy.

BOILERPLATE. A standardized publishing contract. Most authors and agents make many changes on the boilerplate before accepting the contract.

BOOK DOCTOR. A freelance editor hired by a writer, agent, or book editor who analyzes problems that exist in a book manuscript or proposal, and offers solutions to those problems.

BOOK PACKAGER. Someone who draws elements of a book together—from initial concept to writing and marketing strategies—and then sells the book package to a book publisher and/or movie producer. Also known as book producer or book developer.

BOUND GALLEYS. A prepublication, often paperbound, edition of a book, usually prepared from photocopies of the final galley proofs. Designed for promotional purposes, bound galleys serve as the first set of review copies to be mailed out. Also called bound proofs.

CATEGORY FICTION. A term used to include all types of fiction. See *genre*.

CLIMAX. The most intense point in the story line of a fictional work.

CLIPS. Samples, usually from newspapers or magazines, of your published work. Also called tearsheets.

COMMERCIAL FICTION. Novels designed to appeal to a broad audience. These are often broken down into categories such as western, mystery, and romance. See *genre*.

CONFESSION. A first-person story in which the narrator is involved in an emotional situation that encourages sympathetic reader identification, concluding with the affirmation of a morally acceptable theme.

CONFLICT. A prime ingredient of fiction that usually represents some obstacle to the main character's (i.e., the protagonist's) goals.

CONTRIBUTOR'S COPIES. Copies of the book sent to the author. The exact number of contributor's copies is often negotiated in the publishing contract.

CO-PUBLISHING. Arrangement where author and publisher share publication costs and profits of a book. Also called co-operative publishing.

COPYEDITING. Editing of a manuscript for writing style, grammar, punctuation, and factual accuracy.

COPYRIGHT. A means to protect an author's work. A copyright is a proprietary right designed to give the creator of a work the power to control that work's reproduction, distribution, and public display or performance, as well as its adaptation to other forms.

COVER LETTER. A brief letter that accompanies the manuscript being sent to an agent or publisher.

CREATIVE NONFICTION. Type of writing where true stories are told by employing the techniques usually reserved for novelists and poets, such as scenes, character arc, a three-act structure and detailed descriptions. This category is also called narrative nonfiction or literary journalism.

CRITIQUING SERVICE. An editing service offered by some agents in which writers pay a fee for comments on the salability or other qualities of their manuscript. Sometimes the critique includes suggestions on how to improve the work. Fees vary, as does the quality of the critique.

CURRICULUM VITAE (CV). Short account of one's career or qualifications.

DEADLINE. A specified date and/or time that a project or draft must be turned into the editor. A deadline factors into a preproduction schedule, which involves copyediting, typesetting, and production.

DEAL MEMO. The memorandum of agreement between a publisher and author that precedes the actual contract and includes important issues such as royalty, advance, rights, distribution, and option clauses.

DEUS EX MACHINA. A term meaning "God from the machine" that refers to any unlikely, contrived, or trick resolution of a plot in any type of fiction.

DIALOGUE. An essential element of fiction. Dialogue consists of conversations between two or more people, and can be used heavily or sparsely.

DIVISION. An unincorporated branch of a publishing house/company.

ELECTRONIC RIGHTS. Secondary or subsidiary rights dealing with electronic/multimedia formats (the Internet, CD-ROMs, electronic magazines).

EL-HI. Elementary to high school. A term used to indicate reading or interest level.

EROTICA. A form of literature or film dealing with the sexual aspects of love. Erotic content ranges from subtle sexual innuendo to explicit descriptions of sexual acts.

ETHNIC. Stories and novels whose central characters are African American, Native American, Italian American, Jewish, Appalachian, or members of some other specific cultural group. Ethnic fiction usually deals with a protagonist caught between two conflicting ways of life: mainstream American culture and his ethnic heritage.

EVALUATION FEES. Fees an agent may charge to simply evaluate or consider material without further guarantees of representation. Paying upfront evaluation fees to agents is never recommended and strictly forbidden by the Association of Authors' Representations. An agent makes money through a standard commission—taking 15 percent of what you earn through advances, sales of subsidiary rights, and, if applicable, royalties.

EXCLUSIVE. Offering a manuscript, usually for a set period of time such as one month, to just one agent and guaranteeing that agent is the only one looking at the manuscript.

EXPERIMENTAL. Type of fiction that focuses on style, structure, narrative technique, setting, and strong characterization rather than plot. This form depends on the revelation of a character's inner being, which elicits an emotional response from the reader.

FAMILY SAGA. A story that chronicles the lives of a family or a number of related or interconnected families over a period of time.

FANTASY. Stories set in fanciful, invented worlds or in a legendary, mythic past that rely on outright invention or magic for conflict and setting.

FILM RIGHTS. May be sold or optioned by the agent/author to a person in the film industry, enabling the book to be made into a movie.

FLOOR BID. If a publisher is very interested in a manuscript, he may offer to enter a floor bid when the book goes to auction. The publisher sits out of the auction, but agrees to take the book by topping the highest bid by an agreed-upon percentage (usually 10 percent).

FOREIGN RIGHTS. Translation or reprint rights to be sold abroad.

FOREIGN RIGHTS AGENT. An agent who handles selling the rights to a country other than that of the first book agent.

GENRE. Refers to either a general classification of writing, such as a novel, poem, or short story, or to the categories within those classifications, such as problem novels or sonnets.

GENRE FICTION. A term that covers various types of commercial novels, such as mystery, romance, Western, science fiction, fantasy, thriller, and horror.

GHOSTWRITING. A writer puts into literary form the words, ideas or knowledge of another person under that person's name. Some agents offer this service; others pair ghostwriters with celebrities or experts.

GOTHIC. Novels characterized by historical settings and featuring young, beautiful women who win the favor of handsome, brooding heroes while simultaneously dealing with some life-threatening menace—either natural or supernatural.

GRAPHIC NOVEL. Contains comic-like drawings and captions, but deals more with everyday events and issues than with superheroes.

HIGH CONCEPT. A story idea easily expressed in a quick, one-line description.

HI-LO. A type of fiction that offers a high level of interest for readers at a low reading level.

HISTORICAL. A story set in a recognizable period of history. In addition to telling the stories of ordinary people's lives, historical fiction may involve political or social events of the time.

HOOK. Aspect of the work that sets it apart from others and draws in the reader/viewer.

HORROR. A story that aims to evoke some combination of fear, fascination, and revulsion in its readers—either through supernatural or psychological circumstances.

HOW-TO. A book that offers the reader a description of how something is accomplished. It includes both information and advice.

IMPRINT. The name applied to a publisher's specific line of books.

IN MEDIAS RES. A Latin term, meaning "into the midst of things," that refers to the literary device of beginning a narrative at a dramatic point in a story well along in the sequence of events to immediately convey action and capture reader interest.

IRC. International Reply Coupon. Buy at a post office to enclose with material sent outside the country to cover the cost of return postage. The recipient turns them in for stamps in their own country.

ISBN. This acronym stands for International Standard Book Number. ISBN is a tool used for both ordering and cataloging purposes.

JOINT CONTRACT. A legal agreement between a publisher and two or more authors that establishes provisions for the division of royalties their co-written book generates.

LIBEL. A form of defamation, or injury to a person's name or reputation. Written or published defamation is called *libel*, whereas spoken defamation is known as *slander*.

LITERARY. A book where style and technique are often as important as subject matter. In literary fiction, character is typically more important than plot, and the writer's voice and skill with words are both very essential. Also called serious fiction.

LOGLINE. A one-sentence description of a plot.

MAINSTREAM FICTION. Fiction on subjects or trends that transcend popular novel categories like mystery or romance. Using conventional methods, this kind of fiction tells stories about people and their conflicts.

MARKETING FEE. Fee charged by some agents to cover marketing expenses. It may be used to cover postage, telephone calls, faxes, photocopying or any other legitimate expense incurred in marketing a manuscript. Recouping expenses associated with submissions and marketing is the one and only time agents should ask for out-of-pocket money from writers.

MASS MARKET PAPERBACKS. Softcover books, usually 4×7 inches, on a popular subject directed at a general audience and sold in groceries, drugstores and bookstores.

MEMOIR. An author's commentary on the personalities and events that have significantly influenced one phase of his life.

MIDLIST. Those titles on a publisher's list expected to have limited sales. Midlist books are mainstream, not literary, scholarly or genre, and are usually written by new or relatively unknown writers.

MULTIPLE CONTRACT. Book contract that includes an agreement for a future book(s).

MYSTERY. A form of narration in which one or more elements remain unknown or unexplained until the end of the story. Subgenres include: amateur sleuth, caper, cozy, heist, malice domestic, police procedural, etc.

NET RECEIPTS. One method of royalty payment based on the amount of money a book publisher receives on the sale of the book after the booksellers' discounts, special sales discounts and returned copies.

NOVELIZATION. A novel created from the script of a popular movie and published in paperback. Also called a movie tie-in.

NOVELLA. A short novel or long short story, usually 20,000–50,000 words. Also called a novelette.

OCCULT. Supernatural phenomena, including ghosts, ESP, astrology, demonic possession, paranormal elements, and witchcraft.

ONE-TIME RIGHTS. This right allows a short story or portions of a fiction or nonfiction book to be published again without violating the contract.

OPTION. The act of a producer buying film rights to a book for a limited period of time (usually six months or one year) rather than purchasing said rights in full. A book can be optioned multiple times by different production companies.

OPTION CLAUSE. A contract clause giving a publisher the right to publish an author's next book.

OUTLINE. A summary of a book's content (up to fifteen double-spaced pages); often in the form of chapter headings with a descriptive sentence or two under each one to show the scope of the book.

PICTURE BOOK. A type of book aimed at ages two to nine that tells the story partially or entirely with artwork, with up to one thousand words. Agents interested in selling to publishers of these books often handle both artists and writers.

PLATFORM. A writer's speaking experience, interview skills, website, and other abilities that help form a following of potential buyers for his book.

PROOFREADING. Close reading and correction of a manuscript's typographical errors.

PROPOSAL. An offer to an editor or publisher to write a specific work, usually a package consisting of an outline and sample chapters.

PROSPECTUS. A preliminary written description of a book, usually one page in length.

PSYCHIC/SUPERNATURAL. Fiction exploiting—or requiring as plot devices or themes— some contradictions of the commonplace natural world and materialist assumptions about it (including the traditional ghost story).

QUERY. A letter written to an agent or a potential market to elicit interest in a writer's work.

READER. A person employed by an agent to go through the slush pile of manuscripts and scripts, and select those worth considering.

REGIONAL. A book faithful to a particular geographic region and its people, including behavior, customs, speech and history.

RELEASE. A statement that your idea is original, has never been sold to anyone else, and that you are selling negotiated rights to the idea upon payment. Some agents may ask that you sign a release before they request pages and review your work.

REMAINDERS. Leftover copies of an out-of-print or slow-selling book purchased from the publisher at a reduced rate. Depending on the contract, a reduced royalty or no royalty is paid to the author on remaindered books.

REPRINT RIGHTS. The right to republish a book after its initial printing.

ROMANCE. A type of category fiction in which the love relationship between a man and a woman pervades the plot. The story is told from the viewpoint of the heroine, who meets a man (the hero), falls in love with him, encounters a conflict that hinders their relationship, and then resolves the conflict with a happy ending.

ROYALTIES. A percentage of the retail price paid to the author for each copy of the book that is sold. Agents take their percentage from the royalties earned and from the advance.

SASE. Self-addressed, stamped envelope. It should be included with all postal mail correspondence and submissions.

SCHOLARLY BOOKS. Books written for an academic or research audience. These are usually heavily researched, technical, and often contain terms used only within a specific field.

SCIENCE FICTION. Literature involving elements of science and technology as a basis for conflict, or as the setting for a story.

SERIAL RIGHTS. The right for a newspaper or magazine to publish sections of a manuscript.

SIMULTANEOUS SUBMISSION. Sending the same query or manuscript to several agents or publishers at the same time.

SLICE OF LIFE. A type of short story, novel, play or film that takes a strong thematic approach, depending less on plot than on vivid detail in describing the setting and/or environment, and the environment's effect on characters involved in it.

SLUSH PILE. A stack of unsolicited submissions in the office of an editor, agent or publisher.

STANDARD COMMISSION. The commission an agent earns on the sales of a manuscript. The commission percentage (usually fifteen percent) is taken from the advance and royalties paid to the writer.

SUBAGENT. An agent handling certain subsidiary rights, usually working in conjunction with the agent who handled the book rights. The percentage paid the book agent is increased to pay the subagent.

SUBSIDIARY. An incorporated branch of a company or conglomerate (for example, Crown Publishing Group is a subsidiary of Random House, Inc.).

SUBSIDIARY RIGHTS. All rights other than book publishing rights included in a book publishing contract, such as paperback rights, book club rights and movie rights. Part of an agent's job is to negotiate those rights and advise you on which to sell and which to keep.

SUSPENSE. The element of both fiction and some nonfiction that makes the reader uncertain about the outcome. Suspense can be created through almost any element of a story, including the title, characters, plot, time restrictions and word choice.

SYNOPSIS. A brief summary of a story, novel or play. As a part of a book proposal, it is a comprehensive summary condensed in a page or page-and-a-half, single-spaced. Unlike a query letter or logline, a synopsis is a front-to-back explanation of the work—and will give away the story's ending.

TERMS. Financial provisions agreed upon in a contract, whether between writer and agent, or writer and editor.

TEXTBOOK. Book used in school classrooms at the elementary, high school, or college level.

THEME. The point a writer wishes to make. It poses a question—a human problem.

THRILLER. A story intended to arouse feelings of excitement or suspense. Works in this genre are highly sensational, usually focusing on illegal activities, international espionage, sex, and violence.

TOC. Table of Contents. A listing at the beginning of a book indicating chapter titles and their corresponding page numbers. It can also include chapter descriptions.

TRADE BOOK. Either a hardcover or softcover book sold mainly in bookstores. The subject matter frequently concerns a special interest for a more general audience.

TRADE PAPERBACK. A soft-bound volume, usually 5×8 inches, published and designed for the general public; available mainly in bookstores.

TRANSLATION RIGHTS. Sold to a foreign agent or foreign publisher.

UNSOLICITED MANUSCRIPT. An unrequested manuscript sent to an editor, agent, or publisher.

VET. A term used by editors when referring to the procedure of submitting a book manuscript to an outside expert (such as a lawyer) for review before publication. Memoirs are frequently vetted to confirm factually accuracy before the book is published.

WESTERNS/FRONTIER. Stories set in the American West, almost always in the nineteenth century, generally between the antebellum period and the turn of the century.

YOUNG ADULT (YA). The general classification of books written for ages twelve to sixteen. They run forty thousand to eighty thousand words and include category novels—adventure, sports, paranormal, science fiction, fantasy, multicultural, mysteries, romance, etc.

LITERARY AGENTS

Literary agents listed in this section do not charge for reading or considering your ms or book proposal. It's the goal of an agent to find salable manuscripts: Her income depends on finding the best publisher for your manuscript.

Since an agent's time is better spent meeting with editors, she will have little or no time to critique your writing. Agents who don't charge fees must be selective and often prefer to work with established authors, celebrities, or those with professional credentials in a particular field.

SUBHEADS

Each agency listing is broken down into subheads to make locating specific information easier. In the first section, you'll find contact information for each agency. Additional information in this section includes the size of each agency, its willingness to work with new or unpublished writers, and its general areas of interest.

MEMBER AGENTS: Agencies comprised of more than one agent list member agents and their individual specialties. This information will help you determine the appropriate person to whom you should send your query letter.

REPRESENTS: This section allows agencies to specify what nonfiction and fiction subjects they represent. Make sure you query only those agents who represent the type of material you write.

Look for the key icon to quickly learn an agent's areas of specialization. In this portion of the listing, agents mention the specific subject areas they're currently seeking as well as those subject areas they do not consider.

HOW TO CONTACT: Most agents open to submissions prefer an initial query letter that briefly describes your work. You should send additional material only if the agent requests it. In this section, agents also mention if they accept queries by fax or e-mail, if they consider simultaneous submissions, and how they prefer to obtain new clients.

TERMS: Provided here are details of an agent's commission, whether a contract is offered and for how long, and what additional office expenses you might have to pay if the agent agrees to represent you. Standard commissions range from 10–15 percent for domestic sales and 15–25 percent for foreign or dramatic sales (with the difference going to the co-agent who places the work).

RECENT SALES: Some agencies have chosen to list recent book sales in their listing. To get to know an agency better, investigate these published titles and learn about writing styles that the agency has bonded with.

WRITERS CONFERENCES: A great way to meet an agent is at a writers conference. Here agents list the conferences they usually attend. For more information about a specific conference, check the Conferences section starting on page 262.

TIPS: In this section, agents offer advice and additional instructions for writers.

SPECIAL INDEXES

LITERARY AGENTS SPECIALTIES INDEX: This index (page 287) organizes agencies according to the subjects they are interested in receiving. This index should help you compose a list of agents specializing in your areas. Cross-referencing categories and concentrating on agents interested in two or more aspects of your manuscript might increase your chances of success.

AGENTS INDEX: This index (page 321) provides a list of agents' names in alphabetical order, along with the name of the agency for which they work. Find the name of the person you would like to contact, and then check the agency listing.

⊙ A+B WORKS

E-mail: query@aplusbworks.com. **Website:** http://aplusbworks.com. **Contact:** Amy Jameson, Brandon Jameson. Estab. 2004.

○ Amy began her career in New York with the literary agency Janklow & Nesbit Associates.

REPRESENTS Novels. **Considers these fiction areas:** middle-grade, young adult.

HOW TO CONTACT Query via e-mail only. "Please review our submissions policies first. Send queries to query@aplusbworks.com. Due to the high volume of queries we receive, we can't guarantee a response." Accepts simultaneous submissions.

⊘ DOMINICK ABEL LITERARY AGENCY, INC.

146 W. 82nd St., #1A, New York NY 10024. (212)877-0710. **E-mail:** agency@dalainc.com. **Website:** www.dalainc.com. "The agency represents authors of fiction (especially mysteries and suspense novels), narrative nonfiction, and business books. It is a full-service agency, with co-agents in all major countries and in Hollywood. Among the agency's clients are *New York Times* best-selling writers, as well as winners of Edgar, Malice Domestic, Shamus, Anthony, Dilys, Bram Stoker, and other awards." Estab. 1975. Member of AAR. Represents 50 clients.

HOW TO CONTACT Query via e-mail. No attachments. Check the agency website to learn when this agency reopens to new submissions. "If you wish to submit fiction, describe what you have written and what market you are targeting (you may find it useful to compare your work to that of an established author). Include a synopsis of the novel and the first 2-3 chapters. If you wish to submit nonfiction, you should, in addition, detail your qualifications for writing this particular book. Identify the audience for your book and explain how your book will be different from and better than already-published works aimed at the same market." Accepts simultaneous submissions.

ADAMS LITERARY

7845 Colony Rd., C4 #215, Charlotte NC 28226. (704)542-1440. **Fax:** (704)542-1450. **E-mail:** info@adamsliterary.com. **Website:** www.adamsliterary.com. **Contact:** Tracey Adams, Josh Adams. Adams Literary is a full-service literary agency exclusively representing children's and young adult authors and artists. Estab. 2004. Member of AAR. Other memberships include SCBWI and WNBA.

MEMBER AGENTS Tracey Adams, Josh Adams, Samantha Bagood (assistant).

REPRESENTS Considers these fiction areas: middle-grade, picture books, young adult.

☛ Represents "the finest children's book and young adult authors and artists."

HOW TO CONTACT Submit through online form on website only. This agency accepts submissions only through its website submission form. (You can query by e-mail if the website form is not operating correctly.) No snail mail submissions. Before submitting work for consideration, review complete guidelines online, as the agency sometimes closes to new submissions. Accepts simultaneous submissions. "While we have an established client list, we do seek new talent—and we accept submissions from both published and aspiring authors and artists."

TERMS Agent receives 15% commission on domestic sales; 20% on foreign sales. Offers written contract.

RECENT SALES *The Cruelty* by Scott Bergstrom (Feiwel & Friends), *The Little Fire Truck* by Margery Cuyler (Christy Ottaviano), *Unearthed* by Amie Kaufman and Meagan Spooner (Disney-Hyperion), *A Handful of Stars* by Cynthia Lord (Scholastic), *Under Their Skin* by Margaret Peterson Haddix (Simon & Schuster).

TIPS "Guidelines are posted (and frequently updated) on our website."

⊙ BRET ADAMS LTD. ARTISTS AGENCY

448 W. 44th St., New York NY 10036. **E-mail:** literary@bretadamsltd.net. **Website:** www.bretadamsltd.net. **Contact:** Aislinn Frantz. A full service boutique theatrical agency representing writers, directors, and designers. Member of AAR.

MEMBER AGENTS Bruce Ostler; Mark Orsini; Alexis Williams.

REPRESENTS Theatrical stage plays. **Considers these script areas:** stage plays, theatrical stage play.

☛ Handles theater projects. No books. Cannot accept unsolicited material.

HOW TO CONTACT Use the online submission form. Because of this agency's submission policy and interests, it's advised to approach with a professional recommendation from a client. Accepts simultaneous submissions.

NEW AGENT SPOTLIGHT

MICHAEL HOOGLAND
DYSTEL & GODERICH LITERARY MANAGEMENT

www.dystel.com
@mike_hoogland

ABOUT MICHAEL: Michael Hoogland joined Dystel & Goderich Literary Management after completing an internship at Sterling Lord Literistic. Before pursuing a career in publishing, Mike studied at Colgate University and graduated with a degree in political science and the intention to work in government. He interned with the US Department of Homeland Security, but soon realized his interests and passions were better suited to a career in the publishing industry. After Colgate, Mike went on to gain a valuable education at the Columbia Publishing Course and discovered his passion for the agenting side of the business.

HE IS SEEKING: Science fiction, fantasy, thrillers, upmarket women's fiction, and some children's books (picture books, middle-grade, and young adult). He also seeks a wide variety of narrative nonfiction, including science, history, and politics. He is particularly interested in seeing thought-provoking, realistic speculative fiction.

HOW TO CONTACT: Send a query to mhoogland@dystel.com. "Synopses, outlines, or sample chapters (say, one chapter or the first twenty-five pages of your manuscript) should either be included below the cover letter or attached as a separate document. We won't open attachments if they come with a blank e-mail, by the way. We will respond to most query letters within eight weeks. If you don't hear from us within that time frame, chances are we did not receive yours. Feel free to resend it."

THE AHEARN AGENCY, INC.

2021 Pine St., New Orleans LA 70118. (504)861-8395. **Fax:** (504)866-6434. **E-mail:** pahearn@aol.com. **Website:** www.ahearnagency.com. **Contact:** Pamela G. Ahearn. Member of MWA, RWA, International Thriller Writers. Represents 35 clients.

○ Prior to opening her agency, Ms. Ahearn was an agent for 8 years and an editor with Bantam Books.

REPRESENTS Novels. **Considers these fiction areas:** romance, suspense, thriller, women's.

☞ Handles general adult fiction, specializing in women's fiction and suspense. Does not deal with any nonfiction, poetry, juvenile material, or science fiction.

HOW TO CONTACT Query with SASE or via e-mail. Please send a one-page query letter stating the type of book you're writing, word count, where you feel your book fits into the current market, and any writing credentials you may possess. Please do not send ms pages or synopses if they haven't been previously requested. If you're querying via e-mail, send no attachments unless requested. Accepts simultaneous submissions. Responds in 3 months to queries and submissions. Obtains most new clients through recommendations from others, solicitations, conferences.

TERMS Agent receives 15% commission on domestic sales; 20% commission on foreign sales. Offers written contract, binding for 1 year; renewable by mutual consent.

RECENT SALES *Black-Eyed Susans* by Julia Heaberlin, *The Art of Sinning* by Sabrina Jeffries, *The Comfort of Black* by Carter Wilson, *Flirting with Felicity* by Gerri Russell, *The Iris Fan* by Laura Joh Rowland, *The Loner* by Kate Moore, *Can't Find My Way Home* by Carlene Thompson.

TIPS "Be professional! Always send in exactly what an agent/editor asks for—no more, no less. Keep query letters brief and to the point, giving your writing credentials and a very brief summary of your book. If 1 agent rejects you, keep trying—there are a lot of us out there."

⚫ AITKEN ALEXANDER ASSOCIATES

291 Gray's Inn Rd., Kings Cross, London England WC1X 8QJ United Kingdom. (020)7373-8672. **Fax:** (020)7373-6002. **E-mail:** reception@aitkenalexander. co.uk. **Website:** www.aitkenalexander.co.uk. Estab. 1976.

MEMBER AGENTS Gillon Aitken; Clare Alexander (literary, commercial, memoir, narrative nonfiction, history); **Matthew Hamilton** (literary fiction, suspense, music, politics, sports); **Gillie Russell** (middle-grade, young adult); **Mary Pachnos**; **Anthony Sheil**; **Lucy Luck** (quality fiction and nonfiction); **Lesley Thorne**; **Matias Lopez Portillo**; **Shruti Debi**; **Leah Middleton**.

REPRESENTS Nonfiction, novels. **Considers these nonfiction areas:** creative nonfiction, memoirs, music, politics, sports. **Considers these fiction areas:** commercial, literary, mainstream, middle-grade, suspense, thriller, young adult.

☛ "We specialize in literary fiction and nonfiction." Does not represent illustrated children's books, poetry, or screenplays.

HOW TO CONTACT "If you would like to submit your work to us, please e-mail your query letter with a short synopsis and the first 30 pages (as a Word document) to submissions@aitkenalexander.co.uk, indicating if there is a specific agent who you would like to consider your work. Although every effort is made to respond to submissions, if we have not responded within 3 months, please assume that your work is not right for the agency's list. Please note that the Indian office does not accept unsolicited submissions." Accepts simultaneous submissions. Obtains most new clients through recommendations from others, solicitations.

RECENT SALES *A Country Row, A Tree* by Jo Baker (Knopf), *Noonday* by Pat Barker (Doubleday), *Beatlebone* by Kevin Barry (Doubleday), *Spill Simmer Falter Wither* by Sara Baume (Houghton Mifflin).

⊘◎ ALIVE LITERARY AGENCY

7680 Goddard St., Suite 200, Colorado Springs CO 80920. (719)260-7080. **Fax:** (719)260-8223. **E-mail:** submissions@aliveliterary.com. **Website:** www.aliveliterary.com. **Contact:** Rick Christian. Alive is the largest, most influential literary agency for inspirational content and authors. Estab. 1989. Member of AAR. Other memberships include Authors Guild.

MEMBER AGENTS Rick Christian, president (blockbusters, bestsellers); **Andrea Heinecke** (thoughtful or inspirational nonfiction, women's fiction and nonfiction, popular or commercial nonfiction and fiction); **Bryan Norman** (popular nonfiction, biography, memoir, spiritual growth, inspirational, literary fiction); **Lisa Jackson** (popular or women's nonfiction, biography, memoir, spiritual growth, inspirational, literary).

REPRESENTS Nonfiction, novels, short story collections, novellas. **Considers these nonfiction areas:** autobiography, biography, business, child guidance, economics, health, how-to, humor, inspirational, memoirs, parenting, popular culture, politics, religious, self-help, women's issues, young adult. **Considers these fiction areas:** adventure, contemporary issues, family saga, historical, humor, inspirational, literary, mainstream, mystery, religious, romance, satire, sports, suspense, thriller, young adult.

☛ This agency specializes in inspirational fiction, Christian living, how-to, and commercial nonfiction. Actively seeking inspirational, literary fiction, mainstream fiction, inspirational nonfiction, and work from authors with established track records and platforms. Does not want to receive poetry, scripts, or dark themes.

HOW TO CONTACT "Because all our agents have full client loads, they are only considering queries from authors referred by clients and close contacts. Please refer to our guidelines at www.aliveliterary. com/submissions. Authors referred by an Alive client or close contact are invited to send proposals to submissions@aliveliterary.com." Please write the name of the referring Alive client or close contact in the e-mail subject line. In the e-mail, please describe your personal or professional connection to the referring individual. Also include a brief author biography (including recent speaking engagements, media appearances, social media platform statistics, and sales histories of your books); a synopsis of the work for which you are seeking agency representation (including the target audience, sales and marketing hooks, and comparable titles on the market); and the first 3 chapters of your ms. Alive will respond to queries meeting the above guidelines within 10 weeks.

TERMS Agent receives 15% commission on domestic sales. Offers written contract; two-month notice must be given to terminate contract.

TIPS Rewrite and polish until the words on the page shine. Endorsements, a solid platform, and great connections may help, provided you can write with power and passion. Hone your craft by networking with publishing professionals, joining critique groups, and attending writers conferences.

◉ AMBASSADOR LITERARY AGENCY & SPEAKERS BUREAU

P.O. Box 50358, Nashville TN 37205. (615)370-4700. **Website:** www.ambassadorspeakers.com/ACP/about. aspx. **Contact:** Wes Yoder. Represents 25-30 clients.

● Prior to becoming an agent, Mr. Yoder founded a music artist agency in 1973; he established a speakers bureau division of the company in 1984.

REPRESENTS Novels, nonfiction.

⊶ "Ambassador's literary department represents a select list of best-selling authors and writers who are published by the leading religious and general market publishers in the United States and Europe, and who represent television and major motion picture rights for our clients."

HOW TO CONTACT Authors should e-mail a short description of their ms with a request to submit their

work for review. Official submission guidelines will be sent if the agency agrees to review a ms. Speakers should submit a bio, headshot, and speaking demo. Direct all inquiries and submissions to info@ambassadorspeakers.com. Accepts simultaneous submissions.

BETSY AMSTER LITERARY ENTERPRISES

6312 SW Capitol Hwy., #503, Portland OR 97239. **E-mail:** b.amster.assistant@gmail.com (for adult titles), b.amster.kidsbooks@gmail.com (for children's and young adult). **Website:** www.amsterlit.com. **Contact:** Betsy Amster (adult books), Mary Cummings (children's and young adult). Estab. 1992. Member of AAR. Represents 65+ clients.

● Prior to opening her agency, Ms. Amster was an editor at Pantheon and Vintage for 10 years and served as editorial director for the Globe Pequot Press for 2 years.

REPRESENTS Nonfiction, novels, juvenile books. **Considers these nonfiction areas:** business, cooking, creative nonfiction, decorating, gardening, history, horticulture, interior design, investigative, memoirs, money, multicultural, parenting, popular culture, psychology, self-help, women's issues. **Considers these fiction areas:** crime, detective, juvenile, literary, middle-grade, multicultural, mystery, picture books, police, women's, young adult.

⊶ "Actively seeking strong narrative nonfiction, particularly by journalists; outstanding literary fiction (the next Jennifer Haigh or Jess Walter); witty, intelligent commercial women's fiction (the next Elinor Lipman); mysteries that open new worlds to us; and high-profile self-help and psychology, preferably research-based." Does not want to receive poetry, children's books, romances, western, science fiction, action/adventure, screenplays, fantasy, techno-thrillers, spy capers, apocalyptic scenarios, or political or religious arguments.

HOW TO CONTACT For adult titles: b.amster.assistant@gmail.com. "For fiction or memoirs, please [paste] the first 3 pages in the body of your e-mail. For nonfiction, please [paste] your proposal [into the e-mail]." For children's and young adult: b.amster.kidsbooks@gmail.com. See submission requirements online. "For picture books, please [paste] the entire text in the body of your e-mail. For novels, please [paste] the first 3 pages [into the e-mail]." Accepts simultaneous submissions. Responds in 1 month to queries; in 2 months to mss. Obtains most new clients through recommendations from others, solicitations, conferences.

TERMS Agent receives 15% commission on domestic sales; 20% commission on foreign sales. Offers written contract, binding for 1 year. Three-month notice must be given to terminate contract. Charges for photocopying, postage, messengers, galleys/books used in submissions to foreign and film agents and to magazines for first serial rights. (Please note that it is rare to incur much in the way of expenses now that most submissions are made by e-mail.)

RECENT SALES *Kachka: The Recipes, Stories, and Vodka That Started a Russian Food Revolution* by Bonnie Morales (Flatiron), *It Takes One to Tango* by Winifred Reilly (Touchstone), *Plus One* by Christopher Noxon (Prospect Park Books), *Animals Spell Love: I Love You in Sixteen Languages* by David Cundy (David R. Godine), *Monster Trucks* by Joy Keller (Holt Children's).

THE ANDERSON LITERARY AGENCY

(917)363-6829. **E-mail:** giles@andersonliteraryagency.com. **Website:** www.andersonliteraryagency.com. **Contact:** Giles Anderson. Estab. 2000.

Owner and founder Giles Anderson started the agency in 2000 after working several years at The Waxman Literary Agency, Zephyr Press, and The Carnegie Council for Ethics in International Affairs.

MEMBER AGENTS Giles Anderson.

"Over time my interests have increasingly turned to books that help us understand people, ideas, and the possibility of change—from an examination of religious beliefs to the science of motivation, I'm looking for books that surprise, inform, and inspire."

HOW TO CONTACT Query via e-mail. Accepts simultaneous submissions.

RECENT SALES *Mindset: The New Psychology of Success* by Carol S. Dweck, *9 Things Successful People Do Differently* by Heidi Grant Halverson, *Reality-Based Leadership* by C.Y. Wakeman.

ANDERSON LITERARY MANAGEMENT, LLC

244 Fifth Ave., Floor 11, New York NY 10001. (212)645-6045. **Fax:** (212)741-1936. **E-mail:** info@andersonliterary.com. **Website:** www.andersonliter-

ary.com. **Contact:** Kathleen Anderson. Estab. 2006. Member of AAR. Represents 100+ clients.

MEMBER AGENTS Kathleen Anderson, kathleen@andersonliterary.com; **Adam Friedstein**, adam@andersonliterary.com; **Tess Taylor**, tess@andersonliterary.com.

REPRESENTS Nonfiction, novels. **Considers these nonfiction areas:** anthropology, architecture, biography, creative nonfiction, cultural interests, current affairs, environment, ethnic, history, music, politics, psychology, religious, science, spirituality, travel, women's studies, literary journalism, narrative nonfiction, social science, nature. **Considers these fiction areas:** ethnic, historical, humor, literary, middle-grade, multicultural, suspense, thriller, women's, young adult, contemporary, international.

"We do not represent plays or screenplays. We do not represent science fiction, cookbooks, gardening, craft books, or children's picture books. While we love literature in translation, we cannot accept samples of work written in languages other than English."

HOW TO CONTACT Query with SASE. Submit synopsis, first 3 sample chapters, proposal (for nonfiction). Snail mail queries only. Accepts simultaneous submissions. Responds in 6 weeks to queries.

APONTE LITERARY AGENCY

E-mail: agents@aponteliterary.com. **Website:** aponteliterary.com. **Contact:** Natalia Aponte. Member of AAR. Signatory of WGA.

MEMBER AGENTS Natalia Aponte (any genre of mainstream fiction and nonfiction, but she is especially seeking women's novels, historical novels, supernatural and paranormal fiction, fantasy novels, political thrillers, and science thrillers); **Victoria Lea** (any category—especially interested in women's fiction, science fiction, and speculative fiction).

REPRESENTS Novels. **Considers these fiction areas:** fantasy, historical, paranormal, science fiction, supernatural, thriller, women's.

HOW TO CONTACT E-query. Accepts simultaneous submissions. Responds in 6 weeks if interested.

RECENT SALES *The Nightingale Bones* by Ariel Swan, *An Irish Doctor in Peace and at War* by Patrick Taylor, *Siren's Treasure* by Debbie Herbert.

⊘ ARCADIA

31 Lake Place N., Danbury CT 06810. **E-mail:** arcadialit@sbcglobal.net. **Contact:** Victoria Gould Pryor. Member of AAR.

REPRESENTS Considers these nonfiction areas: biography, current affairs, health, history, medicine, psychology, science, investigative journalism, culture, classical music, life-transforming self-help.

☞ "I'm a very hands-on agent, which is necessary in this competitive marketplace. I work with authors on revisions until whatever we present to publishers is as strong as possible. Arcadia represents talented, dedicated, intelligent, and ambitious writers who are looking for a long-term relationship based on professional success and mutual respect." Does not want to receive fiction, true crime, business, science fiction, fantasy, horror, memoirs about addiction or abuse, humor or children's books.

HOW TO CONTACT No unsolicited submissions.

THE AUGUST AGENCY, LLC

Website: www.augustagency.com. **Contact:** Cricket Freeman. Estab. 2004. Represents 25-40 clients.

○ Before opening The August Agency, Ms. Freeman was a freelance writer, magazine editor, and independent literary agent.

REPRESENTS Novels, nonfiction. **Considers these nonfiction areas:** art, biography, business, current affairs, history, memoirs, popular culture, politics, sociology, true crime, narrative nonfiction, academic works. **Considers these fiction areas:** crime, mainstream.

☞ "At this time, we are not accepting the following types of submissions: self-published works, screenplays, children's books, genre fiction, romance, horror, western, fantasy, science fiction, poetry, short story collections."

HOW TO CONTACT Currently closed to unsolicited submissions.

THE AXELROD AGENCY

55 Main St., P.O. Box 357, Chatham NY 12037. (518)392-2100. **E-mail:** steve@axelrodagency.com. **Website:** www.axelrodagency.com. **Contact:** Steven Axelrod. Member of AAR. Represents 15-20 clients.

○ Prior to becoming an agent, Mr. Axelrod was a book club editor.

REPRESENTS Novels. **Considers these fiction areas:** crime, mystery, new adult, romance, women's.

☞ This agency specializes in women's fiction and romance.

HOW TO CONTACT Query via e-mail. Accepts simultaneous submissions. Obtains most new clients through recommendations from others.

TERMS Agent receives 15% commission on domestic sales; 20% commission on foreign sales. No written contract.

AZANTIAN LITERARY AGENCY

E-mail: queries@azantianlitagency.com. **Website:** www.azantianlitagency.com. **Contact:** Jennifer Azantian. Estab. 2014. Member of AAR. Signatory of WGA.

○ Prior to her current position, Ms. Azantian was with Sandra Dijkstra Literary Agency.

REPRESENTS Novels. **Considers these fiction areas:** fantasy, horror, middle-grade, science fiction, young adult.

☞ Actively seeking fantasy, science fiction, and psychological horror for adult, young adult, and middle-grade readers. Does not want to receive nonfiction or picture books.

HOW TO CONTACT Send your query letter, a synopsis of 1-2 pages, and the first 10-15 pages of your ms all pasted in an e-mail (no attachments) to queries@azantianlitagency.com. Please note in the e-mail subject line if your work was requested at a conference, is an exclusive submission, or was referred by a current client. Accepts simultaneous submissions. Responds within 6 weeks. Check the website before submitting to make sure the agency is currently open to queries.

BARONE LITERARY AGENCY

385 North St., Batavia OH 45103. (513)732-6740. **Fax:** (513)297-7208. **E-mail:** baroneliteraryagency@roadrunner.com. **Website:** www.baroneliteraryagency.com. **Contact:** Denise Barone. Represents Anna Snow, Cathy Bennett, Rebekah Purdy, Michele Barrow-Belisle, Gwen Williams, Denise Gwen, Laurie Albano, Pamela McCoy, Yvette Geer, Jennifer Petersen Fraser. Estab. 2010. Member of AAR, RWA. Signatory of WGA. Represents 10 clients.

REPRESENTS Nonfiction, novels. **Considers these nonfiction areas:** memoirs. **Considers these fiction areas:** action, adventure, cartoon, comic books, commercial, confession, contemporary issues, crime, detective, erotica, ethnic, experimental, family saga, fantasy, feminist, frontier, gay, glitz, hi-lo, historical, horror, humor, inspirational, juvenile, lesbian, literary, mainstream, metaphysical, military, multicultural, multimedia, mystery, new adult, New Age, occult, paranormal, plays, police, psychic, regional, religious, romance, satire, science fiction, sports, supernatural, suspense, thriller, urban fantasy, war, westerns, women's, young adult. **Considers these script areas:** action, adventure, animation, cartoon, comedy, contemporary issues, crime, detective, erotica, ethnic, experimental, family saga, fantasy, feminist, gay, glitz, historical, horror, juvenile, lesbian, mainstream, mystery, police, psychic, religious, romantic comedy, romantic drama, science fiction, sports, supernatural, teen, thriller, western.

☞ Actively seeking adult contemporary romance. Does not want textbooks.

HOW TO CONTACT "We are no longer accepting snail mail submissions; send a query letter via e-mail instead. If I like your query letter, I will ask for the first 3 chapters and a synopsis as attachments." Accepts simultaneous submissions.

TERMS Agent receives 15% commission on domestic sales, 20% on foreign sales. Offers written contract.

RECENT SALES *All the Glittering Bones* by Anna Snow (Entangled Publishing), *Melody Massacre to the Rescue* by Anna Snow (Entangled Publishing), *Devon's Choice* by Cathy Bennett (Clean Reads), *Molly's Folly* by Denise Gwen (Clean Reads), *In Deep* by Laurie Albano (Solstice Publishing).

TIPS "The best writing advice I ever got came from a fellow writer, who wrote, 'Learn how to edit yourself,' when signing her book to me."

BAROR INTERNATIONAL, INC.

P.O. Box 868, Armonk NY 10504. **E-mail:** heather@barorint.com. **Website:** www.barorint.com. **Contact:** Danny Baror, Heather Baror-Shapiro. Represents 300 clients.

MEMBER AGENTS Danny Baror, Heather Baror-Shapiro.

REPRESENTS Fiction. **Considers these fiction areas:** fantasy, literary, science fiction, young adult, commerical.

☞ This agency represents authors and publishers in the international market. Currently representing commercial fiction, literary titles, science fiction, young adult, and more.

HOW TO CONTACT Submit by e-mail or mail (with SASE). Include a query letter and a few sample chapters. Accepts simultaneous submissions.

BARRON'S LITERARY MANAGEMENT

4615 Rockland Dr., Arlington TX 76016. **E-mail:** barronsliterary@sbcglobal.net. **Contact:** Adele Brooks, president.

REPRESENTS Nonfiction, novels. **Considers these nonfiction areas:** design, health, memoirs, true crime. **Considers these fiction areas:** crime, mystery, police, romance, thriller.

☞ Barron's Literary Management is a small Dallas/Fort Worth-based agency with good publishing contacts. Seeks tightly written, fast-moving fiction and nonfiction, and authors with a significant platform or subject area expertise. Considers legal, crime, techno, or medical thrillers. Considers all romance. Considers nonfiction in the categories of business, cooking, health, investing, psychology, and true crime.

HOW TO CONTACT Contact by e-mail initially. Send bio and a brief synopsis of story (fiction) or a nonfiction book proposal. Accepts simultaneous submissions. Obtains most new clients through e-mail submissions.

TIPS "Have your book tightly edited, polished, and ready to be seen before contacting agents. I respond quickly and, if interested, may request an electronic or hard-copy mailing."

⬏ LORELLA BELLI LITERARY AGENCY (LBLA)

54 Hartford House, 35 Tavistock Crescent, Notting Hill, London England W11 1AY United Kingdom. (44)(207)727-8547. **Fax:** (44)(870)787-4194. **E-mail:** info@lorellabelliagency.com. **Website:** www.lorellabelliagency.com. **Contact:** Lorella Belli. "LBLA represents best-selling, award-winning, debut and successfully self-published authors of fiction and nonfiction, and is particularly interested in books with a multicultural perspective and a genuine potential to sell internationally." Estab. 2002. Memberships include Crime Writers' Association, Romantic Novelists Association, The Book Society, Women in Publishing.

REPRESENTS Nonfiction, novels, juvenile books. **Considers these nonfiction areas:** autobiography, biography, cooking, current affairs, diet/nutrition, history, memoirs, multicultural, popular culture, psychology, science, self-help, sports, translation, travel, true crime, women's issues, young adult. **Considers these fiction areas:** action, adventure, commercial, contemporary issues, crime, detective, family saga, feminist, historical, inspirational, literary, mainstream, multicultural, mystery, new adult, police, romance, suspense, thriller, women's, young adult.

☞ This agency handles adult fiction, adult nonfiction, and young adult. Does not want to receive children's picture books, fantasy, science fiction, screenplays, short stories, poetry, academic, or specialist books. "We handle full-length fiction (from literary to genre—in particular women's fiction, book club reads, historical and crime/thrillers) and general nonfiction (memoirs, biography, autobiography, mainstream self-help, travel, sport, women's issues, humor, popular music, popular science, popular history, fashion, food, soft business, lifestyle, media personalities, current affairs). Please check what kind of books/authors we represent before submitting to us by following us on Twitter @lblaUK."

HOW TO CONTACT Please send an initial brief query to info@lorellabelliagency.com. Do not send a proposal or ms before it's requested. Accepts simultaneous submissions.

TERMS Agent receives 15% commission on domestic sales; 20% commission on foreign sales.

RECENT SALES Follow us on Twitter and Facebook to see all sales.

THE BENT AGENCY

E-mail: info@thebentagency.com. **Website:** www.thebentagency.com. Estab. 2009. Member of AAR.

💬 Prior to forming her own agency, Ms. Bent was an agent and vice president at Trident Media Group.

MEMBER AGENTS Jenny Bent, queries@thebentagency.com (adult fiction including women's fiction, romance, and crime/suspense; she particularly likes novels with magical or fantasy elements that fall outside of genre fiction; young adult and middle-grade fiction; nonfiction interests are memoir and humor); Susan Hawk, kidsqueries@thebentagency.com (young adult, middle-grade, picture books; within the realm of kids stories, she likes contemporary, mystery, fantasy, science fiction, and historical sto-

ries); **Molly Ker Hawn**, queries@thebentagency.com (young adult and middle-grade books, including contemporary, historical, fantasy, science fiction, thrillers, and mystery); **Gemma Cooper**, cooperqueries@thebentagency.com (all ages of children's and young adult books, including picture books; she likes historical, contemporary, thrillers, mystery, humor, and science fiction); **Louise Fury**, furyqueries@thebentagency.com (picture books, literary middle-grade, all young adult subgenres, speculative fiction, suspense/thriller, commercial fiction, all sub-genres of romance, erotic novels; her nonfiction interest are cookbooks and pop culture); **Brooks Sherman**, shermanqueries@thebentagency.com (speculative and literary adult fiction, select narrative nonfiction, all ages of children's and young adult books; he enjoys historical, contemporary, thrillers, humor, fantasy, and horror); **Beth Phelan**, phelanqueries@thebentagency.com (young adult, thrillers, suspense and mystery, romance, women's fiction, literary fiction, general fiction, cookbooks, lifestyle and pets); **Victoria Lowes**, lowesqueries@thebentagency.com (romance, women's fiction, thrillers, mystery, and young adult); **Heather Flaherty**, flahertyqueries@thebentagency.com (all genres of young adult and middle-grade fiction; she represents select adult fiction upmarket fiction—women's fiction, and female-centric thrillers; she also takes select nonfiction—pop culture, humorous, and social media based projects, as well as teen memoir).

REPRESENTS Nonfiction, novels, juvenile books. **Considers these nonfiction areas:** animals, cooking, creative nonfiction, foods, juvenile nonfiction, popular culture, women's issues, young adult. **Considers these fiction areas:** commercial, crime, erotica, fantasy, feminist, historical, horror, juvenile, literary, mainstream, middle-grade, multicultural, mystery, picture books, romance, suspense, thriller, women's, young adult.

HOW TO CONTACT E-query. "Tell us briefly who you are, what your book is, and why you're the one to write it. Then include the first 10 pages of your material in the body of your e-mail. We respond to all queries; please resend your query if you haven't had a response within 4 weeks." Accepts simultaneous submissions.

RECENT SALES *Caraval* by Stephanie Garber (Flatiron), *The Smell of Other People's Houses* by Bonnie-Sue Hitchcock (Wendy Lamb Books/Random House), *My Perfect Me* by J.M.M. Nuanez (Kathy Dawson

NEW AGENT SPOTLIGHT

PAUL STEVENS
DONALD MAASS LITERARY AGENCY

www.maassagency.com
@pstevens1824

ABOUT PAUL: Paul Stevens joined the Donald Maass Literary Agency in 2016. Previously, he worked as an editor for fifteen years, primarily at Tor Books, where he edited science fiction, fantasy, and mystery. Paul is an Ohio native and a graduate of The Ohio State University. He spent a year in Chile as a high school exchange student.

HE IS SEEKING: Paul is looking for science fiction, fantasy, mystery, suspense, and humor (both fiction and nonfiction). He's looking for strong stories with interesting characters. Well-rounded LGBT characters and characters of color are a plus.

HOW TO SUBMIT: Contact query.pstevens@maassagency.com. "Include a cover letter and a synopsis pasted in the body of the e-mail. (If your book has a twist at the end, please don't reveal the twist in the synopsis. Paul needs to judge how well a twist works in the actual manuscript, and it's better to read the ending cold without spoilers.) Please also include the first five pages of your manuscript pasted into the e-mail. No attachments. For humor books that include images, please send a cover letter and synopsis pasted in the body of the e-mail, and attach one or two representative images. Please make sure that the image files are low resolution so the files are of reasonable size. Responds in three weeks."

Books/Penguin BFYR), *The Square Root of Summer* by Harriet Reuter Hapgood (Roaring Brook/Macmillan), *Dirty Money* by Lisa Renee Jones (Simon & Schuster), *True North* by Liora Blake (Pocket Star).

⊘ **BICOASTAL TALENT**

2600 West Olive Ave., Suite 500, Burbank CA 91505. (818)845-0150. **Fax:** (818)845-0152. **E-mail:** submissions@bicoastaltalent.com. **Website:** www.bicoastaltalent.com/. Estab. 2001.
MEMBER AGENTS Liz Hanley, Niche Martin.

HOW TO CONTACT *Not currently accepting submissions.* "Query letters only are accepted only by our Burbank literary department as an initial step towards representation. Unsolicited materials (scripts, mss, graphics, DVDs, etc.) will not be reviewed. We do not represent authors of self-published mss, treatments, concepts, or TV pilots. A minimum of 3 completed screenplays must be available for review upon request. We also consider new writers with strong placements in industry recognized competitions or by industry referral. Queries should include a list of completed screenplays with title, genre, and a one-paragraph synopsis (4-8 lines)." Accepts simultaneous submissions.

BIDNICK & COMPANY

E-mail: bidnick@comcast.net. **Website:** www.publishersmarketplace.com/members/bidnick.

○ Prior to her time as an agent, Ms. Bidnick was a founding member of Collins Publishers and vice president of HarperCollins, San Francisco.

MEMBER AGENTS Carole Bidnick.

REPRESENTS Nonfiction. **Considers these nonfiction areas:** cooking, commercial.

⌖ This agency specializes in cookbooks and commercial nonfiction.

HOW TO CONTACT Send queries via e-mail only. Accepts simultaneous submissions.

RECENT SALES *Burma Superstar Cookbook* by Desmond Tan and Kate Leahy (Ten Speed), *The Healthiest Diet on the Planet* by Dr. John McDougall and Mary McDougall (Harper One), *Southern Living's Vegetables* by Rebecca Lang (Oxmoor House).

VICKY BIJUR LITERARY AGENCY

27 W. 20th St., Suite 1003, New York NY 10011. **E-mail:** queries@vickybijuragency.com. **Website:** www.vickybijuragency.com. Estab. 1988. Member of AAR.

○ Before starting her own agency, Ms. Bijur worked at Oxford University Press and with the Charlotte Sheedy Literary Agency.

MEMBER AGENTS Vicky Bijur, Alexandra Franklin.

REPRESENTS Nonfiction, novels. **Considers these nonfiction areas:** memoirs. **Considers these fiction areas:** commercial, literary, mystery, new adult, thriller, women's, young adult, campus novels, coming-of-age.

⌖ "We are not the right agency for screenplays, picture books, poetry, self-help, science fiction, fantasy, horror, or romance."

HOW TO CONTACT "Please send a query letter along with the first 10 pages of your ms. Please let us know in your query letter if it is a simultaenous submission, and kindly keep us informed of other agents' interest and offers of representation. If sending electronically, paste the pages in an e-mail, as we don't open attachments from unfamiliar senders. If sending by hard copy, please include a SASE for our response. If you want your material returned, include a SASE large enough to contain pages and enough postage to send back to you." Include a cover letter with a proposal and the first 10 pages for nonfiction projects. Accepts simultaneous submissions. "We generally respond to all queries within 8 weeks of receipt."

RECENT SALES *That Darkness* by Lisa Black, *Long Upon the Land* by Margaret Maron, *Daughter of Ashes* by Marcia Talley.

DAVID BLACK LITERARY AGENCY

335 Adams St., Suite 2707, Brooklyn NY 11201. (718)852-5500. **Fax:** (718)852-5539. **Website:** www.davidblackagency.com. **Contact:** David Black, owner. Member of AAR. Represents 150 clients.

MEMBER AGENTS David Black, Jenny Herrera, Gary Morris, Joy E. Tutela (narrative nonfiction, memoir, history, politics, self-help, investment, business, science, women's issues, LGBT issues, parenting, health, humor, craft, cooking, lifestyle and entertainment, commercial fiction, literary fiction, middle-grade, young adult); Susan Raihofer (commercial fiction and nonfiction, memoir, pop culture, music, inspirational, thrillers, literary fiction); Sarah Smith (memoir, biography, food, music, narrative history, social studies, literary fiction); Heather Jackson, (commercial nonfiction, commercial fiction, popular culture; also seeks fresh narrative voices that inform, entertain, and shift the cultural conversation).

REPRESENTS Nonfiction, novels. **Considers these nonfiction areas:** biography, business, cooking, crafts, gay/lesbian, health, history, humor, inspirational, memoirs, music, parenting, popular culture, politics, science, self-help, sociology, sports, women's issues. **Considers these fiction areas:** commercial, literary, middle-grade, thriller, young adult.

HOW TO CONTACT "To query an individual agent, please follow the specific query guidelines outlined in the agent's profile on our website. Not all agents are currently accepting unsolicited queries. To query the agency, please send a query letter of 1-2 pages describing your book, and include information about any previously published works, your audience, and your platform." Do not e-mail your query unless an agent specifically asks for it. Accepts simultaneous submissions. Responds in 2 months to queries.

RECENT SALES Some of the agency's best-selling authors include Erik Larson, Stuart Scott, Jeff Hobbs, Mitch Albom, Gregg Olsen, Jim Abbott, and John Bacon.

JUDY BOALS, INC.

307 W. 38th St., #812, New York NY 10018. (212)500-1424. **Fax:** (212)500-1426. **E-mail:** info@judyboals.

com. **Website:** www.judyboals.com. **Contact:** Judy Boals.

HOW TO CONTACT Query by referral or invitation only. Accepts simultaneous submissions.

⊘ REID BOATES LITERARY AGENCY

69 Cooks Crossroad, Pittstown NJ 08867. (908)797-8087. **Fax:** (908)788-3667. **E-mail:** reid.boates@gmail.com; boatesliterary@att.net. **Contact:** Reid Boates. Represents 45 clients.

HOW TO CONTACT No unsolicited queries. Obtains new clients by personal referral only. This agency, at the current time, is handling 100% nonfiction.

TERMS Agent receives 15% commission on domestic sales; 20% commission on foreign sales.

RECENT SALES New sales include placements at HarperCollins, Wiley, Random House, and other major general-interest publishers.

BOND LITERARY AGENCY

4340 E. Kentucky Ave., Suite 471, Denver CO 80246. (303)781-9305. **E-mail:** queries@bondliteraryagency.com. **Website:** www.bondliteraryagency.com. **Contact:** Sandra Bond.

○ Prior to her current position, Ms. Bond worked with agent Jody Rein.

MEMBER AGENTS Sandra Bond; Becky LeJeune, associate agent.

REPRESENTS Nonfiction, novels, juvenile books. **Considers these nonfiction areas:** biography, business, history, juvenile nonfiction, popular culture, science, young adult. **Considers these fiction areas:** commercial, crime, detective, family saga, historical, horror, juvenile, literary, mainstream, middle-grade, mystery, police, suspense, thriller, women's, young adult.

➥ The agency represents adult and young adult fiction—both literary and commercial, including mysteries and women's fiction. The agency also seeks many categories of nonfiction, including narrative, health, science, memoir, biography, and business. It does not represent romance, adult fantasy, science fiction, poetry, children's picture books, or screenplays. Becky LeJeune is particularly looking for thriller and horror.

HOW TO CONTACT Please submit query by e-mail (absolutely no attachments unless requested). They will let you know if they are interested in seeing more

material. *No unsolicited mss or phone calls.* Accepts simultaneous submissions.

RECENT SALES *The Ninja's Daughter* by Susan Spann, *Amelia Earhart: Beyond the Grave* by W.C. Jameson, *The Gathering Jar* by Margo Catts.

BOOK CENTS LITERARY AGENCY, LLC

364 Patteson Dr., #228, Morgantown WV 26505. **E-mail:** cw@bookcentsliteraryagency.com. **Website:** www.bookcentsliteraryagency.com. **Contact:** Christine Witthohn. "It is our goal not only to assist our clients in selling their creative work(s), but to also assist them with growing their writing careers and helping them reach their targeted audiences. We will make it our mission to work hard and be diligent, and to keep the lines of communication open with the authors we represent." Estab. 2005. Member of AAR, RWA, MWA, SinC.

MEMBER AGENTS Christine Witthohn.

REPRESENTS **Considers these nonfiction areas:** cooking, gardening, travel, women's issues. **Considers these fiction areas:** commercial, literary, mainstream, multicultural, mystery, new adult, paranormal, romance, suspense, thriller, urban fantasy, women's, young adult.

➥ Actively seeking upmarket fiction, commercial fiction (particularly if it has crossover appeal), women's fiction (emotional and layered), romance (single title or category), mainstream mystery/suspense, thrillers (particularly psychological), and young adult. For a detailed list of what this agency is currently searching for, visit the agency website. Does *not* want to receive third party submissions, previously published titles, short stories, novellas, erotica, inspirational, historical, science fiction, fantasy, horror/pulp/slasher thrillers, middle-grade, children's picture books, poetry, screenplays, or stories with priests/nuns, religion, abuse of children/animals/elderly, rape, or serial killer stories.

HOW TO CONTACT Accepts e-submissions only from agency's website via an online form. Accepts simultaneous submissions.

TIPS Sponsors the International Women's Fiction festival in Matera, Italy. See: www.womensfictionfestival.com for more information. Ms. Witthohn is also the US rights and licensing agent for leading French publisher Bragelonne and German publisher Egmont. For a list of upcoming publications, leading clients, and sales, visit www.publishersmarketplace.com/members/BookCents.

BOOKENDS LITERARY AGENCY

Website: bookendsliterary.com. **Contact:** Jessica Faust, Kim Lionetti, Jessica Alvarez, Moe Ferrara, Beth Campbell. "Representing fiction and nonfiction primarily for the adult, young adult, and middle-grade markets, BookEnds agents continue to live their dreams while helping authors achieve theirs." Estab. 1999. Member of AAR, RWA, MWA, SCBWI. Represents 50+ clients.

MEMBER AGENTS Jessica Faust, jfsubmissions@bookendsliterary.com (women's fiction, mysteries, thrillers, suspense); **Kim Lionetti,** klsubmissions@bookendsliterary.com (contemporary romance, women's fiction, cozies, new adult, and contemporary young adult); **Jessica Alvarez,** jasubmissions@bookendsliterary.com (romance, women's fiction, erotica, romantic suspense); **Beth Campbell,** bcsubmissions@bookendsliterary.com (urban fantasy, science fiction, young adult, suspense, romantic suspense, and mystery); **Moe Ferrara,** mfsubmissions@bookendsliterary.com (adult science fiction and fantasy).

REPRESENTS Nonfiction, novels. **Considers these nonfiction areas:** business, creative nonfiction, ethnic, how-to, money, women's issues. **Considers these fiction areas:** crime, detective, erotica, fantasy, gay, lesbian, mainstream, middle-grade, multicultural, mystery, police, romance, science fiction, thriller, urban fantasy, women's, young adult.

☛ "BookEnds is currently accepting queries from published and unpublished writers in the areas of romance (and all its subgenres), erotica, mystery, suspense, thrillers, science fiction, fantasy, urban fantasy, young adult, middle-grade, and women's fiction." BookEnds does not want to receive children's books, screenplays, poetry, or technical/military thrillers.

HOW TO CONTACT Visit http://bookendsliterary.com/index.php/submissions for the most up-to-date submission instructions, as they change. BookEnds is no longer accepting unsolicited proposal packages or snail mail queries. Send query in the body of e-mail to only 1 agent. No attachments. Accepts simultaneous submissions. "Our response time goals are 6 weeks for queries and 12 weeks on requested partials and fulls."

THE BOOK GROUP

20 W. 20th St., Suite 601, New York NY 10011. (212)803-3360. **E-mail:** submissions@thebookgroup.com. **Website:** www.thebookgroup.com. "The Book Group is a full service literary agency located in the heart of Manhattan. Launched in 2015 by publishing industry veterans, The Book Group cultivates writers and serves as their champions throughout their careers. We represent a wide range of distinguished authors, including critically acclaimed and best-selling novelists." Estab. 2015. Member of AAR. Signatory of WGA.

MEMBER AGENTS Julie Barer; Faye Bender; **Brettne Bloom** (fiction interests include literary fiction, commercial fiction, select young adult; nonfiction interests include cookbooks, lifestyle, investigative journalism, history, biography, memoir, and psychology); **Elisabeth Weed** (upmarket fiction, especially plot-driven novels with a sense of place); **Rebecca Stead** (innovative forms, diverse voices, and open-hearted fiction for children, young adults, and adults); **Dana Murphy** (story-driven fiction with a strong sense of place, narrative nonfiction/essays with a pop culture lean, and young adult with an honest voice).

REPRESENTS **Considers these nonfiction areas:** biography, cooking, history, investigative, memoirs, psychology. **Considers these fiction areas:** commercial, literary, mainstream, women's, young adult.

☛ Please do not send poetry or screenplays.

HOW TO CONTACT Send a query letter and 10 sample pages to submissions@thebookgroup.com, with the first and last name of the agent you are querying in the subject line. All material must be in the body of the e-mail, as the agents do not open attachments. "If we are interested in reading more, we will get in touch with you as soon as possible." Accepts simultaneous submissions.

RECENT SALES *The Family Fang* by Kevin Wilson, *The Violets of March* by Sarah Jio, *The Husband's Secret* by Liane Moriarty.

✚◎ BOOKMARK LITERARY

189 Berdan Ave., #101, Wayne NJ 07470 **E-mail:** teresa@bookmarkliterary.com. **Website:** http://bookmarkliterary.com. **Contact:** Teresa Kietlinski, foundere.

☛ This agency specializes in books for young children, including picture books, early reader books, and chapter books. Seeks submis-

NEW AGENT SPOTLIGHT

ANJALI SINGH
AYESHA PANDE LITERARY

www.pandeliterary.com

ABOUT ANJALI: Before joining Ayesha Pande Literary, Anjali Singh started her career in publishing in 1996 as a literary scout. Most recently editorial director at Other Press, she has also worked as an editor at Simon & Schuster, Houghton Mifflin Harcourt, and Vintage Books. She is a member of the International Committee of the Brooklyn Book Festival.

SHE IS SEEKING: She is looking for new voices, character-driven fiction or nonfiction works that reflect an engagement with the world around us, literary thrillers, memoirs, young adult literature, and graphic novels.

HOW TO SUBMIT: Use the agency's online submissions form here: www.pande literary.com/queries.

---

sions from authors, illustrators, and author-illustrators.

HOW TO CONTACT "Bookmark Literary has an open door policy when it comes to Illustrator submissions. Illustrators are welcome to submit by snail mail with postcards and promo. If submitting a dummy via e-mail, PDF proposals must have a file size under 1MB. Please do not send multiple attachments of art samples. We will automatically delete any e-mails with large files or multiple attachments. We are not accepting self-publishing or previously published projects. Submit to submissions@bookmarkliterary.com." Writers of picture books, beginning readers, and early chapter books can submit to the same e-mail above. Again, no self-publishing or previously published projects. There is also an online submission form.

BOOKS & SUCH LITERARY MANAGEMENT

52 Mission Circle, Suite 122, PMB 170, Santa Rosa CA 95409-5370. **E-mail:** representation@booksandsuch.com. **Website:** www.booksandsuch.com. **Contact:** Janet Kobobel Grant, Wendy Lawton, Rachel Kent, Mary Keeley, Rachelle Gardner. Estab. 1996. Member of CBA (associate), American Christian Fiction Writers. Represents 250 clients.

○ Prior to becoming an agent, Ms. Grant was an editor for Zondervan and managing editor for Focus on the Family before founding the agency. She became an agent in 2005. Ms. Keeley previously was an acquisitions editor for Tyndale publishers. Ms. Kent has worked as an agent for 9 years and is a graduate of UC Davis majoring in English. Ms. Gardner worked as an editor at NavPress, at General Publishing Group in rights and marketing, and at Fox Broadcasting Company as special programming coordinator before becoming an agent in 2007.

REPRESENTS Nonfiction, novels, novellas, juvenile books. **Considers these nonfiction areas:** autobiography, biography, business, cooking, creative nonfiction, cultural interests, current affairs, foods, inspirational, juvenile nonfiction, memoirs, parenting, religious, spirituality, true crime, women's issues, young adult. **Considers these fiction areas:** action, adventure, commercial, crime, family saga, frontier, historical, inspirational, juvenile, literary, mainstream, middle-grade, mystery, new adult, religious, romance, spiritual, suspense, women's, young adult.

☛ This agency specializes in general and inspirational fiction and nonfiction, and in the Christian booksellers market. Actively seeking well-crafted material that presents Judeo-Christian values, if only subtly.

HOW TO CONTACT Query via e-mail only; no attachments. Accepts simultaneous submissions. Responds in 1 month to queries. "If you don't hear from us asking to see more of your writing within 30 days after you have sent your e-mail, please know that we have read and considered your submission but determined that it would not be a good fit for us." Obtains most new clients through recommendations from others, conferences.

TERMS Agent receives 15% commission on domestic sales; 20% commission on foreign sales. Offers written contract; two-month notice must be given to terminate contract. No additional charges.

RECENT SALES A full list of this agency's clients (and the awards they have won) is on the agency website.

TIPS "Our agency highlights personal attention to individual clients that includes coaching on how to thrive in a rapidly changing publishing climate, grow a career, and get the best publishing offers possible."

BOOKSTOP LITERARY AGENCY

67 Meadow View Rd., Orinda CA 94563. (925)254-2664. **E-mail:** info@bookstopliterary.com. **Website:** www.bookstopliterary.com. Represents authors and illustrators of books for children and young adults. Estab. 1984.

REPRESENTS Nonfiction, novels, short story collections, juvenile books, poetry books. **Considers these nonfiction areas:** juvenile nonfiction, young adult. **Considers these fiction areas:** hi-lo, middle-grade, picture books, plays, poetry, young adult.

☛ "Special interest in Hispanic, Asian-American, African-American, and multicultural writers. Also seeking quirky picture books, clever mystery novels, eye-opening nonfiction, heartfelt middle-grade, and unusual teen romance."

HOW TO CONTACT For picture books, send a cover letter and the entire ms. For novels, send a query and the first 10 pages. For nonfiction, send a proposal and sample chapters. E-query info@bookstopliterary.

com. Send sample illustrations only if you are an illustrator. Illustrators, send a postcard or link to online portfolio. Do not send original artwork. Accepts simultaneous submissions.

TERMS Agent receives 15% commission on domestic sales. Offers written contract, binding for 1 year.

Ø GEORGES BORCHARDT, INC.

136 E. 57th St., New York NY 10022. (212)753-5785. **Website:** www.gbagency.com. Estab. 1967. Member of AAR. Represents 200+ clients.

MEMBER AGENTS Anne Borchardt, Georges Borchardt, Valerie Borchardt, Samantha Shea.

REPRESENTS Nonfiction, novels, short story collections, novellas. **Considers these nonfiction areas:** art, biography, creative nonfiction, current affairs, history, literature, philosophy, politics, religious, science.

☛ This agency specializes in literary fiction and outstanding nonfiction.

HOW TO CONTACT *No unsolicited submissions.* Obtains most new clients through recommendations from others.

TERMS Agent receives 15% commission on domestic sales; 20% commission on foreign sales. Offers written contract.

RECENT SALES *Commotion of the Birds* by John Ashbery, *Huck Out West* by Lesley Arimah, *The Midnight Cool* by Lydia Peelle.

BRADFORD LITERARY AGENCY

5694 Mission Center Rd., #347, San Diego CA 92108. (619)521-1201. **E-mail:** queries@bradfordlit.com. **Website:** www.bradfordlit.com. **Contact:** Laura Bradford, Natalie Lakosil, Sarah LaPolla, Monica Odom. "The Bradford Literary Agency is a boutique agency that offers a full range of representation services to authors who are both published and pre-published. Our mission at the Bradford Literary Agency is to form true partnerships with our clients and build long-term relationships that extend from writing the first draft through the length of the author's career." Estab. 2001. Member of AAR, RWA, SCBWI, ALA. Represents 130 clients.

MEMBER AGENTS Laura Bradford (romance [historical, romantic suspense, paranormal, category, contemporary, erotic], mystery, women's fiction, thrillers, suspense, and young adult); **Natalie Lakosil** (children's literature [from picture book through teen and new adult], romance [contemporary and historical], cozy mystery/crime, upmarket women's/general fiction and select children's nonfiction); **Sarah LaPolla** (YA, middle-grade, literary fiction, science fiction, magical realism, dark/psychological mystery, literary horror, and upmarket contemporary fiction); **Monica Odom** (nonfiction by authors with demonstrable platforms in the areas of pop culture, illustrated/graphic design, food and cooking, humor, history, and social issues; she also seeks narrative nonfiction, memoir, literary fiction, upmarket commercial fiction, compelling speculative fiction, magical realism, historical fiction, alternative histories, dark and edgy fiction, literary psychological thrillers, and illustrated/picture books).

REPRESENTS Nonfiction, novels, juvenile books. **Considers these nonfiction areas:** biography, business, cooking, creative nonfiction, cultural interests, foods, history, humor, juvenile nonfiction, memoirs, parenting, popular culture, politics, self-help, women's issues, women's studies, young adult. **Considers these fiction areas:** erotica, juvenile, middle-grade, multicultural, mystery, new adult, paranormal, picture books, romance, science fiction, thriller, women's, young adult.

☞ Laura Bradford does not want to receive poetry, screenplays, short stories, westerns, horror, New Age, religion, crafts, cookbooks, or gift books. Natalie Lakosil does not want to receive inspirational novels, memoir, romantic suspense, adult thrillers, poetry, or screenplays. Sarah LaPolla does not want to receive nonfiction, picture books, inspirational/spiritual novels, romance, or erotica. Monica Odom does not want to receive genre romance, erotica, military, poetry, or inspirational/spiritual works.

HOW TO CONTACT Accepts e-queries only. For submissions to Laura Bradford or Natalie Lakosil, send to queries@bradfordlit.com. For submissions to Sarah LaPolla, send to sarah@bradfordlit.com. For submissions to Monica Odom, send to monica@bradfordlit.com. The entire submission must appear in the body of the e-mail and not as an attachment. The subject line should begin as follows: "QUERY: [the title of the ms]." For fiction: e-mail a query letter along with the first chapter of ms and a synopsis. Include the genre and word count in your query letter. Nonfiction writers should e-mail a full nonfiction proposal, including a query letter and a sample chapter. Accepts simultaneous submissions. Responds in 4 weeks to queries. Obtains most new clients through queries.

TERMS Agent receives 15% commission on domestic sales; 25% commission on foreign sales. Offers written contract.

RECENT SALES Sold 115 titles in the last year, including *All the Secrets We Keep* by Megan Hart (Montlake), *Magnate* by Joanna Shupe (Kensington), *Always and Forever* by Soraya Lane (Amazon), *Billionaire After Dark* by Katie Lane (Grand Central), *Coming Back* by Lauren Dane (Grand Central).

WRITERS CONFERENCES RWA National Conference, Romantic Times Booklovers Convention.

BRANDT & HOCHMAN LITERARY AGENTS, INC.

1501 Broadway, Suite 2310, New York NY 10036. (212)840-5760. **Fax:** (212)840-5776. **Website:** brandthochman.com. **Contact:** Gail Hochman. Member of AAR. Represents 200 clients.

MEMBER AGENTS Gail Hochman (works of literary fiction, idea-driven nonfiction, literary memoir, and children's books); **Marianne Merola** (fiction, nonfiction, and children's books with strong and unique narrative voices); **Bill Contardi** (voice-driven young adult and middle-grade fiction, commercial thrillers, psychological suspense, quirky mysteries, high fantasy, commercial fiction, and memoir); **Emily Forland** (voice-driven literary fiction and nonfiction, memoir, narrative nonfiction, history, biography, food writing, cultural criticism, graphic novels, and young adult fiction); **Emma Patterson** (fiction— from dark, literary novels to upmarket women's and historical fiction; she also seeks narrative nonfiction that includes memoir, investigative journalism, and popular history); **Jody Kahn** (literary and upmarket fiction, narrative nonfiction [particularly books related to sports, food, history, science, and pop culture], literary memoir, and journalism); **Henry Thayer** (nonfiction on a wide variety of subjects and fiction that inclines toward the literary). The e-mail addresses and specific preferences of each of these agents is listed on the agency website.

REPRESENTS Nonfiction, novels. **Considers these nonfiction areas:** biography, cooking, current affairs, foods, health, history, memoirs, music, popular culture, science, sports, narrative nonfiction, journalism. **Considers these fiction areas:** fantasy, histori-

NEW AGENT SPOTLIGHT

DANIELLE BARTHEL
NEW LEAF LITERARY & MEDIA

www.newleafliterary.com
@debarthel

ABOUT DANIELLE: Following her completion of the Denver Publishing Institute after graduation, Danielle began interning at Writers House. While there, she realized she wanted to put her English degree and love of the written word to work at a literary agency. She worked as a full-time assistant for three years, and continues to help keep the New Leaf offices running smoothly in her role of team and client services coordinator, and associate agent.

SHE IS SEEKING: Upper middle-grade, young adult, adult fiction, and adult nonfiction. She'd love to find an amazing middle-grade epistolary, engrossing young adult realistic contemporary stories like *This is What Happy Looks Like* and *Anna and the French Kiss*, well-crafted fantasies, and retellings that truly twist a story from its original version. Adult family dramas akin to *This is Where I Leave You* and upmarket women's fiction are also high on her wish list. A strong romantic subplot, especially with expertly crafted tension, is never a bad thing, and she's particularly fond of historical romance (especially set in England). For nonfiction, she's excited about unique and poignant lifestyle and cookbooks.

HOW TO SUBMIT: Contact query@newleafliterary.com. "The word 'Query' must be in the subject line, plus the agent's name—for example 'Query for Danielle: [Title].' You may include up to five double-spaced sample pages within the body of the e-mail. No attachments, unless specifically requested. We respond if we are interested in seeing more work."

cal, literary, middle-grade, mystery, suspense, thriller, women's, young adult.

☞ No screenplays or textbooks.

HOW TO CONTACT "We accept queries by e-mail and postal mail; however, we cannot guarantee a response to e-mailed queries. For queries via postal mail, be sure to include a SASE for our reply. Query letters should be no more than 2 pages and should include a convincing overview of the book project and information about the author and his or her writing credits. Address queries to the specific Brandt & Hochman agent whom you would like to consider your work. Agent e-mail addresses and query preferences may be found at the end of each agent profile on the 'Agents' page of our website." Accepts simultaneous submissions. Obtains most new clients through recommendations from others.

TERMS Agent receives 15% commission on domestic sales; 20% commission on foreign sales.

RECENT SALES This agency sells 40-60 new titles each year. A full list of their clients is on the agency website.

TIPS "Write a letter that will give the agent a sense of you as a professional writer—your long-term interests, as well as a short description of the work at hand."

THE BRATTLE AGENCY

P.O. Box 380537, Cambridge MA 02238. (617)721-5375. **E-mail:** submissions@thebrattleagency.com. **Website:** thebrattleagency.com. **Contact:** Christopher Vyce. Member of AAR. Signatory of WGA.

○ Prior to being an agent, Mr. Vyce worked for the Beacon Press in Boston as an acquisitions editor.

MEMBER AGENTS Christopher Vyce.

REPRESENTS Nonfiction, fiction. **Considers these nonfiction areas:** art, cultural interests, history, politics, sports, race studies, American studies. **Considers these fiction areas:** literary, graphic novels.

HOW TO CONTACT Query by e-mail. Include cover letter, brief synopsis, brief CV. Accepts simultaneous submissions. Responds to queries in 72 hours. Responds to approved submissions in 8 weeks.

BARBARA BRAUN ASSOCIATES, INC.

7 E. 14th St., #19F, New York NY 10003. **Fax:** (212)604-9023. **E-mail:** bbasubmissions@gmail.com. **Website:** www.barbarabraunagency.com. **Contact:** Barbara Braun. Member of AAR, Authors Guild, PEN Center USA.

MEMBER AGENTS Barbara Braun.

REPRESENTS Nonfiction, novels. **Considers these nonfiction areas:** architecture, art, biography, design, film, history, photography, politics, psychology, women's issues, social issues, cultural criticism, fashion, narrative nonfiction. **Considers these fiction areas:** commercial, historical, literary, multicultural, mystery, thriller, women's, young adult, art-related fiction.

☛ "Our fiction is strong on stories for women, art-related fiction, historical and multicultural stories, and, to a lesser extent, mysteries and thrillers. We are interested in narrative nonfiction and current-affairs books by journalists, as well as young adult literature. We do not represent poetry, science fiction, fantasy, horror, or screenplays."

HOW TO CONTACT "We no longer accept submissions by regular mail. Please send all queries via e-mail, marked 'Query' in the subject line. Your query should include a brief summary of your book, word count, genre, any relevant publishing experience, and the first 5 pages of your ms pasted into the body of the e-mail. (No attachments—we will not open these.)" Accepts simultaneous submissions.

TERMS Agent receives 15% commission on domestic sales; 20% commission on foreign sales. No reading fees.

TIPS "Our clients' books are represented throughout Europe, Asia, and Latin America by various sub-agents. We are also active in selling motion picture rights to the books we represent, and we work with various Hollywood agencies."

BRESNICK WEIL LITERARY AGENCY

115 W. 29th St., 3rd Floor, New York NY 10001. (212)239-3166. **Fax:** (212)239-3165. **E-mail:** query@bresnickagency.com. **Website:** bresnickagency.com. **Contact:** Paul Bresnick.

○ Prior to becoming an agent, Mr. Bresnick spent 25 years as a trade book editor.

MEMBER AGENTS Paul Bresnick; Susan Duff (women's health, food and wine, fitness, humor, memoir); Lisa Kopel (narrative nonfiction, memoir, pop culture, both commercial and literary fiction); Matthew MiGangi (music, American history, sports, politics, weird science, pop/alternative culture, video games, and fiction).

REPRESENTS Nonfiction, novels. **Considers these nonfiction areas:** food, health, history, humor, memoirs, music, popular culture, politics, science, sports, women's issues, fitness, pop/alternative culture, video games. **Considers these fiction areas:** commercial, literary.

☛ Matthew DiGangi does not represent young adult, middle-grade, or books for children.

HOW TO CONTACT Electronic submissions only. For fiction, submit query and 2 chapters. For nonfiction, submit query with proposal. Accepts simultaneous submissions.

⊘⊙ M. COURTNEY BRIGGS

Derrick & Briggs, LLP, 100 N. Broadway Ave., 28th Floor, Oklahoma City OK 73102-8819. (405)235-1900. **Fax:** (405)235-1995. **Website:** www.derrickndbriggs.com.

"M. Courtney Briggs combines her primary work as a literary agent with expertise in intellectual property, entertainment law, estates, and probate. Her clients are published authors (exclusively), theaters, and a variety of small businesses and individuals."

⚙ RICK BROADHEAD & ASSOCIATES LITERARY AGENCY

47 St. Clair Ave. W., Suite 501, Toronto, Ontario M4V 3A5 Canada. (416)929-0516. **E-mail:** info@rbaliterary.com. **E-mail:** submissions@rbaliterary.com. **Website:** www.rbaliterary.com. **Contact:** Rick Broadhead, president. The agency's clients include accomplished journalists, historians, scholars, physicians, television personalities, bloggers, creators of popular websites, successful business executives, and experts in their respective fields. Estab. 2002. Membership includes Authors Guild. Represents 125 clients.

"With an MBA from the Schulich School of Business, Mr. Broadhead is one of the few literary agents in the publishing industry with a business and entrepreneurial background."

MEMBER AGENTS Rick Broadhead.

REPRESENTS Nonfiction. **Considers these nonfiction areas:** biography, business, current affairs, environment, health, history, humor, medicine, military, popular culture, politics, science, self-help, relationships, pop science, security/intelligence, natural history.

The agency is actively seeking compelling proposals from experts in their fields, journalists, and authors with relevant credentials and an established media platform (TV, Internet, radio, print experience/exposure). Does not want to receive fiction, screenplays, children's books, or poetry at this time.

HOW TO CONTACT E-query. Include a brief description of your project, your credentials, and contact information. Accepts simultaneous submissions.

TIPS "Books rarely sell themselves these days, so I look for authors who have a 'platform' (media exposure or experience, university affiliation, recognized expertise, etc.). Remember that a literary agent has to sell your project to an editor, and then the editor has to sell your project internally to his or her colleagues (including the marketing and sales staff), and then the publisher has to sell your book to the book buyers at the chains and bookstores. You're most likely to get my attention if you write a succinct and persuasive query letter that demonstrates your platform and credentials, the market potential of your book, and why your book is different."

CURTIS BROWN, LTD.

10 Astor Place, New York NY 10003-6935. (212)473-5400. **Website:** www.curtisbrown.com. Represents authors and illustrators of fiction, nonfiction, picture books, middle-grade, young adult. Member of AAR. Signatory of WGA.

MEMBER AGENTS Noah Ballard (literary debuts, upmarket thrillers, and narrative nonfiction; he is always on the hunt for honest and provocative new writers); **Ginger Clark** (science fiction, fantasy, paranormal romance, literary horror, young adult, middle-grade); **Kerry D'Agostino** (a wide range of literary and commercial fiction, as well as narrative nonfiction and memoir); **Katherine Fausset** (literary fiction, upmarket commercial fiction, journalism, memoir, popular science, and narrative nonfiction); **Holly Frederick; Peter Ginsberg**, president; **Elizabeth Harding**, vice president (authors and illustrators of juvenile, middle-grade, and young adult fiction); **Steve Kasdin** (mysteries/thrillers, romantic suspense [emphasis on the suspense], historical fiction, young adult fiction [particularly with crossover appeal]; he also seeks narrative nonfiction, including biography, history, and current affairs); **Ginger Knowlton**, executive vice president (authors and illustrators of children's books in all genres); **Timothy Knowlton,** chief executive officer; **Jonathan Lyons** (biographies, history, science, pop culture, sports, general narrative nonfiction, mysteries, thrillers, science fiction, fantasy, and young adult fiction); **Laura Blake Peterson**, vice president (memoir and biography, natural history, literary fiction, mystery, suspense, women's fiction, health and fitness, children's and young adult, faith issues, popular culture); **Maureen Walters**, senior vice president (women's fiction, and nonfiction projects on subjects as eclectic as parenting, popular psychology, inspirational topics, and medical books); **Mitchell Waters** (literary and commercial fiction and nonfiction—including mystery, history, biography, memoir, young adult, cookbooks, self-help, and pop culture).

REPRESENTS Nonfiction, novels. **Considers these nonfiction areas:** biography, computers, cooking, current affairs, ethnic, health, history, humor, memoirs, popular culture, psychology, science, self-help, spirituality, sports. **Considers these fiction areas:** fantasy, horror, humor, juvenile, literary, mainstream, middle-grade, mystery, paranormal, picture books, religious, romance, spiritual, sports, suspense, thriller, women's, young adult.

HOW TO CONTACT Please refer to the "Agents" page on the website for each agent's submission guidelines. Accepts simultaneous submissions. Responds in 3 weeks to queries; 5 weeks to mss. Obtains most new clients through recommendations from others, solicitations, conferences.

TERMS Agent receives 15% commission on domestic sales; 20% on foreign sales. Offers written contract. Seventy-five-day notice must be given to terminate contract. Charges for some postage (overseas, etc.)

RECENT SALES This agency prefers not to share information on specific sales.

CURTIS BROWN (AUST) PTY LTD

P.O. Box 19, Paddington NSW 2021 Australia. (+61)(2)9361-6161. **Fax:** (+61)(2)9360-3935. **E-mail:** reception@curtisbrown.com.au. **Website:** www.curtisbrown.com.au.

○ "Prior to joining Curtis Brown, most of our agents worked in publishing or the film/theater industries in Australia and the United Kingdom."

MEMBER AGENTS Fiona Inglis (managing director/agent), **Tara Wynne** (agent), **Pippa Masson** (agent), **Clare Forster** (agent), **Grace Heifetz** (agent).

☞ "We are Australia's oldest and largest literary agency, representing a diverse range of Australian and New Zealand writers and estates."

HOW TO CONTACT "Please refer to our website for information regarding ms submissions, permissions, theater rights requests, and the clients and estates we represent. We are not currently looking to represent poetry, short stories, stage plays, screenplays, picture books, or translations. We do not accept e-mailed or faxed submissions. No responsibility is taken for the receipt or loss of mss." Accepts simultaneous submissions.

MARIE BROWN ASSOCIATES, INC.

412 W. 154th St., New York NY 10032-6302. (212)939-9725 for Marie Brown; or (678)515-7907 for Janell Walden Agyeman. **Fax:** (212)939-9728. **E-mail:** info@janellwaldenagyeman.com. **Website:** www.janellwaldenagyeman.com. **Contact:** Marie Brown, Janell Walden Agyeman. Estab. 1984. Memberships include Authors Guild, Independent Book Publishers Association, SCBWI.

MEMBER AGENTS Marie Brown, Janell Walden Agyeman.

REPRESENTS Nonfiction, novels, juvenile books. **Considers these nonfiction areas:** creative nonfiction, cultural interests, education, ethnic, history, inspirational, juvenile nonfiction, memoirs, multicultural, popular culture, spirituality, sports, women's studies, young adult. **Considers these fiction areas:** contemporary issues, ethnic, hi-lo, historical, juvenile, literary, mainstream, middle-grade, multicultural, new adult, paranormal, picture books, supernatural, urban fantasy, women's, young adult. "We welcome debut fiction for adults (literary and popular) and for young readers."

☞ Marie Brown does not want to receive genre fiction, poetry, true crime, high fantasy.

HOW TO CONTACT Marie Dutton Brown: Query first via snail mail. For fiction, you may include your first 20-25 pages. With nonfiction, include an annotated table of contents. **Janell Walden Agyeman:** E-submissions only. Queries should include a brief pitch of no more than 150 words. Fiction submissions may also include an attached Word document containing the first 20-25 pages. For nonfiction, attach the completed proposal. Responds within 12 weeks. Obtains most new clients through recommendations from others, conferences

TERMS Agent receives 15% commission on domestic sales; 20% commission on foreign sales. Offers written contract.

RECENT SALES *The Man in 3B* by Carl Weber, *Pushout* by Monique Morris, *Born Bright* by C. Nicole Mason, *Degree Zombie Zone* by Patrick Henry Bass, *Harlem Renaissance Party* by Faith Ringgold, *Stella by Starlight* by Sharon M. Draper, *Grant Park* by Leonard H. Pitts, Jr.

TIPS "Have your project professionally edited and/or critiqued before submitting. Show us your very best work."

BROWNE & MILLER LITERARY ASSOCIATES, LLC

410 S. Michigan Ave., Suite 460, Chicago IL 60605. (312)922-3063. **Fax:** (312)922-1905. **E-mail:** mail@browneandmiller.com. **Website:** www.brownean-

dmiller.com. Estab. 1971. Member of AAR, RWA, MWA. Signatory of WGA.

○ Prior to opening the agency, Ms. Egan-Miller worked as an editor.

MEMBER AGENTS Danielle Egan-Miller; Abby Saul (runs the gamut from literary newbies and classics, to cozy mysteries, to sappy women's fiction, to dark and twisted thrillers); Joanna MacKenzie (women's fiction, thrillers, new adult, and young adult).

REPRESENTS Nonfiction, novels. **Considers these fiction areas:** commercial, crime, historical, inspirational, literary, romance, women's, young adult, Amish fiction, time-travel.

☛ Browne & Miller is most interested in literary fiction, commercial fiction, women's fiction, women's historical fiction, literary-leaning crime fiction, romance, and Amish fiction. We are also interested in time travel stories, Christian/inspirational fiction by established authors, literary and commercial young adult fiction, and a broad array of nonfiction by nationally-recognized author/experts. "We do not represent children's picture books, horror, science fiction, short stories, poetry, original screenplays, articles, or software."

HOW TO CONTACT E-query. No attachments. Do not send unsolicited mss. Accepts simultaneous submissions.

TIPS "We are very hands-on and do much editorial work with our clients. We are passionate about the books we represent and work hard to help clients reach their publishing goals."

ANDREA BROWN LITERARY AGENCY, INC.

Website: www.andreabrownlit.com. Member of AAR.

○ Prior to opening her agency, Ms. Brown served as an editorial assistant at Random House and Dell Publishing and an editor with Knopf.

MEMBER AGENTS Andrea Brown, andrea@andreabrownlit.com (president); Laura Rennert, lauraqueries@gmail.com (executive agent); Caryn Wiseman, caryn@andreabrownlit.com (senior agent); Jennifer Laughran, jennL@andreabrownlit.com (senior agent); Jennifer Rofé, jennifer@andreabrownlit.com (senior agent); Kelly Sonnack, kelly@andreabrownlit.com (agent); Jamie Weiss Chilton, jamie@andreabrownlit.com (agent); Jennifer Mattson, jmatt@andreabrownlit.com (agent); Kathleen Rushall, kathleen@andreabrownlit.com (agent); Lara Perkins,

lara@andreabrownlit.com (associate agent, digital manager); **Jennifer March Soloway**, soloway@andreabrownlit.com (assistant agent).

REPRESENTS Nonfiction, novels, juvenile books. **Considers these nonfiction areas:** juvenile nonfiction, young adult, narrative. **Considers these fiction areas:** picture books, young adult, middle-grade, all juvenile genres.

☛ Specializes in all kinds of children's books—illustrators and authors.

HOW TO CONTACT For picture books, submit a query letter and complete ms in the body of the e-mail. For fiction, submit a query letter and the first 10 pages in the body of the e-mail. For nonfiction, submit proposal, first 10 pages in the body of the e-mail. Illustrators: submit a query letter and 2-3 illustration samples (in JPEG format), link to online portfolio, and text of picture book, if applicable. "We only accept queries via e-mail. No attachments, with the exception of JPEG illustrations from illustrators. Visit the agents' bios on our website and choose only 1 agent to whom you will submit your e-query. Send a short e-mail query letter to that agent with 'QUERY' in the subject line. If we are interested in your work, we will certainly follow up by e-mail or by phone. However, if you haven't heard from us within 8 weeks, please assume that we are passing on your project." Obtains most new clients through referrals from editors, clients, and agents. Check website for guidelines and information. Accepts simultaneous submissions.

TERMS Agent receives 15% commission on domestic sales; 25% commission on foreign sales. Offers written contract.

WRITERS CONFERENCES SCBWI, Asilomar; Maui Writers' Conference, Southwest Writers' Conference, San Diego State University Writers' Conference, Big Sur Children's Writing Workshop, William Saroyan Writers' Conference, Columbus Writers' Conference, Willamette Writers' Conference, La Jolla Writers' Conference, San Francisco Writers' Conference, Hilton Head Writers' Conference, Pacific Northwest Conference, Pikes Peak Conference.

TRACY BROWN LITERARY AGENCY

P.O. Box 772, Nyack NY 10960. (914)400-4147. **Fax:** (914)931-1746. **E-mail:** tracy@brownlit.com. **Contact:** Tracy Brown. Represents 35 clients.

○ Prior to becoming an agent, Mr. Brown was a book editor for 25 years.

REPRESENTS Considers these nonfiction areas: biography, current affairs, health, history, psychology, travel, women's issues, travel, popular history. **Considers these fiction areas:** literary.

☞ Specializes in thorough involvement with clients' books at every stage of the process, from writing to proposals to publication. Actively seeking serious nonfiction and fiction. Does not want to receive young adult, science fiction, or romance.

HOW TO CONTACT Submit query, outline/proposal (for nonfiction), synopsis, author bio. Accepts simultaneous submissions. Responds in 2 weeks to queries. Obtains most new clients through referrals.

TERMS Agent receives 15% commission on domestic sales; 20% commission on foreign sales. Offers written contract.

RECENT SALES *Why Have Kids?* by Jessica Valenti (HarperCollins), *Tapdancing to Work* by Carol J. Loomis (Portfolio), *Mating in Captivity* by Esther Perel.

☯◉ THE BUKOWSKI AGENCY

14 Prince Arthur Ave., Suite 202, Toronto, Ontario M5R 1A9 Canada. (416)928-6728. **Fax:** (416)963-9978. **E-mail:** info@thebukowskiagency.com. **Website:** www.thebukowskiagency.com. **Contact:** Denise Bukowski. Estab. 1986.

○ Prior to becoming an agent, Ms. Bukowski was a book editor.

REPRESENTS Nonfiction, novels. **Considers these fiction areas:** literary.

☞ "The Bukowski Agency specializes in international literary fiction and upmarket nonfiction for adults. The agency looks for Canadian writers whose work can be marketed in many media and territories, and who have the potential to make a living from their work." Actively seeking nonfiction and fiction works from Canadian writers. Does not represent genre fiction, children's literature, plays, poetry, or screenplays.

HOW TO CONTACT "The Bukowski Agency is currently accepting nonfiction submissions, by mail only, from prospective authors who are resident in Canada. We ask for exclusivity for 6 weeks after receipt to allow time for proper consideration. Please see our nonfiction submission guidelines for more details on submitting proposals for nonfiction. You must include a SASE for return of your proposal; if you do not do so, we will not be able to respond to your inquiry. The Bukowski Agency is currently considering fiction submissions, also, by mail only, from prospective authors who are residents in Canada. Please send the first 50 pages of your novel (double-spaced in 12-point type, printed on 1 side of the sheet only) with a brief synopsis and a SASE. Note that if you do not include a SASE, a response to your submission will not be possible." Responds in 6 weeks to queries.

SHEREE BYKOFSKY ASSOCIATES, INC.

P.O. Box 706, Brigantine NJ 08203. **E-mail:** shereebee@aol.com. **E-mail:** submitbee@aol.com. **Website:** www.shereebee.com. **Contact:** Sheree Bykofsky. Estab. 1991. Member of AAR. Other memberships include Authors Guild, Atlantic City Chamber of Commerce, PRC Council.

○ Prior to opening her agency, Ms. Bykofsky served as executive editor of the Stonesong Press and managing editor of Chiron Press. She is also the author or coauthor of more than 30 books, including *The Complete Idiot's Guide to Getting Published, 5th Edition*. As an adjunct professor, Ms. Bykofsky teaches publishing at Rosemont College, NYU, and offers a popular all-day preconference pitch workshop at writers conferences, libraries, and other venues around the country.

MEMBER AGENTS Sheree Bykofsky, Janet Rosen.

REPRESENTS Nonfiction, novels, scholarly books. **Considers these nonfiction areas:** Americana, animals, anthropology, architecture, art, autobiography, biography, business, child guidance, cooking, crafts, creative nonfiction, cultural interests, current affairs, dance, decorating, diet/nutrition, design, economics, education, environment, ethnic, film, foods, gardening, gay/lesbian, government, health, history, hobbies, how-to, humor, inspirational, language, law, literature, medicine, memoirs, metaphysics, military, money, multicultural, music, New Age, parenting, philosophy, photography, popular culture, politics, psychology, recreation, regional, religious, science, self-help, sex, sociology, software, spirituality, sports, technology, theater, translation, travel, true crime, war, women's issues, creative nonfiction. **Considers these fiction areas:** commercial, contemporary issues, crime, detective, literary, mainstream, mystery, suspense, women's.

☛ This agency specializes in prescriptive nonfiction, especially health and business, commercial fiction with a literary quality, and mysteries. "I have wide-ranging interests, but it really depends on quality of writing, originality, and how a particular project appeals to me (or doesn't). I take on fiction when I completely love it—it doesn't matter what area or genre." Does not want to receive poetry, material for children, screenplays, western, or horror.

HOW TO CONTACT "We only accept e-queries now and will only respond to those in which we are interested. E-mail short queries to submitbee@aol.com. Please no attachments, snail mail queries, or phone calls. For fiction, send a one-page query, one-page synopsis, and first page of ms in the body of the e-mail. For nonfiction, send a one-page query in the body of the e-mail. We cannot open attached Word files or any other types of attached files." Accepts simultaneous submissions. Responds in 1 month to requested mss. Obtains most new clients through recommendations from others.

RECENT SALES *ADHD Does Not Exist* by Dr. Richard Saul (HarperCollins), *Be Bold and Win the Sale* by Jeff Shore (McGraw-Hill), *Westlake Girl* by Frieda Wampler and Larry Wampler (Two Dot), *The Essential Executor* by David Hoffman (Career), *Idea to Invention* by Patricia Nolan-Brown (Amacom).

TIPS "Read the agent listing carefully and comply with guidelines."

KIMBERLEY CAMERON & ASSOCIATES

1550 Tiburon Blvd., #704, Tiburon CA 94920. (415)789-9191. **Website:** www.kimberleycameron.com. **Contact:** Kimberley Cameron. Member of AAR. Signatory of WGA.

○ Kimberley Cameron & Associates (formerly The Reece Halsey Agency) has had an illustrious client list of established writers, including Aldous Huxley, Upton Sinclair, William Faulkner, and Henry Miller.

MEMBER AGENTS Kimberley Cameron; Elizabeth Kracht, liz@kimberleycameron.com (literary, commercial, women's, thrillers, mysteries, historical, young adult with crossover appeal, health, science, environment, prescriptive, investigative, true crime, memoir, sexuality, spirituality, animal/pet stories); **Pooja Menon**, pooja@kimberleycameron.com (currently closed to unsolicited submissions); **Amy**
Cloughley, amyc@kimberleycameron.com (literary and upmarket fiction, women's, historical, narrative nonfiction, travel or adventure memoir); **Mary C. Moore** (currently closed to submissions); **Lisa Abellera**, lisa@kimberlycameron.com (currently closed to unsolicited submissions).

REPRESENTS Considers these nonfiction areas: animals, environment, health, memoirs, science, spirituality, travel, true crime, narrative nonfiction. **Considers these fiction areas:** commercial, fantasy, historical, literary, mystery, romance, science fiction, thriller, women's, young adult, LGBT.

☛ "We are looking for a unique and heartfelt voice that conveys a universal truth."

HOW TO CONTACT Prefers e-mail queries. Visit the page for each agent on the agency website to see his or her individual online submission form. Accepts simultaneous submissions. Obtains new clients through recommendations from others, solicitations.

CYNTHIA CANNELL LITERARY AGENCY

54 W. 40th St., New York NY 10018. (212)396-9595. **Website:** www.cannellagency.com. **Contact:** Cynthia Cannell. "The Cynthia Cannell Literary Agency is a full-service literary agency in New York City, active in both the national and the international publishing markets. We represent the authors of literary fiction, memoir, biography, historical fiction, popular science, self-improvement, spirituality, and nonfiction on contemporary issues." Estab. 1997. Member of AAR, Women's Media Group, Authors Guild.

○ Prior to forming the agency, Ms. Cannell was the vice president of Janklow & Nesbit Associates for 12 years.

REPRESENTS Nonfiction, fiction. **Considers these nonfiction areas:** biography, current affairs, memoirs, self-help, spirituality.

☛ Does not represent screenplays, children's books, illustrated books, cookbooks, romance, category mystery, or science fiction.

HOW TO CONTACT "Please query us with an e-mail or letter. If querying by e-mail, send a brief description of your project with relevant biographical information (including any publishing credits) to info@cannellagency.com. Do not send attachments. If querying by postal mail, enclose a SASE." Responds if interested. Accepts simultaneous submissions.

RECENT SALES Check the website for an updated list of authors and sales.

CAPITAL TALENT AGENCY

1330 Connecticut Ave. NW, Suite 271, Washington DC 20036. (202)429-4785. **Fax:** (202)429-4786. **E-mail:** literary.submissions@capitaltalentagency.com. **Website:** http://capitaltalentagency.com/html/literary.shtml. **Contact:** Cynthia Kane. Estab. 2014. Member of AAR. Signatory of WGA.

○ Prior to joining CTA, Ms. Kane was involved in the publishing industry for more than 10 years. She has worked as a development editor for different publishing houses and individual authors, and has seen more than 100 titles to market.

MEMBER AGENTS Cynthia Kane.

REPRESENTS Nonfiction, fiction

HOW TO CONTACT "We accept submissions only by e-mail. For fiction and nonfiction submissions, send a query letter in the body of your e-mail. Please note that while we consider each query seriously, we are unable to respond to all of them. We endeavor to respond within 6 weeks to projects that interest us." Accepts simultaneous submissions.

MARIA CARVAINIS AGENCY, INC.

Rockefeller Center, 1270 Avenue of the Americas, Suite 2320, New York NY 10020. (212)245-6365. **Fax:** (212)245-7196. **E-mail:** mca@mariacarvainisagency.com. **Website:** mariacarvainisagency.com. Estab. 1977. Member of AAR, Authors Guild, Women's Media Group, ABA, MWA, RWA. Signatory of WGA.

○ Prior to opening her agency, Ms. Carvainis spent more than 10 years in the publishing industry as a senior editor with Macmillan Publishing, Basic Books, Avon Books, and Crown Publishers. Ms. Carvainis has served as a member of the AAR Board of Directors and AAR Treasurer, as well as serving as chair of the AAR Contracts Committee.

MEMBER AGENTS Maria Carvainis, president/agent; Elizabeth Copps, associate agent.

REPRESENTS Nonfiction, novels. **Considers these nonfiction areas:** biography, business, history, memoirs, popular culture, psychology, science. **Considers these fiction areas:** action, adventure, commercial, contemporary issues, crime, historical, horror, humor, juvenile, literary, mainstream, middle-grade, multicultural, mystery, romance, suspense, thriller, women's, young adult.

☛ The agency does not represent screenplays, children's picture books, science fiction, or poetry.

HOW TO CONTACT Send us a query letter, a synopsis of the work, the first 5-10 pages of the ms, and an explanation of any writing credentials. E-mail queries to mca@mariacarvainisagency.com. All attachments must be either Word documents or PDF files. "We typically respond to queries within 1 month, if not earlier." Accepts simultaneous submissions. Obtains most new clients through recommendations from others, conferences, query letters.

TERMS Agent receives 15% commission on domestic sales; 20% commission on foreign sales. Offers written contract. Charges clients for foreign postage and bulk copying.

RECENT SALES *Only Beloved* by Mary Balogh (Signet), *Friction* by Sandra Brown (Grand Central), *Enraptured* by Candace Camp (Pocket Books), *The Infinite* by Nicholas Mainieri (Harper Perennial), *If You Only Knew* by Kristan Higgins (HQN Books), *Anatomy of Evil* by Will Thomas (Minotaur Books).

CASTIGLIA LITERARY AGENCY

P.O. Box 1094, Sumerland CA 93067. **E-mail:** castiglia-agency-query@yahoo.com. Member of AAR. Other memberships include PEN. Represents 65 clients.

MEMBER AGENTS Julie Castiglia (not accepting queries at this time); **Win Golden** (fiction: thrillers, mystery, crime, science fiction, young adult, commercial/literary fiction; nonfiction: narrative nonfiction, current events, science, journalism).

REPRESENTS Nonfiction, novels. **Considers these nonfiction areas:** creative nonfiction, current affairs, investigative, science. **Considers these fiction areas:** commercial, crime, literary, mystery, science fiction, thriller, young adult.

☛ "We'd particularly like to hear from you if you are a journalist or published writer in magazines." Does not want to receive horror, screenplays, poetry, or academic nonfiction.

HOW TO CONTACT Query via e-mail to CastigliaAgency-query@yahoo.com. Send no materials via first contact besides a one-page query. No snail mail submissions accepted. Accepts simultaneous submissions. Obtains most new clients through recommendations from others, solicitations, conferences.

TERMS Agent receives 15% commission on domestic sales. Agent receives 25% commission on foreign sales.

Offers written contract; 6-week notice must be given to terminate contract.

WRITERS CONFERENCES Santa Barbara Writers' Conference, Southern California Writers' Conference, Surrey International Writers' Conference, San Diego State University Writers' Conference, Willamette Writers' Conference.

TIPS "Be professional with submissions. Attend workshops and conferences before you approach an agent."

CHALBERG & SUSSMAN

115 W. 29th St., Third Floor, New York NY 10001. (917)261-7550. **Website:** www.chalbergsussman.com. Member of AAR. Signatory of WGA.

Prior to her current position, Ms. Chalberg held a variety of editorial positions and was an agent with The Susan Golomb Literary Agency. Ms. Sussman was an agent with Zachary Shuster Harmsworth. Ms. James was with The Aaron Priest Literary Agency.

MEMBER AGENTS Terra Chalberg; Rachel Sussman (narrative journalism, memoir, psychology, history, humor, pop culture, literary fiction); Nicole James (plot-driven fiction, psychological suspense, uplifting female-driven memoir, upmarket self-help, and lifestyle books); Lana Popovic (young adult, middle-grade, contemporary realism, speculative fiction, fantasy, horror, sophisticated erotica, romance, select nonfiction, international stories).

REPRESENTS Nonfiction, novels. **Considers these nonfiction areas:** history, humor, memoirs, psychology, self-help, narrative journalism, pop culture. **Considers these fiction areas:** erotica, fantasy, horror, literary, middle-grade, romance, science fiction, suspense, young adult, contemporary realism, speculative fiction.

HOW TO CONTACT To query by e-mail, please contact 1 of the following: terra@chalbergsussman. com, rachel@chalbergsussman.com, nicole@chalbergsussman.com, lana@chalbergsussman.com. To query by regular mail, please address your letter to 1 agent and include a SASE. Accepts simultaneous submissions.

RECENT SALES The agents' sales and clients are listed on their website.

CHASE LITERARY AGENCY

242 W. 38th St., Second Floor, New York NY 10018. (212)477-5100. **E-mail:** farley@chaseliterary.com.

Website: www.chaseliterary.com. **Contact:** Farley Chase. "After starting out at *The New Yorker*, I moved to The New Press and later became an editor at Talk Miramax Books. I spent 8 years as a literary agent at the Waxman Literary Agency, and I founded Chase Literary Agency in 2012. I live in NYC with my wife and dog and am a graduate of Macalester College. Over my more than 13 years as a literary agent and 19 years in publishing, I've been fortunate to work with distinguished authors of fiction and nonfiction. They include winners of the Pulitzer Prize, MacArthur Fellows, Members of Congress, Olympic Gold Medalists, and members of the Baseball Hall of Fame."

MEMBER AGENTS Farley Chase.

REPRESENTS Nonfiction, novels. **Considers these nonfiction areas:** agriculture, Americana, animals, anthropology, archeology, architecture, autobiography, biography, business, creative nonfiction, cultural interests, current affairs, design, education, environment, ethnic, film, foods, gay/lesbian, health, history, how-to, humor, inspirational, investigative, juvenile nonfiction, language, law, literature, medicine, memoirs, metaphysics, military, money, multicultural, music, philosophy, popular culture, politics, recreation, regional, satire, science, sex, sociology, sports, technology, translation, travel, true crime, war, women's issues, women's studies. **Considers these fiction areas:** commercial, historical, literary, mystery.

No romance, science fiction, or young adult.

HOW TO CONTACT E-query farley@chaseliterary. com. If submitting fiction, please include the first few pages of the ms with the query. Accepts simultaneous submissions.

RECENT SALES *Devil in the Grove: Thurgood Marshall, the Groveland Boys, and the Dawn of a New America* by Gilbert King (Harper), *Heads in Beds: A Reckless Memoir of Hotels, Hustles, and So-Called Hospitality* by Jacob Tomsky (Doubleday), *And Every Day Was Overcast* by Paul Kwiatowski (Black Balloon), *The Badlands Saloon* by Jonathan Twingley (Scribner).

JANE CHELIUS LITERARY AGENCY

548 Second St., Brooklyn NY 11215. (718)499-0236. **Fax:** (718)832-7335. **E-mail:** jane@janechelius.com. **Website:** www.janechelius.com. Member of AAR.

MEMBER AGENTS Jane Chelius, Mark Chelius.

REPRESENTS **Considers these nonfiction areas:** natural history, narrative nonfiction.

NEW AGENT SPOTLIGHT

STACEY GRAHAM
RED SOFA LITERARY

www.redsofaliterary.com
@staceyigraham

ABOUT STACEY: Stacey is an associate agent for Red Sofa Literary after years of being on the other side of the literary blanket. She is the author of four books, as well as being a freelance editor, ghostwriter, and screenwriter. She works closely with Boundary Stone Films.

SHE IS SEEKING: Humor books, humorous memoir along the lines of Jenny Lawson or John Cleese, dark middle-grade, New Age with a strong platform, quirky nonfiction (young adult, middle-grade, and adult), history, and horror. She is *not* looking for young adult fiction or adult fantasy.

HOW TO SUBMIT: Contact stacey@redsofaliterary.com. If it's a good fit, she will request the first three chapters or a finished book proposal.

HOW TO CONTACT Currently closed to submissions. Responds in 4 weeks.

ELYSE CHENEY LITERARY ASSOCIATES, LLC

78 Fifth Ave., 3rd Floor, New York NY 10011. (212)277-8007. **Fax:** (212)614-0728. **E-mail:** submissions@cheneyliterary.com. **Website:** www.cheneyliterary.com. **Contact:** Elyse Cheney, Adam Eaglin, Alex Jacobs.

○ Prior to her current position, Ms. Cheney was an agent with Sanford J. Greenburger Associates.

MEMBER AGENTS Elyse Cheney; **Adam Eaglin** (literary fiction and nonfiction—including history, politics, current events, narrative reportage, biography, memoir, and popular science); **Alexander Jacobs** (narrative nonfiction [particularly in the areas of history, science, politics, and culture], literary fiction, crime, and memoir); **Sam Freilich** (literary fiction, crime, biography, narrative nonfiction, and anything about Los Angeles).

REPRESENTS Nonfiction, novels. **Considers these nonfiction areas:** biography, cultural interests, current affairs, history, memoirs, politics, science, narrative nonfiction, narrative reportage. **Considers these fiction areas:** commercial, crime, family saga, historical, literary, short story collections, suspense, women's.

HOW TO CONTACT Query by e-mail or snail mail. For a snail mail responses, include a SASE. Include up to 3 chapters of sample material. Do not query more than 1 agent at this agency. Accepts simultaneous submissions.

RECENT SALES *The Love Affairs of Nathaniel P.* by Adelle Waldman (Henry Holt & Co.), *This Town* by Mark Leibovich (Blue Rider Press), *Thunder & Lightning* by Lauren Redniss (Random House).

⊙ THE CHUDNEY AGENCY

72 N. State Rd., Suite 501, Briarcliff Manor NY 10510. (201)758-8739. **E-mail:** steven@thechudneyagency.com. **Website:** www.thechudneyagency.com. **Contact:** Steven Chudney. Estab. 2001.

○ Prior to becoming an agent, Mr. Chudney held various sales positions with major publishers.

REPRESENTS Novels. **Considers these fiction areas:** historical, juvenile, literary, middle-grade, picture books, young adult.

☞ "At this time, the agency is only looking for author/illustrators (1 individual), who can both write and illustrate wonderful picture books. Storylines should be engaging, fun, with a hint of a life lessons and cannot be longer than 800 words. With chapter books, middle-grade, and teen novels, I'm primarily looking for quality, contemporary literary fiction. I seek novels that are exceedingly well-written, with wonderful settings and developed, unforgettable characters. I'm looking for historical fiction that will excite me, young readers, editors, and reviewers, and will introduce us to unique characters in settings and situations, countries, and eras we haven't encountered too often yet in children's and teen literature." Does not want to receive any fantasy, science fiction, board books, fables, fairytales, poetry, "stories for all ages," or stage plays.

HOW TO CONTACT No snail mail submissions. E-queries only. Submit a proposal package and 4-6 sample chapters. For picture books, submit full text and 3-5 illustrations. Accepts simultaneous submissions. Responds if interested. Responds in 3 weeks to queries.

WM CLARK ASSOCIATES

186 Fifth Ave., 2nd Floor, New York NY 10010. (212)675-2784. **E-mail:** general@wmclark.com. **Website:** www.wmclark.com. Estab. 1997. Member of AAR.

🗩 Prior to opening WCA, Mr. Clark was an agent at the William Morris Agency.

REPRESENTS Nonfiction, novels. **Considers these nonfiction areas:** architecture, art, autobiography, biography, cultural interests, current affairs, dance, design, ethnic, film, history, inspirational, memoirs, music, popular culture, politics, religious, science, sociology, technology, theater, translation, travel. **Considers these fiction areas:** contemporary issues, ethnic, historical, literary, mainstream, young adult.

☞ William Clark represents a wide range of titles across all formats to the publishing, motion picture, TV, and multimedia fields. "Offering individual focus and a global reach, we move quickly and strategically on behalf of domestic and international clients ranging from authors of award-winning, best-selling narrative nonfiction, to authors in translation, chefs, musicians, and artists. The agency undertakes to discover, develop, and market today's most interesting content and the talent that creates it, and forge sophisticated and innovative plans for self-promotion, reliable revenue streams, and an enduring creative career. It is advised that before querying you become familiar with the kinds of books we handle by browsing our book list, which is available on our website." Does not represent screenplays or respond to screenplay pitches.

HOW TO CONTACT Accepts queries via online form only. "We will endeavor to respond as soon as possible as to whether or not we'd like to see a proposal or sample chapters from your ms." Responds in 2 months to queries.

TERMS Agent receives 15% commission on domestic sales; 20% commission on foreign sales. Offers written contract.

⊘ COLCHIE AGENCY, GP

8701 Shore Rd., #514, Brooklyn NY 11209. (718)921-7468. **E-mail:** colchieagency@gmail.com. **Contact:** Thomas Colchie, Elaine Colchie. This company handles 100% international fiction. Estab. 1978.

REPRESENTS Fiction.

☞ Does not want to receive nonfiction.

HOW TO CONTACT This listing does not take or respond to unsolicited queries or submissions.

RECENT SALES *Butterfly Skin* by Sergey Kuznetsov (Titan), *Broken Mirrors* by Elias Khoury (Archipelago), *La Templanza* by María Dueñas (Atria), *Pierced by the Sun* by Laura Esquivel (Amazon Crossing), *Remembering Akbar* by Behrooz Ghamari (OR Books), *The Heart Tastes Bitter* by Víctor del Árbol (Scribe Publications).

⊘◉ COMPASS TALENT

(646)376-7747. **Website:** www.compasstalent.com. **Contact:** Heather Schroder. Founded by Heather Schroder after more than 25 years as an agent at ICM Partners, Compass is dedicated to working with authors to shape their work and guide their careers through each stage of the publication process. Member of AAR. Signatory of WGA.

REPRESENTS Considers these nonfiction areas: cooking, creative nonfiction, foods, memoirs. **Considers these fiction areas:** commercial, literary, mainstream.

HOW TO CONTACT This agency is currently closed to unsolicited submissions. Accepts simultaneous submissions.

RECENT SALES A full list of agency clients is available on the agency website.

DON CONGDON ASSOCIATES INC.

110 William St., Suite 2202, New York NY 10038. (212)645-1229. **Fax:** (212)727-2688. **E-mail:** dca@doncongdon.com. **Website:** http://doncongdon.com. **Contact:** Michael Congdon, Susan Ramer, Cristina Concepcion, Maura Kye Casella, Katie Kotchman, Katie Grimm. Member of AAR.

MEMBER AGENTS Christina Concepcion (crime fiction, narrative nonfiction, political science, journalism, history, books about cities or classical music, biography, science for a popular audience, philosophy, food and wine, iconoclastic books on health and human relationships, essays, and arts criticism); **Michael Congdon** (commercial and literary fiction, suspense, mystery, thriller, history, military history, biography, memoir, current affairs, and narrative nonfiction [adventure, medicine, science, and nature]); **Katie Grimm** (literary fiction, historical, women's fiction, short story collections, graphic novels, mysteries, young adult, middle-grade, memoirs, science, academic); **Katie Kotchman** (business [all areas], narrative nonfiction [particularly popular science and cultural issues], self-help, success, motivation, psychology, pop culture, women's fiction, realistic young adult, literary fiction, and psychological thrillers); **Maura Kye-Casella** (narrative nonfiction, cookbooks, self-help, pop culture, sports, humor, and parenting; for fiction, she seeks literary works, women's fiction, horror, multicultural voices, young adult, and middle-grade); **Susan Ramer** (literary fiction, upmarket commercial fiction [contemporary and historical], narrative nonfiction, social history, cultural history, smart pop culture [music, film, food, art], women's issues, psychology and mental health, and memoir).

REPRESENTS Nonfiction, novels, short story collections, graphic novels. **Considers these nonfiction areas:** art, biography, business, cooking, creative nonfiction, cultural interests, current affairs, film, foods, history, humor, medicine, memoirs, military, multicultural, music, parenting, philosophy, popular culture, politics, psychology, science, self-help, sociology, sports, women's issues, journalism, relationships, essays/criticism, nature, adventure, academic, mental health. **Considers these fiction areas:** crime, historical, literary, middle-grade, mystery, suspense, thriller, young adult.

☛ Susan Ramer is not looking for romance, science fiction, fantasy, espionage, mysteries, politics, health/diet/fitness, self-help, or sports. Katie Kotchman is not looking for screenplays or poetry.

HOW TO CONTACT "For queries via e-mail, you must include the word 'Query' and the agent's full name in your subject line. Please also include your query and a sample chapter in the body of the e-mail, as we do not open attachments for security reasons. Please query only 1 agent within the agency at a time. If you are sending your query via regular mail, please enclose a SASE for our reply. If you would like us to return your materials, please make sure your postage will cover their return." Does not accept unsolicited mss. Accepts simultaneous submissions.

RECENT SALES This agency represents many best-selling clients such as David Sedaris and Kathryn Stockett.

CONNOR LITERARY AGENCY

Website: www.connorliteraryagency.webs.com. **Contact:** Marlene Connor Lynch, Deborah Connor Coker.

○ Prior to opening her agency, Ms. Connor served at the Literary Guild of America, Simon & Schuster, and Random House. She is author of *Welcome to the Family: Memories of the Past for a Bright Future* (Broadway Books) and *What is Cool: Understanding Black Manhood in America* (Crown).

MEMBER AGENTS Marlene Connor Lynch; Deborah Coker (young adult, mainstream fiction and nonfiction, suspense, historical fiction, humor, illustrated books, children's books).

REPRESENTS Nonfiction, novels. **Considers these fiction areas:** historical, literary, mainstream, picture books, suspense, young adult.

HOW TO CONTACT Inquire via form on website. "Please include information about your writing experience and your general bio with your inquiry. Whenever submitting sample material, remember to add headers or footers to your material that identify you and the name of your material." Accepts simultaneous submissions.

THE DOE COOVER AGENCY

P.O. Box 668, Winchester MA 01890. (781)721-6000. **E-mail:** info@doecooveragency.com. **Website:** www.doecooveragency.com. Represents 150+ clients.
MEMBER AGENTS Doe Coover (general nonfiction—including business, cooking/food writing, health, and science); **Colleen Mohyde** (literary and commercial fiction, general nonfiction); associate **Frances Kennedy**.
REPRESENTS Considers these nonfiction areas: creative nonfiction. **Considers these fiction areas:** commercial, literary.

☛ The agency specializes in narrative nonfiction, particularly biography, business, cooking and food writing, health, history, popular science, social issues, gardening, and humor. The agency does not represent poetry, screenplays, romance, fantasy, science fiction, or unsolicited children's books.

HOW TO CONTACT Accepts queries by e-mail only. Check website for submission guidelines. No unsolicited mss. Accepts simultaneous submissions. Responds within 6 weeks, only if additional material is required. Obtains most new clients through solicitation and recommendation.
TERMS Agent receives 15% commission on domestic sales; 10% of original advance commission on foreign sales. No reading fees.
RECENT SALES *Jacques Pepin Heart and Soul in the Kitchen* by Jacques Pepin (Houghton Mifflin Harcourt), *The Vermont Country Store Cookbook* by Ellen Ecker Ogden and Andrea Diehl with The Orton Family (Grand Central Publishing), *L.A. Son: My Life, My City, My Food* by Roy Choi (Anthony Bourdain/Ecco), *The Last Love Song: A Biography of Joan Didion* by Tracy Daugherty (St. Martin's Press), *Rosemary: The Hidden Kennedy Daughter* by Kate Clifford Larson (Houghton Mifflin Harcourt).

◉ JILL CORCORAN LITERARY AGENCY

P.O. Box 4116, Palos Verdes Peninsula CA 90274. **E-mail:** query@jillcorcoranliteraryagency.com. **Website:** http://jillcorcoranliteraryagency.com. **Contact:** Jill Corcoran. Ms. Corcoran previously worked with the Herman Agency for 4 years. Estab. 2013. Member of AAR. Signatory of WGA.
REPRESENTS Considers these fiction areas: juvenile, middle-grade, picture books, romance, young adult.

HOW TO CONTACT Send a query and the first 10 pages of your ms embedded into your e-mail, plus a link to your portfolio (illustrators) to query@jillcorcoranliteraryagency.com. Accepts simultaneous submissions.
RECENT SALES *Guy-Write: What Every Guy Writer Needs to Know* by Ralph Fletcher, *Kiss, Kiss Good Night* by Kenn Nesbitt, *The Plot Whisperer: Secrets of Story Structure Any Writer Can Master* by Martha Alderson, *Blind Spot* by Laura Ellen, *How I Lost You* by Janet Gurtler.

CORNERSTONE LITERARY, INC.

4525 Wilshire Blvd., Suite 208, Los Angeles CA 90010. (323)930-6039. **Fax:** (323)930-0407. **E-mail:** info@cornerstoneliterary.com. **Website:** www.cornerstoneliterary.com. **Contact:** Helen Breitwieser. Member of AAR.
REPRESENTS Nonfiction, novels. **Considers these nonfiction areas:** creative nonfiction. **Considers these fiction areas:** commercial, literary.

☛ "We do not consider business, how-to, photography books, poetry, screenplays, self-help, or western."

HOW TO CONTACT "Submissions should consist of a one-page query letter detailing the book, as well as the qualifications of the author. For fiction, submissions may also include the first 10 pages of the novel pasted in the e-mail or 1 short story from a collection. We receive hundreds of queries each month and make every effort to give each one careful consideration. We appreciate your patience in waiting 8 weeks for a response before contacting us with a gentle reminder. We cannot guarantee a response to queries submitted electronically due to the volume of queries received." Accepts simultaneous submissions.

CORVISIERO LITERARY AGENCY

275 Madison Ave., at 40th, 14th Floor, New York NY 10016. **E-mail:** query@corvisieroagency.com. **Website:** www.corvisieroagency.com. **Contact:** Marisa A. Corvisiero, senior agent and literary attorney. Member of AAR. Signatory of WGA.
MEMBER AGENTS Marisa A. Corvisiero, senior agent and literary attorney (contemporary romance, thrillers, adventure, paranormal, urban fantasy, science fiction, middle-grade, young adult, picture books, Christmas themes, time travel, space science fiction, nonfiction, self-help, science busi-

ness); **Saritza Hernandez**, senior agent (all kinds of romance, LGBT, young adult, erotica); **Sarah Negovetich** (young adult); **Doreen McDonald** (no submissions); **Cate Hart** (young adult, fantasy, magical realism, middle-grade, mystery, fantasy, adventure, historical romance, LGBT, erotic, history, biography); **Samantha Bremekamp** (children's, middle-grade, young adult, and new adult—closed to unsolicited queries); **Veronica Park** (dark or edgy young adult and new adult, commercial fiction, romance and romantic suspense, adult nonfiction [funny, current, controversial]); **Vanessa Robins** (new adult, young adult, thrillers, romance, science fiction, sports-centric plots, memoirs, humor, medical narratives); **Kelly Peterson** (middle-grade, fantasy, paranormal, young adult, science fiction, steampunk, historical, dystopian, sword and sorcery, new adult, romance, historical romance, fantasy, romance).

REPRESENTS Nonfiction, novels. **Considers these nonfiction areas:** biography, business, history, medicine, memoirs, science, self-help, spirituality. **Considers these fiction areas:** adventure, erotica, fantasy, gay, historical, lesbian, middle-grade, mystery, paranormal, picture books, romance, science fiction, suspense, thriller, urban fantasy, young adult, magical realism, steampunk, dystopian, sword and sorcery.

HOW TO CONTACT Accepts submissions via e-mail only. Include 5 pages of a complete and polished ms pasted into the body of an e-mail, and a synopsis of 1-2 pages. For nonfiction, include a proposal instead of the synopsis. Put "Query for [Agent]" in the e-mail subject line. Accepts simultaneous submissions.

⊘ RICHARD CURTIS ASSOCIATES, INC.

200 E. 72nd St., Suite 28J, New York NY 10021. (212)772-7363. **Fax:** (212)772-7393. **Website:** www.curtisagency.com. Member of AAR, RWA, MWA, ITW, SFWA. Represents 100 clients.

○ Prior to being an agent, Mr. Curtis authored blogs, articles, and books on the publishing business and help for authors.

REPRESENTS Nonfiction, fiction, juvenile books. **Considers these nonfiction areas:** autobiography, biography, current affairs, dance, diet/nutrition, gay/lesbian, health, history, how-to, investigative, literature, military, music, parenting, politics, psychology, science, sports, theater, true crime, women's issues. **Considers these fiction areas:** commercial, fantasy, romance, science fiction, thriller, young adult.

HOW TO CONTACT Considers only authors already published by national houses. Accepts simultaneous submissions.

TERMS Agent receives 15% commission on domestic sales; 25% commission on foreign sales. Offers written contract. Charges for photocopying, express mail, international freight, book orders.

RECENT SALES *The Library* by DJ MacHale, *War Dogs* by Greg Bear, *The Drafter* by Kim Harrison.

WRITERS CONFERENCES RWA National Conference.

D4EO LITERARY AGENCY

7 Indian Valley Rd., Weston CT 06883. (203)544-7180. **Fax:** (203)544-7160. **Website:** www.d4eoliteraryagency.com. **Contact:** Bob Diforio. Estab. 1990.

○ Prior to opening his agency, Mr. Diforio was a publisher.

MEMBER AGENTS Bob Diforio (prefers to see recommendations from clients and writers with previously published works); **Joyce Holland**; **Pam Howell** (genre fiction, middle-grade, young adult, new adult).

REPRESENTS Nonfiction, novels. **Considers these nonfiction areas:** biography, business, health, history, humor, money, psychology, science, sports. **Considers these fiction areas:** adventure, detective, erotica, juvenile, literary, mainstream, middle-grade, mystery, new adult, romance, sports, thriller, young adult.

HOW TO CONTACT Each of these agents has a different submission e-mail and different tastes regarding how they review material. See all on their individual agent pages on the agency website.

LAURA DAIL LITERARY AGENCY, INC.

350 Seventh Ave., Suite 2003, New York NY 10001. (212)239-7477. **E-mail:** ldail@ldlainc.com. **E-mail:** queries@ldlainc.com. **Website:** www.ldlainc.com. Member of AAR.

MEMBER AGENTS Laura Dail, Tamar Rydzinski, Elana Roth Parker.

REPRESENTS Nonfiction, novels, juvenile books. **Considers these nonfiction areas:** biography, cooking, creative nonfiction, current affairs, government, history, investigative, juvenile nonfiction, memoirs, multicultural, popular culture, politics, psychology, sociology, true crime, war, women's studies, young adult. **Considers these fiction areas:** commercial, crime, detective, fantasy, feminist, historical, juvenile, mainstream, middle-grade, multicultural, mystery, picture book, thriller, women's, young adult.

- Specializes in women's fiction, literary fiction, young adult fiction, as well as both practical and idea-driven nonfiction. Tamar is not interested in prescriptive or practical nonfiction, humor, coffee table books, or children's books (anything younger than middle-grade). She is interested in everything that is well-written and has great characters, including graphic novels. "Due to the volume of queries and mss received, we apologize for not answering every e-mail and letter. None of us handles children's picture books or chapter books. No New Age. We do not handle screenplays or poetry." Elana, who joined the agency in 2016, specializes in children's books.

HOW TO CONTACT "If you would like, you may include a synopsis and no more than 10 pages. If you are mailing your query, please be sure to include a SASE; without it, you may not hear back from us. To save money, time, and trees, we prefer queries by e-mail to queries@ldlainc.com. We get a lot of spam and are wary of computer viruses, so please use the word 'Query' in the subject line and include your detailed materials in the body of your message, not as an attachment." Accepts simultaneous submissions.

DANIEL LITERARY GROUP

601 Old Hickory Blvd., No. 56, Brentwood TN 37027. **E-mail:** submissions@danielliterarygroup.com. **Website:** www.danielliterarygroup.com. **Contact:** Greg Daniel. Represents 45 clients.

- Prior to becoming an agent, Mr. Daniel spent 10 years in publishing—6 at the executive level at Thomas Nelson Publishers.

REPRESENTS Nonfiction. **Considers these nonfiction areas:** autobiography, biography, business, child guidance, current affairs, economics, environment, film, health, history, how-to, humor, inspirational, medicine, memoirs, parenting, popular culture, religious, satire, self-help, sports, theater, women's issues, women's studies.

- "We take pride in our ability to come alongside our authors and help strategize about where they want their writing to take them. Forging close relationships with our authors, we help them with such critical factors as editorial refinement, branding, audience, and marketing."

The agency is open to submissions in almost every popular category of nonfiction, especially if authors are recognized experts in their fields. No fiction, screenplays, poetry, science fiction/fantasy, romance, children's, or short stories.

HOW TO CONTACT Query via e-mail only. Submit publishing history, author bio, key selling points; no attachments. Check the agency's online submissions guidelines before querying or submitting, as they do change. Please do not query via phone. Accepts simultaneous submissions. Responds in 3 weeks to queries.

DARHANSOFF & VERRILL LITERARY AGENTS

133 W. 72nd St., Room 304, New York NY 10023. (917)305-1300. **E-mail:** submissions@dvagency.com. **Website:** www.dvagency.com. "We are most interested in literary fiction, narrative nonfiction, memoir, sophisticated suspense, and both fiction and nonfiction for younger readers. We do not represent theatrical plays or film scripts." Member of AAR.

MEMBER AGENTS Liz Darhansoff, Chuck Verrill, Michele Mortimer, Eric Amling.

REPRESENTS Nonfiction, novels. **Considers these nonfiction areas:** creative nonfiction, juvenile nonfiction, memoirs, young adult. **Considers these fiction areas:** literary, middle-grade, suspense, young adult.

HOW TO CONTACT Send queries via e-mail (submissions@dvagency.com). Accepts simultaneous submissions.

RECENT SALES A full list of clients is available on their website.

LIZA DAWSON ASSOCIATES

350 Seventh Ave., Suite 2003, New York NY 10001. (212)465-9071. **Website:** www.lizadawsonassociates.com. **Contact:** Caitie Flum. Member of AAR, MWA, Women's Media Group. Represents 50+ clients.

- Prior to becoming an agent, Ms. Dawson was an editor for 20 years, spending 11 years at William Morrow as vice president and 2 years at Putnam as executive editor. Ms. Blasdell was a senior editor at HarperCollins and Avon.

MEMBER AGENTS **Liza Dawson**, queryliza@lizadawsonassociates.com (plot-driven literary and popular fiction, historicals, thrillers, suspense, history, psychology [both popular and clinical], politics, narrative nonfiction, and memoirs); **Caitlin Blasdell**, querycaitlin@lizadawsonassociates.com (science fiction, fantasy [both adult and young adult], parenting, business, thrillers, women's fiction); **Hannah Bowman**, queryhannah@lizadawsonassociates.com (commercial fiction—especially science fiction and fantasy, young adult; she also seeks nonfiction in the areas of mathematics, science, spirituality); **Jennifer Johnson-Blalock**, queryjennifer@lizadawsonassociates.com (nonfiction interests include current events, social sciences, women's issues, law, business, history, the arts and pop culture, lifestyle, sports, and food; fiction interests include commercial and upmarket fiction—especially thrillers/mysteries, women's fiction, contemporary romance, young adult, and middle-grade); **Caitie Flum**, querycaitie@lizadawsonassociates.com (commercial fiction—especially historical, women's, mysteries, young adult, middle-grade, and crossover fantasy; her nonfiction interests are theater, memoir, current affairs, pop culture).

REPRESENTS **Considers these nonfiction areas:** agriculture, Americana, animals, anthropology, archeology, architecture, art, autobiography, biography, business, computers, cooking, creative nonfiction, cultural interests, current affairs, environment, ethnic, film, gardening, gay/lesbian, history, humor, investigative, juvenile nonfiction, memoirs, multicultural, parenting, popular culture, politics, psychology, religious, science, sex, sociology, spirituality, theater, travel, true crime, women's issues, women's studies, young adult. **Considers these fiction areas:** action, adventure, commercial, contemporary issues, crime, detective, ethnic, family saga, fantasy, feminist, gay, historical, horror, humor, juvenile, lesbian, mainstream, middle-grade, multicultural, mystery, new adult, police, romance, science fiction, supernatural, suspense, thriller, urban fantasy, women's, young adult.

☞ This agency specializes in readable literary fiction, thrillers, mainstream historicals, women's fiction, young adult, middle-grade, academics, historians, journalists, and psychology.

HOW TO CONTACT Query by e-mail only. No phone calls. Each of these agents has specific submission requirements, which you can find on their website. Accepts simultaneous submissions. Responds in 6 weeks to queries; 8 weeks to mss.

TERMS Agent receives 15% commission on domestic sales; 20% commission on foreign sales. Offers written contract.

THE JENNIFER DE CHIARA LITERARY AGENCY

31 E. 32nd St., Suite 300, New York NY 10016. (212)481-8484. **Fax:** (212)481-9582. **Website:** www.jdlit.com. **Contact:** Jennifer De Chiara. Estab. 2001.
MEMBER AGENTS Jennifer DeChiara, jenndec@aol.com (literary, commercial, women's fiction [no bodice-rippers, please], chick-lit, mysteries, suspense, thrillers, funny/quirky picture books, middle-grade, and young adult; for nonfiction: celebrity memoirs and biographies, LGBT, memoir, books about the arts and performing arts, behind-the-scenes-type books, and books about popular culture); **Stephen Fraser**, fraserstephena@gmail.com (one-of-a-kind picture books; strong chapter book series; whimsical, dramatic, or humorous middle-grade; dramatic or high-concept young adult; powerful and unusual nonfiction; nonfiction with a broad audience on topics as far reaching as art history, theater, film, literature, and travel); **Marie Lamba**, marie.jdlit@gmail.com (young adult and middle-grade fiction, along with general and women's fiction and some memoir; interested in established illustrators and picture book authors); **Roseanne Wells**, queryroseanne@gmail.com (literary fiction, young adult, middle-grade, narrative nonfiction, select memoir, science [popular or trade, not academic], history, religion [not inspirational], travel, humor, food/cooking, and similar subjects); **Victoria Selvaggio**, vselvaggio@windstream.net (lyrical picture books, middle-grade, young adult, mysteries, suspense, thrillers, paranormal, fantasy, narrative nonfiction); **Alex Weiss**.
REPRESENTS Nonfiction, novels, juvenile books. **Considers these nonfiction areas:** art, autobiography, biography, child guidance, cooking, creative nonfiction, cultural interests, current affairs, dance, film, foods, gay/lesbian, health, history, humor, investigative, juvenile nonfiction, literature, memoirs, multicultural, parenting, philosophy, popular culture, politics, psychology, religious, science, self-help, sex, spirituality, theater, travel, true crime, war, women's issues, women's studies, young adult. **Considers these fiction areas:** commercial, contemporary issues, crime, ethnic, family saga, fantasy, feminist, gay, historical, horror, humor, inspirational, juvenile, lesbian, literary, mainstream, middle-grade, multicultural, mystery, new adult, New Age, paranormal, picture books, suspense, thriller, urban fantasy, women's, young adult.

NEW AGENT SPOTLIGHT

TANUSRI PRASANNA
HANNIGAN SALKY GELTZER

www.hsgagency.com
@tanusriprasanna

ABOUT TANUSRI: A lawyer by training, Tanusri Prasanna has a PhD in legal philosophy and human rights from Oxford University, and a master's degree from Harvard Law School. Along the way, she worked in the legal department of the World Bank in Washington and as a fellow at Columbia Law School. An avid fan of children's literature, Tanusri joined a book club devoted to kidlit in 2012, which sowed the seeds of her decision to become a literary agent specializing in children's books. To this end, before joining HSG, she gained valuable experience interning at Knopf Young Readers and Foundry Literary + Media. Tanusri was born and raised in India, though she has lived in the United Kingdom and New York for the past fourteen years.

SHE IS SEEKING: All sorts of kidlit, ranging from picture books and middle-grade to young adult (including young adult/adult crossovers). And while her primary interest is kidlit, she is also open to selective domestic suspense (Tana French and Sophie Hannah are two of her favorite authors in the genre) and voice-driven narrative nonfiction on social justice issues.

HOW TO SUBMIT: Send a query letter and the first five pages of your manuscript (within the e-mail—no attachments) to tprasanna@hsgagency.com. If it is a picture book, please include the entire manuscript. "If you were referred to us, please mention it in the first line of your query. We generally respond to queries within six weeks, although we do get behind occasionally."

HOW TO CONTACT Each agent has an individual e-mail submission address and submission instructions. Check the website for the current updates, as policies do change. Accepts simultaneous submissions. Obtains most new clients through recommendations from others, conferences, query letters.
TERMS Agent receives 15% commission on domestic sales; 20% commission on foreign sales. Offers written contract.

DEFIORE & CO. LITERARY MANAGEMENT, INC.

47 E. 19th St., Third Floor, New York NY 10003. (212)925-7744. **Fax:** (212)925-9803. **E-mail:** info@defliterary.com; submissions@defliterary.com. **Website:** www.defliterary.com. Member of AAR. Signatory of WGA.

○ Prior to becoming an agent, Mr. DeFiore was publisher of Villard Books (1997-1998), editor-in-chief of Hyperion (1992-1997), editorial director of Delacorte Press (1988-1992), and an editor at St. Martin's Press (1984-88).

MEMBER AGENTS Brian DeFiore (popular nonfiction, business, pop culture, parenting, commercial fiction); **Laurie Abkemeier** (memoir, parenting, business, how-to, self-help, popular science); **Matthew Elblonk** (young adult, popular culture, narrative nonfiction); **Caryn Karmatz-Rudy** (popular fiction, self-help, narrative nonfiction); **Adam Schear** (commercial fiction, humor, young adult, smart thrillers, historical fiction, and quirky debut literary novels; for nonfiction: popular science, politics, popular culture, and current events); **Meredith Kaffel Simonoff** (smart upmarket women's fiction, literary fiction [especially debut], literary thrillers, narrative nonfiction, nonfiction about science and tech, sophisticated pop culture, humor books); **Rebecca Strauss** (literary and commercial fiction, women's fiction, urban fantasy, romance, mystery, young adult, memoir, pop culture, and select nonfiction); **Lisa Gallagher** (fiction and nonfiction); **Nicole Tourtelot** (narrative and prescriptive nonfiction, food, lifestyle, wellness, pop culture, history, humor, memoir, select young adult and adult fiction); **Ashley Collum** (women's fiction, books for kids and teens, psychological thrillers, memoir, politics, photography, cooking, narrative nonfiction, LGBT issues, feminism, and the occult); **Colin Farstad** (literary fiction, upmarket fiction, young adult, narrative nonfiction, graphic novels, science fiction, fantasy); **Miriam Altshuler** (adult literary and commercial fiction, narrative nonfiction, middle-grade, young adult, memoir, narrative nonfiction, self-help, family sagas, historical novels); **Reiko Davis** (adult literary and upmarket fiction, narrative nonfiction, young adult, middle-grade, memoir).

REPRESENTS Novels, nonfiction. **Considers these nonfiction areas:** autobiography, biography, business, child guidance, cooking, economics, foods, how-to, inspirational, money, multicultural, parenting, photography, popular culture, politics, psychology, religious, science, self-help, sports, technology, travel, women's issues, young adult. **Considers these fiction areas:** commercial, ethnic, literary, mainstream, middle-grade, mystery, paranormal, picture books, romance, short-story collections, suspense, thriller, urban fantasy, women's, young adult.

HOW TO CONTACT Query with a SASE or e-mail to submissions@defliterary.com. "Please include the word 'Query' in the subject line. All attachments will be deleted; please insert all text in the body of the e-mail. For more information about our agents, their individual interests, and their query guidelines, please visit our 'About Us' page on our website." Accepts simultaneous submissions. Obtains most new clients through recommendations from others.

TERMS Agent receives 15% commission on domestic sales; 20% commission on foreign sales. Offers written contract; 10-day notice must be given to terminate contract. Charges clients for photocopying and overnight delivery (deducted only after a sale is made).

JOELLE DELBOURGO ASSOCIATES, INC.

101 Park St., Montclair NJ 07042 USA. (973)773-0836. **Fax:** (973)783-6802. **E-mail:** joelle@delbourgo.com. **E-mail:** submissions@delbourgo.com. **Website:** www.delbourgo.com. "We are a boutique agency representing a wide range of nonfiction and fiction."

Prior to becoming an agent, Ms. Delbourgo was an editor and senior publishing executive at HarperCollins and Random House. She began her editorial career at Bantam Books where she discovered the Choose Your Own Adventure series. Ms. Flynn was executive editor at Amacom for more than 15 years.

MEMBER AGENTS Joelle Delbourgo, Jacqueline Flynn.

REPRESENTS Novels, nonfiction. **Considers these nonfiction areas:** Americana, animals, anthropology, archeology, autobiography, biography, business, child guidance, cooking, creative nonfiction, current affairs, dance, decorating, diet/nutrition, design, economics, education, environment, film, gardening, gay/lesbian, government, health, history, how-to, humor, inspirational, interior design, investigative, juvenile nonfiction, literature, medicine, memoirs, military, money, multicultural, music, parenting, philosophy, popular culture, politics, psychology, science, self-help, sex, sociology, spirituality, sports, translation, travel, true crime, war, women's issues, women's studies. **Considers these fiction areas:** adventure, commercial, contemporary issues, crime, detective, fantasy, feminist, juvenile, literary, mainstream, middle-grade, military, mystery, new adult, New Age, romance, science fiction, thriller, urban fantasy, women's, young adult.

"We are former publishers and editors with deep knowledge and an insider perspective. We have a reputation for individualized attention to clients, strategic management of authors' careers, and creating strong partnerships with publishers for our clients."

HOW TO CONTACT Submit via e-mail to a specific agent. Query 1 agent only. No attachments. Put the word "Query" in the subject line. "While we do our best to respond to each query, if you have not received a response in 60 days, you may consider that a pass. Please do not send us copies of self-published books unless requested. Let us know if you are sending your query to us exclusively or if this is a multiple submission. For nonfiction, let us know if a proposal and sample chapters are available. If not, you should probably wait to send your query when you have a completed proposal. For fiction and memoir, embed the *first* 10 pages of the ms into the e-mail after your query letter. Please no attachments. If we like your first pages, we may ask to see your synopsis and more ms. Please do not cold call us or make a follow-up call unless we call you." Accepts simultaneous submissions.

TERMS Agent receives 15% commission on domestic sales; 20% commission on foreign sales. Offers written contract. Charges clients for postage and photocopying.

RECENT SALES *Searching for Sappho* by Philip Freeman (Norton), *UnSelfie: The Habits of Empathy* by Dr. Michele Borba (Touchstone/Simon & Schuster), *Underground Airlines* by Ben H. Winters (Mulholland/Little Brown).

TIPS "Do your homework. Do not cold call. Read and follow submission guidelines before contacting us. Do not call to find out if we received your material. No e-mail queries. Treat agents with respect, as you would any other professional, such as a doctor, lawyer, or financial advisor."

SANDRA DIJKSTRA LITERARY AGENCY

1155 Camino del Mar, PMB 515, Del Mar CA 92014. **E-mail:** elise@dijkstraagency.com. **E-mail:** queries@dijkstraagency.com. **Website:** www.dijkstraagency.com. The Dijkstra Agency was established more than 30 years ago and is known for guiding the careers of many best-selling fiction and nonfiction authors, including Amy Tan, Lisa See, Maxine Hong Kingston, Chitra Divakaruni, Eric Foner, Marcus Rediker, and many more. "We handle nearly all genres, except for poetry." Member of AAR, Authors Guild, Organization of American Historians, RWA. Represents 100+ clients.

MEMBER AGENTS Sandra Dijkstra; Elise Capron (adult books only); **Jill Marr** (adult books only); **Thao Le** (adult books and young adult); **Roz Foster** (adult books and young adult); **Jessica Watterson** (subgenres of adult and new adult romance, as well as women's fiction).

REPRESENTS Nonfiction, novels, short story collections, juvenile books, scholarly books. **Considers these nonfiction areas:** Americana, anthropology, art, biography, business, creative nonfiction, cultural interests, current affairs, design, economics, environment, ethnic, gardening, government, health, history, juvenile nonfiction, literature, memoirs, multicultural, popular culture, politics, psychology, science, self-help, true crime, young adult, narrative. **Considers these fiction areas:** commercial, horror, literary, middle-grade, new adult, romance, science fiction, suspense, thriller, women's, young adult.

HOW TO CONTACT "Please see submission guidelines on our website, as they can change. Please note that we accept only e-mail submissions. Due to the large number of unsolicited submissions we receive, we are able to respond only to those submissions in which we are interested." Accepts simultaneous submissions. Responds to queries of interest within 6 weeks.

TERMS Works in conjunction with foreign and film agents. Agent receives 15% commission on domestic sales; 20% commission on foreign sales. Offers written contract.

TIPS "Remember that publishing is a business. Do your research and present your project in as professional a way as possible. Only submit your work when you are confident that it is polished and ready. Make yourself a part of the active writing community by getting stories and articles published, networking with other writers, and getting a good sense of where your work fits in the market."

◉ DONADIO & OLSON, INC.

40 W. 27th St., 5th Floor, New York NY 10001. (212)691-8077. **Fax:** (212)633-2837. **E-mail:** neil@donadio.com. **E-mail:** mail@donadio.com. **Website:** http://donadio.com. **Contact:** Neil Olson. Member of AAR.

MEMBER AGENTS Neil Olson (no queries); **Edward Hibbert** (no queries); **Carrie Howland**, carrie@donadio.com (adult literary fiction, narrative nonfiction, young adult, middle-grade, picture books).

REPRESENTS Nonfiction, novels. **Considers these nonfiction areas:** creative nonfiction. **Considers these fiction areas:** literary, middle-grade, picture books, young adult.

☛ This agency represents mostly fiction and is very selective.

HOW TO CONTACT "Please send a query letter and the first 3 chapters (or first 25 pages) of the ms to mail@donadio.com. Please allow a minimum of 1 month for a reply. Accepts simultaneous submissions.

DONAGHY LITERARY GROUP

6-14845 Yonge St., Suite # 123, Aurora, Ontario L4G 6H8, Canada, (647)527-4353. **E-mail:** stacey@donaghyliterary.com. **E-mail:** query@donaghyliterary.com. **Website:** www.donaghyliterary.com. **Contact:** Stacey Donaghy. "Donaghy Literary Group provides full-service literary representation to our clients at every stage of their writing career. Specializing in commercial fiction, we seek young adult, new adult, and adult novels."

○ Prior to opening her agency, Ms. Donaghy served as an agent at the Corvisiero Literary Agency. Ms. Noble interned for Jessica Sinsheimer of Sarah Jane Freymann Literary Agency. Ms. Miller previously worked in children's publishing with Scholastic Canada and also interned with Bree Ogden during her time at the D4EO Agency.

MEMBER AGENTS Stacey Donaghy (romantic suspense, LGBT, thriller, mystery, contemporary romance, erotic romance, young adult, and quirky middle-grade); **Valerie Noble** (historical, science fiction and fantasy [think Kristin Cashore and Suzanne Collins] for young adults and adults); **Sue Miller** (young adult, urban fantasy, contemporary romance).

REPRESENTS **Considers these fiction areas:** commercial, erotica, ethnic, fantasy, gay, juvenile, lesbian, mainstream, multicultural, mystery, new adult, police, psychic, romance, science fiction, sports, suspense, thriller, urban fantasy, young adult.

HOW TO CONTACT Query via e-mail with no attachments. Visit agency website for submission guidelines to view agent bios. Do not e-mail agents directly. Accepts simultaneous submissions. Responds in 8 weeks to queries. Time may vary during holidays and closures.

TERMS Agent receives 15% commission on domestic sales; 20% commission on foreign sales.

WRITERS CONFERENCES Toronto Writing Workshop, Romantic Times Booklovers Convention, Windsor International Writers Conference, OWC Ontario Writers Conference.

TIPS "Submit to only 1 DLG agent. We work collaboratively and often share projects that may be better suited to another agent at the agency."

JANIS A. DONNAUD & ASSOCIATES, INC.

525 Broadway, Suite 201, New York NY 10012. (212)431-2664. **Fax:** (212)431-2667. **E-mail:** jdonnaud@aol.com; donnaudassociate@aol.com. **Website:** www.publishersmarketplace.com/members/Janis-Donnaud/. **Contact:** Janis A. Donnaud. This agency specializes in nonfiction. Member of AAR. Signatory of WGA. Represents 40 clients.

REPRESENTS Nonfiction. **Considers these nonfiction areas:** animals, biography, business, cooking, creative nonfiction, cultural interests, current affairs, diet/nutrition, film, foods, health, history, humor, inspirational, memoirs, money, psychology, self-help.

☛ Seeks the following kinds of nonfiction books: culinary subjects, narrative nonfiction, wellness, medical topics for a general audience, contemporary issues, and "big idea" books. Does not want to receive fiction, poetry, mysteries, juvenile books, romances, science fiction, young adult, religious, or fantasy.

HOW TO CONTACT Query via e-mail with a detailed description of project. Send more materials if requested.

TERMS Agent receives 15% commission on domestic and film sales; 20% commission on foreign sales. Offers written contract; 1-month notice must be given to terminate contract.

RECENT SALES *The Skinnytaste Cookbook* by Gina Homolka, *Fat Chance* by Robert Lustig, *50 Shades of Chicken: A Parody in a Cookbook* by F.L. Fowler, *The Dogist* by Elias Weiss Friedman, *Immune System Recovery Plan* by Susan Blum.

◎ JIM DONOVAN LITERARY

5635 SMU Blvd., Suite 201, Dallas TX 75206. **E-mail:** jdliterary@sbcglobal.net. **Contact:** Melissa Shultz, agent. Estab. 1993.

MEMBER AGENTS **Jim Donovan** (history—particularly American, military and western, biography, sports, popular reference, popular culture; fiction interests include literary, thrillers, and mystery); **Me-**

lissa **Shultz** (all Jim's subjects listed above, along with parenting and women's issues).

REPRESENTS Nonfiction, novels. **Considers these nonfiction areas:** current affairs, health, history, investigative, literature, parenting, popular culture, science, sports, war, women's issues. **Considers these fiction areas:** action, adventure, commercial, crime, detective, frontier, historical, mainstream, multicultural, mystery, police, suspense, thriller, war, westerns.

☛ This agency specializes in commercial fiction and nonfiction. "Does not want to receive poetry, children's, science fiction, fantasy, short stories, memoir, inspirational, or anything else not listed above."

HOW TO CONTACT "For nonfiction, I need a query letter telling me about the book—what it does, how it does it, why it's needed now, why it's better or different than what's out there on the subject, and why the author is the perfect writer for it. For fiction, include a synopsis (2-5 pages) and the first 30-50 pages. This material should be polished to as close to perfection as possible." Accepts simultaneous submissions.

TERMS Agent receives 15% commission on domestic sales; 20% commission on foreign sales. Offers written contract, binding for 1 year; 30-day notice must be given to terminate contract. This agency charges for things such as overnight delivery and ms copying. Charges are discussed beforehand.

RECENT SALES *Manson* by Jeff Guinn (S&S), *The Last Outlaws* by Thom Hatch (NAL), *Rough Riders* by Mark Lee Gardner (Morrow), *James Monroe* by Tim McGrath (NAL), *What Lurks Beneath* by Ryan Lockwood (Kensington), *Battle for Hell's Island* by Stephen Moore (NAL), *Powerless* by Tim Washburn (Kensington).

TIPS "Get published in short form—magazine reviews, journals, etc.—first. This will increase your credibility considerably and make it much easier to sell a full-length book."

DOYEN LITERARY SERVICES, INC.

E-mail: bestseller@barbaradoyen.com. **Website:** www.barbaradoyen.com. **Contact:** (Ms.) B.J. Doyen, president.

❍ Prior to opening her agency, Ms. Doyen worked as a published author, teacher, and guest speaker. She is also the author of *The Everything Guide to Writing a Book Proposal*

and *The Everything Guide to Getting Published* (both Adams Media).

REPRESENTS Nonfiction. **Considers these nonfiction areas:** business, crafts, current affairs, diet/nutrition, economics, gardening, health, history, hobbies, horticulture, law, medicine, military, money, parenting, psychology, science, self-help, women's issues.

☛ This agency specializes in nonfiction. Seeking business, health, science, how-to, self-help—adult nonfiction suitable for the major trade publishers. Does not want to receive pornography, screenplays, children's books, fiction, or poetry.

HOW TO CONTACT Send an e-query initially. "Please read the website before submitting a query. Send no unsolicited attachments." Accepts simultaneous submissions.

TERMS Agent receives 15% commission on domestic sales. Offers written contract.

TIPS Please read our website to better understand how we work and what we are looking for in a query. No snail mail queries.

DUNHAM LITERARY, INC.

110 William St., Suite 2202, New York NY 10038. (212)929-0994. **E-mail:** query@dunhamlit.com. **Website:** www.dunhamlit.com. **Contact:** Jennie Dunham. Estab. 2000. Member of AAR, SCBWI.

❍ Prior to opening her agency, Ms. Dunham worked as a literary agent for Russell & Volkening. The Rhoda Weyr Agency is now a division of Dunham Literary, Inc.

MEMBER AGENTS Jennie Dunham, Bridget Smith.

REPRESENTS Nonfiction, novels, juvenile books. **Considers these nonfiction areas:** anthropology, archeology, biography, creative nonfiction, cultural interests, environment, health, history, language, literature, medicine, memoirs, multicultural, parenting, popular culture, politics, psychology, science, technology, women's issues, women's studies, young adult. **Considers these fiction areas:** fantasy, historical, humor, juvenile, literary, mainstream, middle-grade, multicultural, mystery, picture books, science fiction, women's, young adult.

HOW TO CONTACT E-queries preferred, with all materials pasted in the body of the e-mail. Attachments will not be opened. Paper queries are also accepted. Please include a SASE for response and return of materials. If submitting to Bridget, please include the first 5 pages with the query. Accepts simultaneous submissions. Responds in 4 weeks to queries; 2 months to mss. Obtains most new clients through recommendations from others, solicitations.

TERMS Agent receives 15% commission on domestic sales; 20% commission on foreign sales.

RECENT SALES *The White House* by Robert Sabuda (Simon & Schuster), *The Gollywhopper Games* and sequels by Jody Feldman (HarperCollins), *First & Then* by Emma Mills (Macmillan).

DUNOW, CARLSON, & LERNER AGENCY

27 W. 20th St., Suite 1107, New York NY 10011. (212)645-7606. **E-mail:** mail@dclagency.com. **E-mail:** mail@dclagency.com. **Website:** www.dclagency.com. Member of AAR.

MEMBER AGENTS Jennifer Carlson (narrative nonfiction by journalists covering current events, ideas, and cultural history; she also seeks literary and upmarket commercial novelists); **Henry Dunow** (quality fiction—literary, historical, strongly written commercial—and with voice-driven nonfiction across a range of areas [narrative history, biography, memoir, current affairs, cultural trends and criticism, science, sports]); **Erin Hosier** (popular culture, music, sociology, and memoir); **Betsy Lerner** (nonfiction writers in the areas of psychology, history, cultural studies, biography, current events, business; fiction interests include literary, dark, funny, voice-driven works); **Yishai Seidman** (broad range of fiction: literary, postmodern, and thrillers; nonfiction interests include sports, music, and pop culture); **Amy Hughes** (history, cultural studies, memoir, current events, wellness, health, food, pop culture, biography, literary fiction); **Eleanor Jackson** (literary, commercial, memoir, art, food, science, history); **Julia Kenny** (fiction—adult, middle-grade, and young adult—and is especially interested in dark thrillers and suspense); **Edward Necarsulmer IV** (strong new voices in teen and middle-grade, as well as picture books); **Stacia Decker**; **Arielle Datz** (young adult, middle-grade, literary, commercial; nonfiction interests include essays, unconventional memoir, pop culture, and sociology).

REPRESENTS Nonfiction, novels. **Considers these nonfiction areas:** art, biography, creative nonfiction, cultural interests, current affairs, foods, health, history, memoirs, music, popular culture, psychology, science, sociology, sports. **Considers these fiction**

areas: commercial, literary, mainstream, middle-grade, mystery, picture books, thriller, young adult.

HOW TO CONTACT Query via snail mail with SASE, or by e-mail. Paste 10 sample pages below your query letter. No attachments. Will respond only if interested. Accepts simultaneous submissions.

RECENT SALES A full list of agency clients is on the website.

⊘ DUPREE/MILLER AND ASSOCIATES INC. LITERARY

4311 Oak Lawn Ave., Suite 650, Dallas TX 75219. (214)559-BOOK. **Fax:** (214)559-PAGE. **E-mail:** editorial@dupreemiller.com. **Website:** www.dupreemiller.com. "Global literary agency for leading-edge authors and communicators." Member of ABA. Represents 200 clients.

REPRESENTS Nonfiction, novels. **Considers these nonfiction areas:** animals, art, autobiography, biography, business, child guidance, cooking, current affairs, diet/nutrition, design, economics, education, ethnic, foods, gardening, government, health, history, how-to, humor, literature, medicine, memoirs, money, multicultural, music, parenting, philosophy, photography, popular culture, psychology, recreation, science, self-help, sex, sociology, spirituality, sports, technology, translation, true crime, women's issues. **Considers these fiction areas:** literary, mainstream, picture books.

☛ This agency specializes in commercial fiction and nonfiction.

HOW TO CONTACT This agency does not review unsolicited submissions and meets their new clients through referrals or face-to-face events. Accepts simultaneous submissions. Obtains all new clients through recommendations from current clients.

TERMS Agent receives 15% commission on domestic sales. Offers written contract.

DYSTEL & GODERICH LITERARY MANAGEMENT

1 Union Square W., Suite 904, New York NY 10003. (212)627-9100. **Fax:** (212)627-9313. **Website:** www.dystel.com. Estab. 1994. Member of AAR, SCBWI. Represents 600+ clients.

MEMBER AGENTS Jane Dystel; Miriam Goderich, miriam@dystel.com (literary and commercial fiction, some genre fiction, narrative nonfiction, pop culture, psychology, history, science, art, business books, and biography/memoir); **Stacey Kendall Glick**, sglick@dystel.com (adult narrative nonfiction [including memoir, parenting, cooking, and food], psychology, science, health and wellness, lifestyle, current events, pop culture, young adult, middle-grade, children's nonfiction, and select adult contemporary fiction); **Michael Bourret**, mbourret@dystel.com (middle-grade and young adult fiction, commercial adult fiction; varied nonfiction interests, such as food and cocktail books, memoir, popular history, politics, religion [though not spirituality], popular science, and current events); **Jim McCarthy**, jmccarthy@dystel.com (literary women's fiction, underrepresented voices, mysteries, romance, paranormal fiction, narrative nonfiction, memoir, and paranormal nonfiction); **Jessica Papin**, jpapin@dystel.com (plot-driven literary and smart commercial fiction, narrative nonfiction across a range of subjects [history, medicine, science, economics, and women's issues]); **Lauren E. Abramo**, labramo@dystel.com (humorous middle-grade, contemporary young adult, upmarket commercial fiction, and well-paced literary fiction; she's also interested in adult narrative nonfiction—especially pop culture, psychology, pop science, reportage, media, and contemporary culture); **John Rudolph**, jrudolph@dystel.com (picture book author/illustrators, middle-grade, young adult, select commercial fiction, and narrative nonfiction [music, sports, history, popular science], performing arts, health, business, memoir, military history, and humor); **Sharon Pelletier**, spelletier@dystel.com (smart commercial fiction, upmarket women's fiction, domestic suspense, literary thrillers, strong contemporary romance novels; she seeks compelling nonfiction projects, especially feminism and religion); **Michael Hoogland**, mhoogland@dystel.com (thriller, science fiction, fantasy, young adult, upmarket women's fiction, narrative nonfiction); **Erin Young**, eyoung@dystel.com (young adult, middle-grade, literary and intellectual commercial thrillers, memoirs, biographies, sport and science narratives); **Amy Bishop**, abishop@dystel.com (commercial and literary women's fiction, fiction from diverse authors, historical fiction, young adult, personal narratives, and biographies); **Kemi Faderin**, kfaderin@dystel.com (plot-driven young adult, historical fiction and nonfiction, contemporary women's fiction, literary fiction); **Eric Myers**, emyers@dystel.com (young adult and middle-grade;

he also seeks adult nonfiction in the categories of history, biography, psychology, health and wellness, pop culture, thriller, and memoir).

REPRESENTS Considers these nonfiction areas: animals, art, autobiography, biography, business, cooking, cultural interests, current affairs, ethnic, foods, gay/lesbian, health, history, humor, inspirational, investigative, medicine, memoirs, metaphysics, military, New Age, parenting, popular culture, politics, psychology, religious, science, sports, women's issues, women's studies. **Considers these fiction areas:** commercial, ethnic, gay, lesbian, literary, mainstream, middle-grade, mystery, paranormal, romance, suspense, thriller, women's, young adult.

☞ "We are actively seeking fiction for all ages, in all genres." No plays, screenplays, or poetry.

HOW TO CONTACT Query via e-mail and put "Query" in the subject line. "Synopses, outlines, or sample chapters (for example, 1 chapter or the first 25 pages of your ms) should either be included below the cover letter or attached as a separate document. We won't open attachments if they come with a blank e-mail." Accepts simultaneous submissions. Responds in 8 weeks to queries; within 8 weeks to mss. Obtains most new clients through recommendations from others, solicitations, conferences.

TIPS "DGLM prides itself on being a full-service agency. We're involved in every stage of the publishing process, from offering substantial editing on mss and proposals, to coming up with book ideas for authors looking for their next project, to negotiating contracts and collecting monies for our clients. We follow a book from its inception through its sale to a publisher, its publication, and beyond. Our commitment to our writers does not, by any means, end when we have collected our commission. This is one of the many things that makes us unique in a very competitive business."

EDEN STREET LITERARY

P.O. Box 30, Billings NY 12510. **E-mail:** info@edenstreetlit.com. **E-mail:** submissions@edenstreetlit.com. **Website:** www.edenstreetlit.com. **Contact:** Liza Voges. Eden Street represents more than 40 authors and author-illustrators of books for young readers from pre-school through young adult. Their books have won numerous awards over the past 30 years. Member of AAR. Signatory of WGA.

REPRESENTS Novels, juvenile books. **Considers these fiction areas:** juvenile, middle-grade, picture books, young adult.

HOW TO CONTACT Check the website before submitting, as the agency will close itself off to submissions sometimes. When open, contact submissions@edenstreetlit.com. Accepts simultaneous submissions. Responds only to submissions of interest.

RECENT SALES *Dream Dog* by Lou Berger, *Biscuit Loves the Library* by Alyssa Capucilli, *The Scraps Book* by Lois Ehlert, *Two Bunny Buddies* by Kathryn O. Galbraith, *Between Two Worlds* by Katherine Kirkpatrick.

EDUCATIONAL DESIGN SERVICES LLC

5750 Bou Ave., Suite 1508, N. Bethesda MD 20852. (301)881-8611. **E-mail:** blinder@educationaldesign-services.com. **Website:** www.educationaldesignser-vices.com. **Contact:** B. Linder. Estab. 1981. Member of AAR. Signatory of WGA.

REPRESENTS Nonfiction, textbooks. **Considers these nonfiction areas:** education.

☛ "We specialize in educational materials to be used in classrooms (in class sets), for staff development or in teacher education classes." Actively seeking educational text materials. Not looking for picture books, story books, fiction; no illustrators. Does not want children's fiction with educational messages.

HOW TO CONTACT Query by e-mail or with SASE. Send outline and 1 sample chapter. Considers simultaneous queries and submissions if so indicated. Returns material only with SASE. Prefers e-submissions (Word format). Accepts simultaneous submissions. Responds in 8 weeks to queries/mss.

TERMS Agent receives 15% commission on domestic sales; 25% on foreign sales.

JUDITH EHRLICH LITERARY MANAGEMENT, LLC

146 Central Park W., 20E, New York NY 10023. (646)505-1570. **Fax:** (646)505-1570. **E-mail:** jehrlich@judithehrlichliterary.com. **Website:** www.judithehrlichliterary.com. Estab. 2002. Member of the Authors Guild, American Society of Journalists and Authors.

🔲 Prior to her current position, Ms. Ehrlich was a senior associate at the Linda Chester Agency and is an award-winning journalist; she is the co-author of *The New Crowd: The Chang-*

ing of the Jewish Guard on Wall Street (Little, Brown).

MEMBER AGENTS Judith Ehrlich jehrlich@judithehrlichliterary.com (upmarket, literary fiction, quality commercial fiction; nonfiction interests include narrative, women's, business, prescriptive, health-related topics, history, current events); **Sophia Seidner** sseidner@judithehrlichliterary.com (upmarket fiction and nonfiction—including prescriptive, narrative nonfiction, memoir, and biography; areas of special interest include health-related topics, science [popular, political and social], animal welfare, current events, politics, law, history, ethics, parody and humor, sports, and business self-help).

REPRESENTS Nonfiction, novels, short story collections, juvenile books. **Considers these nonfiction areas:** animals, art, autobiography, biography, business, creative nonfiction, cultural interests, current affairs, diet/nutrition, health, history, how-to, humor, inspirational, investigative, juvenile nonfiction, memoirs, parenting, photography, popular culture, politics, psychology, science, self-help, sociology, true crime, women's issues, young adult. **Considers these fiction areas:** adventure, commercial, contemporary issues, crime, detective, family saga, historical, humor, juvenile, literary, middle-grade, mystery, picture books, short story collections, suspense, thriller, women's, young adult.

☛ "We represent nonfiction and fiction, both literary and commercial for the mainstream trade market. Special areas of interest include compelling narrative nonfiction, outstanding biographies and memoirs, lifestyle books, works that reflect our changing culture, women's issues, psychology, science, social issues, current events, parenting, health, history, business, and prescriptive books offering fresh information and advice. We also seek and represent stellar commercial and literary fiction, including romance and other women's fiction, historical fiction, literary mysteries, and select thrillers." Does not want to receive novellas, poetry, textbooks, plays, or screenplays.

HOW TO CONTACT E-query with a synopsis and some sample pages. The agency will respond only if interested. Accepts simultaneous submissions.

RECENT SALES *The Bicycle Spy* by Yona Zeldis McDonough (Scholastic), *The House on Primrose Pond* by Yona McDonough (NAL/Penguin), *Once We Were:*

The Hybrid Chronicles by Kat Zhang (HarperCollins), *Little Author in the Big Woods: A Biography of Laura Ingalls Wilder* by Yona McDonough (Christy Ottaviano Books/Henry Holt).

EINSTEIN LITERARY MANAGEMENT

27 W. 20th St., No. 1003, New York NY 10011. **E-mail:** submissions@einsteinliterary.com. **Website:** http://einsteinliterary.com. **Contact:** Susanna Einstein. Estab. 2015. Member of AAR. Signatory of WGA.

○ Prior to her current position, Ms. Einstein was with LJK Literary Management and the Einstein Thompson Agency.

MEMBER AGENTS Susanna Einstein.

REPRESENTS Nonfiction, fiction. **Considers these nonfiction areas:** cooking, creative nonfiction, memoirs, blog-to-book projects. **Considers these fiction areas:** commercial, crime, historical, literary, romance, women's.

☛ "We represent a broad range of literary and commercial fiction, including upmarket women's fiction, crime fiction, historical fiction, romance, and books for middle-grade and young adults. We also handle nonfiction, including cookbooks, memoir and narrative, and blog-to-book projects." Does not want picture books, poetry, textbooks, or screenplays.

HOW TO CONTACT Please submit a query letter and the first 10 double-spaced pages of your ms in the body of the e-mail (no attachments). Does not respond to snail mail queries, phone queries, or queries that are not specifically addressed to this agency. Accepts simultaneous submissions. Responds in 6 weeks if interested.

⊙ THE LISA EKUS GROUP, LLC

57 North St., Hatfield MA 01038. (413)247-9325. **Fax:** (413)247-9873. **E-mail:** info@lisaekus.com. **Website:** www.lisaekus.com. **Contact:** Lisa Ekus. This agency specializes in cookbooks. Member of AAR.

MEMBER AGENTS Lisa Ekus, Sally Ekus.

REPRESENTS **Considers these nonfiction areas:** cooking, diet/nutrition, foods, health, and women's issues.

☛ "Note that we do not handle fiction, poetry, or children's books. If we receive a query for titles in these categories, understand that we do not have the time or resources to respond."

HOW TO CONTACT "Submit a query via e-mail or through our contact form on the website. You can also

submit a complete hard copy proposal with title page, proposal contents, concept, bio, marketing, TOC, etc. Include a SASE for the return of materials." Accepts simultaneous submissions.

RECENT SALES "Please see the regularly updated client listing on our website."

ETHAN ELLENBERG LITERARY AGENCY

155 Suffolk St., No. 2R, New York NY 10002. (212)431-4554. **E-mail:** agent@ethanellenberg.com. **Website:** http://ethanellenberg.com. **Contact:** Ethan Ellenberg. This agency specializes in commercial fiction and nonfiction. Estab. 1984. Member of AAR, Science Fiction and Fantasy Writers of America, SCBWI, RWA, MWA.

MEMBER AGENTS Ethan Ellenberg, president; Evan Gregory, senior agent; Bibi Lewis, associate agent (young adult and women's fiction).

REPRESENTS Nonfiction, fiction. **Considers these nonfiction areas:** biography, cooking, current affairs, health, history, memoirs, New Age, popular culture, psychology, science, spirituality, true crime, adventure. **Considers these fiction areas:** commercial, ethnic, fantasy, literary, middle-grade, mystery, picture books, romance, science fiction, thriller, women's, young adult, general.

☛ "We specialize in commercial fiction and children's books. In commercial fiction, we want to see science fiction, fantasy, romance, mystery, thriller, and women's fiction. In children's books, we want to see everything: picture books, early reader, middle-grade, and young adult. We do some nonfiction: history, biography, military, popular science, and cutting edge books about any subject." Does not want to receive poetry, short stories, or screenplays.

HOW TO CONTACT Query by e-mail. Paste all of the material in the order listed. Fiction: query letter, synopsis, first 50 pages. Nonfiction: query letter, book proposal. Picture books: query letter, complete ms, 4-5 sample illustrations (if available), link to online portfolio (if available). Will not respond unless interested. Accepts simultaneous submissions. Responds in 2 weeks.

⊕ EMERALD CITY LITERARY AGENCY

2522 N. Proctor St., Suite 359, Tacoma WA 98406. **Website:** http://emeraldcityliterary.com.

NEW AGENT SPOTLIGHT

ROB KIRKPATRICK
THE STUART AGENCY

www.stuartagency.com
@ wrappedupinboox

ABOUT ROB: Rob Kirkpatrick joined The Stuart Agency after working as a senior editor at multiple publishing houses for more than a dozen years. Titles he has helped publish include *The Wrecking Crew: The Inside Story of Rock and Roll's Best-Kept Secret; Shrinkage; Manhood, Marriage, and the Tumor that Tried to Kill Me; Vagos, Mongols, and Outlaws* (basis for the miniseries "Gangland Undercover"); and others. Rob completed a PhD in English and also is the author of several books himself.

HE IS SEEKING: His specialties include memoir, biography, sports, music, pop culture, current events, and history. Please note that as of 2016, he is no longer accepting fiction submissions of any kind.

HOW TO CONTACT: Submissions should be sent to rob@stuartagency.com. Please send a query letter outlining your credentials along with full nonfiction book proposal.

MEMBER AGENTS Mandy Hubbard, querymandy@emeraldcityliterary.com (young adult, middle-grade, adult romance; she has specific tastes for each genre, and those are available on the website); **Linda Epstein**, querylinda@emeraldcityliterary.com (picture books, middle-grade, young adult, and children's nonfiction; she does not represent adult literature); **Lindsay Mealing** (agency assistant).
REPRESENTS Nonfiction, fiction. **Considers these nonfiction areas:** juvenile. **Considers these fiction areas:** middle-grade, picture books, romance, young adult.
HOW TO CONTACT Each agent has different submission guidelines. Those guidelines are explained on the agency website.

FELICIA ETH LITERARY REPRESENTATION

555 Bryant St., Suite 350, Palo Alto CA 94301. **E-mail:** feliciaeth.literary@gmail.com. **Website:** http://eth-literary.com. **Contact:** Felicia Eth. Member of AAR.

REPRESENTS Novels, nonfiction. **Considers these nonfiction areas:** cooking, creative nonfiction, investigative, memoirs, parenting, popular culture, psychology, sociology, travel, women's issues. **Considers these fiction areas:** historical, literary, mainstream, suspense.

☛ This agency specializes in quality fiction (preferably mainstream/contemporary) and provocative, intelligent, and thoughtful nonfiction on a wide array of commercial subjects. The agency does not represent genre ficiton, including romance novels, science fiction and fantasy, westerns, anime and graphic novels, or mysteries."

HOW TO CONTACT For fiction, please write a query letter introducing yourself, your book, your writing background. Don't forget to include degrees you may have, publishing credits, or awards and endorsements.

Please wait for a response before including sample pages. For nonfiction, a query letter is best, introducing the idea and what you have written already (proposal, ms, etc.). "For writerly nonficiton (narratives, biography, memoir), please let us know if you have a finished ms. Also, it's important you include information about yourself, your background and expertise, and your platform and notoriety, if any. We do not ask for exclusivity in most instances but do ask that you inform us if other agents are considering the same material." Accepts simultaneous submissions.

TERMS Agent receives 15% commission on domestic sales; 20% commission on foreign sales. Charges clients for photocopying and express mail service.

RECENT SALES *Bumper Sticker Philosophy* by Jack Bowen (Random House), *Boys Adrift* by Leonard Sax (Basic Books), *The Memory Thief* by Emily Colin (Ballantine Books), *The World is a Carpet* by Anna Badkhen (Riverhead).

MARY EVANS INC.

242 E. Fifth St., New York NY 10003. (212)979-0880. **Fax:** (212)979-5344. **E-mail:** info@maryevansinc.com. **Website:** http://maryevansinc.com. Member of AAR.

MEMBER AGENTS Mary Evans (progressive politics, alternative medicine, science and technology, social commentary, American history and culture); Julia Kardon (literary and upmarket fiction, narrative nonfiction, journalism, history); Mary Gaule (picture books, middle-grade, young adult).

REPRESENTS Nonfiction, novels. **Considers these nonfiction areas:** creative nonfiction, cultural interests, history, medicine, politics, science, technology, social commentary, journalism. **Considers these fiction areas:** literary, middle-grade, picture books, young adult, upmarket.

☞ No screenplays or stage plays.

HOW TO CONTACT Query by mail or e-mail. If querying by mail, include a SASE. If querying by e-mail, put "Query" in the subject line. For fiction, include the first few pages or opening chapter of your novel as a single Word attachment. For nonfiction, include your book proposal as a single Word attachment. Accepts simultaneous submissions. Responds within 8 weeks.

FAIRBANK LITERARY REPRESENTATION

P.O. Box 6, Hudson NY 12534-0006. (617)576-0030. **Fax:** (617)576-0030. **E-mail:** queries@fairbankliter-ary.com. **Website:** www.fairbankliterary.com. **Contact:** Sorche Fairbank. Member of AAR.

MEMBER AGENTS Sorche Fairbank (narrative nonfiction, commercial and literary fiction, humor books, memoir, food and wine); Matthew Frederick, matt@fairbankliterary.com (scout for sports nonfiction, architecture, design).

REPRESENTS Novels, nonfiction, short-story collections. **Considers these nonfiction areas:** agriculture, architecture, art, autobiography, biography, cooking, crafts, cultural interests, current affairs, decorating, diet/nutrition, design, environment, ethnic, foods, gay/lesbian, government, hobbies, horticulture, how-to, interior design, investigative, law, memoirs, photography, popular culture, politics, science, sociology, sports, technology, true crime, women's issues, women's studies. **Considers these fiction areas:** action, adventure, feminist, gay, lesbian, literary, mainstream, mystery, sports, suspense, thriller, women's, Southern voices.

☞ "I tend to gravitate toward literary fiction and narrative nonfiction, with a strong interest in women's issues and women's voices, international voices, class and race issues, and projects that simply teach me something new about the greater world and society around us. We have a good reputation for working closely and developmentally with our authors and love what we do." Actively seeking literary fiction, international and culturally diverse voices, narrative nonfiction, topical subjects (politics, current affairs), history, sports, architecture/design, and pop culture. Does not want to receive romance, poetry, science fiction, pirates, vampire, young adult, or children's works.

HOW TO CONTACT E-query or snail mail query with SASE. Submit author bio. Accepts simultaneous submissions.

TERMS Agent receives 15% commission on domestic sales; 20% commission on foreign sales. Offers written contract, binding for 12 months; 45-day notice must be given to terminate contract.

RECENT SALES *When Clowns Attack* by Chuck Sambuchino (Ten Speed Press), 101 Things I Learned in School series by Matthew Fredericks. Many recent sales available on website.

TIPS "Be professional from the very first contact. There shouldn't be a single typo or grammatical flub in your query. Have a reason for contacting me about your project other than I was the next name listed on some website. Please do not use form query software. Show me that you know your audience—and your competition. Have the writing and/or proposal at the very, very best it can be before starting the querying process. Don't assume that if someone likes it enough they'll 'fix' it. The biggest mistake new writers make is starting the querying process before they and the work are ready. Take your time and do it right."

DIANA FINCH LITERARY AGENCY

116 W. 23rd St., Suite 500, New York NY 10011. (917)544-4470. **E-mail:** diana.finch@verizon.net. **Website:** http://dianafinchliteraryagency.blogspot. com. **Contact:** Diana Finch. Estab. 2003. Member of AAR. Represents 40 clients.

○ Seeking to represent books that change lives. Prior to opening her agency in 2003, Ms. Finch worked at Ellen Levine Literary Agency for 18 years.

REPRESENTS Nonfiction, novels. **Considers these nonfiction areas:** autobiography, biography, business, child guidance, computers, cultural interests, current affairs, dance, economics, environment, ethnic, film, government, health, history, how-to, humor, investigative, juvenile nonfiction, law, medicine, memoirs, military, money, music, parenting, photography, popular culture, politics, psychology, satire, science, self-help, sports, technology, theater, translation, true crime, war, women's issues, women's studies. **Considers these fiction areas:** action, adventure, contemporary issues, crime, detective, ethnic, historical, literary, mainstream, police, sports, thriller, young adult.

⊶ "Does not want romance, mysteries, or children's picture books."

HOW TO CONTACT This agency prefers submissions via its online form: https://dianafinchliterary-agency.submittable.com/submit. Accepts simultaneous submissions.

TERMS Agent receives 15% commission on domestic sales; 20% commission on foreign sales. Offers written contract. "I charge for overseas postage, galleys, and books purchased, and try to recoup these costs from earnings received for a client, rather than charging outright."

TIPS "Do as much research as you can on agents before you query. Have someone critique your query letter before you send it. It should be only 1 page and describe your book clearly—and why you are writ-

ing it—but also demonstrate creativity and a sense of your writing style."

FINEPRINT LITERARY MANAGEMENT

115 W. 29th, Third Floor, New York NY 10001. (212)279-1282. **Website:** www.fineprintlit.com. Member of AAR.

MEMBER AGENTS Peter Rubie, CEO, peter@fineprintlit.com (nonfiction interests include narrative nonfiction, popular science, spirituality, history, biography, pop culture, business, technology, parenting, health, self help, music, and food; fiction interests include literary thrillers, crime fiction, science fiction and fantasy, military fiction, literary fiction, middle-grade, and boy-oriented young adult); **Stephany Evans**, stephany@fineprintlit.com (nonfiction interests include health and wellness, spirituality, lifestyle [including home renovating, decorating, food and drink, and sustainability], running and fitness, memoir, and narrative nonfiction; fiction interests include women's fiction [from literary to romance, including mystery, historical, and romantic suspense]); **Janet Reid**, janet@fineprintlit.com (crime fiction and narrative nonfiction); **Laura Wood**, laura@fineprintlit.com (serious nonfiction—especially in the areas of science and nature, business, history, religion, and other areas by academics and professionals; she seeks select genre fiction [no poetry, literary fiction, or memoir] in the categories of science fiction, fantasy, and mystery); **June Clark**, june@fineprintlit.com (nonfiction projects in the areas of entertainment, self-help, parenting, reference, how-to books, food and wine, style/beauty, and prescriptive business titles); **Penny Moore**, penny@fineprintlit.com (all genres of middle-grade and young adult fiction; she seeks adult fiction in the genres of upmarket, speculative, science fiction, fantasy, psychological thrillers, and select romance; nonfiction projects in the realm of pop culture, humor, travel, food, and pets); **Jacqueline Murphy**, jacqueline@fineprintlit.com.

REPRESENTS **Considers these nonfiction areas:** biography, business, foods, health, history, how-to, humor, memoirs, music, parenting, popular culture, science, self-help, spirituality, technology, travel, fitness, lifestyle. **Considers these fiction areas:** commercial, crime, fantasy, historical, middle-grade, mystery, romance, science fiction, suspense, thriller, women's, young adult.

HOW TO CONTACT E-query. For fiction, send a query, synopsis, bio, and 30 pages pasted into the e-mail. No attachments. For nonfiction, send a query only, with the proposal requested later if the agent is interested. Accepts simultaneous submissions. Obtains most new clients through recommendations from others, solicitations.

TERMS Agent receives 15% commission on domestic sales; 20% commission on foreign sales.

JAMES FITZGERALD AGENCY

118 Waverly Place, #1B, New York NY 10011. **E-mail:** submissions@jfitzagency.com. **Website:** www.jfitzagency.com. **Contact:** James Fitzgerald. "As an agency, we primarily represent books that reflect the popular culture of today being in the forms of fiction, nonfiction, graphic, and packaged books."

Prior to his current position, Mr. Fitzgerald was an editor at St. Martin's Press and Doubleday.

MEMBER AGENTS James Fitzgerald, Alice Bauer.
REPRESENTS Nonfiction, fiction, graphic novels, packaged books.

HOW TO CONTACT Query via e-mail or snail mail. This agency's online submission guidelines page explains all the elements they want to see when you submit a nonfiction book proposal. Accepts simultaneous submissions.

RECENT SALES A full and diverse list of titles are on this agency's website.

FLANNERY LITERARY

1140 Wickfield Court, Naperville IL 60563. **E-mail:** jennifer@flanneryliterary.com. **Contact:** Jennifer Flannery. "Flannery Literary is a Chicago-area literary agency representing writers of books for children and young adults." Estab. 1992. Represents 40 clients.
REPRESENTS Nonfiction, novels, juvenile books. **Considers these nonfiction areas:** young adult. **Considers these fiction areas:** juvenile, middle-grade, new adult, picture books, young adult.

This agency specializes in children's and young adult fiction and nonfiction. It also accepts picture books. 100% juvenile books.

HOW TO CONTACT Query by e-mail. "Simultaneous submissions are fine, but please inform us. No attachments. If you're sending a query about a novel, please include, in the e-mail, the first 5-10 pages. If it's a picture book, please include the entire text." Accepts simultaneous submissions. Responds in 2 weeks to queries; 1 month to mss.

TERMS Agent receives 15% commission on domestic sales; 20% commission on foreign sales.
TIPS "Write an engrossing, succinct query describing your work. We are always looking for a fresh new voice."

FLETCHER & CO.

E-mail: info@fletcherandco.com. **Website:** www.fletcherandco.com. **Contact:** Christy Fletcher. Today, Fletcher & Co. is a full-service literary management and production company dedicated to writers of upmarket nonfiction as well as commercial and literary fiction. Estab. 2003. Member of AAR.
MEMBER AGENTS Christy Fletcher (referrals only); **Melissa Chinchillo** (select list of her own authors); **Rebecca Gradinger** (literary fiction, upmarket commercial fiction, narrative nonfiction, self-help, memoir, women's studies, humor, pop culture); **Gráinne Fox** (literary fiction and quality commercial authors, award-winning journalists and food writers, American voices, international, literary crime, upmarket fiction, narrative nonfiction); **Lisa Grubka** (literary fiction, upmarket women's, young adult, narrative nonfiction, food, science); **Sylvie Greenberg** (literary fiction, business, sports, science, memoir, and history); **Donald Lamm** (history, biography, investigative journalism, politics, current affairs, and business); **Todd Sattersten** (business books).
REPRESENTS Nonfiction, novels. **Considers these nonfiction areas:** biography, business, creative nonfiction, current affairs, foods, history, humor, investigative, memoirs, popular culture, politics, science, self-help, sports, women's studies. **Considers these fiction areas:** commercial, crime, literary, women's, young adult.

HOW TO CONTACT Send queries to info@fletcherandco.com. Please do not include e-mail attachments with your initial query, as they will be deleted. Address your query to a specific agent. No snail mail queries. Accepts simultaneous submissions.

RECENT SALES *The Profiteers* by Sally Denton, *The Longest Night* by Andrea Williams, *Disrupted: My Misadventure in the Start-Up Bubble* by Dan Lyons.

FOLIO LITERARY MANAGEMENT, LLC

The Film Center Building, 630 Ninth Ave., Suite 1101, New York NY 10036. (212)400-1494. **Fax:** (212)967-0977. **Website:** www.foliolit.com. Member of AAR. Represents 100+ clients.

Prior to creating Folio Literary Management, Mr. Hoffman worked for several years at another agency; Mr. Kleinman was an agent at Graybill & English.

MEMBER AGENTS Claudia Cross (romance novels, commercial women's fiction, cooking and food writing, serious nonfiction on religious and spiritual topics); **Scott Hoffman** (literary and commercial fiction, journalistic or academic nonfiction, narrative nonfiction, pop culture books, business, history, politics, spiritual or religious fiction and nonfiction, science fiction, fantasy, literary fiction, heartbreaking memoirs, humorous nonfiction); **Jeff Kleinman** (bookclub fiction [not genre commercial, like mysteries or romances], literary fiction, thrillers and suspense, narrative nonfiction, memoir); **Dado Derviskadic** (nonfiction interests include cultural history, biography, memoir, pop science, motivational self-help, health, pop culture, cookbooks; also seeks fiction that's gritty, introspective, or serious); **Frank Weimann** (biography, business, finance, history, religious, health, lifestyle, cookbooks, sports, African-American, science, memoir, military, prescriptive nonfiction, humor, celebrity; also seeks adult and children's fiction); **Michael Harriot** (commercial nonfiction [both narrative and prescriptive], fantasy, science fiction); **Erin Harris** (book club, historical fiction, literary, narrative nonfiction, psychological suspense, young adult); **Molly Jaffa** (middle-grade, young adult, select nonfiction); **Katherine Latshaw** (blog-to-book projects, food/cooking, middle-grade, narrative and prescriptive nonfiction); **Annie Hwang** (literary and upmarket fiction with commercial appeal; select nonfiction in the areas of popular science, health, lifestyle, narrative nonfiction, pop culture, and humor); **Erin Niumata** (commercial women's fiction, romance, historical fiction, mysteries, psychological thrillers, suspense, humor, self-help, women's issues, pop culture and humor, pets, memoirs, and anything by successful bloggers); **Ruth Pomerance** (narrative nonfiction and commercial fiction); **Marcy Posner** (commercial women's fiction, historical fiction, mystery, biography, history, health, lifestyle, thrillers, narrative nonfiction; for kidlit, she seeks contemporary young adult and middle-grade, mystery series for boys, and select historical fiction and fantasy); **Jeff Silberman** (narrative nonfiction, biography, history, politics, current affairs, health, lifestyle, humor, food, memoir, pop culture, sports, science, technology; his fiction interests include commercial, literary, and book club fiction); **Steve Troha**; **Emily van Beek** (young adult, middle-grade, picture books), **Melissa White** (general nonfiction, literary and commercial fiction, middle-grade, young adult); **John Cusick** (middle-grade, picture books, young adult).

REPRESENTS Nonfiction, novels. **Considers these nonfiction areas:** animals, art, biography, business, cooking, creative nonfiction, economics, environment, foods, health, history, how-to, humor, inspirational, memoirs, military, parenting, popular culture, politics, psychology, religious, satire, science, self-help, technology, war, women's issues, women's studies. **Considers these fiction areas:** commercial, fantasy, horror, literary, middle-grade, mystery, picture books, religious, romance, thriller, women's, young adult.

No poetry, stage plays, or screenplays.

HOW TO CONTACT Query via e-mail only (no attachments). Read agent bios online for specific submission guidelines and e-mail addresses, and to check if someone is closed to queries. "All agents respond to queries as soon as possible, whether interested or not. If you haven't heard back from the individual agent within the time period that they specify on their bio page, it's possible that something has gone wrong, and you can e-mail a follow-up."

TIPS "Please do not submit simultaneously to more than 1 agent at Folio. If you're not sure which of us is exactly right for your book, don't worry. We work closely as a team, and if 1 of our agents gets a query that might be more appropriate for someone else, we'll always pass it along. It's important that you check each agent's bio page for clear directions as to how to submit, as well as when to expect feedback."

FOUNDRY LITERARY + MEDIA

33 W. 17th St., PH, New York NY 10011. (212)929-5064. **Fax:** (212)929-5471. **Website:** www.foundry-media.com.

MEMBER AGENTS Peter McGuigan, pmsubmissions@foundrymedia.com (smart, offbeat voices in all genres of fiction and nonfiction); **Yfat Reiss Gendell**, yrgsubmissions@foundrymedia.com (practical nonfiction in the areas of health and wellness, diet, lifestyle, how-to, and parenting; seeks a range of narrative nonfiction that includes humor, memoir, history, science, pop culture, psychology, and adventure/travel stories; seeks unique commercial fiction, including young adult fiction, speculative fiction, thrillers, and historical fiction); **Chris Park**, cpsubmissions@foundrymedia.com (memoirs, narrative nonfiction, sports books, Christian nonfiction, Christian character-driven fiction); **Hannah Brown Gordon**, hbgsubmissions@foundrymedia.com (stories and narratives that blend genres, including thriller, suspense, historical, literary, speculative, memoir, pop-science, psychology, humor, and pop culture); **Brandi Bowles**, bbsubmissions@foundrymedia.com (nonfiction ranges from cookbooks to prescriptive books, science, pop culture, and real-life inspirational stories; seeks high-concept novels that feature strong female bonds and psychological or scientific themes); **Kirsten Neuhaus**, knsubmissions@foundrymedia.com (platform-driven narrative nonfiction in the areas of memoir, business, lifestyle [fashion/relationships], current events, history, and stories with strong female voices; seeks smart fiction that appeals to a wide market); **Jessica Regel**, jrsubmissions@foundrymedia.com (young adult and middle-grade books, as well as a select list of adult general fiction, women's fiction, and adult nonfiction); **Anthony Mattero**, amsubmissions@foundrymedia.com (smart, platform-driven nonfiction in the areas of pop culture, humor, music, sports, and popular business); **Peter Steinberg**, pssubmissions@foundrymedia.com (narrative nonfiction, commercial and literary fiction, memoir, health, history, lifestyle, humor, sports, and young adult); **Roger Freet**, rfsubmissions@foundrymedia.com (narrative and idea-driven nonfiction clients in the areas of religion, spirituality, memoir, and cultural issues; represents leading scholars, pastors, historians, activists, and musicians); **Adriann Ranta** arsubmissions@foundrymedia.com (accepts all genres and age groups; loves gritty, realistic, true-to-life narratives, women's fiction and nonfiction, accessible pop nonfiction [science, history, and craft], and fresh genre-bending works for children).

REPRESENTS Considers these nonfiction areas: creative nonfiction, current affairs, diet/nutrition, health, history, how-to, humor, medicine, memoirs, music, parenting, popular culture, psychology, science, sports, travel. **Considers these fiction areas:** commercial, historical, humor, literary, middle-grade, suspense, thriller, women's, young adult.

HOW TO CONTACT Target 1 Foundry agent only. Send queries to the specific submission e-mail of the agent. For fiction, send a query, synopsis, author bio, and the first 3 chapters—all pasted in the e-mail. For nonfiction, send a query, sample chapters, table of contents, and author bio (all pasted). "If you do not receive a response within 8 weeks, your submission is not right for our lists at this time." Accepts simultaneous submissions.

RECENT SALES *The Last September* by Nina de Gramont, *The Hired Girl* by Laura Amy Schlitz, *The Power of Broke* by Daymond John with Daniel Paisner, *The Suja Juice Solution* by Annie Lawless and Jeff Church, *NFL Confidential* by Johnny Anonymous.

TIPS "Consult our website for each agent's individual submission instructions."

FOX LITERARY

110 W. 40th St., Suite 2305, New York NY 10018. **E-mail:** submissions@foxliterary.com. **Website:** www.publishersmarketplace.com/members/fox/. Fox Literary is a boutique agency that represents commercial fiction, along with select works of literary fiction and nonfiction with broad commercial appeal.

MEMBER AGENTS Diana Fox.

REPRESENTS Nonfiction, fiction, graphic novels. **Considers these nonfiction areas:** biography, creative nonfiction, history, popular culture, mind/body. **Considers these fiction areas:** fantasy, historical, romance, science fiction, thriller, young adult, general.

HOW TO CONTACT E-mail a query and first 5 pages in body of e-mail. No attachments. Accepts simultaneous submissions.

RECENT SALES *Black Ships* by Jo Graham (Orbit), Evernight series by Claudia Gray (HarperCollins), October Daye series by Seanan McGuire (DAW), *Salt and Silver* by Anna Katherine (Tor), *Alcestis* by Katharine Beutner (Soho Press).

LYNN C. FRANKLIN ASSOCIATES, LTD.

1350 Broadway, Suite 2015, New York NY 10018. (212)868-6311. **E-mail:** agency@franklinandsiegal.com. **Website:** www.publishersmarketplace.com/members/LynnCFranklin/. **Contact:** Lynn Franklin, president; Claudia Nys, foreign rights.

REPRESENTS Nonfiction. **Considers these nonfiction areas:** biography, current affairs, memoirs, psychology, self-help, spirituality, alternative medicine.

☛ Primary interest lies in nonfiction (memoir, biography, current affairs, spirituality, psychology/self-help, alternative medicine, etc.).

HOW TO CONTACT E-query us at agency@ franklinandsiegal.com. No unsolicited mss or attachments. For nonfiction, send a query letter with short outline and synopsis. For fiction, send a query letter with short synopsis and a maximum of 10 sample pages (in the body of the e-mail). Accepts simultaneous submissions.

RECENT SALES *The Wahls Protocol: How I Beat Progressive MS Using Paleo Principles and Functional Medicine* by Terry Wahls (Avery/Penguin), *The Book of Forgiving: The Four-Fold Path To Healing For Ourselves and Our World* by Archbishop Desmond Tutu and Reverend Mpho Tutu (US: HarperOne, UK: Collins), *The Customer Rules: 39 Essential Practices for Delivering Sensational Service* by Lee Cockerell (Crown Business/Random House).

⊕ FRASER-BUB LITERARY, LLC

410 Park Ave. S, Tenth Floor, New York NY 10016. (917)524-6982. **E-mail:** mackenzie@fraserbubliterary.com . **Website:** www.fraserbubliterary.com . **Contact:** MacKenzie Fraser-Bub. Estab. 2015.

○ Prior to forming her own agency, Ms. Fraser-Bub worked as an editor before becoming an agent at Trident Media Group..

REPRESENTS Nonfiction, novels. **Considers these nonfiction areas:** cookbooks (especially healthy eating and baking), design, diet, fashion, food, popular psychology, relationships, self-help, true crime. **Considers these fiction areas:** crime, historical fiction, mystery (female-driven), new adult, romance, thriller, women's fiction, young adult (with crossover appeal).

⊶ Does not want to receive children's picture books, middle-grade, screenplays, poetry, graphic novels, or comics. Rarely represents or requests science fiction, fantasy, westerns, philosophy, or sports.

HOW TO CONTACT "I only accept e-queries. Please do not query via phone. Include the world 'Query' in your subject line. For fiction submissions, your query may include the first chapter in the body of the e-mail. I will not open attachments. For nonfiction submissions, your query may include the first 10 pages in the body of the e-mail."

JEANNE FREDERICKS LITERARY AGENCY, INC.

221 Benedict Hill Rd., New Canaan CT 06840. (203)972-3011. **Fax:** (203)972-3011. **E-mail:** jeanne.

fredericks@gmail.com. **Website:** www.jeannefredericks.com. **Contact:** Jeanne Fredericks. "The Jeanne Fredericks Literary Agency, Inc. has specialized in representing quality adult nonfiction by experts in their fields. We particularly enjoy working with authors who communicate important new information that will make a positive difference in the lives of a sizable population." Estab. 1997. Member of AAR, Authors Guild.

○ Prior to opening her agency in 1997, Ms. Fredericks was an agent and acting director with the Susan P. Urstadt, Inc. Agency. Previously she was the editorial director of Ziff-Davis Books and managing editor and acquisitions editor at Macmillan Publishing Company.

REPRESENTS Nonfiction. **Considers these nonfiction areas:** Americana, animals, autobiography, biography, child guidance, cooking, decorating, foods, gardening, health, history, how-to, interior design, medicine, parenting, photography, psychology, self-help, women's issues.

⊶ This agency specializes in quality adult nonfiction by authorities in their fields. "We do not handle the following: fiction, true crime, juvenile, textbooks, poetry, essays, screenplays, short stories, science fiction, pop culture, guides to computers and software, politics, horror, pornography, books on overly depressing or violent topics, romance, teacher manuals, or memoir."

HOW TO CONTACT Query first by e-mail, then send outline, proposal, and 1-2 sample chapters, if requested and after you have consulted the submission guidelines on the agency website. If you do send requested submission materials, include the word "Requested" in the subject line. Accepts simultaneous submissions. Responds in 5 weeks to queries. Responds in 4 months to mss.

TERMS Agent receives 15% commission on domestic sales; 25% commission on foreign sales with co-agent.

RECENT SALES *Greenhouse Gardener's Manual* by Roger Marshall (Timber), *M.D.'s Guide to Alternative Medicine* by Lloyd May, M.D. (Basic Health), *Yoga Nidra for Stress Relief* by Julie Lusk (New Harbinger), *The Epidural Book* by Rich Siegenfeld, M.D. (Johns Hopkins University Press), *A Place in the Sun* by Stephen Snyder (Rizzoli), *American Quilts* by Bob Shaw (Sterling).

NEW AGENT SPOTLIGHT

RACHEL BURKOT
HOLLOWAY LITERARY

www.hollowayliteraryagency.com
@Rachel_Burkot

ABOUT RACHEL: Rachel Burkot of Holloway Literary has been in the publishing industry since 2009. After completing an internship with two literary agencies, she worked as an editor for Harlequin. Rachel's career highlights include helping her authors achieve prestigious romance book nominations and two selective awards, including the National Readers' Choice Award, and several top reviews in *Romantic Times* magazine for her writers' books.

SHE IS SEEKING: Voice-driven fiction, particularly in young adult books. She enjoys quirky, three-dimensional, flawed characters—especially secondary characters. She seeks beautiful writing, books that explore good people in morally complicated situations, and complex, detailed plots. Rachel is interested in representing women's fiction, upmarket/book club fiction (e.g., Emily Giffin and Diane Chamberlain), young adult (no fantasy or paranormal unless it's very light), contemporary romance (i.e., Kristan Higgins), category romance with unique plots (e.g., Natalie Charles), Southern fiction, "dark" women's thrillers (e.g., Gillian Flynn or Mary Kubica), urban fiction, and literary fiction

HOW TO SUBMIT: Send your query to submissions@hollowayliteraryagency.com. E-mail a brief query and the first five pages of your manuscript pasted in the body of your e-mail. In the e-mail subject header, write "Query: [Title/Genre]." If Rachel is interested, she'll respond via e-mail with a request for more material.

TIPS "Be sure to research competition for your work and be able to justify why there's a need for your book. I enjoy building an author's career, particularly if he/she is professional, hardworking, and courteous, and actively involved in establishing a marketing platform. Aside from 25 years of agenting experience, I've had 10 years of editorial experience in adult trade book publishing that enables me to help an author polish a proposal so that it's more appealing to prospective editors. My MBA in marketing also distinguishes me from other agents."

GRACE FREEDSON'S PUBLISHING NETWORK

7600 Jericho Turnpike, Suite 300, Woodbury NY 11797. (516)931-7757. **Fax:** (516)931-7759. **E-mail:** gfreedson@gmail.com. **Contact:** Grace Freedson. Estab. 2000. Member of AAR, Women's Media Group, Authors Guild. Represents 100 clients.

○ Prior to becoming an agent, Ms. Freedson was a managing editor and director of acquisition for Barron's Educational Series.

REPRESENTS Nonfiction, scholarly books. **Considers these nonfiction areas:** animals, business, child guidance, computers, cooking, crafts, creative nonfiction, current affairs, diet/nutrition, economics, education, environment, foods, gardening, health, history, hobbies, horticulture, how-to, humor, inspirational, interior design, juvenile nonfiction, language, law, memoirs, metaphysics, money, multicultural, parenting, philosophy, popular culture, psychology, recreation, regional, satire, science, self-help, sports, technology, true crime, war, women's issues, women's studies.

HOW TO CONTACT Query. Agency responds in 6 weeks to queries. Obtains most new clients through recommendations from others.

TERMS Agent receives 15% commission on domestic sales. Offers written contract; 30-day notice must be given to terminate contract.

RECENT SALES *The 25 Most Influential Aircraft of All Time* by Colonel Walter Boyne and Philip Handleman (Globe Pequot), *Murder in Plain English* by Mike Arntfield and Marcel Danesi (Prometheus Books).

WRITERS CONFERENCES BookExpo of America.

TIPS "At this point, I am reviewing only proposals on nonfiction topics by credentialed authors with platforms."

SARAH JANE FREYMANN LITERARY AGENCY

(212)362-9277. **E-mail:** sarah@sarahjanefreymann. com. **E-mail:** submissions@sarahjanefreymann.com. **Website:** www.sarahjanefreymann.com.

MEMBER AGENTS Sarah Jane Freymann (nonfiction interests include spiritual, psychology, self-help, women/men's issues, books by health experts [conventional and alternative], cookbooks, narrative nonfiction, natural science, nature, memoirs, cutting-edge journalism, travel, multicultural issues, parenting, lifestyle; fiction interests include literary, mainstream, young adult); **Jessica Sinsheimer**, jessica@sarahjanefreymann.com (young adult, thrillers, picture books); **Steven Schwartz**, steve@sarahjanefreymann.com (popular fiction [crime, thrillers, and historical novels], world and national affairs, business books, self-help, psychology, humor, sports and travel).

REPRESENTS Nonfiction, novels. **Considers these nonfiction areas:** business, cooking, creative nonfiction, current affairs, health, humor, memoirs, multicultural, parenting, psychology, science, self-help, spirituality, sports, travel, women's issues, men's issues, nature, journalism, lifestyle. **Considers these fiction areas:** crime, historical, literary, mainstream, thriller, young adult, popular fiction.

HOW TO CONTACT Query via e-mail. No attachments. Below the query, please paste the first 10 pages of your work. Accepts simultaneous submissions.

TERMS Charges clients for long distance, overseas postage, photocopying. 100% of business is derived from commissions on ms sales.

RECENT SALES *Your Life is a Book: How to Craft and Publish Your Memoir* by Brenda Peterson and Sarah Jane Freymann (Sasquatch Books), *The Soul of an Octopus: A Surprising Exploration into the Wonder of Consciousness* by Sy Montgomery (Atria Books), *The Bird Has My Wings: The Autobiography of an Innocent Man on Death Row* by Jarvis Jay Masters (HarperOne).

FREDRICA S. FRIEDMAN AND CO., INC.

857 Fifth Ave., New York NY 10065. (212)829-9600. **Fax:** (212)829-9669. **E-mail:** submissions@fredricafriedman.com. **Website:** www.fredricafriedman. com. **Contact:** Ms. Chandler Smith.

○ Prior to establishing her own literary management firm, Ms. Friedman was the editorial director of Little, Brown & Co., a division of Time Warner, and the first woman to hold the position.

REPRESENTS Nonfiction, fiction.

☛ Does not want poetry, plays, screenplays, children's picture books, science fiction, fantasy, or horror.

HOW TO CONTACT Submit e-query, synopsis. "Be concise and include any pertinent author information, including relevant writing history. If you are a fiction writer, submit the first 10 pages of your ms. Keep all material in the body of the e-mail." Accepts simultaneous submissions. Responds in 6 weeks.

REBECCA FRIEDMAN LITERARY AGENCY

E-mail: Abby@rfliterary.com. **Website:** www.rfliterary.com. Estab. 2013. Member of AAR. Signatory of WGA.

○ Prior to opening her agency in 2013, Ms. Friedman was with Sterling Lord Literistic from 2006 to 2011, then with Hill Nadell Agency.

MEMBER AGENTS Rebecca Friedman, brandie@rfliterary.com (commercial and literary fiction with a focus on literary novels of suspense, women's fiction, contemporary romance, young adult, as well as journalistic nonfiction and memoir); **Kimberly Brower**, kimberly@rfliterary.com (commercial and literary fiction, with an emphasis in contemporary romance, women's fiction, mysteries/thrillers, young adult); **Rachel Marks**, rachel@rfliterary.com (young adult, fantasy, science fiction, new adult, and romance); **Susan Finesman**, susan@rfliterary.com (fiction, cookbooks, lifestyle); **Jess Dallow**, jess@rfliterary.com (young adult and adult literary and commercial fiction—with a focus in romance, thrillers, and women's fiction).

REPRESENTS Nonfiction, fiction. **Considers these nonfiction areas:** memoirs, journalistic nonfiction. **Considers these fiction areas:** commercial, fantasy, literary, mystery, new adult, romance, science fiction, suspense, women's, young adult.

HOW TO CONTACT Please submit your query letter and first chapter (no more than 15 pages, double-spaced). If querying Kimberly, paste a full synopsis into the e-mail submission. No attachments. Accepts simultaneous submissions. Tries to respond in 8 weeks.

RECENT SALES A complete list of agency authors is available online.

THE FRIEDRICH AGENCY

19 W. 21st St., Suite 201, New York NY 10010. (212)317-8810. **Website:** www.friedrichagency.com. **Contact:** Molly Friedrich, Lucy Carson, Kent D. Wolf. Estab. 2006. Member of AAR. Signatory of WGA. Represents 50+ clients.

○ Prior to her current position, Ms. Friedrich was an agent at the Aaron Priest Literary Agency.

MEMBER AGENTS Molly Friedrich, founder and agent, mfriedrich@friedrichagency.com (open to queries); **Lucy Carson**, TV/film rights director and agent, lcarson@friedrichagency.com (open to queries); **Kent D. Wolf**, foreign rights director and agent, kwolf@friedrichagency.com (open to queries).

REPRESENTS Nonfiction, novels, short story collections. **Considers these nonfiction areas:** creative nonfiction, memoirs. **Considers these fiction areas:** commercial, literary.

HOW TO CONTACT Query by e-mail only. Please query only 1 agent at this agency. Accepts simultaneous submissions.

RECENT SALES *W is For Wasted* by Sue Grafton, *Olive Kitteridge* by Elizabeth Strout. Other clients include Frank McCourt, Jane Smiley, Esmeralda Santiago, Terry McMillan, Cathy Schine, Ruth Ozeki, Karen Joy Fowler, and more.

FULL CIRCLE LITERARY, LLC

Website: www.fullcircleliterary.com. **Contact:** Stefanie Von Borstel. Estab. 2005. Member of AAR, SCBWI, Authors Guild. Represents 100+ clients.

○ Please read the "Our Agents" page on our website and determine the Full Circle Literary agent who is the best fit for your work.

MEMBER AGENTS Stefanie Von Borstel; **Adriana Dominguez**; **Taylor Martindale** (multicultural voices); **Lilly Ghahremani**.

REPRESENTS Considers these nonfiction areas: creative nonfiction, how-to, interior design, multicultural, women's issues, young adult. **Considers these fiction areas:** literary, middle-grade, multicultural, picture books, women's, young adult.

⚊ Actively seeking nonfiction by authors with a unique voice and strong platform, projects that offer new and diverse viewpoints, and literature with a global or multicultural perspective. We are particularly interested in books with a Latino or Middle Eastern angle.

HOW TO CONTACT Online submissions only via the submissions form at www.fullcircleliterary.com Please complete the form and submit a cover letter, author information, and sample writing. Concerning the sample writing, fiction submissions should include the first 10 ms pages. For nonfiction, include a proposal with 1 sample chapter. Accepts simultaneous submissions. "Due to the high volume of submissions, please keep in mind we are no longer able to personally respond to every submission. If you have not heard from us in 8 weeks, your project is not right for our agency at the current time."

TERMS Agent receives 15% commission on domestic sales; 25% commission on foreign sales. Offers written contract which outlines responsibilities of the author and the agent.

RECENT SALES "Please visit our website to learn about our latest deals and book news. Follow our agency on Twitter @fullcirclelit."

FUSE LITERARY

Website: www.fuseliterary.com. Member of AAR. Signatory of WGA.

MEMBER AGENTS Laurie McLean (only accepting referral inquiries and submissions requested at conferences or online events, with the exception of unsolicited adult and children's science fiction); **Gordon Warnock**, querygordon@fuseliterary.com (fiction interests include high-concept commercial fiction, literary fiction [adult and young adult], graphic novels [adult, young adult, middle-grade]; nonfiction interests include memoir [adult, young adult, new adult, graphic novels], cookbooks, food, illustrated art and photography [especially graphic nonfiction], political and current events, pop science, pop culture [especially punk culture and geek culture], self-help, how-to, humor, pets, business, career); **Connor Goldsmith**, queryconnor@fuseliterary.com (fiction interests include science fiction, fantasy, horror, thrillers, and upmarket commercial fiction with a unique and memorable hook; seeks books by and about people from marginalized perspectives, such as LGBT people and/or racial minorities; seeks nonfiction from recognized experts with established platforms in the areas of history [particularly of the ancient world], theater, cinema, music, television, mass media, popular culture, feminism and gender studies, LGBT issues, race relations, and the sex industry); **Sara Sciuto**, querysara@fuseliterary.com (middle-grade, young adult, standout picture books); **Michelle Richter**, querymichelle@fuseliterary.com (book club reads, literary fiction, mystery, suspense, thrillers; for nonfiction, she seeks fashion, pop culture, science, medicine, sociology, and economics); **Emily S. Keyes**, queryemily@fuseliterary.com (young adult, middle-grade, fantasy, science fiction, women's fiction, new adult fiction, pop culture, and humor); **Tricia Skinner**, querytricia@fuseliterary.com (romance in the subgenres of science fiction, futuristic, fantasy, military/special ops, medieval historical, diversity); **Jennifer Chen Tran**, queryjennifer@fuseliterary.com (literary fiction, commercial fiction, women's fiction, upmarket fiction, contemporary romance, mature young adult, new adult, suspense, thriller, select graphic novels [adult, young adult, middle-grade], memoir; seeks narrative nonfiction in the areas of adventure, biography, business, current affairs, medical, history, how-to, pop culture, psychology, social entrepreneurism, social justice, travel, and lifestyle books [home, design, fashion, food]).

HOW TO CONTACT E-query an individual agent. Check the website to see if any individual agent has closed themselves to submissions, as well as each agent's individual query preferences. Accepts simultaneous submissions.

WRITERS CONFERENCES Agents from this agency attend many conferences. A full list of their appearances is available on the agency website.

THE G AGENCY, LLC

P.O. Box 374, Bronx NY 10471. (718)664-4505. **E-mail:** gagencyquery@gmail.com. **Website:** www.publishersmarketplace.com/members/jeffg. **Contact:** Jeff Gerecke. Estab. 2012. Member of AAR. Signatory of WGA.

MEMBER AGENTS Jeff Gerecke.

REPRESENTS Considers these nonfiction areas: biography, business, computers, history, military, money, popular culture, technology. **Considers these fiction areas:** mainstream, mystery.

☞ "I am interested in commercial and literary fiction, as well as serious nonfiction and pop culture. My focus as an agent has always been on working with writers to shape their work for its greatest commercial potential. I provide lots of editorial advice in sharpening mss and proposals before submission." Does not want screenplays, science fiction, fantasy, or romance.

HOW TO CONTACT E-mail submissions preferred, Attach sample chapters or proposal if you wish. Enter "Query" along with your title in the subject line of e-mails or on the envelope of snail mail. "I cannot guarantee replies to every submission. If you do not hear from me the first time, you may send me 1 reminder." Accepts simultaneous submissions.

RECENT SALES *The Race for Paradise* by Paul Cobb (Oxford UP), *Nothin' But Blue Skies* by Edward McClelland (Bloomsbury), *Tear Down* by Gordon Young.

◉ NANCY GALLT LITERARY AGENCY

273 Charlton Ave., South Orange NJ 07079. (973)761-6358. **Website:** www.nancygallt.com. **Contact:** Nancy Gallt, Marietta Zacker. "At the Nancy Gallt Literary Agency, we represent people, not projects, and we focus solely on writers and illustrators of children's books." Estab. 2000. Represents 60 clients.

NEW AGENT SPOTLIGHT

MITCH HOFFMAN
AARON PRIEST LITERARY AGENCY

www.aaronpriest.com
@mitch_hoffman

ABOUT MITCH: Mitch Hoffman joined the Aaron Priest Literary Agency as a senior agent in 2015. A twenty-year veteran of the publishing industry, he was most recently vice president and executive editor at Grand Central Publishing. As an editor, Mitch published two hundred books, more than sixty of which were *New York Times* bestsellers.

HE IS SEEKING: Mitch is actively building a client list of authors writing across the spectrum of fiction and nonfiction—including thrillers, suspense, crime fiction, literary fiction, narrative nonfiction, politics, popular science, history, memoir, current events, and pop culture.

HOW TO SUBMIT: Send a one-page query to queryhoffman@aaronpriest.com. Please do not send attachments; however, a first chapter pasted into the body of an e-mail query is acceptable. "We will get back to you within four weeks if interested in seeing more."

Prior to opening her agency, Ms. Gallt was subsidiary rights director of the children's book division at Morrow, Harper, and Viking.
MEMBER AGENTS Nancy Gallt, Marietta Zacker.
REPRESENTS Considers these fiction areas: juvenile, middle-grade, picture books, young adult.
Actively seeking picture books, middle-grade, and young adult novels. No adult fiction.
HOW TO CONTACT Submit through online submission form on agency website. No e-queries, please. Accepts simultaneous submissions.
TERMS Agent receives 15% commission on domestic sales; 20% commission on foreign sales. Offers written contract; 30-day notice must be given to terminate contract.
RECENT SALES *Toya* by Randi Revill, Rick Riordan's books (Hyperion), *Something Extraordinary* by Ben Clanton (Simon & Schuster), *The Baby Tree* by Sophie Blackall (Nancy Paulsen Books/Penguin), *Fenway and Hattie* by Victoria J. Coe (Putnam/Penguin).
TIPS "Writing and illustrations stand on their own, so submissions should tell the most compelling stories possible—whether visually, in words, or both."

⊙ THE GARAMOND AGENCY, INC.

1840 Columbia Rd. NW, #503, Washington DC 20009. **E-mail:** query@garamondagency.com. **Website:** www.garamondagency.com.
MEMBER AGENTS Lisa Adams, David Miller.
REPRESENTS Nonfiction, scholarly books. **Considers these nonfiction areas:** anthropology, archeology, biography, business, creative nonfiction, current affairs, economics, environment, government, history, law, medicine, parenting, politics, psychology, science, sociology, sports, technology, women's issues.
"We work closely with our authors through each stage of the publishing process, first in

developing their books and then in presenting themselves and their ideas effectively to publishers and to readers. We represent our clients throughout the world in all languages, media, and territories through an extensive network of subagents." No proposals for children's or young adult books, fiction, poetry, or memoir.

HOW TO CONTACT "Queries sent by e-mail may not make it through the spam filters on our server. Please e-mail a brief query letter only. We do not read unsolicited mss or attachments submitted by e-mail under any circumstances. See our website." Accepts simultaneous submissions.

RECENT SALES *$2.00 a Day* by Kathryn Edin and H. Luke Shaefer (Houghton Mifflin Harcourt), *The Gulf* by Jack Davis (Norton), *Downhill From Here* by Katherine S. Newman (Metropolitan Books), *Free and Equal* by Jeremy Popkin (Basic Books).

TIPS "Query us first if you have any questions about whether we are the right agency for your work."

MAX GARTENBERG LITERARY AGENCY

912 N. Pennsylvania Ave., Yardley PA 19067, (215)295-9230. **Website:** www.maxgartenberg.com. **Contact:** Anne Devlin. Estab. 1954. Represents 100 clients.

MEMBER AGENTS Anne G. Devlin (current events, politics, true crime, women's issues, sports, parenting, biography, environment, narrative nonfiction, health, lifestyle, literary fiction, romance, and celebrity); Dirk Devlin (thrillers, science fiction, mysteries, and humor).

REPRESENTS Novels, nonfiction. **Considers these nonfiction areas:** animals, art, biography, current affairs, film, health, history, money, music, psychology, science, sports, true crime.

HOW TO CONTACT Query by e-mail to agdevlin@aol.com. Accepts simultaneous submissions. Obtains most new clients through recommendations from others, following up on good query letters.

TERMS Agent receives 15% commission on domestic sales; 20% commission on foreign sales.

RECENT SALES *Blazing Ice: Pioneering the 21st Century's Road to the South Pole* by John H. Wright, *Beethoven for Kids: His Life and Music* by Helen Bauer, *Slaughter on North LaSalle* by Robert L. Snow, *What Patients Taught Me* by Audrey Young (Sasquatch Books).

TIPS "We have recently expanded to allow more access for new writers."

GELFMAN SCHNEIDER / ICM PARTNERS

850 Seventh Ave., Suite 903, New York NY 10019. **E-mail:** mail@gelfmanschneider.com. **Website:** www.gelfmanschneider.com. **Contact:** Jane Gelfman, Deborah Schneider. Member of AAR. Represents 300+ clients.

MEMBER AGENTS Deborah Schneider (all categories of literary and commercial fiction and nonfiction); Jane Gelfman; Victoria Marini, victoria.gsliterary@gmail.com (literary fiction, commercial fiction, pop culture nonfiction, young adult and middle-grade fiction; she has a particular interest in engaging literary fiction and mysteries/suspense, commercial women's fiction [suspense, mystery, thriller, magical realism, fantasy], and young adult [contemporary and speculative]); Heather Mitchell (particularly interested in narrative nonfiction, historical fiction, and young debut authors with strong voices); Penelope Burns, penelope.gsliterary@gmail.com (literary and commercial fiction and nonfiction, as well as a variety of young adult and middle-grade).

REPRESENTS Nonfiction, fiction, juvenile books. **Considers these nonfiction areas:** creative nonfiction, popular culture. **Considers these fiction areas:** commercial, fantasy, historical, literary, mainstream, middle-grade, mystery, science fiction, suspense, women's, young adult.

Does not currently accept screenplays or scripts, poetry, or picture book queries.

HOW TO CONTACT Query. Check the submissions page of the website to see which agents are open to queries and further instructions. To query Victoria or Penelope, please send a query letter and 1-3 sample chapters (pasted, no attachments) to their individual e-mails. Please include "Query" in the subject line. If you are contacting Victoria, please check victoriamarini.com/submissions for updates and response times, as they may vary. Accepts simultaneous submissions.

TERMS Agent receives 15% commission on domestic sales; 20% commission on foreign sales. Offers written contract. Charges clients for photocopying and messengers/couriers.

THE GERNERT COMPANY

136 E. 57th St., New York NY 10022. (212)838-7777. **E-mail:** info@thegernertco.com. **Website:** www.thegernertco.com. **Contact:** Sarah Burnes.

Prior to her current position, Ms. Burnes was with Burnes & Clegg, Inc.

MEMBER AGENTS Sarah Burnes (literary fiction and nonfiction, children's fiction); **Stephanie Cabot** (represents a variety of genres, including crime/thrillers, commercial and literary fiction, latte lit, and nonfiction); **Chris Parris-Lamb** (nonfiction, literary fiction); **Seth Fishman** (looking for the new voice, the original idea, the entirely breathtaking creative angle in both fiction and nonfiction); **Logan Garrison** (young adult fiction); **Will Roberts** (smart, original thrillers with distinctive voices, compelling backgrounds, and fast-paced narratives); **Erika Storella** (nonfiction projects that make an argument, narrate a history, and/or provide a new perspective); **Flora Hackett** (thrillers with a twist, science fiction, fantasy, and women's fiction); **Andy Kifer** (literary fiction, smart genre fiction [especially science fiction], and nonfiction by brilliant writers who can make you fall in love with a subject you never knew you cared about); **Anna Worrall** (smart women's literary and commercial fiction, psychological thrillers, narrative nonfiction); **Ellen Goodson** (women's literary and commercial fiction, historical fiction, narrative nonfiction, and smart thrillers; she also seeks well-written Southern gothic anything). At this time, **Courtney Gatewood** and **Rebecca Gardner** are closed to queries. See the website to find out further tastes of each agent.

REPRESENTS Nonfiction, novels. **Considers these fiction areas:** commercial, crime, fantasy, historical, literary, middle-grade, science fiction, thriller, women's, young adult.

HOW TO CONTACT Please send us a query letter by e-mail to info@thegernertco.com describing the work you'd like to submit, along with some information about yourself and a sample chapter if appropriate. Please indicate in your letter which agent you are querying. Please do not send e-mails directly to individual agents. "It's our policy to respond to your query only if we are interested in seeing more material, usually within 6 weeks." See company website for more instructions. Accepts simultaneous submissions. Obtains most new clients through recommendations from others, solicitations.

RECENT SALES *Partners* by John Grisham, *The River Why* by David James Duncan, *The Thin Green Line* by Paul Sullivan, *A Fireproof Home for the Bride* by Amy Scheibe.

GHOSH LITERARY

E-mail: submissions@ghoshliterary.com. **Website:** www.ghoshliterary.com. Member of AAR. Signatory of WGA.

○ Prior to opening her own agency, Ms. Ghosh was previously a partner at Scovil Galen Ghosh.

REPRESENTS Nonfiction, fiction.

☛ "Anna's literary interests are wide and eclectic, and she is known for discovering and developing writers. She is particularly interested in literary narratives and books that illuminate some aspect of human endeavor or the natural world. Anna does not typically represent genre fiction but is drawn to compelling storytelling in most guises."

HOW TO CONTACT E-query. Please send an e-mail to submissions@ghoshliterary.com briefly introducing yourself and your work. Although no specific format is required, it is helpful to know the following: your qualifications for writing your book, including any publications and recognition for your work; who you expect to buy and read your book; similar books and authors. Accepts simultaneous submissions.

GLASS LITERARY MANAGEMENT

138 W. 25th St., 10th Floor, New York NY 10001. (646)237-4881. **E-mail:** submissions@glassliterary.com. **Website:** www.glassliterary.com. **Contact:** Alex Glass. Mr. Glass is a generalist and takes submissions for virtually all kinds of fiction and nonfiction (except children's picture books). Estab. 2014. Member of AAR. Signatory of WGA.

REPRESENTS Nonfiction, novels.

☛ Represents general fiction, mystery, suspense, thriller, biography, history, health, lifestyle, cookbooks, sports, literary fiction, memoir, narrative nonfiction, and pop culture. "We do not represent picture books for children."

HOW TO CONTACT "Please send your query letter in the body of an e-mail, and if we are interested, we will respond and ask for the complete ms or proposal. No attachments." Accepts simultaneous submissions.

RECENT SALES *100 Days of Cake* by Shari Goldhagen, *The Red Car* by Marcy Dermansky, *The Overnight Solution* by Dr. Michael Breus, *So That Happened: A Memoir* by Jon Cryer, *Bad Kid* by David Crabb, *Finding Mr. Brightside* by Jay Clark, *Strange Animals* by Chad Kultgen.

GLOBAL LION INTELLECTUAL PROPERTY MANAGEMENT, INC.

P.O. Box 669238, Pompano Beach FL 33066. **E-mail:** queriesgloballionmgt@gmail.com. **Website:** www. globallionmanagement.com. **Contact:** Peter Miller. Estab. 2013. Member of AAR. Signatory of WGA.

○ Prior to his current position, Mr. Miller was formerly the founder of PMA Literary & Film Management Inc. of New York.

☛ "I look for cutting-edge authors of both fiction and nonfiction with global marketing and motion picture (or TV) production potential."

HOW TO CONTACT E-query. Global Lion Intellectual Property Management, Inc. accepts exclusive submissions only. If your work is under consideration by another agency, please do not submit it to us." Below the query, paste a one-page synopsis, a sample of your book (20 pages is typical), a short author bio, and any impressive social media links.

BARRY GOLDBLATT LITERARY LLC

320 Seventh Ave. #266, Brooklyn NY 11215. **E-mail:** query@bgliterary.com. **Website:** www.bgliterary.com. **Contact:** Barry Goldblatt. Estab. 2000. Member of AAR. Signatory of WGA.

MEMBER AGENTS Barry Goldblatt; Jennifer Udden, query.judden@gmail.com (speculative fiction of all stripes [especially innovative science fiction or fantasy], romance [contemporary, erotic, LGBT, paranormal, historical], contemporary or speculative young adult, mysteries, thrillers, and urban fantasies).

REPRESENTS Fiction. **Considers these fiction areas:** fantasy, middle-grade, mystery, romance, science fiction, thriller, young adult.

☛ "Please see our website for specific submission guidelines and information on our particular tastes."

HOW TO CONTACT "E-mail queries can be sent to query@bgliterary.com and should include the word 'Query' in the subject line. To query Jen specifically, e-mail queries can be sent to query.judden@gmail. com. Please know that we will read and respond to every e-query that we receive, provided it is properly addressed and follows the submission guidelines below. We will not respond to e-queries that are addressed to no one or to multiple recipients. While we do not require exclusivity, exclusive submissions will receive priority review. If your submission is exclu-

sive to Barry Goldblatt Literary, please indicate so by including the word 'Exclusive' in the subject line of your e-mail. Your e-query should include the following within the body of the e-mail: your query letter, a synopsis of the book, and the first 5 pages of your ms. We will not open or respond to any e-mails that have attachments. Our response time is 4 weeks on queries, 8 weeks on full mss. If you haven't heard from us within that time, feel free to check in via e-mail." Accepts simultaneous submissions. Obtains clients through referrals, queries, conferences.

TERMS Agent receives 15% commission on domestic sales; 20% on foreign and dramatic sales. Offers written contract.

RECENT SALES *Other Broken Things* by C. Desir, *Masks and Shadows* by Stephanie Burgis, *Wishing Day* by Lauren Myracle, *Mother-Daughter Book Camp* by Heather Vogel Frederick.

TIPS "We're a hands-on agency, focused on building an author's career, not just making an initial sale. We don't care about trends or what's hot; we just want to sign great writers."

FRANCES GOLDIN LITERARY AGENCY, INC.

214 W. 29th St., Suite 410, New York NY 10001. (212)777-0047. **Fax:** (212)228-1660. **Website:** www. goldinlit.com. Estab. 1977. Member of AAR.

MEMBER AGENTS Frances Goldin, founder/president; Ellen Geiger, vice president/principal (nonfiction interests include history, biography, progressive politics, photography, science and medicine, women, religion, and serious investigative journalism; fiction interests include literary thrillers, novels in general that provoke and challenge the status quo, as well as historical and multicultural works; does not seek New Age, romance, how-to, or right-wing politics); Matt McGowan, agent/rights director, mm@goldinlit. com (literary fiction, essays, history, memoir, journalism, biography, music, popular culture, popular science, sports [particularly soccer], narrative nonfiction, cultural studies, literary travel, crime, food, suspense, and science fiction); Sam Stoloff, vice president/principal (literary fiction, memoir, history, accessible sociology and philosophy, cultural studies, serious journalism, narrative and topical nonfiction with a progressive orientation); Ria Julien, agent/counsel; Nina Cochran, literary assistant.

REPRESENTS Nonfiction, novels. **Considers these nonfiction areas:** biography, creative nonfiction, cultural interests, foods, history, investigative, medicine, memoirs, music, philosophy, photography, popular culture, politics, science, sociology, sports, travel, women's issues, crime. **Considers these fiction areas:** historical, literary, mainstream, multicultural, suspense, thriller.

☛ "We work intensively with clients on proposal and ms development. Please note that we do not handle screenplays, romances, most genre fiction, or poetry. We do not handle work that is racist, sexist, ageist, homophobic, or pornographic."

HOW TO CONTACT There is an online submission process you can find here: www.goldinlit.com/contact.html. Responds in 6 weeks to queries.

IRENE GOODMAN LITERARY AGENCY

27 W. 24th St., Suite 700B, New York NY 10010. **Website:** www.irenegoodman.com. Member of AAR.
MEMBER AGENTS Irene Goodman, irene.queries@irenegoodman.com; Miriam Kriss, miriam.queries@irenegoodman.com; Barbara Poelle, barbara.queries@irenegoodman.com; Rachel Ekstrom, rachel.queries@irenegoodman.com; Beth Vesel, beth.queries@irenegoodman.com; Kim Perel, kim.queries@irenegoodman.com; Anne Baltazar; Brita Lundberg.
REPRESENTS Nonfiction, novels, juvenile books. **Considers these nonfiction areas:** parenting, social issues, francophilia, anglophilia, Judaica, lifestyles, cooking, memoir. **Considers these fiction areas:** crime, detective, historical, mystery, romance, thriller, women's, young adult.

☛ Seeking commercial fiction, literary fiction, and commercial nonfiction. No children's picture books, screenplays, poetry, or inspirational fiction.

HOW TO CONTACT Query. Also submit a synopsis and the first 10 pages pasted into the body of the e-mail. E-mail queries only. No attachments. Query 1 agent only. Accepts simultaneous submissions. Responds in 2 months to queries. Consult website for each agent's specific submission guidelines.
TIPS "We are receiving an unprecedented amount of e-queries. If you find that the mailbox is full, please try again in 2 weeks. E-queries to our personal inboxes will be deleted."

DOUG GRAD LITERARY AGENCY, INC.

68 Jay St., Suite N3, Brooklyn NY 11201. (718)788-6067. **E-mail:** query@dgliterary.com. **Website:** www.

dgliterary.com. **Contact:** Doug Grad. Estab. 2008. Member of AAR. Signatory of WGA.

○ Prior to being an agent, Mr. Grad spent 22 years as an editor at imprint at 4 major publishing houses—Simon & Schuster, Random House, Penguin, and HarperCollins.

MEMBER AGENTS Doug Grad (narrative nonfiction, military, sports, celebrity memoir, thrillers, mysteries, historical fiction, music, style, business, home improvement, cookbooks, science, and theater).
REPRESENTS Nonfiction, novels. **Considers these nonfiction areas:** Americana, autobiography, business, cooking, creative nonfiction, current affairs, diet/nutrition, design, film, government, history, humor, military, music, popular culture, politics, science, sports, technology, theater, travel, true crime, war. **Considers these fiction areas:** action, adventure, commercial, crime, detective, historical, horror, literary, mainstream, military, mystery, police, science fiction, suspense, thriller, war, young adult.

☛ Does not want fantasy, young adult, or children's picture books.

HOW TO CONTACT Query by e-mail. No sample material unless requested; no printed submissions by mail. Accepts simultaneous submissions.
RECENT SALES *The Earthend Saga* by Gillian Anderson and Jeff Rovin (Simon451), *Bounty* by Michael Byrnes (Bantam), *Sports Idioms and Words* by Josh Chetwynd (Ten Speed Press).

ASHLEY GRAYSON LITERARY AGENCY

1342 W. 18th St., San Pedro CA 90732. **E-mail:** graysonagent@earthlink.net. **Website:** www.publishersmarketplace.com/members/CGrayson. Estab. 1976. Member of AAR.
MEMBER AGENTS Ashley Grayson (fantasy, mystery, thrillers, young adult); Carolyn Grayson, carolyngraysonagent@earthlink.net (women's fiction, romance, urban fantasy, paranormal romance, mysteries, thrillers, children's books, nonfiction); Lois Winston, lois.graysonagent@earthlink.net (women's fiction, romance, chick lit, mystery).
REPRESENTS Nonfiction, novels. **Considers these nonfiction areas:** business, parenting, popular culture, science, spirituality, true crime. **Considers these fiction areas:** fantasy, juvenile, middle-grade, mystery, romance, thriller, women's, young adult.

☛ "We represent literary and commercial fiction, as well as nonfiction for adults (self-help, par-

NEW AGENT SPOTLIGHT

CAITLIN MCDONALD
DONALD MAASS LITERARY AGENCY

www.maassagency.com
@literallycait

ABOUT CAITLIN: Caitlin McDonald joined the agency in 2015, and was previously at Sterling Lord Literistic. She represents adult and young adult speculative fiction, primarily science fiction, fantasy, horror, and related subgenres, as well as contemporary fiction about geeky characters. She also handles a small amount of nonfiction in geeky areas, with a focus on feminist theory, women's issues, and pop culture. Caitlin grew up overseas and has a bachelor of arts in creative writing from Columbia University.

SHE IS SEEKING: All science fiction and fantasy fiction (and subgenres) for adult, young adult, and middle-grade—especially secondary world fantasy and alternate history. She enjoys genre-bending or cross-genre fiction, and stories that examine tropes from a new angle. She especially likes diversity of all kinds, including (but not limited to) race, gender, sexuality, and ability, in both characters and world-building.

HOW TO CONTACT: Contact query.cmcdonald@maassagency.com with the query letter, synopsis, and first ten pages of your novel pasted into the body of the e-mail. Responds to queries within four weeks.

enting, pop culture, mind/body/spirit, true crime, business, science). We also represent fiction for younger readers (chapter books through young adult). We are seeking more mysteries and thrillers."

HOW TO CONTACT "The agency is temporarily closed to queries from fiction writers who are not previously published at book length (self-published or print-on-demand titles do not count). However, we will take contacts through client referrals, conference meetings, and from unpublished authors who have received an offer from a reputable publisher (who need an agent before beginning contract negotiations). Nonfiction authors who are recognized within their field or area may still query with proposals. We cannot review self-published, subsidy-published, and POD-published works to evaluate moving them to mainstream publishers. If you meet the criteria above, send a query letter with a list of your publication credits. Do not include attachments to your e-mail unless requested. Do not query more than 1 agent in our agency, whether by e-mail or post." Accepts simultaneous submissions.

TERMS Agent receives 15% commission on domestic sales; 20% commission on foreign sales.

SANFORD J. GREENBURGER ASSOCIATES, INC.

55 Fifth Ave., New York NY 10003. (212)206-5600. **Fax:** (212)463-8718. **Website:** www.greenburger.com. Member of AAR. Represents 500 clients.

MEMBER AGENTS Matt Bialer, lribar@sjga.com (fantasy, science fiction, thrillers, mysteries, select group of literary writers; also seeks smart narrative nonfiction—including books about current events, popular culture, biography, history, music, race, and sports); **Brenda Bowen**, querybb@sjga.com (literary fiction, writers and illustrators of picture books, chapter books, middle-grade, young adult); **Faith Hamlin**, fhamlin@sjga.com (submissions by referral only); **Heide Lange**, queryhl@sjga.com (submissions by referral only); **Daniel Mandel**, querydm@sjga.com (literary and commercial fiction, memoirs; seeks nonfiction about business, art, history, politics, sports, and popular culture); **Courtney Miller-Callihan**, cmiller@sjga.com (young adult, middle-grade, women's fiction, romance, historical novels; seeks nonfiction projects on unusual topics, humor, pop culture, and lifestyle); **Nicholas Ellison**, nellison@sjga.com; **Chelsea Lindman**, clindman@sjga.com (playful literary fiction, upmarket crime fiction, and forward-thinking or boundary-pushing nonfiction); **Rachael Dillon Fried**, rfried@sjga.com (both fiction and nonfiction authors—with a keen interest in unique literary voices, women's fiction, narrative nonfiction, memoir, and comedy); **Lindsay Ribar**, co-agents with Matt Bialer (young adult and middle-grade fiction); **Bethany Buck,** querybbuck@sjga.com (middle-grade, chapter books, teen fiction, and a select list of picture book authors and illustrators); **Stephanie Delman,** sdelman@sjga.com (literary/upmarket contemporary fiction, psychological thrillers and suspense, atmospheric near-historical fiction); **Ed Maxwell,** emaxwell@sjga.com (expert and narrative nonfiction authors, novelists and graphic novelists, as well as children's book authors and illustrators).

REPRESENTS Nonfiction, novels, juvenile books. **Considers these nonfiction areas:** art, biography, business, creative nonfiction, current affairs, ethnic, history, humor, memoirs, music, popular culture, politics, sports. **Considers these fiction areas:** commercial, crime, family saga, fantasy, feminist, historical, literary, middle-grade, multicultural, mystery, picture books, romance, science fiction, thriller, women's, young adult.

HOW TO CONTACT E-query. "Please look at each agent's profile page for current information about what each agent is looking for and for the correct e-mail address to use for queries to that agent. Please be sure to use the correct query e-mail address for each agent." Agents will respond within 8 weeks if interested.

TERMS Agent receives 15% commission on domestic sales; 20% commission on foreign sales.

RECENT SALES *Inferno* by Dan Brown, *Sweet Pea and Friends: A Sheepover* by John Churchman and Jennifer Churchman, *Code of Conduct* by Brad Thor.

⊙ THE GREENHOUSE LITERARY AGENCY

E-mail: submissions@greenhouseliterary.com. **Website:** www.greenhouseliterary.com. Member of AAR, SCBWI. Represents 20 clients.

Ms. Davies has had an editorial and management career in children's publishing spanning 25 years.

MEMBER AGENTS Sarah Davies (fiction by North American authors—from middle-grade through young adult); **Polly Nolan** (fiction by authors in the United Kingdom, Ireland, and the Commonwealth [including Australia, New Zealand, and India], plus European authors writing in English—from picture books (fewer than 1,000 words) to young adult).

"We exclusively represent authors writing fiction for children and teens. The agency has offices in both the US and the United Kingdom. Does not want to receive picture books texts (i.e., written by writers who aren't also illustrators), short stories, educational works, religious/inspirational work, preschool material, novelty material, screenplays, or writing aimed at adults."

HOW TO CONTACT Query 1 agent only. Put the target agent's name in the subject line. Paste the first 5 pages of your story (or your complete picture book) after the query. Accepts simultaneous submissions.

TERMS Agent receives 15% commission on domestic sales; 25% commission on foreign sales. Offers written contract.

RECENT SALES *Hour of the Bees* by Lindsay Eager (Candlewick), *Triangles: The Points of Love* by Natalie C. Parker (HarperCollins), *Maudeville* by Michelle Schusterman (Random House), *The Radiant Man* by Tami Lewis Brown (FSG, Macmillan).

TIPS "Before submitting material, authors should read the Greenhouse's 'Top 10 Tips for Authors of Children's Fiction' on our website and carefully follow our online submission guidelines."

KATHRYN GREEN LITERARY AGENCY, LLC

250 W. 57th St., Suite 2302, New York NY 10107. (212)245-4225. **Fax:** (212)245-4042. **E-mail:** query@kgreenagency.com. **Website:** www.kathryngreenlit-

eraryagency.com. **Contact:** Kathy Green. Represents approximately 20 clients.

○ Prior to becoming an agent, Ms. Green was a book and magazine editor.

REPRESENTS **Considers these nonfiction areas:** history, humor, memoirs, parenting, popular culture, psychology. **Considers these fiction areas:** crime, detective, family saga, historical, humor, juvenile, literary, mainstream, middle-grade, mystery, police, romance, satire, suspense, thriller, women's, young adult.

☞ Considers all types of fiction but particularly likes historical fiction, cozy mysteries, young adult, and middle-grade. "For nonfiction, I am interested in memoir, parenting, humor with a pop culture bent, and history. Quirky nonfiction is also a particular favorite." Does not want to receive science fiction, fantasy, children's picture books, screenplays, or poetry.

HOW TO CONTACT Send a query to query@kgreenagency.com. Send no attachments unless requested. Do not send queries via postal mail. Responds in 4 weeks. "Queries do not have to be exclusive; however, if further material is requested, please be in touch before accepting other representation."

TERMS Agent receives 15% commission on domestic sales; 20% commission on foreign sales.

GREYHAUS LITERARY

3021 20th St., Pl. SW, Puyallup WA 98373. **E-mail:** scott@greyhausagency.com. **E-mail:** submissions@greyhausagency.com. **Website:** www.greyhausagency.com. **Contact:** Scott Eagan. Estab. 2003. Member of AAR, RWA. Signatory of WGA.

REPRESENTS Novels. **Considers these fiction areas:** romance, women's.

☞ Greyhaus only focuses on romance and women's fiction. Please review submission information found on the website to know exactly what Greyhaus is looking for within these categories. Stories should be 75,000-120,000 words or meet the word count requirements for Harlequin found on its website. Does not want fantasy, single title inspirational, young adult, middle-grade, picture books, memoirs, biographies, erotica, urban fantasy, science fiction, screenplays, poetry, or authors interested in only e-publishing or self-publishing.

HOW TO CONTACT Submissions to Greyhaus can be done by any of the following: 1) A standard query letter via e-mail. If using this method, do not attach documents or send anything else other than a query letter. 2) Use the submission form found on the website on the "Contact" page. Or 3) send a query, the first 3 pages, and a synopsis of no more than 3-5 pages (and a SASE), using a snail mail submission. Accepts simultaneous submissions.

JILL GRINBERG LITERARY MANAGEMENT

392 Vanderbilt Ave., Brooklyn NY 11238. (212)620-5883. **E-mail:** info@jillgrinbergliterary.com. **Website:** www.jillgrinbergliterary.com. Estab. 1999.

○ Prior to her current position, Ms. Grinberg was at Anderson Grinberg Literary Management.

MEMBER AGENTS Jill Grinberg; Cheryl Pientka, cheryl@jillgrinbergliterary.com; Katelyn Detweiler, katelyn@jillgrinbergliterary.com.

REPRESENTS Nonfiction, novels. **Considers these nonfiction areas:** biography, cooking, ethnic, history, science, travel. **Considers these fiction areas:** fantasy, juvenile, literary, mainstream, middle-grade, romance, science fiction, young adult.

HOW TO CONTACT Please send your query letter to info@jillgrinbergliterary.com and attach the first 50 pages (fiction) or full proposal (nonfiction) as a Word doc file. All submissions will be read, but electronic submissions are preferred. Accepts simultaneous submissions.

RECENT SALES *Cinder* by Marissa Meyer, *The Hero's Guide to Saving Your Kingdom* by Christopher Healy, *Kiss and Make Up* by Katie Anderson and T.J. Stiles, *Eon* and *Eona* by Alison Goodman, *American Nations* by Colin Woodard, HALO trilogy by Alexandra Adornetto, *Liar* by Justine Larbalestier, *Turtle in Paradise* by Jennifer Holm, *Wisdom's Kiss* and *Dairy Queen* by Catherine Gilbert Murdock.

TIPS "We prefer submissions by e-mail."

JILL GROSJEAN LITERARY AGENCY

1390 Millstone Rd., Sag Harbor NY 11963. (631)725-7419. **E-mail:** JillLit310@aol.com. **Contact:** Jill Grosjean. Estab. 1999.

○ Prior to becoming an agent, Ms. Grosjean managed an independent bookstore. She also worked in publishing and advertising.

REPRESENTS Novels. **Considers these fiction areas:** historical, literary, mainstream, mystery, thriller, women's.

☞ Actively seeking literary novels and mysteries.

NEW AGENT SPOTLIGHT

TRACY MARCHINI
BOOKENDS LITERARY AGENCY

www.bookendsliterary.com
@tracymarchini

ABOUT TRACY: After four years as an agency assistant at Curtis Brown, Tracy Marchini left to pursue her own editorial business and to earn her MFA in writing for children from Simmons College. Her editorial clients have gone on to secure representation, sell books to traditional publishers, win awards, and become bestsellers in the United Kingdom. She's looking forward to being able to work with her BookEnds clients throughout their careers and to see them grow as authors in the same way. Growing up, Tracy made it a personal goal to read every Nancy Drew Case Files title in her school's library and still has a soft spot for a good girl detective story. As an adult, she loves the sense of possibility in children's and young adult literature—and can still empathize with the soul-crushing feeling that is mandatory gym class.

SHE IS SEEKING: Picture books, middle-grade, and young adult manuscripts across most genres—including contemporary, mysteries, thrillers, magical realism, historical fiction, and nonfiction. For picture books, she's particularly interested in manuscripts that are laugh-out-loud funny or deliciously dark. For middle-grade and young adult, she's interested in underdogs, strong female characters, and/or unreliable narrators. She believes that it's important for readers of all backgrounds to see themselves reflected in the media they consume, and is looking to bring that diversity to her list. She is *not* a good fit for young adult horror, true crime, hard science fiction, or high fantasy. At this time, she is also not looking for board books, early chapter books, or nonfiction for the educational market.

HOW TO CONTACT: Contact tmsubmissions@bookendsliterary.com.

HOW TO CONTACT E-queries preferred, with no attachments. No cold calls, please. Accepts simultaneous submissions, though when a ms is requested, the agency requires exclusive reading time. Accepts simultaneous submissions. Responds in 1 week to queries; month to mss. Obtains most new clients through recommendations and solicitations.

TERMS Agent receives 15% commission on domestic sales; 20% commission on foreign and film sales.

RECENT SALES *The Edison Effect* by Bernadette Pajer (Poison Pen Press), *Neutral Ground* by Greg Garrett (Bondfire Books), *Threading the Needle* by Marie Bostwick (Kensington Publishing), *Tim Cratchit's Christmas Carol: A Novel of Scrooge's Legacy* by Jim Piecuch (Simon & Schuster), *A Murder in Time* by Julie McElwain (Pegasus Books).

LAURA GROSS LITERARY AGENCY

E-mail: assistant@lg-la.com. **Website:** www.lg-la.com. Estab. 1988. Represents 30 clients.

- Prior to becoming an agent, Ms. Gross was an editor and ran a reading series.

REPRESENTS Nonfiction, novels.

- "I represent a broad range of both fiction and nonfiction writers. I am particularly interested in history, politics, and current affairs, and also love beautifully written literary fiction and intelligent thrillers."

HOW TO CONTACT Queries accepted via online form: https://lg-la.submittable.com/submit. No e-queries. "On the submission form, please include a concise but substantive query letter. You may include the first 6,000 words of your ms in the form as well. We will request further sample chapters from you at a later date if we think your work suits our list." There may be a delay of several weeks in responding to your query. Accepts simultaneous submissions.

TERMS Agent receives 15% commission on domestic sales; 20% commission on foreign sales. Offers written contract.

THE JOY HARRIS LITERARY AGENCY, INC.

1501 Broadway, Suite 2310, New York NY 10036. (212)924-6269. **Fax:** (212)540-5776. **E-mail:** submissions@joyharrisliterary.com. **Website:** www.joyharrisliterary.com. **Contact:** Joy Harris. Estab. 1990. Member of AAR. Represents more than 100 clients.

MEMBER AGENTS Joy Harris (literary fiction, well-written commercial fiction, narrative nonfiction across a broad range of topics, memoir, and biography); **Adam Reed** (literary fiction, science and technology, pop culture).

REPRESENTS Nonfiction, fiction. **Considers these nonfiction areas:** art, biography, creative nonfiction, memoir, popular culture, science, technology. **Considers these fiction areas:** commercial, literary.

- "We are not accepting poetry, screenplays, genre fiction, or self-help submissions at this time."

HOW TO CONTACT Please e-mail all submissions, comprised of a query letter, outline, or sample chapter, to submissions@joyharrisliterary.com. Accepts simultaneous submissions. Obtains most new clients through recommendations from clients and editors.

TERMS Agent receives 15% commission on domestic sales; 20% commission on foreign sales. Charges clients for some office expenses.

RECENT SALES *Smash Cut* by Brad Gooch, *The Other Paris* by Luc Sante, *The Past* by Tessa Hadley, *In a Dark Wood* by Joseph Luzzi.

HARTLINE LITERARY AGENCY

123 Queenston Dr., Pittsburgh PA 15235-5429. (412)829-2483. **E-mail:** joyce@hartlineliterary.com. **Website:** www.hartlineliterary.com. **Contact:** Joyce A. Hart. Many of the agents at this agency are generalists. This agency also handles inspirational and Christian works. Member of ACFW. Represents 200 clients.

MEMBER AGENTS Joyce A. Hart, principal agent (no unsolicited queries); **Jim Hart**, jim@hartlineliterary.com; **Diana Flegal**, diana@hartlineliterary.com; **Linda Glaz**, linda@hartlineliterary.com; **Andy Scheer**, andy@hartlineliterary.com; **Cyle Young**, cyle@hartlineliterary.com.

REPRESENTS Nonfiction, novels, novellas, juvenile books, scholarly books. **Considers these nonfiction areas:** diet/nutrition, health, history, parenting, philosophy, popular culture, recreation, religious, spirituality, women's issues. **Considers these fiction areas:** contemporary issues, family saga, humor, inspirational, new adult, religious, romance, suspense, women's, young adult.

- "This agency specializes in the Christian bookseller market." Actively seeking adult fiction, self-help, nutritional books, Christian living, devotional, and business. Does not want to receive erotica, LGBT, fantasy, horror.

HOW TO CONTACT E-queries preferred. Target one agent only. "All e-mail submissions sent to Hartline Agents should be sent as a Word doc (or in rich text file format from another word processing program) attached to an e-mail with 'Submission: [title, author's name, and word count]' in the subject line. A proposal is a single document, not a collection of files. Place the query letter in the e-mail itself. Do not send the entire proposal in the body of the e-mail or send PDF files." Further guidelines online. Accepts simultaneous submissions. Responds in 2 months to queries. Responds in 3 months to mss.

TERMS Agent receives 15% commission on domestic sales. Offers written contract.

JOHN HAWKINS & ASSOCIATES, INC.

80 Maiden Lane, Suite 1503, New York NY 10038. (212)807-7040. **E-mail:** jha@jhalit.com. **Website:** www.jhalit.com. **Contact:** Moses Cardona (rights and translations); Liz Free (permissions); William Reiss, literary agent; Warren Frazier, literary agent; Anne Hawkins, literary agent. Member of AAR. Represents 100+ clients.

MEMBER AGENTS William Reiss, reiss@jhalit. com (historical narratives, biography, slightly offbeat fiction and nonfiction, children's books, nature writing); Moses Cardona, moses@jhalit.com (commercial fiction, suspense, business, science, and multicultural fiction); Warren Frazier, frazier@jhalit.com (fiction; nonfiction interests include technology, history, world affairs, and foreign policy); Anne Hawkins ahawkins@jhalit.com (thrillers, literary fiction, serious nonfiction [science, history, public policy, medicine, and women's issues]).

REPRESENTS Novels, nonfiction. **Considers these nonfiction areas:** biography, business, history, medicine, politics, science, technology, women's issues. **Considers these fiction areas:** commercial, historical, literary, multicultural, suspense, thriller.

HOW TO CONTACT Query. Include the word "Query" in the subject line. For fiction, include 1-3 chapters of your book as a single Word attachment. For nonfiction, include your proposal as a single attachment. E-mail a particular agent directly if you are targeting one. Accepts simultaneous submissions. Responds in 1 month to queries.

TERMS Agent receives 15% commission on domestic sales; 20% commission on foreign sales. Charges clients for photocopying.

RECENT SALES *Forty Rooms* by Olga Grushin, *The Man Without a Shadow* by Joyce Carol Oates, *After Alice* by Gregory Maguire, *The Adventuress* by Tasha Alexander, *Harbour Street* by Ann Cleeves, *What Philosophy Can Do* by Gary Gutting.

✪ HELEN HELLER AGENCY, INC.

4-216 Heath St. W, Toronto, Ontario M5P 1N7 Canada. (416)489-0396. **E-mail:** info@helenhelleragency. com. **Website:** www.helenhelleragency.com. **Contact:** Helen Heller. Represents 30+ clients.

○ Prior to her current position, Ms. Heller worked for Cassell & Co. (England), was an editor for Harlequin Books, a senior editor for Avon Books, and editor in chief for Fitzhenry & Whiteside.

MEMBER AGENTS Helen Heller, helen@helen-helleragency.com (thrillers and front-list general fiction); Sarah Heller, sarah@helenhelleragency.com (front list commercial young adult and adult fiction, with a particular interest in high-concept historical fiction); Barbara Berson, barbara@helenhelleragency. com (literary fiction, nonfiction, young adult).

REPRESENTS Nonfiction, novels. **Considers these fiction areas:** commercial, crime, historical, literary, mainstream, thriller, young adult.

HOW TO CONTACT E-mail info@helenheller agency.com. Submit a brief synopsis, publishing history, author bio, and writing sample—pasted in the body of the e-mail. No attachments. Accepts simultaneous submissions. Responds within 3 months if interested. Accepts simultaneous submissions. Obtains most new clients through recommendations from others, solicitations.

RECENT SALES *Broken Promise* by Linwood Barclay, *When the Moon is Low* by Nadia Hashimi, *Fear the Darkness* by Becky Masterman.

TIPS "Whether you are an author searching for an agent, or whether an agent has approached you, it is in your best interest to first find out who the agent represents, what publishing houses has that agent sold to recently, and what foreign sales have been made. You should be able to go to the bookstore or search online and find the books the agent refers to. Many authors acknowledge their agents in the front or back or their books."

RICHARD HENSHAW GROUP

145 W. 28th St., 12th Floor, New York NY 10001. (212)414-1172. **E-mail:** submissions@henshaw.com. **Website:** www.richardhenshawgroup.com. **Contact:** Rich Henshaw. Member of AAR.

○ Prior to opening his agency, Mr. Henshaw served as an agent with Richard Curtis Associates, Inc.

REPRESENTS Novels. **Considers these fiction areas:** fantasy, historical, horror, literary, mainstream, mystery, police, romance, science fiction, thriller, young adult.

☛ "We specialize in popular fiction and nonfiction and are affiliated with a variety of writers' organizations. Our clients include *New*

York Times bestsellers and recipients of major awards in fiction and nonfiction. We only consider works between 65,000–150,000 words. We do not represent children's books, screenplays, short fiction, poetry, textbooks, scholarly works, or coffee-table books."

HOW TO CONTACT "Please feel free to submit a query letter in the form of an e-mail of fewer than 250 words to submissions@henshaw.com." No snail mail queries. Accepts simultaneous submissions.

TERMS Agent receives 15% commission on domestic sales; 20% commission on foreign sales. No written contract. Charges clients for photocopying and book orders.

TIPS "While we do not have any reason to believe that our submission guidelines will change in the near future, writers can find up-to-date submission policy information on our website. Always include a SASE with correct return postage."

THE JEFF HERMAN AGENCY, LLC

P.O. Box 1522, Stockbridge MA 01262. (413)298-0077. **Fax:** (413)298-8188. **E-mail:** jeff@jeffherman.com. **Website:** www.jeffherman.com. **Contact:** Jeffrey H. Herman. Estab. 1987. Represents 100 clients.

○ Prior to opening his agency, Mr. Herman served as a public relations executive.

MEMBER AGENTS Deborah Levine, vice president (nonfiction book doctor); Jeff Herman.

REPRESENTS Nonfiction. **Considers these nonfiction areas:** biography, business, computers, crafts, creative nonfiction, cultural interests, current affairs, diet/nutrition, economics, government, health, history, hobbies, how-to, humor, inspirational, investigative, law, medicine, metaphysics, money, multicultural, New Age, parenting, politics, psychology, regional, religious, science, self-help, sex, sociology, software, spirituality, technology, true crime, popular reference.

☛ This agency specializes in adult nonfiction.

HOW TO CONTACT Query with a SASE. Accepts simultaneous submissions.

TERMS Agent receives 15% commission on domestic sales. Offers written contract.

RONNIE ANN HERMAN

350 Central Park West, New York NY 10025. **E-mail:** ronnie@hermanagencyinc.com. **E-mail:** ronnie@hermanagencyinc.com. **Website:** www.hermanagencyinc.com. **Contact:** Ronnie Ann Herman. "We are a small boutique literary agency that represent authors and artists for the children's book market. We are only accepting submissions for middle-grade and young adult books at this time." Estab. 1999. Member of SCBWI. Represents 19 clients.

MEMBER AGENTS Ronnie Ann Herman, Katia Herman.

REPRESENTS Juvenile books. **Considers these nonfiction areas:** juvenile nonfiction. **Considers these fiction areas:** juvenile.

☛ Middle-grade and young adult (all genres).

HOW TO CONTACT Submit via e-mail Accepts simultaneous submissions.

HIDDEN VALUE GROUP

27758 Santa Margarita Pkwy., #361, Mission Viejo CA 92691. **E-mail:** bookquery@hiddenvaluegroup.com. **Website:** www.hiddenvaluegroup.com. **Contact:** Nancy Jernigan. Represents 55 clients.

MEMBER AGENTS Jeff Jernigan, Nancy Jernigan.

☛ The Hidden Value Group represents previously published Christian authors specializing in family, marriage, parenting, fiction, inspirational, self-help, business, and women's and men's issues. No poetry or short stories.

HOW TO CONTACT If you have been previously published (not including self-publishing), please include the following in your submission: a summary of ms (1-2 pages; it should include description of ms, target audience, and positioning statement that differentiates you from the rest), biography (background, experience, speaking experience, book sales history), marketing summary (how you will help support sales and marketing), and 2-3 sample chapters. Accepts queries to bookquery@hiddenvaluegroup.com or by postal mail with SASE. "Due to the volume of submissions we receive, we are unable to respond to all mail and e-mail inquiries."

TERMS Agent receives 15% commission on domestic sales; 15% commission on foreign sales. Offers written contract.

JULIE A. HILL AND ASSOCIATES, LLC

12997 Caminito Del Pasaje, Del Mar CA 92014. (858)259-2595. **Fax:** (858)259-2777. **E-mail:** Hillagent@aol.com. **Website:** www.publishersmarketplace/members/hillagent. **Contact:** Julie Hill.

MEMBER AGENTS Julie Hill, agent and principal.

REPRESENTS Nonfiction. **Considers these nonfiction areas:** architecture, art, biography, health, memoirs, New Age, self-help, technology, travel, women's issues, technology books, both for professionals and laypersons.

⌛ Specialties of the house are memoir, health, self-help, art, architecture, business/technology, both literary and reference travel. "We also do contract and sale consulting for authors who are working unagented. Consulting inquiries welcome."

HOW TO CONTACT E-query, or query via snail mail with SASE. Accepts simultaneous submissions. Responds in 4-6 weeks to queries.

TIPS A secondary website for this agency is www.publishersmarketplace.com/members/destiny, titled "Astrology for Writers."

HILL NADELL LITERARY AGENCY

6442 Santa Monica Blvd., Suite 201, Los Angeles CA 90038. (310)860-9605. **E-mail:** queries.hillnadell@gmail.com. **Website:** www.hillnadell.com. Represents 100 clients.

MEMBER AGENTS Bonnie Nadell (current affairs, food, memoir, narrative nonfiction; in fiction, she represents thrillers, upmarket women's, literary fiction); Dara Hyde (literary and genre fiction, narrative nonfiction, graphic novels, memoir, and the occasional young adult novel).

REPRESENTS Novels, nonfiction. **Considers these nonfiction areas:** biography, current affairs, environment, government, health, history, language, literature, medicine, popular culture, politics, science, technology, biography, narrative. **Considers these fiction areas:** literary, mainstream, thriller, women's, young adult.

HOW TO CONTACT Send a query and SASE. If you would like your materials returned, please include adequate postage. To submit electronically, send your query letter and the first chapter (no more than 15 pages double-spaced) to queries@hillnadell.com. No attachments. Due to the high volume of submissions the agency receives, it cannot guarantee a response to all e-queries. Accepts simultaneous submissions.

RECENT SALES *S Street Rising* by Ruben Castaneda; *Spare Parts* by Joshua Davis; *Men Explain Things to Me* by Rebecca Solnit; *Bellweather Rhapsody* by Kate Racculia.

HOLLOWAY LITERARY

Raleigh NC. **E-mail:** submissions@hollowayliteraryagency.com. **Website:** http://hollowayliteraryagency.com. **Contact:** Nikki Terpilowski. Estab. 2011. Member of AAR, ITW, RWA. Signatory of WGA.

MEMBER AGENTS Nikki Terpilowski (romance, women's fiction, Southern fiction, historical fiction, cozy mysteries); Rachel Burkot (young adult contemporary, women's fiction, upmarket/book club fiction, contemporary romance, Southern fiction, urban fiction, literary fiction); Ryann Wahl (literary fiction, upmarket fiction, and young adult).

REPRESENTS Fiction. **Considers these fiction areas:** erotica, ethnic, fantasy, glitz, historical, literary, mainstream, middle-grade, multicultural, regional, romance, thriller, women's, young adult.

⌛ "Note to self-published authors: While we are happy to receive submissions from authors who have previously self-published novels, we do not represent self-published works. Send us your unpublished mss only." Nikki is open to submissions and is selectively reviewing queries for cozy mysteries with culinary, historical or book/publishing industry themes written in the vein of Jaclyn Brady, Laura Childs, Julie Hyzy, and Lucy Arlington. Nikki also seeks women's fiction with strong magical realism similar to Meena van Praag's *The Dress Shop of Dreams*. She would love to find a wine-themed mystery series similar to Nadia Gordon's Sunny McCoskey series or Ellen Crosby's Wine County mysteries that combine culinary themes with lots of great Southern history.

HOW TO CONTACT Send your query and the first 15 pages of your ms pasted into the body of your e-mail to submissions@hollowayliteraryagency.com. In the subject header, write: "[agent name]/[title]/[genre]." You can expect a response in 4-6 weeks. Responds if interested. Accepts simultaneous submissions.

RECENT SALES A list of agency clients is available on the website.

THE HOLMES AGENCY

1942 Broadway, Suite 314, Boulder CO 80302. (720)443-8550. **E-mail:** kristina@holmesliterary.com. **Website:** www.holmesliterary.com. **Contact:** Kristina A. Holmes. "The Holmes Agency represents a wide range of nonfiction books, specializing in the categories of health and wellness, spirituality, psychology, relationships, sex, science, nature, environmental issues, business, women's issues, literary nonfiction,

NEW AGENT SPOTLIGHT

ALEXANDRA WEISS
JENNIFER DE CHIARA LITERARY AGENCY

www.jdlit.com
@akaweiss

ABOUT ALEXANDRA: Alexandra Weiss recently joined the agency as an associate agent and is currently building her client list. She's also a writer for www.bustle.com and PR manager for a Chicago circus. She previously worked as an acquisitions editor for an award-winning anthology and holds a BFA in creative writing and publishing from Columbia College Chicago.

SHE IS SEEKING: In young adult, she seeks realism, magical realism, science fiction (especially if it includes real science and or astronomy), paranormal, historical fiction, and fantasy. She's searching for beautiful writing, diverse voices, and subjects that go beyond the coming-of-age story. Pirates are cool, space travelers are awesome, and talented magicians are the way to her heart. For middle-grade and children's fiction, she is open to all genres. She loves adventurous, silly, out-of-the-box, and character-driven stories. Adult literary fiction and magical realism are welcome. She's *not* interested in nonfiction, heavy mysteries, horror, or thriller novels. If you have a short story collection, essay collection, or happen to use unique forms in your novel (letters, how-to, photos, poetry, or screenplays) and fit her other criteria, she's interested to hear from you.

HOW TO CONTACT: E-mail a query letter with the word "Query" in the subject line to alexweiss.jdlit@gmail.com. Send the first twenty pages in the body of the e-mail, along with a one-paragraph bio and one-paragraph pitch. Established picture book authors should e-mail a query and bio with the complete picture book manuscript pasted into the body of the e-mail.

memoir, cookbooks, and gift books." Member of AAR. Signatory of WGA.
MEMBER AGENTS Kristina A. Holmes.
REPRESENTS Considers these nonfiction areas: business, cooking, environment, foods, health, memoirs, psychology, science, sex, spirituality, women's issues.
HOW TO CONTACT E-mail your query and full book proposal to submissions@holmesliterary.com. Please note that this agency does not represent fiction

of any kind, true crime, poetry, or children's books. "In your query, please briefly describe your book (content, vision, purpose, and audience), as well as a bit about your background as an author (including notable platform highlights such as national media, a popular blog or website, speaking career, etc.)." Accepts simultaneous submissions.
TIPS "With 7 years of experience as a literary agent, I have had the privilege of working with many gifted

and inspiring writers. Some of them are best-selling authors and experts in their field, but what makes them truly special, from my perspective, is their deep passion for their work, and their commitment to guiding, educating, and inspiring people around the world. At The Holmes Agency, I am seeking authors focused on inspiring and helping positively transform readers' lives. I am open to queries, but please be aware that I don't generally represent authors without a platform."

HORNFISCHER LITERARY MANAGEMENT

P.O. Box 50544, Austin TX 78763. **E-mail:** queries@ hornfischerlit.com. **Website:** www.hornfischerlit. com. **Contact:** James D. Hornfischer, president.

○ Prior to opening his agency, Mr. Hornfischer held editorial positions at HarperCollins and McGraw-Hill. "My New York editorial background is useful in this regard. In 17 years as an agent, I've handled 12 *New York Times* nonfiction bestsellers."

REPRESENTS Nonfiction.

☛ Hornfischer Literary Management, L.P., is a literary agency with a strong track record handling a broad range of serious and commercial nonfiction.

HOW TO CONTACT E-queries preferred. Responds if interested. Accepts simultaneous submissions. Responds in 5-6 weeks to mailed submissions with SASE.

TERMS Agent receives 15% commission on domestic sales; receives 25% commission on foreign sales. Offers written contract.

TIPS "When you query agents and send out proposals, present yourself as someone who's in command of his material and comfortable in his own skin. Too many writers have a palpable sense of anxiety and insecurity. Take a deep breath and realize that—if you're good— someone in the publishing world will want you."

HSG AGENCY

37 W. 28th St, Eighth Floor, New York NY 10001. **E-mail:** channigan@hsgagency.com, jsalky@hsgagency.com, jgetzler@hsgagency.com, dburby@hsgagency.com, tprasanna@hsgagency.com, leigh@hsgagency.com. **Website:** http://hsgagency.com. Estab. 2011. Member of AAR. Signatory of WGA.

○ Prior to opening HSG Agency, Ms. Hannigan, Ms. Salky, and Mr. Getzler were agents at Russell & Volkening.

MEMBER AGENTS Carrie Hannigan (fiction and nonfiction children's books in the picture book and middle-grade age range, as well as adult women's fiction and select photography projects that would appeal to a large audience); **Jesseca Salky** (literary and mainstream fiction); **Josh Getzler** (foreign and historical fiction, women's fiction, straight-ahead historical fiction, thrillers, mysteries); **Danielle Burby** (young adult, women's fiction, mysteries, fantasy); **Tanusri Prasanna** (picture books, middle-grade, young adult, voice-driven narrative nonfiction on social justice issues); **Leigh Eisenman** (literary and commercial fiction, foodie/cookbooks, health and fitness, lifestyle, select narrative nonfiction).

REPRESENTS Nonfiction, novels, juvenile books. **Considers these nonfiction areas:** business, creative nonfiction, current affairs, diet/nutrition, education, environment, foods, memoirs, multicultural, photography, politics, psychology, science, self-help, women's issues, women's studies. **Considers these fiction areas:** adventure, commercial, contemporary issues, crime, detective, ethnic, family saga, historical, juvenile, literary, mainstream, middle-grade, multicultural, mystery, picture books, thriller, translation, women's, young adult.

HOW TO CONTACT Electronic submissions only. Send query letter and the first 5 pages of ms within an e-mail to the appropriate agent. Avoid submitting to multiple agents within the agency. Picture books submissions should include the entire ms. Accepts simultaneous submissions. Responds in 4-6 weeks.

RECENT SALES *The Beginner's Goodbye* by Anne Tyler (Knopf), *Blue Sea Burning* by Geoff Rodkey (Putnam), *The Partner Track* by Helen Wan (St. Martin's Press), *The Thrill of the Haunt* by E.J. Copperman (Berkley), *Aces Wild* by Erica Perl (Knopf Books for Young Readers), *Steve & Wessley: The Sea Monster* by Jennifer Morris (Scholastic), *Infinite Worlds* by Michael Soluri (Simon & Schuster).

⊘ ICM PARTNERS

730 Fifth Ave., New York NY 10019. (212)556-5600. **Website:** www.icmtalent.com. **Contact:** Literary Department. Member of AAR. Signatory of WGA. **REPRESENTS** Nonfiction, novels. **HOW TO CONTACT** The best way to query this agency is through a referral or by meeting an agent at an industry event, such as a writers conference.

NEW AGENT SPOTLIGHT

KELLY PETERSON
CORVISIERO LITERARY AGENCY

www.corvisieroagency.com
@yafantasyfan

ABOUT KELLY: Kelly Peterson has spent her whole life with a book in her hands. Whether it's from reading, writing, or daydreaming, her mind has always been up in the clouds wishing her fantasy stories would come true. A graduate of West Chester University, she earned her BSEd in English.

SHE IS SEEKING: Kelly is seeking middle-grade in the areas of fantasy, paranormal, and science fiction. She seeks young adult in the areas of fantasy (all types), steampunk, science fiction, paranormal, historical (nineteenth century and earlier, with strong heroines), dystopian (hold the cyborgs, the scorch, and diseases, please), sword and sorcery, a very selective few for contemporary romance, and any combination of the above with strong female main characters. In new adult, she likes the areas of fantasy, paranormal, romance, and historical romance. Lastly, she seeks adult fantasy and adult romance. Her truest passion is for young adult fantasy.

HOW TO CONTACT: Contact query@corvisieroagency.com. In the e-mail subject line, write "Query for Kelly: [Title]." For fiction, provide a query letter pasted into the body of your e-mail along with a short synopsis and the first five pages of your manuscript either attached as two separate Word files or pasted into the query e-mail.

INKLINGS LITERARY AGENCY

3419 Virginia Beach Blvd., #183, Virginia Beach VA 23452. (757)340-1070. **Fax:** (904)758-5440. **E-mail:** michelle@inklingsliterary.com. **E-mail:** query@inklingsliterary.com. **Website:** www.inklingsliterary.com. Inklings Literary Agency is a full-service, hands-on literary agency seeking submissions from established authors, as well as talented new authors. "We represent a broad range of commercial and literary fiction, as well as memoirs and true crime. We are not seeking other nonfiction, short stories, poetry, screenplays, or children's picture books." Estab. 2013. Member of RWA, SinC, HRW.

"We offer our clients interactive representation for their work, as well as developmental guidance for their author platforms, working with them as they grow."

MEMBER AGENTS Michelle Johnson, michelle@inklingsliterary.com (adult and young adult fiction interests include contemporary, suspense, thriller, mystery, horror, fantasy [including paranormal and supernatural elements within those genres],

romance of every level; also seeks nonfiction in the areas of memoir and true crime); **Dr. Jamie Bodnar Drowley**, jamie@inklingsliterary.com (new adult fiction in the areas of romance [all subgenres], fantasy [urban fantasy, light science fiction, steampunk], mystery, thrillers, young adult [all subgenres], and middle-grade); **Margaret Bail**, margaret@inklingsliterary.com (romance, science fiction, mystery, thrillers, action adventure, historical fiction, western, some fantasy, memoir, cookbooks, true crime); **Naomi Davis**, naomi@inklingsliterary.com (romance of any variety [including paranormal, fresh urban fantasy, general fantasy, new adult and light science fiction], young adult in any of those same genres, memoirs about living with disabilities, facing criticism, and mental illness); **Whitley Abell**, whitley@inklingsliterary.com (young adult, middle-grade, and select upmarket women's fiction); **Alex Barba**, alex@inklingsliterary.com (young adult); **Amanda Jain** (historical fiction [in all genres], women's, book club fiction, upmarket fiction, romance [particularly historical, suspenseful, or with a comedic bent], mysteries [particularly historical or cozy, or historical cozies]; also seeks narrative nonfiction in the areas of social history, archaeology, art history, and material culture).
REPRESENTS Nonfiction, novels, juvenile books. **Considers these nonfiction areas:** cooking, creative nonfiction, diet/nutrition, gay/lesbian, memoirs, true crime, women's issues. **Considers these fiction areas:** action, adventure, commercial, contemporary issues, crime, detective, erotica, ethnic, fantasy, feminist, gay, historical, horror, juvenile, lesbian, mainstream, metaphysical, middle-grade, military, multicultural, multimedia, mystery, new adult, New Age, occult, paranormal, police, psychic, regional, romance, science fiction, spiritual, sports, supernatural, suspense, thriller, urban fantasy, war, women's, young adult.
HOW TO CONTACT E-queries only. To query, type "Query (Agent Name)" plus the title of your novel in the subject line, then please send your query letter, short synopsis, and first 10 pages pasted into the body of the e-mail to query@inklingsliterary.com. Check the agency website to make sure that your targeted agent is currently open to submissions. Accepts simultaneous submissions. For queries, no response in 3 months is considered a rejection.

INKWELL MANAGEMENT, LLC

521 Fifth Ave., 26th Floor, New York NY 10175. (212)922-3500. **Fax:** (212)922-0535. **E-mail:** submissions@inkwellmanagement.com. **Website:** www.inkwellmanagement.com. Represents 500 clients.
MEMBER AGENTS Stephen Barbara (select adult fiction and nonfiction); William Callahan (nonfiction of all stripes—especially American history and memoir, pop culture and illustrated books, as well as voice-driven fiction that stands out from the crowd); Michael V. Carlisle; Catherine Drayton (books for children, young adults, and women readers); David Forrer (literary, commercial, historical, crime fiction, suspense/thriller, humorous nonfiction, and popular history); Alexis Hurley (literary and commercial fiction, memoir, narrative nonfiction); Nathaniel Jacks (memoir, narrative nonfiction, social sciences, health, current affairs, business, religion, popular history; fiction interests include literary, commercial, women's, young adult, historical, short stories); Jacqueline Murphy (fiction, children's books, graphic novels and illustrated works, compelling narrative nonfiction); Richard Pine; Eliza Rothstein (literary and commercial fiction, narrative nonfiction, memoir, popular science, and food writing); Emma Schlee (literary fiction, the occasional thriller, travel and adventure books, popular culture, and philosophy books); Hannah Schwartz; David Hale Smith; Lauren Smythe (smart narrative nonfiction [narrative journalism, modern history, biography, cultural criticism, personal essay, humor], personality-driven practical nonfiction [cookbooks, fashion, and style], and contemporary literary fiction); Kimberly Witherspoon; Monika Woods (literary and commercial fiction, young adult, memoir; also seeks compelling nonfiction in popular culture, science, and current affairs); Lena Yarbrough (literary fiction, upmarket commercial fiction, memoir, narrative nonfiction, history, investigative journalism, and cultural criticism); Jenny Witherell; Charlie Olson; Liz Parker (commercial and upmarket women's fiction; also seeks narrative, practical, and platform-driven nonfiction); George Lucas; Alyssa diPierro.
REPRESENTS Novels, nonfiction. **Considers these nonfiction areas:** biography, business, cooking, creative nonfiction, current affairs, foods, health, history, humor, memoirs, popular culture, religious, science. **Considers these fiction areas:** commercial, crime, historical, literary, middle-grade, picture books,

romance, short story collections, suspense, thriller, women's, young adult.

HOW TO CONTACT "In the body of your e-mail, please include a query letter and a short writing sample (1-2 chapters). We currently accept submissions in all genres except screenplays. Due to the volume of queries we receive, our response time may take up to 2 months. Feel free to put 'Query for [Agent Name]: [Your Book Title]' in the e-mail subject line." Accepts simultaneous submissions. Obtains most new clients through recommendations from others.

TERMS Agent receives 15% commission on domestic sales; 20% commission on foreign sales. Offers written contract.

TIPS "We will not read a ms before receiving a letter of inquiry."

INTERNATIONAL TRANSACTIONS, INC.

P.O. Box 97, Gila NM 88038-0097. (845)373-9696. **Fax:** (480)393-5162. **E-mail:** submission-nonfiction@intltrans.com; submission-fiction@intltrans.com. **Website:** www.intltrans.com. **Contact:** Peter Riva. Since 1975, Peter and Sandra Riva have specialized in international idea and intellectual property brokerage catering to multinational, multilingual, licensing and rights' representation of authors and publishers.

MEMBER AGENTS Peter Riva (nonfiction, fiction, illustrated, TV and movie rights placement); **Sandra Riva** (fiction, juvenile, biographies); **JoAnn Collins** (fiction, women's fiction, medical fiction).

REPRESENTS Nonfiction, novels, short story collections, juvenile books, illustrated books, anthologies. **Considers these nonfiction areas:** Americana, anthropology, archeology, architecture, art, autobiography, biography, business, computers, cooking, cultural interests, current affairs, diet/nutrition, design, environment, ethnic, film, foods, gay/lesbian, government, health, history, humor, inspirational, investigative, language, law, literature, medicine, memoirs, military, multicultural, music, photography, popular culture, politics, religious, satire, science, self-help, sports, technology, translation, true crime, war, women's issues, women's studies, young adult. **Considers these fiction areas:** action, adventure, commercial, crime, detective, erotica, experimental, family saga, feminist, gay, historical, humor, inspirational, lesbian, literary, mainstream, middle-grade, military, multicultural, mystery, new adult, police, satire, science fiction, spiritual, sports, sus-

pense, thriller, translation, war, westerns, women's, young adult, chick lit.

☛ "We specialize in large and small projects, helping qualified authors perfect material for publication." Always actively seeking intelligent, well-written innovative material that breaks new ground. Does not want to receive material influenced by TV (too much dialogue), a rehash of previous successful novels' themes, or poorly prepared material.

HOW TO CONTACT First, e-query and include an outline or synopsis. Put "Query: [Title]" in the e-mail subject line. Responds in 3 weeks to queries.

TERMS Agent receives 15% (25% on illustrated books) commission on domestic sales.

RECENT SALES Averaging 20+ book placements per year.

JABBERWOCKY LITERARY AGENCY

49 W. 45th St., New York NY 10036. (917)388-3010. **Website:** www.awfulagent.com. **Contact:** Joshua Bilmes. Memberships include SFWA. Represents 40 clients.

MEMBER AGENTS Joshua Bilmes, Eddie Schneider, Lisa Rodgers, Sam Morgan.

REPRESENTS Nonfiction, novels. **Considers these nonfiction areas:** autobiography, biography, business, cooking, current affairs, economics, film, foods, gay/lesbian, government, health, history, humor, language, law, literature, medicine, money, popular culture, politics, satire, science, sociology, sports, theater, war, women's issues, women's studies, young adult. **Considers these fiction areas:** action, adventure, contemporary issues, crime, detective, ethnic, family saga, fantasy, gay, glitz, historical, horror, humor, lesbian, literary, mainstream, middle-grade, police, psychic, regional, satire, science fiction, sports, supernatural, thriller, young adult.

☛ This agency represents quite a lot of genre fiction and is actively seeking to increase the amount of nonfiction projects. It does not handle children's or picture books. Book-length material only—no poetry, articles, or short fiction.

HOW TO CONTACT "We are currently open to unsolicited queries. No e-mail, phone, or fax queries, please. Query with a SASE. Please check our website, as there may be times during the year when we are not accepting queries. Only send a query letter; no ms material unless requested." Accepts simultaneous submissions. Responds in 3 weeks to queries. Obtains most new clients through solicitations, recommendation by current clients.

TERMS Agent receives 15% commission on domestic sales; 20% commission on foreign sales. Offers written contract, binding for 1 year. Charges clients for book purchases, photocopying, international book/ms mailing.

JANKLOW & NESBIT ASSOCIATES

445 Park Ave., New York NY 10022. (212)421-1700. **Fax:** (212)980-3671. **E-mail:** submissions@janklow. com. **Website:** www.janklowandnesbit.com. Estab. 1989.

MEMBER AGENTS Morton L. Janklow; Anne Sibbald; Lynn Nesbit; Luke Janklow; Cullen Stanley; PJ Mark (interests are eclectic—including short stories and literary novels; his nonfiction interests include journalism, popular culture, memoir/narrative, essays, and cultural criticism); **Richard Morris** (books that challenge our common assumptions—be it in the fields of cultural history, business, food, sports, science, or faith); **Paul Lucas** (literary and commercial fiction—focusing on literary thrillers, science fiction, and fantasy; also seeks narrative histories of ideas and objects, as well as biographies and popular science); **Emma Parry** (nonfiction by experts; also considers outstanding literary fiction and upmarket commercial fiction; not looking for children's books, middle-grade, or fantasy); **Alexandra Machinist; Kirby Kim** (formerly of WME); **Allison Hunter** (literary and commercial fiction, memoir, narrative nonfiction, cultural studies, and pop culture; she is always looking for funny female writers, great love stories, family epics, and for nonfiction projects that speak to the current cultural climate).

REPRESENTS Nonfiction, fiction.

HOW TO CONTACT Query via snail mail or e-mail. Include a cover letter, synopsis, and the first 10 pages if sending fiction (no attachments). For nonfiction, send a query and full outline. Address your submission to an individual agent. Accepts simultaneous submissions. Responds in 8 weeks to queries/mss. Obtains most new clients through recommendations from others.

J DE S ASSOCIATES, INC.

9 Shagbark Rd., Wilson Point, South Norwalk CT 06854. (203)838-7571. **E-mail:** Jdespoel@aol.com.

Website: www.jdesassociates.com. **Contact:** Jacques de Spoelberch.

○ Prior to opening his agency, Mr. de Spoelberch was an editor with Houghton Mifflin.

REPRESENTS Novels, nonfiction. **Considers these nonfiction areas:** biography, business, cultural interests, current affairs, economics, ethnic, government, health, history, law, medicine, metaphysics, military, New Age, politics, self-help, sociology, sports, translation. **Considers these fiction areas:** crime, detective, frontier, historical, juvenile, literary, mainstream, mystery, New Age, police, suspense, westerns, young adult.

HOW TO CONTACT "Brief queries by regular mail and e-mail are welcomed for fiction and nonfiction, but kindly do not include sample proposals or other material unless specifically requested to do so." Accepts simultaneous submissions. Responds in 2 months to queries.

TERMS Agent receives 15% commission on domestic sales; 20% commission on foreign sales. Charges clients for foreign postage and photocopying.

RECENT SALES Joshilyn Jackson's new novel *A Grown-Up Kind of Pretty* (Grand Central), Margaret George's final Tudor historical *Elizabeth I* (Penguin), the fifth in Leighton Gage's series of Brazilian thrillers *A Vine in the Blood* (Soho), Genevieve Graham's romance *Under the Same Sky* (Berkley Sensation).

THE CAROLYN JENKS AGENCY

30 Cambridge Park Dr., #3150, Cambridge MA 02140. (617)354-5099. **E-mail:** queries@carolynjenksagency. com. **Website:** www.carolynjenksagency.com. **Contact:** Carolyn Jenks. "This is a boutique agency, which means we give special attention to all of our clients. We act as a mentor to young professionals and students who are entering the profession, in addition to representing established writers." Estab. 1987. Member of AAR. Signatory of WGA.

MEMBER AGENTS Carolyn Jenks, Eric Wing. "See agency website for current member preferences" as well as a list of junior agents.

REPRESENTS Considers these nonfiction areas: architecture, art, autobiography, biography, business, cultural interests, current affairs, design, education, ethnic, gay/lesbian, government, history, juvenile nonfiction, language, law, literature, memoirs, metaphysics, military, money, music, New Age, religious, science, technology, translation, true crime, women's issues, women's studies. **Considers these fiction areas:** action, adventure, ethnic, experimental, family saga, fantasy, feminist, frontier, gay, historical, horror, humor, inspirational, juvenile, lesbian, literary, mainstream, mystery, psychic, regional, religious, science fiction, supernatural, thriller, westerns, women's, young adult.

HOW TO CONTACT Please submit a one-page query (including a brief bio) via the form on the agency website. "Due to the high volume of queries we receive, we are unable to respond to everyone. Queries are reviewed on a rolling basis, and we will follow up directly with the author if there is interest in a full ms. Queries should not be addressed to specific agents. All queries go directly to the director for distribution." Accepts simultaneous submissions.

TERMS Offers written contract, 1-3 years depending on the project. Requires 60-day notice before terminating contract.

TIPS "Do not make cold calls to the agency. E-mail contact only. Do not query for more than 1 project at a time. If possible, have a professional photograph of yourself ready to submit with your query, as it is important to be media-genic in today's marketplace. Be ready to discuss platform."

JERNIGAN LITERARY AGENCY

P.O. Box 741624, Dallas TX 75374. (972)722-4838. **E-mail:** jerniganliterary@gmail.com. **Contact:** Barry Jernigan. Estab. 2010. Represents 45 clients.

MEMBER AGENTS Barry Jernigan (eclectic tastes in nonfiction and fiction; nonfiction interests include women's issues, gay/lesbian, ethnic/cultural, memoirs, true crime; fiction interests include mystery, suspense, and thriller).

REPRESENTS Nonfiction, novels, movie scripts, feature film. **Considers these nonfiction areas:** biography, business, child guidance, current affairs, education, ethnic, health, history, how-to, memoirs, military, psychology, self-help, true crime. **Considers these fiction areas:** historical, mainstream, mystery, romance, thriller.

HOW TO CONTACT E-mail your query with a synopsis, brief bio, and the first few pages embedded (no attachments). No snail mail submissions or unsolicited full mss. Accepts simultaneous submissions. Responds in 2 weeks to queries.

TERMS Agent receives 15% commission.

JET LITERARY ASSOCIATES

941 Calle Mejia, #507, Santa Fe NM 87501. (505)780-0721. **E-mail:** etp@jetliterary.com. **Website:** www.jetliterary.wordpress.com. **Contact:** Liz Trupin-Pulli. Estab. 1975.

MEMBER AGENTS Liz Trupin-Pulli (adult fiction/nonfiction; romance, mysteries, parenting); **Jim Trupin** (adult fiction/nonfiction, military history, pop culture).

REPRESENTS Nonfiction, novels, short story collections.

☞ "JET was founded in New York in 1975, so we bring a wealth of knowledge and contacts, as well as quite a bit of expertise to our representation of writers." JET represents the full range of adult fiction and nonfiction, including humor and cookbooks. Does not want to receive young adult, science fiction, fantasy, horror, poetry, children's, how-to, or religious books.

HOW TO CONTACT E-query only at first. Accepts simultaneous submissions. Responds in 1 week to queries. Obtains most new clients through recommendations from others, solicitations, conferences.

TIPS "Do not write cute queries. Stick to a straightforward message that includes the title and what your book is about, why you are suited to write this particular book, and what you have written in the past (if anything), along with a bit of a bio."

⊙ KELLER MEDIA, INC.

578 Washington Blvd., No. 745, Marina del Rey CA 90292. (800)278-8706. **Website:** www.KellerMedia.com. **Contact:** Wendy Keller, senior agent (nonfiction only); Megan Close Zavala, associate agent (nonfiction and fiction). Estab. 1989. Member of the National Speakers Association.

○ Prior to becoming an agent, Ms. Keller was an award-winning journalist and worked for PR Newswire. Prior to her agenting career, Ms. Close Zavala read, reviewed, edited, rejected, and selected thousands of book and script projects for agencies, film companies, and publishing companies. She uses her background in entertainment and legal affairs in negotiating the best deals for her clients and in helping them think outside of the box.

REPRESENTS Nonfiction, fiction. **Considers these nonfiction areas:** archeology, autobiography, biography, business, crafts, creative nonfiction, current affairs, diet/nutrition, economics, environment, foods, gardening, health, history, hobbies, how-to, literature, money, parenting, popular culture, politics, psychology, science, self-help, sociology, true crime, women's issues. **Considers these fiction areas:** action, adventure, commercial, family saga, historical, literary, multicultural, mystery, new adult, police, regional, romance, suspense, thriller, women's.

☞ "All of our authors are highly credible experts, who have or want to create a significant platform in media, academia, politics, paid professional speaking, syndicated columns, and/or regular appearances in the media. For fiction submissions, we are interested in working with authors who have strong, fresh voices and who have unique stories (especially in the mystery/thriller/suspense and literary fiction genres)." Does not respond to scripts, teleplays, poetry, juvenile, anything religious or overtly political, picture books, illustrated books, young adult, science fiction, fantasy, first-person stories of mental or physical illness, wrongful incarceration, abduction by aliens, books channeled by aliens, demons, or dead celebrities.

HOW TO CONTACT To query, go to www.KellerMedia.com/query and fill in the form. "Please do not mail us anything unless requested to do so by a staff member." Accepts simultaneous submissions.

TIPS "Don't send a query to any agent (including us) unless you're certain they handle the type of book you're writing. Have your proposal in order before you query. Never make apologies for 'bad writing' or sloppy content. Please just get it right before you waste your 1 shot with us. Have something new, different, or interesting to say and be ready to dedicate your whole heart to marketing it. Marketing is everything in publishing these days. If you are submitting fiction to us, please make sure that your unique voice shines through."

NATASHA KERN LITERARY AGENCY

Website: www.natashakern.com. **Contact:** Natasha Kern. Memberships include RWA, MWA, SinC, The Authors Guild, and American Society of Journalists and Authors.

○ Prior to opening her agency, Ms. Kern worked as an editor and publicist for Simon & Schuster, Bantam, and Ballantine. This agency has sold more than 1,000 books.

REPRESENTS Nonfiction, novels. **Considers these nonfiction areas:** animals, child guidance, cultural interests, current affairs, environment, ethnic, gardening, health, inspirational, medicine, metaphysics, New Age, parenting, popular culture, psychology, religious, self-help, spirituality, women's issues, women's studies, investigative journalism. **Considers these fiction areas:** commercial, historical, inspirational, mainstream, multicultural, mystery, romance, suspense, women's.

☞ "This agency specializes in commercial fiction and nonfiction for adults. We are a full-service agency." Seeks historical novels from any country or time period, contemporary fiction (including novels with romance or suspense elements), and multicultural fiction. "We are also seeking inspirational fiction in a broad range of genres. Does not represent horror, true crime, erotica, children's books, short stories or novellas, poetry, screenplays, technical, photography, art/craft books, cookbooks, travel, or sports books.

HOW TO CONTACT This agency is currently closed to unsolicited fiction and nonfiction submissions. Accepts simultaneous submissions.

TERMS Agent receives 15% commission on domestic sales; 20% commission on foreign sales; 15% commission on film sales.

TIPS "Your chances of being accepted for representation will be greatly enhanced by going to our website first. Our idea of a dream client is someone who participates in a mutually respectful business relationship, is clear about needs and goals, and communicates about career planning. If we know what you need and want, we can help you achieve it. A dream client has a storytelling gift, a commitment to a writing career, a desire to learn and grow, and a passion for excellence. We want clients who are expressing their own unique voice and truly have something of their own to communicate. This client understands that many people have to work together for a book to succeed and that everything in publishing takes far longer than one imagines. Trust and communication are truly essential."

VIRGINIA KIDD LITERARY AGENCY, INC.

P.O. Box 278, Milford PA 18337. (570)296-6205. **Fax:** (570)296-7266. **E-mail:** subs@vk-agency.com. **Web-**

NEW AGENT SPOTLIGHT

ALBERT LEE
ZACHARY SHUSTER HARMSWORTH / KUHN PROJECTS

www.zshliterary.com
@albertbrooklyn

ABOUT ALBERT: Albert Lee brings nearly two decades of entertainment and publishing experience to Zachary Shuster Harmsworth / Kuhn Projects. Albert was the executive editor of *US Weekly* for 14 years. Before that, he was the founding editor in chief of www.mediabistro.com, associate editor at www.nerve.com, and wrote for *The Village Voice, Dance Magazine,* and more.

HE IS SEEKING: Nonfiction—especially narrative journalism, current affairs, pop culture, music, business and technology—and actively seeks titles with strong book-to-film/TV potential.

HOW TO CONTACT: Submit online: www.kuhnprojections.com/submissions.

---

site: www.vk-agency.com. Memberships include SFWA, SFRA. Represents 80 clients.
REPRESENTS Novels. **Considers these fiction areas:** fantasy, science fiction, speculative.

☞ This agency specializes in science fiction and fantasy. "The Virginia Kidd Literary Agency is one of the longest established, science fiction specialized literary agencies in the world—with almost half a century of rich experience in the science fiction and fantasy genres. Our client list reads like a top notch 'who's-who' of science fiction: Beth Bernobich, Gene Wolfe, Anne McCaffrey, Ted Chiang, Alan Dean Foster, and others set the bar very high indeed. We welcome queries from prospective and published authors."

HOW TO CONTACT Snail mail queries only. Accepts simultaneous submissions.
TERMS Agent receives 15% commission on domestic sales; 20-25% commission on foreign sales; 20% commission on film sales.
RECENT SALES *Sagramanda* by Alan Dean Foster (Pyr), *Incredible Good Fortune* by Ursula K. Le Guin (Shambhala), *The Wizard and Soldier of Sidon* by Gene Wolfe (Tor), *Voices and Powers* by Ursula K. Le Guin (Harcourt), *Galileo's Children* by Gardner Dozois (Pyr).
TIPS "If you have a completed novel that is of extraordinary quality, please send us a query."

HARVEY KLINGER, INC.

300 W. 55th St., Suite 11V, New York NY 10019. (212)581-7068. **E-mail:** queries@harveyklinger.com. **Website:** www.harveyklinger.com. **Contact:** Harvey Klinger. Always interested in considering new clients, both published and unpublished. Member of AAR. Represents 100 clients.
MEMBER AGENTS Harvey Kliinger; David Dunton (popular culture, music-related books, literary fiction, young adult, fiction, memoirs); **Sara Crowe** (children's and young adult authors, adult fiction and nonfiction, foreign rights sales); **Andrea Somberg** (literary fiction, commercial fiction, romance, science fiction, fantasy, mysteries/thrillers, young adult, middle-grade, quality narrative nonfiction, popular culture, how-to, self-help, humor, interior design, cookbooks, health/fitness); **Wendy Levinson** (literary

and commercial fiction, occasional children's young adult or middle-grade, wide variety of nonfiction).

REPRESENTS Nonfiction, novels, juvenile books. **Considers these nonfiction areas:** autobiography, biography, business, child guidance, cooking, crafts, creative nonfiction, cultural interests, current affairs, diet/nutrition, foods, health, history, how-to, investigative, literature, medicine, memoirs, psychology, science, self-help, spirituality, sports, technology, true crime, women's issues, women's studies, young adult. **Considers these fiction areas:** action, adventure, commercial, crime, detective, erotica, family saga, fantasy, gay, glitz, historical, horror, juvenile, lesbian, literary, mainstream, middle-grade, mystery, police, suspense, thriller, women's, young adult.

☛ This agency specializes in big, mainstream, contemporary fiction and nonfiction.

HOW TO CONTACT Use submission form on the website, or query with SASE via snail mail. No phone or fax queries. Don't send unsolicited mss or e-mail attachments. Make submission letter to the point and as brief as possible. Accepts simultaneous submissions. Responds in 4 weeks to queries, if interested. Obtains most new clients through recommendations from others.

TERMS Agent receives 15% commission on domestic sales; 25% commission on foreign sales.

RECENT SALES *Land of the Afternoon Sun* by Barbara Wood, *I Am Not a Serial Killer* by Dan Wells, *Me, Myself and Us* by Brian Little, *The Secret of Magic* by Deborah Johnson, *Children of the Mist* by Paula Quinn.

THE KNIGHT AGENCY

570 East Ave., Madison GA 30650. **E-mail:** submissions@knightagency.net. **Website:** http://knightagency.net/. **Contact:** Elaine Spencer. The Knight Agency is a full-service literary agency with a focus on genre-based adult fiction, young adult, middle-grade and select nonfiction projects. Estab. 1996. Member of AAR, SCWBI, WFA, SFWA, RWA. Represents 200+ clients.

MEMBER AGENTS Deidre Knight (romance, women's fiction, erotica, commercial fiction, inspirational, memoir and nonfiction narrative, personal finance, true crime, business, popular culture, self-help, religion, and health); **Pamela Harty** (romance, women's fiction, young adult, business, motivational, diet and health, memoir, parenting, pop culture, and true crime); **Elaine Spencer** (romance [single title and

category], women's fiction, commercial "book-club" fiction, cozy mysteries, young adult, and middle-grade); **Lucienne Diver** (fantasy, science fiction, romance, suspense, and young adult); **Nephele Tempest** (literary fiction, commercial fiction, women's fiction, fantasy, science fiction, romantic suspense, paranormal romance, contemporary romance, historical fiction, young adult, and middle-grade); **Melissa Jeglinski** (romance [contemporary, category, historical, inspirational], young adult, middle-grade, women's fiction, mystery); **Kristy Hunter** (romance, women's fiction, commercial fiction, young adult, and middle-grade), **Travis Pennington** (young adult, middle-grade, mysteries, thrillers, commercial fiction, and romance [nothing paranormal/fantasy in any genre for now]).

REPRESENTS Nonfiction, novels. **Considers these nonfiction areas:** current affairs, diet/nutrition, design, economics, gay/lesbian, health, juvenile nonfiction, memoirs, politics, self-help, sociology, travel, true crime, women's issues, young adult. **Considers these fiction areas:** commercial, fantasy, middle-grade, new adult, romance, science fiction, thriller, women's, young adult.

☛ Actively seeking romance in all subgenres (both category and single-title), science fiction, fantasy, historical fiction, mysteries in both traditional and cozy arena, middle-grade, young adult, nonfiction, and memoir. Does not want to receive screenplays, short stories, poetry, essays, or children's picture books.

HOW TO CONTACT E-queries only. "Your submission should include a one-page query letter and the first 5 pages of your ms. All text must be contained in the body of your e-mail. Attachments will not be opened nor included in the consideration of your work. Queries must be addressed to a specific agent. Please do not query multiple agents at our agency." Accepts simultaneous submissions.

LINDA KONNER LITERARY AGENCY

10 W. 15th St., Suite 1918, New York NY 10011. (212)691-3419. **E-mail:** ldkonner@cs.com. **Website:** www.lindakonnerliteraryagency.com. **Contact:** Linda Konner. Member of AAR, ASJA. Signatory of WGA. Represents 85 clients.

REPRESENTS Nonfiction. **Considers these nonfiction areas:** gay/lesbian, health, medicine, money, parenting, popular culture, psychology, science, self-help, women's issues, biography (celebrity), African American and Latino issues, relationships, popular science.

☛ This agency specializes in health, self-help, and how-to books. Authors/co-authors must be top experts in their field with a substantial media platform.

HOW TO CONTACT Query by e-mail or by mail with SASE. Include a synopsis, author bio, and (if applicable) sufficient return postage. Prefers to read materials exclusively for 2 weeks. Obtains most new clients through recommendations from others, occasional solicitation among established authors/journalists.

TERMS Agent receives 15% commission on domestic sales; 25% commission on foreign sales. Offers written contract. Charges one-time fee for domestic expenses; additional expenses may be incurred for foreign sales.

RECENT SALES *How Bad Do You Want It?* by Matt Fitzgerald (Velo), *What to Eat When You're Pregnant* by Nicole Avena (Ten Speed Press), *1920: The Year that Made the Decade Roar* by Eric Burns (Pegasus Books).

STUART KRICHEVSKY LITERARY AGENCY, INC.

6 E. 39th St., Suite 500, New York NY 10016. (212)725-5288. Fax: (212)725-5275. **Website:** www.skagency.com. Member of AAR.

MEMBER AGENTS Stuart Krichevsky, query@skagency.com (narrative nonfiction, literary journalism, and literary and commercial fiction); Ross Harris, rhquery@skagency.com (voice-driven humor and memoir, books on popular culture and our society, narrative nonfiction, and literary fiction); David Patterson, dp@skagency.com (upmarket narrative nonfiction and literary fiction—written by historians, journalists, and thought leaders).

REPRESENTS Novels, nonfiction. **Considers these nonfiction areas:** creative nonfiction, humor, memoirs, popular culture. **Considers these fiction areas:** commercial, contemporary issues, literary.

HOW TO CONTACT Please send a query letter and up to 10 pages of your ms or proposal in the body of an e-mail (not an attachment) to 1 of the e-mail addresses. No attachments. Responds if interested. Accepts simultaneous submissions.

EDITE KROLL LITERARY AGENCY, INC.

20 Cross St., Saco ME 04072. (207)283-8797. **Fax:** (207)283-8799. **E-mail:** ekroll@maine.rr.com. **Contact:** Edite Kroll. Represents 45 clients.

○ Prior to opening her agency, Ms. Kroll served as a book editor and translator.

☛ "We represent writers and writer-artists of both adult and children's books. We have a special focus on international feminist writers, women writers of nonfiction, and artists who write their own books (including children's and humor books)." Actively seeking artists who write their own books and international feminists who write in English. Does not represent genre fiction (mysteries, thrillers, diet, cookery, etc.), photography books, coffee table books, romance, or commercial fiction.

HOW TO CONTACT Query with SASE or by e-mail. Submit outline/proposal, synopsis, 1-2 sample chapters, author bio, and the entire ms (or dummy) if sending a picture book. No phone queries. Accepts simultaneous submissions.

TERMS Agent receives 15% commission on domestic sales; 20% commission on foreign sales.

RECENT SALES Sold 12 domestic titles and 30 foreign titles in the last year. Clients include Shel Silverstein and Charlotte Zolotow estates.

TIPS "Please do your research so you won't send me books/proposals I specifically excluded."

THE LA LITERARY AGENCY

P.O. Box 46370, Los Angeles CA 90046. (323)654-5288. **E-mail:** ann@laliteraryagency.com; mail@laliteraryagency.com. **Website:** www.laliteraryagency.com. **Contact:** Ann Cashman.

○ Prior to opening the agency, Ms. Lasher worked in New York at Prentice-Hall, Liveright, and Random House.

MEMBER AGENTS Ann Cashman, Eric Lasher, Maureen Lasher.

REPRESENTS Nonfiction, novels. **Considers these nonfiction areas:** Americana, animals, anthropology, archeology, art, autobiography, biography, business, child guidance, cooking, crafts, creative nonfiction, cultural interests, current affairs, education, government, health, history, investigative, literature, memoirs, multicultural, music, parenting, popular culture, politics, psychology, recreation, science, sports, technology, true crime. **Considers these fiction areas:** action, adventure, commercial, contemporary issues, crime, detective, family saga, feminist, historical, literary, mainstream, mystery, suspense, thriller, women's.

HOW TO CONTACT To submit nonfiction, send a query letter and book proposal. To submit fiction, send a query letter and full ms as an attachment. Accepts simultaneous submissions.

RECENT SALES *The Fourth Trimester* by Susan Brink (University of California Press), *Rebels in Paradise* by Hunter Drohojowska-Philp (Holt), *La Cucina Mexicana* by Marilyn Tausend (UC Press), *The Orpheus Clock* by Simon Goodman (Scribner).

PETER LAMPACK AGENCY, INC.

The Empire State Building, 350 Fifth Ave., Suite 5300, New York NY 10118. (212)687-9106. **Fax:** (212)687-9109. **E-mail:** andrew@peterlampackagency.com. **Website:** www.peterlampackagency.com. **Contact:** Andrew Lampack. "The Peter Lampack Agency specializes in both commercial and literary fiction, as well as nonfiction by recognized experts in a given field."

REPRESENTS Nonfiction, novels. **Considers these fiction areas:** action, adventure, commercial, crime, detective, family saga, literary, mainstream, mystery, police, suspense, thriller.

⌐ "This agency specializes in commercial fiction and nonfiction by recognized experts." Actively seeking literary and commercial fiction in the following categories: adventure, action, thrillers, mysteries, suspense, and psychological thrillers. Does not want to receive horror, romance, science fiction, westerns, historical literary fiction, or academic material.

HOW TO CONTACT The Peter Lampack Agency no longer accepts material through postal mail. E-queries only. When submitting, you should include a cover letter, author biography, and a synopsis of 1-2 pages. Please do not send more than 1 sample chapter of your ms at a time. "Due to the extremely high volume of submissions, we ask that you allow 4-6 weeks for a response."

TERMS Agent receives 15% commission on domestic sales; 20% commission on foreign sales.

RECENT SALES *The Assassin* by Clive Cussler and Justin Scott, *The Solomon Curse* by Clive Cussler and Russell Blake, *Patriot* by Ted Bell, *The Good Story* by J.M. Coetzee and Arabella Kurtz, *Police State: How America's Cops Get Away With Murder* by Gerry Spence.

TIPS "Submit only your best work for consideration. Have a very specific agenda of goals you wish your prospective agent to accomplish for you. Provide the agent with a comprehensive statement of your credentials—educational and professional accomplishments."

LAURA LANGLIE, LITERARY AGENT

147-149 Green St., Hudson NY 12534. (518)828-4708. **Fax:** (518)828-4787. **E-mail:** laura@lauralanglie.com. **Contact:** Laura Langlie. Represents 25 clients.

⭕ Prior to opening her agency, Ms. Langlie worked in publishing for 7 years and as an agent at Kidde, Hoyt & Picard for 6 years.

REPRESENTS **Considers these nonfiction areas:** autobiography, biography, cultural interests, current affairs, environment, film, gay/lesbian, history, humor, language, law, literature, memoirs, music, popular culture, politics, psychology, theater, women's studies. **Considers these fiction areas:** commercial, crime, detective, ethnic, feminist, gay, historical, humor, juvenile, lesbian, literary, mainstream, multicultural, mystery, police, romance, suspense, thriller, young adult, mainstream.

⌐ "I'm very involved with and committed to my clients. Most of my clients come to me via recommendations from other agents, clients, and editors. I've met very few at conferences. I've often sought out writers for projects, and I still find new clients via the traditional query letter." Does not want to receive how-to, children's picture books, hardcore science fiction, poetry, men's adventure, or erotica.

HOW TO CONTACT Query with SASE. Accepts queries via fax. Accepts simultaneous submissions. Responds in 1 week to queries. Responds in 1 month to mss. Obtains most new clients through recommendations, submissions.

TERMS Agent receives 15% commission on domestic sales; 20% commission on foreign and dramatic sales. No written contract.

RECENT SALES *The Evening Spider* by Emily Arsenault (William Morrow), *The Swans of 5th Avenue* by Melanie Benjamin (Delacorte Press).

TIPS "Be complete, forthright, and clear in your communications. Do your research as to what a particular agent represents."

⊘ MICHAEL LARSEN/ELIZABETH POMADA, LITERARY AGENTS

1029 Jones St., San Francisco CA 94109. (415)673-0939. **E-mail:** larsenpoma@aol.com. **Website:** www.larsen-pomada.com. **Contact:** Mike Larsen, Elizabeth Pomada. Member of AAR, Authors Guild, ASJA, WNBA, California Writers Club, National Speakers Association. Represents 100 clients.

MEMBER AGENTS Michael Larsen (nonfiction), Elizabeth Pomada (fiction and narrative nonfiction). **REPRESENTS** Nonfiction, novels. **Considers these nonfiction areas:** biography, business, current affairs, economics, health, history, how-to, inspirational, medicine, memoirs, money, New Age, popular culture, politics, self-help, sociology, futurism. **Considers these fiction areas:** literary, mainstream, mystery, romance, thriller, women's.

☞ We have diverse tastes. We look for fresh voices and new ideas. We handle literary, commercial, genre fiction, and the full range of nonfiction books. Does not want to receive children's books, plays, short stories, screenplays, pornography, poetry, or stories of abuse.

HOW TO CONTACT As of early 2016, this agency is closed to submissions for some time.

TERMS Agent receives 15% commission on domestic sales; 20% (30% for Asia) commission on foreign sales. May charge for printing, postage for multiple submissions, foreign mail, foreign phone calls, galleys, books, legal fees.

WRITERS CONFERENCES This agency organizes the annual San Francisco Writers Conference (www.sfwriters.org).

TIPS "We love helping writers get the rewards and recognition they deserve. If you can write books that meet the needs of the marketplace and you can promote your books, now is the best time ever to be a writer. We must find new writers to make a living, so we are very eager to hear from new writers whose work will interest large houses, and nonfiction writers who can promote their books. For a list of recent sales, helpful info, and ways to make yourself irresistible to any publisher, please visit our website."

◎ THE STEVE LAUBE AGENCY

24 W. Camelback Rd., A-635, Phoenix AZ 85013. (602)336-8910. **Website:** www.stevelaube.com. Memberships include CBA, RWA, Authors Guild. Represents 250+ clients.

○ Prior to becoming an agent, Mr. Laube worked as a Christian bookseller and for 11 years as editorial director of nonfiction with Bethany House Publishers (named editor of the year

by AWSA). Mrs. Murray was an accomplished novelist and agent for 15 years. Mrs. Ball was an executive editor with Tyndale, Multnomah, Zondervan, and B&H Publishing. Mr. Balow was marketing director for the Left Behind series at Tyndale.

MEMBER AGENTS Steve Laube (president), Tamela Hancock Murray, Karen Ball, Dan Balow.

REPRESENTS Nonfiction, novels. **Considers these nonfiction areas:** inspirational, religious, spirituality. **Considers these fiction areas:** fantasy, inspirational, religious, science fiction.

☞ Primarily serves the Christian market (CBA). Actively seeking Christian fiction and Christian nonfiction. Does not want to receive children's picture books, poetry, or cookbooks.

HOW TO CONTACT Submit proposal package, outline, 3 sample chapters, SASE. For e-mail submissions, attach the entire submission proposal as a Word doc or PDF. Consult website for more guidelines, because queries are sent to assistants, and the assistants' e-mail addresses may change. Accepts simultaneous submissions. Responds in 6-8 weeks to queries.

TERMS Agent receives 15% commission on domestic sales; 20% commission on foreign sales. Offers written contract; 30-day notice must be given to terminate contract.

RECENT SALES Clients include Cindy Woodsmall, Susan May Warren, Lisa Bergren, Lynette Eason, Deborah Raney, Allison Bottke, H. Norman Wright, Ellie Kay, Karol Ladd, Stephen M. Miller, Judith Pella, Nancy Pearcey, William Lane Craig, Elizabeth Goddard, Pamela Tracy, Kim Vogel Sawyer, Mesu Andrews, Mary Hunt, Hugh Ross, Roseanna White, Bill and Pam Farrel, and Ronie Kendig.

LAUNCHBOOKS LITERARY AGENCY

E-mail: david@launchbooks.com. **Website:** www.launchbooks.com. **Contact:** David Fugate. Represents 45 clients.

○ Mr. Fugate has been an agent for 20 years and has successfully represented more than 1,000 book titles. He left another agency to start LaunchBooks in 2005.

REPRESENTS Nonfiction, novels. **Considers these nonfiction areas:** autobiography, biography, business, creative nonfiction, current affairs, diet/nutrition, environment, health, history, how-to, humor, investigative, medicine, memoirs, money, parenting, popular culture, politics, psychology, recreation, science, self-help, sex, sociology, sports, technology, travel. **Considers these fiction areas:** action, adventure, crime, fantasy, horror, mainstream, military, satire, science fiction, suspense, thriller, urban fantasy, war, westerns, young adult.

☛ "We're looking for genre-breaking fiction. Do you have the next *The Martian*? Or maybe the next *Red Rising*, *Ready Player One*, *Ancillary Sword*, or *The Bone Clocks*? We're on the lookout for fun, engaging, contemporary novels that appeal to a broad audience. In nonfiction, we're interested in a broad range of topics. Check www.launchbooks.com/submissions for a complete list."

HOW TO CONTACT Query via e-mail. Accepts simultaneous submissions. Responds in 1 week to queries. Responds in 4 weeks to mss. Obtains most new clients through recommendations from others, solicitations.

TERMS Agent receives 15% commission on domestic sales; 25% commission on foreign sales. Offers written contract; 30-day notice to terminate contract. Charges occur very seldom. This agency's agreement limits any charges to $50 unless the author gives a written consent.

RECENT SALES *The Martian* by Andy Weir (Random House), *The Remaining: Allegiance* by DJ Molles (Orbit), *The Fold* by Peter Clines (Crown), *Faster, Higher, Stronger* by Mark McClusky (Hudson Street Press), *Fluent in Three Months* by Benny Lewis (HarperOne).

◎ SARAH LAZIN BOOKS

19 W. 21st St., Suite 501, New York NY 10010. (212)989-5757. **Fax:** (212)989-1393. **E-mail:** julia@lazinbooks.com. **Website:** www.lazinbooks.com. **Contact:** Julia Conrad. Estab. 1984. Member of AAR.
MEMBER AGENTS Sarah Lazin, Julia Conrad (subsidiary rights).
REPRESENTS Nonfiction, novels. **Considers these nonfiction areas:** autobiography, biography, business, current affairs, environment, history, investigative, memoirs, music, parenting, photography, popular culture, politics, women's studies. **Considers these fiction areas:** commercial, literary, short story collections.

☛ Works with companies who package their books; handles some photography.

HOW TO CONTACT As of 2016: "We accept submissions through referral only." Only accepts queries on referral.
TERMS Agent receives 15% commission on domestic sales; 20% commission on foreign sales.

⊘ THE NED LEAVITT AGENCY

70 Wooster St., Suite 4F, New York NY 10012. (212)334-0999. **Website:** www.nedleavittagency.com. **Contact:** Ned Leavitt, Jillian Sweeney. Member of AAR. Represents 40+ clients.
MEMBER AGENTS Ned Leavitt, founder and agent; **Britta Alexander**, agent; **Jillian Sweeney**, agent.
REPRESENTS Novels.

☛ "We are small in size, but intensely dedicated to our authors and to supporting excellent and unique writing."

HOW TO CONTACT This agency now only takes queries/submissions through referred clients. Do *not* cold query.
TIPS Look online for this agency's recently changed submission guidelines. "For guidance in the writing process, we strongly recommend the following books: *Writing Down The Bones* by Nathalie Goldberg and *Bird by Bird* by Anne Lamott.

ROBERT LECKER AGENCY

4055 Melrose Ave., Montreal, Quebec H4A 2S5 Canada. **E-mail:** robert.lecker@gmail.com. **Website:** www.leckeragency.com. **Contact:** Robert Lecker. Represents 20 clients.

◖ Prior to becoming an agent, Mr. Lecker was the co-founder and publisher of ECW Press, and professor of English literature at McGill University. He has 30 years of experience in book and magazine publishing.

MEMBER AGENTS Robert Lecker (popular culture, music); **Mary Williams** (travel, food, popular science).
REPRESENTS Nonfiction, novels. **Considers these nonfiction areas:** autobiography, biography, cooking, cultural interests, dance, diet/nutrition, ethnic, film, foods, how-to, language, literature, music, popular culture, science, technology, theater. **Considers these fiction areas:** action, adventure, crime, detective, erotica, literary, mainstream, mystery, police, suspense, thriller.

☛ RLA specializes in books about popular culture, popular science, music, entertainment, food, and travel. The agency responds to articulate, innovative proposals within 2 weeks. We do not represent children's literature, screenplays, poetry, self-help books, or spiritual guides.

HOW TO CONTACT E-query. In the subject line, write: "New Submission QUERY." Accepts simultaneous submissions. Obtains most new clients through recommendations from others, conferences, interest in website.

TERMS Agent receives 15% commission on domestic sales; 15-20% commission on foreign sales.

THE LESHNE AGENCY

16 W. 23rd St., Fourth Floor, New York NY 10010. **E-mail:** info@leshneagency.com. **E-mail:** submissions@leshneagency.com. **Website:** www.leshneagency.com. **Contact:** Lisa Leshne, agent and owner. "We are a full-service literary agency committed to the success of our authors. We represent a select and growing number of established and new writers interested in developing long-term relationships. We work closely with authors to develop their ideas for impact and audience reach, across print, digital, and other formats—providing hands-on guidance and networking for success. We also offer our services to authors who may wish to explore the self-publishing route via a variety of platforms." Member of AAR. Signatory of WGA.

○ Prior to founding the agency, Ms. Leshne was a literary agent at LJK Literary.

MEMBER AGENTS Lisa Leshne, agent and owner; Sandy Hodgman, director of foreign rights.

REPRESENTS Considers these nonfiction areas: business, creative nonfiction, health, memoirs, parenting, politics, sports. Considers these fiction areas: commercial, middle-grade, young adult.

☞ Wants authors across all genres. "We are interested in narrative, memoir, and prescriptive nonfiction—with a particular interest in sports, wellness, business, politics, and parenting topics. We will also look at truly terrific commercial fiction, young adult, and middle-grade books."

HOW TO CONTACT "Submit all materials in the body of an e-mail. No attachments. Be sure to include the word 'QUERY' and the title of your ms in the subject line. Include brief synopsis, table of contents or chapter outline, 10 sample pages, bio, any previous publications, word count, how much of the ms is complete, and the best way to reach you." Accepts simultaneous submissions.

LEVINE GREENBERG ROSTAN LITERARY AGENCY, INC.

307 Seventh Ave., Suite 2407, New York NY 10001. (212)337-0934. **Fax:** (212)337-0948. **E-mail:** submit@lgrliterary.com. **Website:** www.lgrliterary.com. Member of AAR. Represents 250 clients.

○ Prior to opening his agency, Mr. Levine served as vice president of the Bank Street College of Education.

MEMBER AGENTS Jim Levine (nonfiction—including business, science, narrative nonfiction, social and political issues, psychology, health, spirituality, parenting); Stephanie Rostan (adult and young adult fiction; nonfiction interests include parenting, health and wellness, sports, memoir); Melissa Rowland; Daniel Greenberg (popular culture, narrative nonfiction, memoir, humor; also seeks literary fiction); Victoria Skurnick; Danielle Svetcov (nonfiction); Lindsay Edgecombe (narrative nonfiction, memoir, lifestyle and health, illustrated books; also seeks literary fiction); Monika Verma (nonfiction interests include humor, pop culture, memoir, narrative nonfiction, style, and fashion; also represents some young adult fiction [paranormal, historical, contemporary]); Kerry Sparks (young adult, middle-grade, select adult fiction, and occasional nonfiction); Tim Wojcik (food narratives, humor, pop culture, popular history, science, literary fiction); Arielle Eckstut (no queries).

REPRESENTS Nonfiction, novels. **Considers these nonfiction areas:** business, creative nonfiction, health, history, humor, memoirs, parenting, popular culture, science, spirituality, sports. **Considers these fiction areas:** literary, mainstream, middle-grade, young adult.

HOW TO CONTACT E-query to submit@lgrliterary.com, or use the agency's online submission form. "If you would like to direct your query to 1 of our agents specifically, please feel free to name them in the online form or in the e-mail you send." Cannot respond to submissions by mail. Do not attach more than 50 pages. "Due to the volume of submissions we receive, we are unable to respond to each individually. If we would like more information about your project, we'll contact you within 3 weeks (though we do get backed up on occasion)." Accepts simultaneous submissions.

Obtains most new clients through recommendations from others.

TERMS Agent receives 15% commission on domestic sales; 20% commission on foreign sales. Offers written contract.

TIPS "We focus on editorial development, business representation, publicity, and marketing strategy."

PAUL S. LEVINE LITERARY AGENCY

(310)450-6711. **Fax:** (310)450-0181. **E-mail:** paul@paulslevinelit.com. **Website:** www.paulslevinelit.com. **Contact:** Paul S. Levine. Other memberships include the State Bar of California. Represents 100 clients.

MEMBER AGENTS Paul S. Levine (children's and young adult fiction; also seeks adult fiction and nonfiction excluding science fiction, fantasy, and horror); **Loren R. Grossman** (archeology, art/photography, architecture, parenting, coffee table books, gardening, education, health, science, law, religion, memoir, sociology).

HOW TO CONTACT E-mail queries preferred. Send a one-page, single-spaced query letter. In your query letter, note your target market with a summary of specifics on how your work differs from other authors' previously published work. Accepts simultaneous submissions.

TERMS Agent receives 15% commission on domestic sales. Offers written contract. Charges for postage and actual, out-of-pocket costs only.

WRITERS CONFERENCES Willamette Writers Conference, San Francisco Writers Conference, Santa Barbara Writers Conference, Las Vegas Writing Workshop, and many others.

LIPPINCOTT MASSIE MCQUILKIN

27 W. 20th St., Suite 305, New York NY 10011. **E-mail:** info@lmqlit.com. **Website:** www.lmqlit.com.

MEMBER AGENTS Laney Katz Becker, laney@lmqlit.com (book club fiction, upmarket women's fiction, suspense, thrillers, and memoir); **Ethan Bassoff**, ethan@lmqlit.com (literary fiction, crime fiction; also seeks narrative nonfiction in the areas of history, sports writing, journalism, science writing, pop culture, humor, and food writing); **Jason Anthony**, jason@lmqlit.com (commercial fiction of all types including young adult; also seeks nonfiction in the areas of memoir, pop culture, true crime, general psychology, and sociology); **Will Lippincott**, will@lmqlit.com (narrative nonfiction and prescriptive nonfiction in the areas of politics, history, biography, foreign affairs, and health); **Rob McQuilkin**, rob@lmqlit.com (literary fiction; also seeks narrative nonfiction and nonfiction in the areas of memoir, history, biography, art history, cultural criticism, popular sociology, and psychology); **Rayhane Sanders**, rayhane@lmqlit.com (literary fiction, historical fiction, upmarket commercial fiction [including select young adult], narrative nonfiction [including essays], and select memoir); **Stephanie Abou** (literary and upmarket commercial fiction [including select young adult and middle-grade], crime fiction, memoir, and narrative nonfiction).

REPRESENTS Nonfiction, novels. **Considers these nonfiction areas:** art, biography, cultural interests, foods, health, history, humor, memoirs, popular culture, politics, psychology, science, sociology, sports, true crime. **Considers these fiction areas:** commercial, crime, literary, mainstream, middle-grade, suspense, thriller, women's.

⌐ "Lippincott Massie McQuilkin is a full-service literary agency that focuses on bringing fiction and nonfiction of quality to the largest possible audience."

HOW TO CONTACT E-queries preferred. Include the word "Query" in the subject line of your e-mail. Review the agency's online page of agent bios (www.lmqlit.com/contact.html), as some agents want sample pages with their submissions and some do not. If you have not heard back from the agency in 4 weeks, assume they are not interested in seeing more. Accepts simultaneous submissions. Obtains most new clients through recommendations from others, solicitations, conferences.

TERMS Agent receives 15% commission on domestic sales; 20% commission on foreign sales. Offers written contract; 30-day notice must be given to terminate contract. Only charges for reasonable business expenses upon successful sale.

RECENT SALES Clients include Peter Ho Davies, Kim Addonizio, Natasha Trethewey, David Sirota, Katie Crouch, Uwen Akpan, Lydia Millet, Tom Perrotta, Jonathan Lopez, Chris Hayes, and Caroline Weber.

◉ LITERARY AND CREATIVE ARTISTS, INC.

3543 Albemarle St., NW, Washington DC 20008-4213. (202)362-4688. **Fax:** (202)362-8875. **E-mail:** lca9643@lcadc.com. **Website:** www.lcadc.com. **Contact:** Muri-

NEW AGENT SPOTLIGHT

VANESSA ROBINS
CORVISIERO LITERARY LITERARY

www.corvisieroagency.com
@vanessarobins7

ABOUT VANESSA: Vanessa is a writer, reader, and lover of food. From Lancaster, Pennsylvania (no, she's not Amish), she graduated from York College of Pennsylvania with a degree in English literary studies and a minor in professional writing. Vanessa was managing editor of her college's undergraduate literary magazine for two years, where her love of literature thrived, and her passion for the publishing world was created. When she isn't reading or working, Vanessa can be found playing rec league softball, experimenting in the kitchen, knitting, or screaming at her favorite sports teams.

SHE IS SEEKING: Fiction genres of interest include smart thrillers, romance novels with strong female leads, science fiction with lots of science, sports-centric plots, new adult fiction (all types, especially humorous), and young adult (gritty plots and diverse characters). Nonfiction areas of interest include memoir—coming of age, cultural/ethnic/sexuality, survivor, and humorous. Bonus points for medical narratives (characters with medical illnesses and chronic diseases, or manuscripts told through a medical professional's viewpoint). She does *not* want to receive picture books, middle-grade, screenplays, or erotica.

HOW TO CONTACT: Contact query@corvisieroagency.com and put "ATTN: Vanessa Robins—Query [Title]" in the subject line. Vanessa prefers if you write a brief query letter in the body of your e-mail and attach a short synopsis as well as the first five pages of your manuscript in separate Word .doc files. Your query letter should include links to any social media or author websites. Please do not query Vanessa via her personal agency e-mail unless specifically requested to do so.

---

el Nellis. Member of AAR, Authors Guild, American Bar Association, American Booksellers Association. **MEMBER AGENTS** Prior to becoming an agent, Mr. Powell was in sales and contract negotiation.

REPRESENTS Considers these nonfiction areas: autobiography, biography, business, cooking, economics, foods, government, health, how-to, law, medicine, memoirs, philosophy, politics.

☛ Actively seeking quality projects by authors with a vision of where they want to be in 10 years and a plan of how to get there. "We do not handle poetry or purely academic/technical work."

HOW TO CONTACT Query via e-mail and include a synopsis. No attachments. Accepts simultaneous submissions. Responds in 3 weeks to queries. Responds in 1 week to mss. Obtains new clients through recommendations from others.

TERMS Agent receives 15% commission on domestic sales; 25% commission on foreign sales. Offers written contract. Charges clients for long-distance phone/fax, photocopying, shipping.

TIPS "If you are an unpublished author, join a writers group, even if it is on the Internet. You need good, honest feedback. Don't send a ms that has not been read by at least 5 people. Don't send a ms cold to any agent without first asking if they want it. Try to meet the agent face to face before signing. Make sure the fit is right."

LITERARY SERVICES, INC.

P.O. Box 888, Barnegat NJ 08005. **E-mail:** jwlitagent@msn.com. **Website:** www.LiteraryServicesInc.com. **Contact:** John Willig. "We're fortunate to represent many award-winning authors but always enjoy discovering new talent with unique research, creative approaches, and an engaging writer's voice." Estab. 1991. Memberships include Authors Guild. Represents 90 clients.

REPRESENTS Nonfiction. **Considers these nonfiction areas:** architecture, art, biography, business, child guidance, cooking, crafts, creative nonfiction, current affairs, diet/nutrition, design, economics, environment, foods, gardening, health, history, hobbies, humor, inspirational, interior design, language, literature, medicine, military, money, parenting, popular culture, politics, psychology, regional, science, self-help, sex, sociology, spirituality, sports, technology, travel, true crime, war, women's issues.

☛ Works primarily with nonfiction and historical crime fiction authors. "Our publishing experience and 'inside' knowledge of how companies and editors really work sets us apart from many agencies. Our specialties are noted here, but we are open to unique research, creative approaches, and presentations in all nonfiction topic areas." Actively seeking science, history, science,

current events, health, work/life topics, psychology, business, food and travel, story-driven narratives. Does not want to receive fiction (except historical crime fiction), religion, or memoirs.

HOW TO CONTACT "For starters, a one-page outline sent via e-mail is acceptable. See our website and our 'Submissions' section to learn more about our process." Do not send a ms unless requested. Accepts simultaneous submissions. Obtains most new clients through recommendations from others, solicitations, writers conferences.

RECENT SALES *Winning the Brain* by Matthew May, *The Amazing Cell* by Josh Rappaport, *John Lennon vs. the U.S.A.* by Leon Wildes.

WRITERS CONFERENCES ASJA, Writer's Digest Conference (NYC), Thrillerfest.

TIPS "Be focused. In all likelihood, your work is not going to be of interest to 'a very broad audience' or 'every parent,' so I appreciate when writers research and do some homework. Positioning benefits your work. Be a marketer. How have you tested your ideas and writing (beyond your inner circle of family and friends)? Have you received any key awards for your work or endorsements from influential persons in your field? What steps, especially through social media and speaking, have you taken to increase your presence in the market?"

LIVING WORD LITERARY AGENCY

P.O. Box 40974, Eugene OR 97414. **E-mail:** livingwordliterary@gmail.com. **Website:** livingwordliterary.wordpress.com. **Contact:** Kimberly Shumate, agent. Estab. 2009. Member of AAR, Evangelical Christian Publishers Association. Signatory of WGA.

○ Ms. Shumate began her employment with Harvest House Publishers as the assistant to the national sales manager as well as the international sales director, continued into the editorial department.

REPRESENTS **Considers these nonfiction areas:** health, parenting, self-help, relationships. **Considers these fiction areas:** inspirational, adult fiction, Christian living.

☛ Does not want to receive young adult fiction, cookbooks, children's books, science fiction, fantasy, memoirs, screenplays, or poetry.

HOW TO CONTACT Submit a query with short synopsis and first chapter via Word document. Agency only responds if interested.

LKG AGENCY

465 West End Ave., 2A, New York NY 10024. **E-mail:** query@lkgagency.com. **Website:** http://lkgagency. com. The LKG Agency was founded in 2005 and is based on the Upper West Side of Manhattan. "We are a boutique literary agency that specializes in middle-grade and young adult fiction, as well as nonfiction, both practical and narrative, with a particular interest in women-focused how-to. We invest a great deal of care and personal attention in each of our authors with the aim of developing long-term relationships that last well beyond the sale of a single book." Estab. 2005. Member of AAR. Signatory of WGA.

MEMBER AGENTS Lauren Galit (nonfiction, middle-grade, young adult); Caitlen Rubino-Bradway (middle-grade and young adult, some nonfiction).

REPRESENTS Nonfiction, juvenile books. **Considers these nonfiction areas:** animals, child guidance, creative nonfiction, diet/nutrition, design, health, how-to, humor, juvenile nonfiction, memoirs, parenting, popular culture, psychology, women's issues, young adult. **Considers these fiction areas:** middle-grade, young adult.

☛ Seeking books on parenting, beauty, celebrity, dating and relationships, entertainment, fashion, health, diet and fitness, home and design, lifestyle, memoir, narrative, pets, psychology, middle-grade, and young adult fiction.

HOW TO CONTACT For nonfiction submissions, send a query letter to nonfiction@lkgagency.com, along with a table of contents and 2 sample chapters. The table of contents should be fairly detailed, with 1-2 paragraphs for an overview of the content of each chapter. Please also make sure to mention any publicity you have at your disposal. For middle-grade and young adult submissions, send a query, synopsis, and 3 chapters, and address all submissions to mgya@lkgagency.com. On a side note, while both Lauren and Caitlen consider young adult and middle-grade, Lauren tends to look more for middle-grade, while Caitlen deals more with young adult fiction. Responds if interested. Accepts simultaneous submissions.

STERLING LORD LITERISTIC, INC.

65 Bleecker St., New York NY 10012. **Fax:** (212)780-6095. **E-mail:** info@sll.com. **Website:** www.sll.com. Estab. 1987. Member of AAR. Signatory of WGA.

MEMBER AGENTS Philippa Brophy (represents journalists, nonfiction writers, and novelists; she is most interested in current events, memoir, science, politics, biography, and women's issues); **Laurie Liss** (represents authors of commercial and literary fiction and nonfiction whose perspectives are well developed and unique); **Sterling Lord**; **Peter Matson** (abiding interest in storytelling, whether in the service of history, fiction, or the sciences); **Douglas Stewart** (fiction for all ages, from the innovatively literary to the unabashedly commercial); **Neeti Madan** (memoir, journalism, popular culture, lifestyle, women's issues, multicultural books, and virtually any intelligent writing on intriguing topics); **Robert Guinsler** (literary and commercial fiction [including young adult], journalism, narrative nonfiction with an emphasis on pop culture, science and current events, memoirs and biographies); **Jim Rutman**; **Celeste Fine** (expert, celebrity, and corporate clients with strong national and international platforms, particularly in the health, science, self-help, food, business, and lifestyle fields); **Erica Rand Silverman** (represents picture books through young adult novels, both fiction and nonfiction; adult interests include parenting and humor nonfiction); **Martha Millard** (fiction and nonfiction, including well-written science fiction and young adult); **Mary Krienke** (literary fiction, memoir, and narrative nonfiction [psychology, popular science, and cultural commentary]); **Jenny Stephens** (nonfiction interests include cookbooks, practical lifestyle projects, transportive travel and nature writing, and creative nonfiction; fiction interests include contemporary literary narratives strongly rooted in place); **Alison MacKeen** (idea-driven research books in the categories of social scientific, scientific, historical, relationships, parenting, learning and education, sexuality, technology, health, the environment, politics, economics, psychology, geography, and culture; also seeks literary fiction, literary nonfiction, memoirs, essays, and travel writing); **John Maas** (serious nonfiction—specifically business, personal development, science, self-help, health, fitness, and lifestyle); **Sarah Passick** (commercial nonfiction in the categories of celebrity, food, blogger, lifestyle, health, diet, fitness, and fashion).

REPRESENTS Nonfiction, fiction. **Considers these nonfiction areas:** biography, business, cooking, creative nonfiction, current affairs, economics, education, foods, gay/lesbian, history, humor, memoirs, multicultural, parenting, popular culture, politics, psychology, science, technology, travel, women's issues, fitness. **Considers these fiction areas:** commercial, juvenile, literary, middle-grade, picture books, science fiction, young adult.

HOW TO CONTACT Query via snail mail. "Please submit a query letter, a synopsis of the work, a brief proposal or the first 3 chapters of the ms, a brief bio, and a SASE for reply. Original artwork is not accepted. Enclose sufficient postage if you wish to have your materials returned to you. We do not respond to unsolicited e-mail inquiries." Accepts simultaneous submissions.

TERMS Agent receives 15% commission on domestic sales; 20% commission on foreign sales. Offers written contract.

LOWENSTEIN ASSOCIATES INC.

115 E. 23rd St., Floor 4, New York NY 10010. (212)206-1630. **Fax:** (212)727-0280. **E-mail:** assistant@bookhaven.com. **Website:** www.lowensteinassociates.com. **Contact:** Barbara Lowenstein. Member of AAR.

MEMBER AGENTS **Barbara Lowenstein**, president (nonfiction interests include narrative nonfiction, health, money, finance, travel, multicultural, popular culture, and memoir; fiction interests include literary fiction, and women's fiction); **Mary South** (literary fiction and nonfiction on subjects such as neuroscience, bioengineering, women's rights, design, and digital humanities; also seeks investigative journalism, essays, and memoir).

REPRESENTS Nonfiction, novels. **Considers these nonfiction areas:** creative nonfiction, health, memoirs, money, multicultural, popular culture, travel. **Considers these fiction areas:** commercial, fantasy, literary, middle-grade, science fiction, women's, young adult.

➣ Barbara Lowenstein is currently looking for writers who have a platform and are leading experts in their field, including business, women's issues, psychology, health, science, and social issues, and is particularly interested in strong new voices in fiction and narrative nonfiction. Does not want westerns, textbooks, children's picture books, or books in need of translation.

HOW TO CONTACT "For fiction, please send us a one-page query letter, along with the first 10 pages pasted in the body of the message to assistant@bookhaven.com. If submitting nonfiction, please send a one-page query letter, a table of contents, and, if available, a proposal pasted into the body of the e-mail. Please put the word 'QUERY' and the title of your project in the subject field of your e-mail and address it to the agent of your choice. Please do not send an attachment as the message will be deleted without being read and no reply will be sent." Accepts simultaneous submissions. Responds in 6 weeks to queries. Obtains most new clients through recommendations from others, solicitations, conferences.

TERMS Agent receives 15% commission on domestic sales; 20% commission on foreign sales. Offers written contract. Charges for large photocopy batches, messenger service, international postage.

TIPS "Know the genre you are working in, and read!"

GINA MACCOBY LITERARY AGENCY

P.O. Box 60, Chappaqua NY 10514. (914)238-5630. **E-mail:** query@maccobylit.com. **Website:** www.publishersmarketplace.com/members/GinaMaccoby/. **Contact:** Gina Maccoby. Member of AAR, Authors Guild. Represents 25 clients.

MEMBER AGENTS Gina Maccoby.

REPRESENTS Nonfiction, novels. **Considers these nonfiction areas:** autobiography, biography, cultural interests, current affairs, ethnic, history, juvenile nonfiction, popular culture, women's issues, women's studies. **Considers these fiction areas:** juvenile, literary, mainstream, mystery, thriller, young adult.

HOW TO CONTACT Query by e-mail only. Accepts simultaneous submissions. Owing to volume of submissions, may not respond to queries unless interested. Obtains most new clients through recommendations from clients and publishers.

TERMS Agent receives 15% commission on domestic sales; 20-25% commission on foreign sales, which includes subagents commissions. May recover certain costs, such as legal fees or the cost of shipping books by air to Europe or Japan.

⊘ MACGREGOR LITERARY, INC.

P.O. Box 1316, Manzanita OR 97130. (503)389-4803. **Website:** www.macgregorliterary.com. **Contact:** Chip MacGregor. Signatory of WGA. Represents 40 clients.

○ Prior to his current position, Mr. MacGregor was the senior agent with Alive Communications. Most recently, he was associate publisher for Time-Warner Book Group's Faith Division, and helped put together their Center Street imprint.

MEMBER AGENTS Chip MacGregor; **Amanda Luedeke** (nonfiction, literary fiction, romance, some speculative fiction); **Holly Lorincz** (literary mystery, political or conspiracy thrillers, fast-paced suspense, some historical fiction, and literary westerns); **Erin Buterbaugh** (children's, middle-grade, and young adult fiction, as well as women's fiction, suspense, and nonfiction); **Brian Tibbetts** (literary fiction, young adult titles, new adult titles, science fiction, fantasy, horror, art and music memoirs, natural foods, alternative healing, and sustainability issues).

REPRESENTS Nonfiction, novels. **Considers these nonfiction areas:** inspirational, memoirs. **Considers these fiction areas:** fantasy, horror, inspirational, literary, mainstream, middle-grade, mystery, new adult, religious, romance, science fiction, suspense, thriller, westerns, women's, young adult.

8→ "My specialty has been in career planning with authors—finding commercial ideas, then helping authors bring them to market, and in the midst of that assisting the authors as they get firmly established in their writing careers. I'm probably best known for my work with Christian books over the years, but I've done a fair amount of general market projects, as well."

HOW TO CONTACT MacGregor Literary is not currently accepting submissions. Do not query this agency without an invitation or referral.

WRITERS CONFERENCES Blue Ridge Christian Writers' Conference, Write to Publish.

TIPS "Seriously consider attending a good writers conference. It will give you the chance to be face-to-face with people in the industry. Also, if you're a novelist, consider joining one of the national writers organizations. The American Christian Fiction Writers (ACFW) is a wonderful group for new as well as established writers. And if you're a Christian writer of any kind, check into The Writers View, an online writing group. All of these have proven helpful to writers."

ANDREW MANN, LTD

39-41 North Rd., London England N7 9DP United Kingdom. **E-mail:** info@andrewmann.co.uk. **Website:** www.andrewmann.co.uk. **Contact:** Tina Betts and Louise Burns. Estab. 1975. Members of the Association of Authors' Agents, Writers' Guild of Great Britain, and Crime Writers' Association (CWA).

REPRESENTS Nonfiction, novels. **Considers these nonfiction areas:** creative nonfiction. **Considers**

these fiction areas: commercial, crime, fantasy, juvenile, middle-grade, women's, young adult.

8→ Actively seeking upmarket commercial fiction, literary fiction, women's commercial fiction, crime, thrillers, historical fiction, commercial picture books, children's fiction 8+ to young adult (including adventure middle-grade series), and narrative nonfiction. No poetry, theater or film submissions, spiritual, or self-help.

HOW TO CONTACT Submit via e-mail only. Submit brief synopsis and first 3 chapters. Accepts simultaneous submissions. Usually responds in 9 weeks.

CAROL MANN AGENCY

55 Fifth Ave., New York NY 10003. (212)206-5635. **Fax:** (212)675-4809. **E-mail:** submissions@carolmannagency.com. **Website:** www.carolmannagency.com. **Contact:** Isabella Ruggiero. Member of AAR. Represents roughly 200 clients.

MEMBER AGENTS **Carol Mann** (health, medical, religion, spirituality, self-help, parenting, narrative nonfiction, current affairs); **Laura Yorke**; **Gareth Esersky**; **Myrsini Stephanides** (nonfiction areas of interest include pop culture, music, humor, narrative nonfiction and memoir, cookbooks; fiction areas of interest include offbeat literary fiction, graphic works, and edgy young adult fiction); **Joanne Wyckoff** (nonfiction areas of interest include memoir, narrative nonfiction, personal narrative, psychology, women's issues, education, health and wellness, parenting, serious self-help, natural history; also accepts fiction); **Lydia Shamah** (edgy modern fiction; also seeks timely nonfiction in the areas of business, self-improvement, relationship, and gift books; she is particularly interested in female voices and experiences).

REPRESENTS Nonfiction, novels. **Considers these nonfiction areas:** anthropology, archeology, architecture, art, autobiography, biography, business, child guidance, cultural interests, current affairs, design, ethnic, government, health, history, law, medicine, money, music, parenting, popular culture, politics, psychology, self-help, sociology, sports, women's issues, women's studies. **Considers these fiction areas:** commercial, literary, young adult, graphic works.

8→ Does not want to receive genre fiction (romance, mystery, etc.).

HOW TO CONTACT Please see website for submission guidelines. Accepts simultaneous submissions. Responds in 4 weeks to queries.

TERMS Agent receives 15% commission on domestic sales; 20% commission on foreign sales. Offers written contract.

MANSION STREET LITERARY MANAGEMENT

Website: http://mansionstreet.com. **Contact:** Jean Sagendorph, Michelle Witte. Member of AAR. Signatory of WGA.

MEMBER AGENTS **Jean Sagendorph**, querymansionstreet@gmail.com (pop culture, gift books, cookbooks, general nonfiction, lifestyle, design, brand extensions); **Michelle Witte**, querymichelle@mansionstreet.com (young adult, middle-grade, early readers, picture books [especially from author-illustrators], juvenile nonfiction).

REPRESENTS Nonfiction, novels. **Considers these nonfiction areas:** cooking, design, popular culture. **Considers these fiction areas:** juvenile, middle-grade, young adult.

- Jean is not interested in memoirs or medical/reference. Typically sports, travel, and self-help books are also not a good fit. Michelle is not interested in fiction or nonfiction for adults.

HOW TO CONTACT Send a query letter and no more than the first 10 pages of your ms in the body of an e-mail. Query 1 specific agent at this agency. No attachments. You must list the genre in the subject line. If the genre is not in the subject line, your query will be deleted. Accepts simultaneous submissions. Responds in up to 6 weeks.

RECENT SALES *Shake and Fetch* by Carli Davidson, *Bleed, Blister, Puke, and Purge* by J. Marin Younker, *Spectrum* by Ginger Johnson, *I Left You a Present* and *Movie Night Trivia* by Robb Pearlman, *Open Sesame!* by Ashley Evanson, *Fox Hunt* by Nilah Magruder, *ABC Now You See Me* by Kim Siebold.

MANUS & ASSOCIATES LITERARY AGENCY, INC.

425 Sherman Ave., Suite 200, Palo Alto CA 94306. (650)470-5151. **Fax:** (650)470-5159. **E-mail:** manuslit@manuslit.com. **Website:** www.manuslit.com. **Contact:** Jillian Manus, Jandy Nelson, Penny Nelson. Member of AAR.

- Prior to becoming an agent, Ms. Manus was associate publisher of 2 national magazines and director of development at Warner Bros. and Universal Studios. She has been a literary agent for 20 years.

MEMBER AGENTS Jandy Nelson (currently not taking on new clients); **Jillian Manus**, jillian@manuslit.com (political, memoirs, self-help, history, sports, women's issues, thrillers); **Penny Nelson**, penny@manuslit.com (memoirs, self-help, sports, nonfiction).

REPRESENTS Nonfiction, novels. **Considers these nonfiction areas:** cooking, history, inspirational, memoirs, politics, psychology, religious, self-help, sports, women's issues. **Considers these fiction areas:** thriller.

- "Our agency is unique in the way that we not only sell the material, but we edit, develop concepts, and participate in the marketing effort. We specialize in large, conceptual fiction and nonfiction, and always value a project that can be sold in the TV/film market." Actively seeking high-concept thrillers, commercial literary fiction, women's fiction, celebrity biographies, memoirs, multicultural fiction, popular health, women's empowerment, and mysteries. No horror, romance, science fiction, fantasy, western, young adult, children's, poetry, cookbooks, or magazine articles.

HOW TO CONTACT Snail mail submissions welcome. E-queries also accepted. For nonfiction, send a full proposal via snail mail. For fiction, send a query letter and 30 pages (unbound) if submitting via snail mail. Send only an e-query if submitting fiction via e-mail. If querying by e-mail, submit directly to one of the agents. Accepts simultaneous submissions.

TERMS Agent receives 15% commission on domestic sales; 20-25% commission on foreign sales. Offers written contract, binding for 2 years; 60-day notice must be given to terminate contract. Charges for photocopying and postage/UPS.

RECENT SALES *Nothing Down for the 2000s* and *Multiple Streams of Income for the 2000s* by Robert Allen, *Missed Fortune 101* by Doug Andrew, *Cracking the Millionaire Code* by Mark Victor Hansen and Robert Allen, *Stress Free for Good* by Dr. Fred Luskin and Dr. Ken Pelletier, *The Mercy of Thin Air* by Ronlyn Domangue, *The Fine Art of Small Talk* by Debra Fine, *Bone Men of Bonares* by Terry Tamoff.

MARCH TENTH, INC.

24 Hillside Terrace, Montvale NJ 07645. (201)387-6551. **Fax:** (201)387-6552. **E-mail:** hchoron@aol.com;

schoron@aol.com. **Website:** www.marchtenthinc.com. **Contact:** Harry Choron, vice president. Represents 40 clients.

REPRESENTS Nonfiction. **Considers these nonfiction areas:** Americana, autobiography, biography, current affairs, film, health, history, humor, language, literature, medicine, music, popular culture, satire, theater.

☞ "We prefer to work with published/established writers." Does not want to receive children's or young adult novels, plays, screenplays, or poetry.

HOW TO CONTACT Send queries via e-mail. Include your proposal, a short bio, and contact information. Detailed submission guidelines are on the agency website. Accepts simultaneous submissions. Responds in 1 month to queries.

TERMS Agent receives 15% commission on domestic sales; 20% commission on foreign sales; 20% commission on film sales. Does not require expense money upfront.

⊙ **THE DENISE MARCIL LITERARY AGENCY, LLC**

483 Westover Rd., Stamford CT 06902. (203)327-9970. **E-mail:** dmla@DeniseMarcilAgency.com; AnneMarie@denisemarcilagency.com. **Website:** www.denisemarcilagency.com. **Contact:** Denise Marcil, Anne Marie O'Farrell. Member of AAR, Women's Media Group.

◑ Prior to opening her agency, Ms. Marcil served as an editorial assistant with Avon Books and as an assistant editor with Simon & Schuster.

MEMBER AGENTS Denise Marcil (self-help and popular reference books in the categories of wellness, health, women's issues, self-help, and popular reference); **Anne Marie O'Farrell** (books that convey and promote innovative, practical, and cutting edge information and ideas which help people increase their self-awareness and fulfillment; she is eager to represent a great basketball book).

REPRESENTS Nonfiction and novels. **Considers these nonfiction areas:** business, cooking, diet/nutrition, education, health, how-to, New Age, psychology, self-help, spirituality, women's issues. **Considers these fiction areas:** commercial, suspense, thriller, women's.

☞ "In nonfiction we are looking for self-help, personal growth, popular psychology, how-to, business, and popular reference; we want to represent books that help people's lives."

HOW TO CONTACT E-query. Accepts simultaneous submissions.

TERMS Agent receives 15% commission on domestic sales; 20% commission on foreign sales. Offers written contract, binding for 2 years.

RECENT SALES *Dogwood Hill* by Sherryl Woods, *The Healthy Pregnancy Book* by William Sears and Martha Sears, *The Girls of Ennismore* by Patricia Falvey, *Irresistible Force* and *Force of Attraction* by D.D. Ayres.

MARSAL LYON LITERARY AGENCY, LLC

PMB 121, 665 San Rodolfo Dr. 124, Solana Beach CA 92075. **Website:** www.marsallyonliteraryagency.com. **Contact:** Kevan Lyon, Jill Marsal. Member of AAR. Signatory of WGA.

MEMBER AGENTS Kevan Lyon, kevan@marsallyonliteraryagency.com (commercial women's fiction, young adult fiction, and all genres of romance); **Jill Marsal**, jill@marsallyonliteraryagency.com (all types of women's fiction, all types of romance, mysteries, cozies, suspense, and thrillers; also seeks nonfiction in the areas of current events, business, health, self-help, relationships, psychology, parenting, history, science, and narrative nonfiction); **Patricia Nelson**, patricia@marsallyonliteraryagency.com (literary fiction, commercial fiction, all types of women's fiction, contemporary and historical romance, young adult, middle-grade, and LGBTQ fiction for both young adult and adult); **Deborah Ritchkin**, deborah@marsallyonliteraryagency.com (lifestyle books [specifically in the areas of food, design and entertaining], pop culture, women's issues, biography, and current events; her niche interest is projects about France, including fiction); **Shannon Hassan,** shannon@marsallyonliteraryagency.com (literary and commercial fiction, young adult and middle-grade fiction, and select nonfiction).

REPRESENTS Nonfiction, novels, juvenile books. **Considers these nonfiction areas:** animals, biography, business, cooking, creative nonfiction, current affairs, diet/nutrition, history, investigative, memoirs, parenting, popular culture, politics, psychology, science, self-help, sports, women's issues, women's studies. **Considers these fiction areas:** commercial, juvenile, literary, mainstream, middle-grade, multicultural, mystery, paranormal, romance, suspense, thriller, women's, young adult.

NEW AGENT SPOTLIGHT

AMANDA JAIN
INKLINGS LITERARY AGENCY

www.inklingsliterary.com
@wensday95

ABOUT AMANDA: After earning a bachelor of arts in English, Amanda Jain worked in the trade department at W.W. Norton for seven years before leaving to pursue graduate studies. She graduated in 2011 with a master of arts in the history of decorative arts. Amanda joined Inklings in 2014. She is now building her client list and seeking submissions.

SHE IS SEEKING: Historical fiction (in all genres), women's fiction, book club/upmarket fiction, romance (particularly historical, suspenseful, or with a comedic bent), and mysteries (particularly historical, cozy, or historical cozies). She also seeks narrative nonfiction in the areas of social history, archaeology, art history, and material culture. She is interested in select young adult and middle-grade projects with unique hooks and a strong voice. In all cases, what Amanda is most looking for is a story that completely immerses the reader in the world of the book. Amanda is *not* the agent to query with picture books, memoirs, self-help, poetry, erotica, science fiction, fantasy, horror, or inspirational fiction.

HOW TO CONTACT: Type "Query for Amanda: [Title]" in the subject line to query@inklingsliterary.com. No attachments. In the body of the e-mail, send a query letter that includes the title, genre, and word count of your project. Also include a brief pitch about the story, a brief bo (including any publishing credits), the first 10 pages of your manuscript, and a brief synopsis (one or two pages). "Our response time varies, but the general response time is within three months for queries, and four months for manuscripts. If you have not received an answer for your query after three months," the agency is not interested in the project."

HOW TO CONTACT Query by e-mail. Query only 1 agent at this agency at a time. "Please visit our website to determine who is best suited for your work. Write 'Query' in the subject line of your e-mail. Please allow up to several weeks to hear back on your query." Accepts simultaneous submissions.

TIPS "Our agency's mission is to help writers achieve their publishing dreams. We want to work with authors not just for a book but for a career. We are dedicated to building long-term relationships with our authors and publishing partners. Our goal is to help find homes for books that engage, entertain, and make a difference."

THE EVAN MARSHALL AGENCY

Indie Rights Agency, 1 Pacio Court, Roseland NJ 07068-1121. (973)287-6216. **Fax:** (973)488-7910. **E-mail:** evan@evanmarshallagency.com. **Website:** www.evanmarshallagency.com. **Contact:** Evan Marshall. Founded in 1987, the Evan Marshall Agency is a leading literary management firm specializing in adult and young adult fiction. "We handle a wide-ranging roster of writers in numerous genres, from romance to mystery and thriller to literary fiction. We take pride in providing careful career guidance and strategizing to our clients." Member of AAR, Novelists, Inc. Represents 50+ clients.

○ Prior to becoming an agent, Mr. Marshall held senior editorial positions at Houghton Mifflin, Ariel Books, New American Library, and Everest House, where he acquired national and international bestsellers.

MEMBER AGENTS Evan Marshall.

REPRESENTS Fiction. **Considers these fiction areas:** action, adventure, crime, detective, erotica, ethnic, family saga, fantasy, feminist, frontier, gay, glitz, historical, horror, humor, inspirational, lesbian, literary, mainstream, military, multicultural, multimedia, mystery, new adult, New Age, occult, paranormal, police, psychic, regional, religious, satire, science fiction, spiritual, sports, supernatural, suspense, thriller, translation, urban fantasy, war, westerns, women's, young adult, romance (contemporary, gothic, historical, regency).

☛ We represent all genres of adult and young adult full-length fiction. Does not want to receive articles, children's books, essays, memoirs, nonfiction, novellas, poetry, screenplays, short stories, or stage plays.

HOW TO CONTACT Actively seeking new clients. E-mail a query letter, synopsis, and the first 3 chapters of your novel within the body of an e-mail. Accepts simultaneous submissions.

TERMS Agent receives 15% commission on domestic sales; 20% commission on foreign sales. Offers written contract.

RECENT SALES *The Language of Sisters* by Cathy Lamb (Kensington), *A Husband for Mari* by Emma Miller (Love Inspired), *A Taste of Fire* by Hannah Howell (Kensington), *Murder Has Nine Lives* by Laura Levine (Kensington), *Fortune's Secret Husband* by Karen Rose Smith (Harlequin).

THE MARTELL AGENCY

1350 Avenue of the Americas, Suite 1205, New York NY 10019. **Fax:** (212)317-2676. **E-mail:** submissions@themartellagency.com. **Website:** www.themartellagency.com. **Contact:** Alice Martell.

REPRESENTS Nonfiction, novels. **Considers these nonfiction areas:** "big idea" books, business, current affairs, economics, health/diet, history, medicine, memoirs, multicultural, politics, personal finance, psychology, science for the general reader, self-help, women's issues.

☛ Seeks the following genres in fiction: literary and commercial—including mystery, suspense, and thrillers. Does not want to receive romance, genre mysteries, genre historical fiction, or children's books.

HOW TO CONTACT E-query. This should include a summary of the project, a short biography, and any information, if appropriate, as to why you are qualified to write on the subject of your book, including any publishing credits. Accepts simultaneous submissions.

RECENT SALES *Defending Jacob* by William Landay, *The Forest Unseen: A Year's Watch in Nature* by David Haskell, *How Paris Became Paris: The Birth of the Modern City* by Joan Dejean, *Waiting for Snow in Havana* by Carlos Eire, *The Boy Kings of Texas* by Domingo Martinez.

MARTIN LITERARY MANAGEMENT

914 164th St. SE, Suite B12, #307, Mill Creek WA 98012. **E-mail:** sharlene@martinliterarymanagement.com. **Website:** www.MartinLit.com. **Contact:** Sharlene Martin. "Please see our website at www.MartinLit.com for company overview, testimonials, bios of literary managers." Estab. 2002.

○ Prior to becoming an agent, Ms. Martin worked in film/TV production and acquisitions.

MEMBER AGENTS Sharlene Martin (nonfiction); Clelia Gore (children's, middle-grade, young adult).

REPRESENTS Nonfiction, juvenile books. **Considers these nonfiction areas:** autobiography, biography, business, child guidance, current affairs, economics, health, history, how-to, humor, inspirational, investigative, medicine, memoirs, parenting, popular culture, psychology, satire, self-help, true crime, war, women's issues, women's studies. **Considers these fiction areas:** juvenile, middle-grade, young adult.

☞ This agency has strong ties to film/TV. Actively seeking nonfiction that is highly commercial and that can be adapted to film. "We are being inundated with queries and submissions that are wrongfully being submitted to us, which only results in more frustration for the writers."

HOW TO CONTACT Query via e-mail with no attachments; place text in the body of the e-mail. Accepts simultaneous submissions. Responds in 2 weeks to queries. Obtains most new clients through recommendations from others.

TERMS Agent receives 15% commission on domestic sales. Offers written contract, binding for 1 year; 1-month notice must be given to terminate contract.

RECENT SALES *Breakthrough* by Jack Andraka, *In the Matter of Nikola Tesla: A Romance of the Mind* by Anthony Flacco, *Honor Bound: My Journey to Hell and Back With Amanda Knox* by Raffaele Sollecito.

TIPS "Have a strong platform for nonfiction. Please don't call. (I can't tell how well you write by the sound of your voice.) I welcome e-mail. I'm very responsive when I'm interested in a query and work hard to get my clients' materials in the best possible shape before submissions. Do your homework prior to submission and only submit your best efforts. Please review our website carefully to make sure we're a good match for your work. If you read my book, *Publish Your Nonfiction Book: Strategies For Learning the Industry, Selling Your Book and Building a Successful Career* (Writer's Digest Books), you'll know exactly how to charm me."

MARGRET MCBRIDE LITERARY AGENCY

P.O. Box 9128, La Jolla CA 92038. (858)454-1550. **Fax:** (858)454-2156. **E-mail:** staff@mcbridelit.com. **Website:** www.mcbrideliterary.com. **Contact:** Michael Daley, submissions manager. Member of AAR, Authors Guild.

○ Prior to opening her agency, Ms. McBride worked at Random House, Ballantine Books, and Warner Books.

MEMBER AGENTS Margret McBride, Faye Atchinson.

REPRESENTS Nonfiction, novels. **Considers these nonfiction areas:** autobiography, biography, business, cooking, cultural interests, current affairs, economics, ethnic, foods, government, health, history, how-to, law, medicine, money, popular culture, politics, psychology, science, self-help, sociology, technology, women's issues, style. **Considers these fiction areas:** action, adventure, crime, detective, historical, humor, literary, mainstream, mystery, police, satire, suspense, thriller.

☞ This agency specializes in mainstream fiction and nonfiction. Actively seeking commercial fiction and nonfiction, business, health, self-help. Please do not send screenplays, romance, poetry, or children's.

HOW TO CONTACT Submit a query letter via e-mail. In your letter, provide a brief synopsis of your work, as well as any pertinent information about yourself. There are detailed nonfiction proposal guidelines online. Accepts simultaneous submissions. Responds in 8 weeks to queries.

RECENT SALES *Value Tales Treasure: Stories for Growing Good People* by Spencer Johnson (Simon & Schuster Children's), *The 6 Reasons You'll Get the Job: What Employers Really Want—Whether They Know it or Not* by Debra MacDougall and Elisabeth Harney Sanders-Park (Tarcher), *The Solution: Conquer Your Fear, Control Your Future* by Lucinda Bassett (Sterling).

TIPS "Our office does not accept e-mail queries!"

⊙ E.J. MCCARTHY AGENCY

(415)383-6639. **E-mail:** ejmagency@gmail.com. **Website:** http://www.publishersmarketplace.com/members/ejmccarthy/. Signatory of WGA.

○ Prior to his current position, Mr. McCarthy was a former executive editor with more than 20 years publishing experience (Bantam Doubleday Dell, Presidio Press, Ballantine/Random House).

REPRESENTS **Considers these nonfiction areas:** biography, history, memoirs, military, sports.

☞ This agency specializes in nonfiction.

HOW TO CONTACT Query first by e-mail. Accepts simultaneous submissions.

RECENT SALES *One Bullet Away* by Nathaniel Fick, *The Unforgiving Minute* by Craig Mullaney, *The Sling and the Stone* by Thomas X. Hammes, *The Heart and* *the First* by Eric Greitens, *When Books Went to War* by Molly Guptill Manning.

THE MCCARTHY AGENCY, LLC

456 Ninth St., No. 28, Hoboken NJ 07030. **E-mail:** McCarthylit@aol.com. **Contact:** Shawna McCarthy. Member of AAR.

MEMBER AGENTS Shawna McCarthy.

REPRESENTS Novels. **Considers these fiction areas:** fantasy, middle-grade, mystery, new adult, science fiction, women's, young adult.

☛ This agency represents mostly novels. No picture books.

HOW TO CONTACT E-queries only. Accepts simultaneous submissions.

MCCARTHY CREATIVE SERVICES

625 Main St., Suite 834, New York NY 10044-0035. (212)832-3428. **Fax:** (212)829-9610. **E-mail:** paulmccarthy@mccarthycreative.com. **Website:** www.mccarthycreative.com. **Contact:** Paul D. McCarthy. "Represents several No. 1 international best-selling, award-winning, and elite authors." Memberships include the Authors Guild, American Society of Journalists & Authors, National Book Critics Circle, Authors League of America.

○ Prior to his current position, Mr. McCarthy was a professional writer, literary agent at the Scott Meredith Literary Agency, senior editor at publishing companies (Simon & Schuster, HarperCollins, and Doubleday), and a public speaker.

MEMBER AGENTS Paul D. McCarthy.

REPRESENTS Nonfiction, novels. **Considers these nonfiction areas:** animals, anthropology, art, biography, business, current affairs, education, ethnic, government, health, history, humor, language, memoirs, military, money, music, popular culture, psychology, science, sociology, sports, translation, true crime. **Considers these fiction areas:** adventure, confession, detective, erotica, ethnic, fantasy, feminist, gay, glitz, historical, horror, humor, literary, mainstream, mystery, regional, romance, sports, thriller, women's.

☛ "Actively seeking established authors of serious and popular nonfiction, who want the value of being one of the agency's very exclusive authors who receive special attention. No first novels please. Novels by established novelists will be considered very selectively."

HOW TO CONTACT Queries and submissions by e-mail only. Send as e-mail attachment. Also submit an outline and 1 chapter (either first or best). Responds in 4 weeks to queries. Obtains most new clients through recommendations from others.

TERMS Agent receives 15% commission on domestic sales; 20% commission on foreign sales. Offers written contract; 30-day notice must be given to terminate contract.

TIPS "Always keep in mind that your query letter and proposal is only one of hundreds and thousands that are competing for the agent's attention. Therefore, your presentation of your book and yourself as author has to be immediate, intense, compelling, and concise. Make the query letter 1 page, and after a short, introductory paragraph, write a 150-word keynote description of your ms."

SEAN MCCARTHY LITERARY AGENCY

E-mail: submissions@mccarthylit.com. **Website:** www.mccarthylit.com. **Contact:** Sean McCarthy. Estab. 2013.

○ Prior to his current position, Mr. McCarthy began his publishing career as an editorial intern at Overlook Press and then moved over to the Sheldon Fogelman Agency.

REPRESENTS **Considers these nonfiction areas:** juvenile nonfiction, young adult. **Considers these fiction areas:** juvenile, middle-grade, picture books, young adult.

☛ Sean is drawn to flawed, multifaceted characters with devastatingly concise writing in young adult, and boy-friendly mysteries or adventures in middle-grade. In picture books, he looks more for unforgettable characters, off-beat humor, and especially clever endings. He is not currently interested in high fantasy, message-driven stories, or query letters that pose too many questions.

HOW TO CONTACT E-query. "Please include a brief description of your book, your biography, and any literary or relevant professional credits in your query letter. If you are a novelist, submit the first 3 chapters of your ms (or roughly 25 pages) and a one-page synopsis in the body of the e-mail or as a Word or PDF attachment. If you are a picture book author, submit the complete text of your ms. We are not currently accepting picture book mss of more than 1,000 words. If you are an illustrator, attach up to 3 JPEGs or

PDFs of your work, along with a link to your website." Accepts simultaneous submissions.

MCCORMICK LITERARY

37 W. 20th St., New York NY 10011. (212)691-9726. **Website:** http://mccormicklit.com. "McCormick Literary is an independent literary agency specializing in literary and commercial fiction and quality nonfiction—including memoir, history, narrative, biography, lifestyle, sports, self-help, and pop culture." Member of AAR. Signatory of WGA.
MEMBER AGENTS David McCormick; **Pilar Queen** (narrative nonfiction, practical nonfiction, and commercial women's fiction); **Bridget McCarthy** (literary and commercial fiction, narrative nonfiction, memoir, and cookbooks); **Alia Hanna Habib** (literary fiction, narrative nonfiction, memoir, and cookbooks); **Edward Orloff** (literary fiction and narrative nonfiction, especially cultural history, politics, biography, and the arts); **Daniel Menaker**.
HOW TO CONTACT Snail mail queries only. Send a SASE. Accepts simultaneous submissions.

✪ ANNE MCDERMID & ASSOCIATES LITERARY, LTD

320 Front St. W, Suite 1105, Toronto, Ontario M5V 3B6 Canada. (647)788-4016. **Fax:** (416)324-8870. **E-mail:** info@mcdermidagency.com. **Website:** www.mcdermidagency.com. **Contact:** Anne McDermid. Estab. 1996.
MEMBER AGENTS Anne McDermid, Martha Webb, Monica Pacheco, and Chris Bucci.
REPRESENTS Nonfiction, novels.

☞ The agency represents literary novelists and commercial novelists of high quality, and also writers of nonfiction in the areas of memoir, biography, history, literary travel, narrative science, and investigative journalism. "We also represent a certain number of children's and young adult writers and writers in the genres of science fiction and fantasy."

HOW TO CONTACT Query via e-mail or mail with a brief bio, description, and first 5 pages of project only. Accepts simultaneous submissions. *No unsolicited mss.* Obtains most new clients through recommendations from others.

MCINTOSH & OTIS, INC.

353 Lexington Ave., New York NY 10016. (212)687-7400. **Fax:** (212)687-6894. **E-mail:** info@mcintoshan-dotis.com. **Website:** www.mcintoshandotis.com. **Contact:** Eugene H. Winick, Esq. McIntosh & Otis has a long history of representing authors of adult and children's books. The children's department is a separate division. Estab. 1927. Member of AAR, SCBWI. Signatory of WGA.
MEMBER AGENTS Elizabeth Winick Rubinstein, ewrquery@mcintoshandotis.com (literary fiction, women's fiction, historical fiction, mystery/suspense, narrative nonfiction, spiritual, self-help, history, and current affairs); **Shira Hoffman**, shquery@mcintoshandotis.com (young adult, middle-grade, mainstream commercial fiction, mystery, literary fiction, women's fiction, romance, urban fantasy, fantasy, science fiction, horror, and dystopian); **Christa Heschke**, chquery@mcintoshandotis.com (picture books, middle-grade, young adult, and new adult); **Adam Muhlig**, amquery@mcintoshandotis.com (music books [from jazz to classical to punk], popular culture, natural history, travel and adventure, and sports); **Eugene Winick**; **Shannon Powers**, spquery@mcintoshandotis.com (literary fiction, mystery, horror, popular history, and romance; also seeks young adult, middle-grade, mysteries and thrillers with high emotional stakes, projects with romantic elements, horror, light science fiction or fantasy, and contemporary fiction with a unique premise); **Amelia Appel**, aaquery@mcintoshandotis.com (literary fiction, mystery, thriller, historical fiction, science fiction, fantasy, horror, and some young adult).
REPRESENTS Considers these nonfiction areas: creative nonfiction, current affairs, history, popular culture, self-help, spirituality, sports, travel. Considers these fiction areas: fantasy, historical, horror, literary, middle-grade, mystery, new adult, paranormal, picture books, romance, science fiction, suspense, urban fantasy, women's, young adult.

☞ Actively seeking "books with memorable characters, distinctive voices, and great plots."

HOW TO CONTACT E-mail submissions only. For fiction, please send a query letter, synopsis, author bio, and the first 3 consecutive chapters (no more than 30 pages) of your novel. For nonfiction, please send a query letter, proposal, outline, author bio, and 3 sample chapters (no more than 30 pages) of the ms. For children's and young adult, please send a query letter, synopsis, and the first 3 consecutive chapters (not to exceed 25 pages) of the ms. Accepts simultaneous submissions. Obtains clients through recommendations from others, editors, conferences, and queries.

SALLY HILL MCMILLAN, LLC

429 E. Kingston Ave., Charlotte NC 28203. (704)334-0897. **E-mail:** mcmagency@aol.com. **Website:** www.publishersmarketplace.com/members/McMillanAgency. **Contact:** Sally Hill McMillan. Member of AAR.

REPRESENTS Considers these nonfiction areas: creative nonfiction, health, history, women's issues, women's studies. **Considers these fiction areas:** commercial, literary, mainstream, mystery.

☞ Do not send science fiction, military, horror, fantasy/adventure, children's, or cookbooks.

HOW TO CONTACT "Please query first with SASE and await further instructions. E-mail queries will be read, but not necessarily answered." Accepts simultaneous submissions.

BOB MECOY LITERARY AGENCY

460 W. 24th St., Suite 3E, New York NY 10011. (212)226-1936. **E-mail:** bob.mecoy@gmail.com. **Website:** bobmecoy.com. **Contact:** Bob Mecoy.

MEMBER AGENTS Bob Mecoy.

☞ Seeking fiction (literary, crime, romance) and nonfiction (true crime, finance, memoir, prescriptive self-help). No westerns.

HOW TO CONTACT Query with sample chapters and synopsis. Accepts simultaneous submissions.

MENDEL MEDIA GROUP, LLC

115 W. 30th St., Suite 800, New York NY 10001. (646)239-9896. **Fax:** (212)685-4717. **E-mail:** scott@mendelmedia.com. **Website:** www.mendelmedia.com. Member of AAR. Represents 40-60 clients.

○ Prior to becoming an agent, Mr. Mendel was an academic. "I taught American literature, Yiddish, Jewish studies, and literary theory at the University of Chicago and the University of Illinois at Chicago while working on my PhD in English. I also worked as a freelance technical writer and as the managing editor of a healthcare magazine. In 1998, I began working for the late Jane Jordan Browne, a long-time agent in the book publishing world."

REPRESENTS Nonfiction, novels. **Considers these nonfiction areas:** Americana, animals, anthropology, architecture, art, biography, business, child guidance, cooking, current affairs, dance, education, environment, ethnic, foods, gardening, gay/lesbian, government, health, history, how-to, humor, investigative, language, medicine, memoirs, military, money, multicultural, music, parenting, philosophy, popular culture, psychology, recreation, regional, religious, science, self-help, sex, sociology, software, spirituality, sports, true crime, war, women's issues, women's studies, Jewish topics; creative nonfiction. **Considers these fiction areas:** action, adventure, contemporary issues, crime, detective, erotica, ethnic, feminist, gay, glitz, historical, humor, inspirational, juvenile, lesbian, literary, mainstream, mystery, picture books, police, religious, romance, satire, sports, thriller, young adult, Jewish fiction.

☞ "I am interested in major works of history, current affairs, biography, business, politics, economics, science, major memoirs, narrative nonfiction, and other sorts of general nonfiction." Actively seeking new, major, or definitive work on a subject of broad interest, or a controversial, but authoritative, new book on a subject that affects many people's lives. "I also represent more light hearted nonfiction projects, such as gift or novelty books, when they suit the market particularly well." Does not want "queries about projects written years ago that were unsuccessfully shopped to a long list of trade publishers by either the author or another agent. I am specifically not interested in reading short, category romances (regency, time travel, paranormal, etc.), horror novels, supernatural stories, poetry, original plays, or film scripts."

HOW TO CONTACT Query with SASE. Do not e-mail or fax queries. For nonfiction, include a complete, fully edited book proposal with sample chapters. For fiction, include a complete synopsis and no more than 20 pages of sample text. Responds in 2 weeks to queries. Obtains most new clients through recommendations from others.

TERMS Agent receives 15% commission on domestic sales; 20% commission on foreign sales.

TIPS "While I am not interested in being flattered by a prospective client, it does matter to me that she knows why she is writing to me in the first place. Is one of my clients a colleague of hers? Has she read a book by one of my clients that led her to believe I might be interested in her work? Authors of descriptive nonfiction should have real credentials and expertise in their subject areas, either as academics, journalists, or policy experts. Authors of prescriptive nonfiction should have legitimate expertise and considerable experience communicating their ideas in seminars and workshops, in a successful business, through the media, etc."

SCOTT MEREDITH LITERARY AGENCY

One Exchange Plaza, Suite 2002, 55 Broadway, New York NY 10006. (646)274-1970. **Fax:** (212)977-5997. **E-mail:** info@scottmeredith.com. **Website:** www.scottmeredith.com. **Contact:** Arthur Klebanoff, CEO. Adheres to the AAR canon of ethics. Represents 20 clients.

- Prior to becoming an agent, Mr. Klebanoff was a lawyer.
- This agency's specialty lies in category nonfiction publishing programs. Actively seeking category leading nonfiction. Does not want to receive first fiction projects.

HOW TO CONTACT Query, and submit a proposal package and author bio. Accepts simultaneous submissions.

TERMS Agent receives 15% commission on domestic sales. Offers written contract.

RECENT SALES *The Conscience of a Liberal* and *End This Depression Now* by Paul Krugman, *The King of Oil: The Secret Lives of Marc Rich* by Daniel Ammann, *Ten* by Sheila Lukins.

ROBIN MIZELL LITERARY REPRESENTATION

1600 Burnside St., Suite 205, Beaufort SC 29902. (614)774-7405. **E-mail:** mail@robinmizell.com. **Website:** www.robinmizell.com. **Contact:** Robin Mizell. Member of AAR. Signatory of WGA.

REPRESENTS Nonfiction, novels. **Considers these nonfiction areas:** popular culture, psychology, sociology. **Considers these fiction areas:** literary, young adult.

- This agency specializes in prescriptive nonfiction, long-form narrative journalism, neuroscience, psychology, sociology, pop culture books, literary and upmarket commercial fiction, and young adult.

HOW TO CONTACT E-query with the first 5 pages of your work pasted in the e-mail. More specific submission instructions can be found on the agency web-

site. You should receive a response to your e-mail query within 30 days. Accepts simultaneous submissions.

HOWARD MORHAIM LITERARY AGENCY

30 Pierrepont St., Brooklyn NY 11201. (718)222-8400. **Fax:** (718)222-5056. **Website:** www.morhaimliterary.com. Member of AAR.

MEMBER AGENTS Howard Morhaim (no unsolicited submissions), **Kate McKean**, kmckean@morhaimliterary.com (fiction interests include contemporary romance, contemporary women's fiction, literary fiction, historical fiction set in the 20th century, high fantasy, magical realism, science fiction, middle-grade, young adult; nonfiction interests include books by authors with demonstrable platforms in the areas of sports, food writing, humor, design, creativity, and craft [sewing, knitting, etc.]; also seeks narrative nonfiction by authors with or without an established platform, and some memoir); **DongWon Song**, dongwon@morhaimliterary.com (science fiction, fantasy; nonfiction interests include food writing, science, pop culture); **Kim-Mei Kirtland**, kimmei@morhaimliterary.com (hard science fiction, literary fiction, history, biography, business, economics).

REPRESENTS **Considers these nonfiction areas:** biography, business, cooking, crafts, creative nonfiction, design, economics, foods, health, humor, memoirs, parenting, self-help, sports. **Considers these fiction areas:** fantasy, historical, literary, middle-grade, new adult, romance, science fiction, women's, young adult, LGBTQ young adult, magical realism.

- Kate is open to many subgenres and categories of young adult and middle-grade fiction. Check the website for the most details. Actively seeking fiction, nonfiction, and young adult novels.

HOW TO CONTACT Query via e-mail with cover letter and 3 sample chapters. See each agent's website listing for further specifics. Accepts simultaneous submissions.

MOVEABLE TYPE MANAGEMENT

244 Madison Ave., Suite 334, New York NY 10016. **E-mail:** AChromy@MovableTM.com. **Website:** www.MovableTM.com. **Contact:** Adam Chromy.

REPRESENTS Nonfiction, novels. **Considers these nonfiction areas:** Americana, business, creative nonfiction, film, foods, history, how-to, humor, literature, memoirs, money, popular culture, politics, psychology, satire, science, self-help, sex, sports, technology, theater, true crime, war, women's issues, women's studies. **Considers these fiction areas:** commercial, crime, detective, erotica, literary, mainstream, mystery, romance, science fiction, sports, suspense, thriller, women's.

☛ Mr. Chromy is a generalist, meaning that he accepts fiction submissions of virtually any kind (except juvenile books aimed for middle-grade and younger), as well as nonfiction. He has sold books in the following categories: new adult, women's, romance, memoir, pop culture, young adult, lifestyle, horror, how-to, general fiction, and more.

HOW TO CONTACT E-queries only. Responds if interested. For nonfiction, send a query letter in the body of an e-mail that precisely introduces your topic and approach, and includes a descriptive bio. For journalists and academics, please also feel free to include a CV. For fiction, send your query letter and the first 10 pages of your novel in the body of an e-mail. Your subject line needs to contain the word "Query" or your message will not reach the agency. No attachments and no snail mail. Accepts simultaneous submissions.

RECENT SALES *The Wedding Sisters* by Jamie Brenner (St. Martin's Press), *Sons Of Zeus* by Noble Smith (Thomas Dunne Books), *World Made by Hand* by James Howard Kunstler (Grove/Atlantic Press), *Dirty Rocker Boys* by Bobbie Brown (Gallery/S&S).

DEE MURA LITERARY

P.O. Box 131, Massapequa NY 11762. (516)795-1616. **E-mail:** info@deemuraliterary.com. **E-mail:** query@deemuraliterary.com. **Website:** www.deemuraliterary.com. "We focus on developing our clients' careers to publication and beyond by providing personalized editorial feedback, social media and platform marketing, and thorough rights management. Both new and experienced authors are welcome to submit." Signatory of WGA. Member of Women's National Book Association, GrubStreet.

○ Prior to opening her agency, Ms. Mura was a public relations executive with a roster of film and entertainment clients. She is the president and CEO of both Dee Mura Literary and Dee Mura Entertainment.

MEMBER AGENTS Dee Mura, Kimiko Nakamura, Kaylee Davis.

REPRESENTS Nonfiction, novels, short story collections, juvenile books. **Considers these nonfiction areas:** agriculture, Americana, animals, anthropology, archeology, architecture, art, autobiography, biography, business, child guidance, cooking, crafts, creative nonfiction, cultural interests, current affairs, dance, decorating, diet/nutrition, design, economics, education, environment, ethnic, film, foods, gardening, gay/lesbian, government, health, history, hobbies, horticulture, how-to, humor, inspirational, interior design, investigative, juvenile nonfiction, language, law, literature, medicine, memoirs, metaphysics, military, money, multicultural, music, New Age, parenting, photography, popular culture, politics, psychology, recreation, religious, science, self-help, sex, sociology, spirituality, sports, technology, travel, true crime, war, women's issues, women's studies, young adult, Judaism. **Considers these fiction areas:** action, adventure, comic books, commercial, contemporary issues, crime, detective, erotica, ethnic, family saga, fantasy, feminist, frontier, gay, glitz, historical, horror, humor, inspirational, juvenile, lesbian, literary, mainstream, metaphysical, middle-grade, military, multicultural, multimedia, mystery, new adult, New Age, occult, paranormal, police, psychic, regional, religious, romance, satire, science fiction, short story collections, spiritual, sports, supernatural, suspense, thriller, translation, urban fantasy, war, westerns, women's, young adult, espionage, magical realism, speculative.

☛ No screenplays, poetry, or children's picture books.

HOW TO CONTACT E-mail query@deemuraliterary.com. Please include the first 25 pages in the body of the e-mail, as well as a short author bio and synopsis of the work. Responds to queries in 5 weeks.

TERMS Agent receives 15% commission on domestic sales; 20% commission on foreign sales. Offers written contract.

RECENT SALES *An Infinite Number of Parallel Universes* by Randy Ribay, *The Number 7* by Jessica Lidh.

WRITERS CONFERENCES BookExpo America, New England Crime Bake, New England SCBWI Agent Day, The Writer's Institute Conference at UW-Madison, Writer's Digest Annual Conference.

⊘◎ ERIN MURPHY LITERARY AGENCY

824 Roosevelt Trail, #290, Windham ME 04062. **Website:** http://emliterary.com. **Contact:** Erin Murphy,

president; Ammi-Joan Paquette, senior agent; Tricia Lawrence, agent.

REPRESENTS Considers these fiction areas: middle-grade, picture books, young adult.

☛   Specializes in children's books only.

HOW TO CONTACT This agency does not take unsolicited submissions. Query only after a referral or meeting an agent at a conference.

JEAN V. NAGGAR LITERARY AGENCY, INC.

JVNLA, Inc., 216 E. 75th St., Suite 1E, New York NY 10021. (212)794-1082. **Website:** www.jvnla.com. **Contact:** Jennifer Weltz. Estab. 1978. Member of AAR, Women's Media Group, SCBWI. Represents 450 clients.

MEMBER AGENTS Jennifer Weltz (well researched and original historicals, thrillers with a unique voice, wry dark humor, voice-driven young adult, middle-grade, magical realism; also seeks enthralling narrative nonfiction); **Alice Tasman** (literary, commercial, young adult, middle-grade; seeks nonfiction in the categories of narrative, biography, music, and pop culture); **Laura Biagi** (literary fiction, magical realism, psychological thrillers, young adult novels, middle-grade novels, and picture books).

REPRESENTS Nonfiction, novels, short story collections, novellas, juvenile books, scholarly books, poetry books.

☛   This agency specializes in mainstream fiction and nonfiction and literary fiction with commercial potential. The agency also seeks young adult, middle-grade, and picture books. Does not want to receive screenplays.

HOW TO CONTACT "Visit our website to send submissions [via an online form] and see what our individual agents are looking for. No snail mail submissions." Accepts simultaneous submissions. Responds if interested.

TERMS Agent receives 15% commission on domestic sales; 20% commission on foreign sales.

RECENT SALES *Mort(e)* by Robert Repino, *The Paying Guests* by Sarah Waters, *Violent Crimes* by Phillip Margolin, *An Unseemly Wife* by E.B. Moore, *The Man Who Walked Away* by Maud Casey, *Dietland* by Sarai Walker, *In the Land of Armadillos* by Helen Maryles Shankman, *Not If I See You First* by Eric Lindstrom.

TIPS "We recommend the courage to be true to your own vision, the fortitude to finish a novel and polish it again and again before sending it out, and the patience to accept rejection gracefully and wait for the stars to align themselves appropriately for success."

NELSON LITERARY AGENCY

1732 Wazee St., Suite 207, Denver CO 80202. (303)292-2805. **E-mail:** querykristin@nelsonagency.com. **Website:** http://nelsonagency.com. **Contact:** Kristin Nelson, President. Kristin Nelson established Nelson Literary Agency, LLC, in 2002 and over the last decade of her career, she has represented 35 *New York Times* best-selling titles and many *USA Today* bestsellers. Member of AAR, RWA, SCBWI, SFWA. Represents 33 clients.

REPRESENTS Fiction. **Considers these fiction areas:** commercial, fantasy, literary, mainstream, middle-grade, romance, science fiction, women's, young adult.

☛   NLA specializes in representing commercial fiction and high-caliber literary fiction. They represent many pop genre categories, including things like historical romance, steampunk, and all subgenres of young adult—good stories well told. Please remember that NLA does not look at submissions for nonfiction, memoir, screenplays, short story collections, poetry, children's picture books, early reader chapter books, or material for the Christian/inspirational market.

HOW TO CONTACT "Please visit our website to carefully read our submission guidelines." Kristin does not accept any queries by Facebook or Twitter. Query by e-mail only. Put the word "Query" in the e-mail subject line along with the title of your novel. No attachments, but it is OK to include the first 10 pages of your novel in the body of the e-mail. Accepts simultaneous submissions. Tries to respond to all queries within 10 business days. Full ms requests can take 2 months or more.

NEW LEAF LITERARY & MEDIA, INC.

110 W. 40th St., Suite 2201, New York NY 10018. (646)248-7989. **Fax:** (646)861-4654. **E-mail:** query@newleafliterary.com. **Website:** www.newleafliterary.com. Estab. 2012. Member of AAR.

MEMBER AGENTS Joanna Volpe (women's fiction, thriller, horror, speculative fiction, literary fiction, historical fiction, young adult, middle-grade, art-focused picture books); **Kathleen Ortiz**, director of subsidiary rights and literary agent (new voices in

NEW AGENT SPOTLIGHT

LORI GALVIN
ZACHARY SHUSTER HARMSWORTH / KUHN PROJECTS

www.zshliterary.com
@galvinlori

ABOUT LORI: Lori Galvin knows cookbooks. For over a decade, she helped lead a team that produced dozens of landmark cookbooks for the multimedia publisher America's Test Kitchen. Just a few of her titles include *The Cook's Illustrated Cookbook, The Complete Cooking for Two Cookbook, Kitchen Hacks,* and *Cook's Country Eats Local.* With her in-depth experience working for a powerful multi-platform brand (books, magazines, web, TV, and radio), she knows what it takes to make a book a success from conception to publication and beyond. Before working at ATK, Lori edited cookbooks for Houghton Mifflin, cooked in restaurant kitchens, and ran a bed-and-breakfast in Maine. She joined Zachary Schuster Harmsworth in 2015. Lori is a member of the International Association of Culinary Professionals (IACP) and Women Chefs and Restaurateurs (WCR). She earned her bachelor of arts in English literature from Northeastern University and is a graduate of the culinary certificate program at Boston University..

SHE IS SEEKING: Lori seeks cookbook authors with a strong point of view, a solid grounding in their field, and a talent for motivating cooks of all stripes to get into the kitchen. She is also on the lookout for compelling narratives about food and drink, whether memoir or cultural commentary, serious or steeped in humor. Lifestyle topics, including motivational self-help, are also of interest.

HOW TO CONTACT: Use the agency's online form (see the website) to send an e-query to Lori.

young adult, as well as animator/illustrator talent); **Suzie Townsend** (new adult, young adult, middle-grade, romance [all subgenres], fantasy [urban fantasy, science fiction, steampunk, epic fantasy], and crime fiction [mysteries, thrillers]); **Pouya Shahbazian**, director of film and television (no unsolicited queries); **Mackenzie Brady** (science books, memoirs,

"lost history" nonfiction, epic sports narratives, true crime, and gift/lifestyle books; she represents select adult and young adult fiction projects, as well); **Peter Knapp** (middle-grade, young adult, general adult fiction, grounded science fiction, genre-agnostic for all); **Jaida Temperly** (magical realism, historical fiction, literary fiction, stories that are quirky and fantastical;

nonfiction interests include niche, offbeat books, or anything that is a bit strange); **J.L. Stermer** (nonfiction and some fiction).

REPRESENTS Nonfiction, novels, novellas, juvenile books, poetry books. **Considers these nonfiction areas:** cooking, crafts, creative nonfiction, science, technology, women's issues, young adult. **Considers these fiction areas:** crime, fantasy, historical, horror, literary, mainstream, middle-grade, mystery, new adult, paranormal, picture books, romance, thriller, women's, young adult.

HOW TO CONTACT Send a query to query@newleafliterary.com. Please do not query via phone. The word "Query" must be in the subject line, plus the agent's name. You may include up to 5 double-spaced sample pages within the body of the e-mail. No attachments unless specifically requested. Include all necessary contact information. You will receive an auto-response confirming receipt of your query. Responds only if interested. All queries read within 2 weeks.

RECENT SALES *Red Queen* by Victoria Aveyard (HarperCollins), *Lobster is the Best Medicine* by Liz Climo (Running Press), *Six of Crows* by Leigh Bardugo (Henry Holt), *A Snicker of Magic* by Natalie Lloyd (Scholastic).

DANA NEWMAN LITERARY

9720 Wilshire Blvd., Fifth Floor, Beverly Hills CA 90212. **Fax:** (866)636-7585. **E-mail:** dananewmanliterary@gmail.com. **Website:** http://dananewman.com. **Contact:** Dana Newman. Dana Newman Literary, LLC, is a boutique literary agency in Los Angeles. Estab. 2009. Member of AAR, California State Bar. Represents 28 clients.

○ Prior to being an agent, Ms. Newman was an attorney in the entertainment industry for 14 years.

REPRESENTS Nonfiction, novels, short story collections. **Considers these nonfiction areas:** architecture, art, autobiography, biography, business, child guidance, cooking, creative nonfiction, cultural interests, current affairs, diet/nutrition, design, education, ethnic, film, foods, gay/lesbian, government, health, history, how-to, inspirational, investigative, language, law, literature, medicine, memoirs, money, multicultural, music, parenting, popular culture, politics, psychology, science, self-help, sociology, sports, technology, theater, travel, true crime, women's is-sues, women's studies. **Considers these fiction areas:** commercial, contemporary issues, family saga, feminist, historical, horror, literary, multicultural, sports, women's.

⌐ Ms. Newman has a background as an attorney in contracts, licensing, and intellectual property law. She is experienced in digital content creation and distribution and embraces the changing publishing environment. Actively seeking narrative nonfiction, practical nonfiction, historical and contemporary literary fiction, or commercial fiction with literary sensibilities. Does not want religious, children's, poetry, horror, mystery, thriller, romance, or science fiction.

HOW TO CONTACT E-queries only. For both nonfiction and fiction, please submit a query letter including a description of your project and a brief biography. "If we are interested in your project, we will contact you and request a full book proposal (nonfiction) or a synopsis and the first 25 pages (fiction)." Accepts simultaneous submissions. "If we have requested your materials after receiving your query, we usually respond within 4 weeks." Obtains new clients through recommendations from others, queries, and submissions.

TERMS Obtains 15% commission on domestic sales; 20% on foreign sales. Offers written contract. Notice must be given 30 days prior to terminate a contract.

RECENT SALES *Native Advertising* by Mike Smith (McGraw-Hill), *Breakthrough: The Making of America's First Woman President* by Nancy L. Cohen (Counterpoint), *Just Add Water* by Clay Marzo and Robert Yehling (Houghton Mifflin Harcourt), *A Stray Cat Struts* by Slim Jim Phantom (St. Martin's Press).

ALLEN O'SHEA LITERARY AGENCY

615 Westover Rd., Stamford CT 06902. (203)359-9965. **Fax:** (203)357-9909. **E-mail:** marilyn@allenoshea.com; coleen@allenoshea.com. **Website:** www.allenoshea.com. **Contact:** Marilyn Allen.

○ Prior to becoming agents, both Ms. Allen and Ms. O'Shea held senior positions in publishing.

MEMBER AGENTS Marilyn Allen, Coleen O'Shea.

REPRESENTS Nonfiction. **Considers these nonfiction areas:** autobiography, biography, business, cooking, crafts, creative nonfiction, current affairs, decorating, diet/nutrition, design, film, foods, gardening, health, history, how-to, humor, inspirational, interior design, medicine, military, money, New Age, parenting, popular culture, psychology, regional, science, self-help, interior design/decorating.

☞ "This agency specializes in practical nonfiction including health, cooking and cocktails, business, and pop culture. We look for passionate clients with strong marketing platforms and new ideas coupled with writing talent." Actively seeking narrative nonfiction, health, popular science, cookbooks, and history writers. The agency is very interested in writers who have large media platforms and interesting topics. Does not want to receive fiction, memoirs, poetry, textbooks, or children's.

HOW TO CONTACT Query via e-mail or mail with SASE. Submit book proposal with sample chapters, competitive analysis, outline, author bio, marketing page. No phone or fax queries. Accepts simultaneous submissions. Obtains most new clients through recommendations from others, conferences.

TERMS Agent receives 15% commission on domestic sales. Offers written contract, binding for 2 years; one-month notice must be given to terminate contract.

TIPS "Prepare a strong overview, with competition, marketing, and bio. We will consider your project when your proposal is ready."

HAROLD OBER ASSOCIATES

425 Madison Ave., New York NY 10017. (212)759-8600. **Fax:** (212)759-9428. **Website:** www.haroldober.com. **Contact:** Appropriate agent. Member of AAR. Represents 250 clients.

○ Mr. Elwell was previously with Elwell & Weiser.

MEMBER AGENTS Phyllis Westberg, Pamela Malpas, Craig Tenney, Jake Elwell (previously with Elwell & Weiser).

HOW TO CONTACT Submit a concise query letter addressed to a specific agent, the first 5 pages of the ms or proposal, and a SASE. No fax or e-mail. Does not handle filmscripts or plays. Responds as promptly as possible. Obtains most new clients through recommendations from others.

TERMS Agent receives 15% commission on domestic sales; 20% commission on foreign sales.

PARK LITERARY GROUP, LLC

270 Lafayette St., Suite 1504, New York NY 10012. (212)691-3500. **Fax:** (212)691-3540. **E-mail:** queries@parkliterary.com. **Website:** www.parkliterary.com. Estab. 2005.

MEMBER AGENTS Theresa Park (plot-driven fiction and serious nonfiction); Abigail Koons (popular science, history, politics, current affairs and art, and women's fiction).

REPRESENTS Novels, nonfiction. **Considers these nonfiction areas:** art, current affairs, history, politics, science. **Considers these fiction areas:** middle-grade, suspense, thriller, women's, young adult.

☞ The Park Literary Group represents fiction and nonfiction with a boutique approach—an emphasis on servicing a relatively small number of clients, with the highest professional standards and focused personal attention. Does not want to receive poetry or screenplays.

HOW TO CONTACT Please specify the first and last name of the agent to whom you are submitting in the subject line of the e-mail. Send your query letter and accompanying material to queries@parkliterary.com. All materials must be in the body of the e-mail. Responds if interested. For fiction submissions, please include a short synopsis and the first 3 chapters of your work. Accepts simultaneous submissions.

RECENT SALES This agency's client list is on their website. It includes bestsellers Nicholas Sparks, Soman Chainani, Emily Giffin, and Debbie Macomber.

⊘◎ PAVILION LITERARY MANAGEMENT

660 Massachusetts Ave., Suite 4, Boston MA 02118. (617)792-5218. **E-mail:** jeff@pavilionliterary.com. **Website:** www.pavilionliterary.com. **Contact:** Jeff Kellogg.

○ Prior to his current position, Mr. Kellogg was a literary agent with The Stuart Agency, and an acquiring editor with HarperCollins.

REPRESENTS Novels, nonfiction. **Considers these nonfiction areas:** creative nonfiction, memoirs, science. **Considers these fiction areas:** adventure, fantasy, juvenile, mystery, thriller.

HOW TO CONTACT No unsolicited submissions. If the agency has requested your submission, you can query first by e-mail (no attachments). The subject line should specify fiction or nonfiction and include the title of the work. If submitting nonfiction, include a book proposal (no longer than 75 pages), with sample chapters. Accepts simultaneous submissions.

JAMES PETER ASSOCIATES, INC.

P.O. Box 358, New Canaan CT 06840. (203)972-1070. **E-mail:** gene_brissie@msn.com. **Website:** www.

NEW AGENT SPOTLIGHT

MOLLY O'NEILL
WAXMAN LEAVELL LITERARY AGENCY

www.waxmanleavell.com
@molly_oneill

ABOUT MOLLY: Prior to becoming an agent, Molly O'Neill spent thirteen years working in various roles inside the publishing industry. She served as an editor at HarperCollins Children's Books, where she acquired Veronica Roth's juggernaut Divergent series, among many other fantastic projects. She also served as head of editorial at Storybird, a publishing/tech startup. She loves the creative process and project development, is invigorated by business strategy and entrepreneurial thinking, and is fascinated by the intersections of art, commerce, creativity, and innovation. Molly is especially passionate about the people behind books, and takes pride in discovering and evangelizing talented authors and illustrators, expanding the global reach of their work, and finding new ways to build connections and community among creators, readers, stories, and their champions. Molly is an alum of Marquette University, an erstwhile Texan, and a current dweller of Brooklyn.

SHE IS SEEKING: Young adult and middle-grade fiction. She is also seeking a select number of children's illustrators (illustrators who write are especially welcome), and authors of juvenile nonfiction (any age), early readers, chapter books, and children's graphic novels. She is *not* currently seeking picture book texts unless the author is also a professional illustrator, a writer of nonfiction, or a referral from an industry contact that she knows personally.

HOW TO CONTACT: E-mail your query to mollysubmit@waxmanleavell.com and include a description of your project, biographical information (including details about any relevant credentials, subject area expertise, stats, or existing platform), and a pitch summary. If applicable, speak of prior published works, agent representation, and/or publisher submission history. Please also be sure to include your phone number, e-mail address, and any relevant Internet/social media links.

jamespeterassociates.com. **Contact:** Gene Brissie. Represents 75 individual and 6 corporate clients.

REPRESENTS Considers these nonfiction areas: anthropology, archeology, architecture, art, biography, business, current affairs, dance, design, ethnic, film, gay/lesbian, government, health, history, language, literature, medicine, military, money, music, popular culture, psychology, self-help, theater, travel, war, women's issues, women's studies, memoirs (political, business).

☛ "We are especially interested in general, trade, and reference nonfiction." Does not want to receive children's or young adult books, poetry, or fiction.

HOW TO CONTACT Send a query letter with SASE for reply. Accepts simultaneous submissions. Responds in 1 month to queries.

TERMS Agent receives 15% commission on domestic sales, 20% commission on foreign sales. Offers written contract.

✪◎ RUBIN PFEFFER CONTENT

648 Hammond St., Chestnut Hill MA 02467. **E-mail:** info@rpcontent.com. **Website:** www.rpcontent.com. **Contact:** Rubin Pfeffer. Rubin Pfeffer Content is a literary agency exclusively representing children's and young adult literature, as well as content that will serve educational publishers and digital developers. Estab. 2014. Member of AAR. Signatory of WGA.

○ Mr. Pfeffer has previously worked as the vice president and publisher of Simon & Schuster Children's Books and as an independent agent at East West Literary Agency.

REPRESENTS Considers these fiction areas: juvenile, middle-grade, picture books, young adult.

HOW TO CONTACT *This agent accepts submissions by referral only. Specify the contact information of your reference when submitting.* Authors/illustrators should send a query and 1-3 chapters of their ms via e-mail (no postal submissions). The query, placed in the body of the e-mail, should include a pitch, as well as any relevant information regarding previous publications, referrals, websites, and biographies. The ms may be attached as a .doc or a PDF file. Specifically for illustrators, attach a PDF of the dummy or artwork to the e-mail. Accepts simultaneous submissions. Responds within 8 weeks.

RECENT SALES *Marti Feels Proud* by Micha Archer, *Burning* by Elana K. Arnold, *Junkyard* by Mike Austin, *Little Dog, Lost* by Marion Dane Bauer, *Not Your Typical Dragon* by Tim Bowers, *Ghost Hawk* by Susan Cooper.

◎ PIPPIN PROPERTIES, INC.

110 W. 40th St., Suite 1704, New York NY 10018. (212)338-9310. **Fax:** (212)338-9579. **E-mail:** info@pippinproperties.com. **Website:** www.pippinproperties.com. **Contact:** Holly McGhee.

○ Prior to becoming an agent, Ms. McGhee was an editor for 7 years and in book marketing for 4 years.

MEMBER AGENTS Holly McGhee, Elena Giovinazzo, Heather Alexander. Although each of the agents take children's books, you can find in-depth preferences for each agency on their website.

REPRESENTS Juvenile books. **Considers these fiction areas:** middle-grade, picture books, young adult.

☛ "We are strictly a children's literary agency devoted to the management of authors and artists in all media. We are small and discerning in choosing our clientele."

HOW TO CONTACT Query via e-mail. Include a synopsis of the work(s), your background and/or publishing history, and anything else you think is relevant. Accepts simultaneous submissions. Obtains most new clients through recommendations from others.

TIPS "Please do not start calling after sending a submission."

LINN PRENTIS LITERARY

155 E. 116th St., #2F, New York NY 10029. **Fax:** (212)875-5565. **Website:** www.linnprentis.com. **Contact:** Amy Hayden, acquisitions; Linn Prentis, agent. Represents 18-20 clients.

○ Prior to becoming an agent, Ms. Prentis was a nonfiction writer and editor, primarily in magazines. She also worked in book promotion in New York. Ms. Prentis then worked for and later ran the Virginia Kidd Agency. She is known particularly for her assistance with ms development.

REPRESENTS Considers these nonfiction areas: biography, current affairs, ethnic, humor, memoirs, popular culture, women's issues. **Considers these fiction areas:** adventure, ethnic, fantasy, gay, glitz, historical, horror, humor, lesbian, literary, mainstream, thriller.

☛ "Because of the Virginia Kidd connection and the clients I brought with me at the start, I have a special interest in science fiction and fantasy, but fiction is what truly interests me. As for nonfiction projects, they are books I just couldn't resist." Actively seeking hard science fiction, family saga, mystery, memoir, mainstream, literary, women's. Does not want to receive children's picture books.

HOW TO CONTACT This agency is closed to submissions as of 2016. Check the website before submitting.

TIPS "Consider query letters and synopses as writing assignments. Spell names correctly."

AARON M. PRIEST LITERARY AGENCY

200 W. 41st St., 21st Floor, New York NY 10036. (212)818-0344. **Fax:** (212)573-9417. **E-mail:** info@aaronpriest.com. **Website:** www.aaronpriest.com. Estab. 1974. Member of AAR.

MEMBER AGENTS Aaron Priest, querypriest@aaronpriest.com (thrillers, commercial fiction, biographies); **Lisa Erbach Vance**, queryvance@aaronpriest.com (contemporary fiction, thrillers/suspense, international fiction, narrative nonfiction); **Lucy Childs Baker**, querychilds@aaronpriest.com (literary and commercial fiction, memoir, edgy women's fiction); **Melissa Edwards**, queryedwards@aaronpriest.com (middle-grade, young adult, women's fiction, thrillers); **Mitch Hoffman** (thrillers, suspense, crime fiction, and literary fiction, as well as narrative nonfiction, politics, popular science, history, memoir, current events, and pop culture).

REPRESENTS Considers these nonfiction areas: biography, current affairs, history, memoirs, popular culture, politics, science. **Considers these fiction areas:** commercial, contemporary issues, crime, literary, middle-grade, suspense, thriller, women's, young adult.

☛ Does not want to receive poetry, screenplays, horror, or science fiction.

HOW TO CONTACT "Please do not submit to more than 1 agent at this agency. We urge you to check our website and consider each agent's emphasis before submitting. Your query letter should be about 1 page long and describe your work, as well as your background. You may also paste the first chapter of your work in the body of the e-mail. Do not send attachments." Accepts simultaneous submissions. Responds in 4 weeks, only if interested.

TERMS Agent receives 15% commission on domestic sales.

RECENT SALES *The Hit* by David Baldacci, *Six Years* by Harlan Coben, *Suspect* by Robert Crais, *Permanent Record* by Leslie Stella.

PROSPECT AGENCY

551 Valley Rd., PMB 377, Upper Montclair NJ 07043. (718)788-3217. **Fax:** (718)360-9582. **Website:** www.prospectagency.com. "Prospect Agency focuses on adult and children's literature, and is currently looking for the next generation of writers and illustrators to shape the literary landscape." Estab. 2005. Member of AAR. Signatory of WGA.

MEMBER AGENTS Emily Sylvan Kim, esk@prospectagency.com (romance, women's, commercial, young adult, new adult); **Rachel Orr**, rko@prospectagency.com (picture books, illustrators, middle-grade, young adult); **Becca Stumpf**, becca@prospectagency.com (young adult and middle-grade [all genres for both, especially novels featuring diverse protagonists and life circumstances]; also seeks adult science fiction and fantasy, upmarket women's fiction, spicy romance novels); **Carrie Pestritto**, carrie@prospectagency.com (narrative nonfiction, general nonfiction, biography, and memoir; fiction interests include commercial fiction with a literary twist, women's fiction, romance, upmarket, historical fiction, high-concept young adult and upper middle-grade); **Linda Camacho**, linda@prospectagency.com (middle-grade, young adult, and adult fiction across all genres—especially women's fiction/romance, horror, fantasy, science fiction, graphic novels, contemporary, select literary fiction, and fiction featuring diverse/marginalized groups); **Kirsten Carleton**, kcarleton@prospectagency.com (upmarket speculative, thriller, and literary fiction for adult and young adult).

REPRESENTS Nonfiction, novels, novellas, juvenile books. **Considers these nonfiction areas:** biography, memoirs. **Considers these fiction areas:** commercial, contemporary issues, crime, ethnic, family saga, fantasy, feminist, gay, historical, horror, humor, juvenile, lesbian, literary, mainstream, middle-grade, multicultural, mystery, new adult, picture books, romance, science fiction, suspense, thriller, urban fantasy, women's, young adult.

☛ "We're looking for strong, unique voices and unforgettable stories and characters."

HOW TO CONTACT Note that each agent at this agency has a different submission e-mail address and different submission policies. Check the agency website for the latest formal guideline per each agent. Accepts simultaneous submissions. Obtains new clients through conferences, recommendations, queries, and some scouting.

⊘ JOANNA PULCINI LITERARY MANAGEMENT

E-mail: info@jplm.com. **Website:** www.jplm.com. **Contact:** Joanna Pulcini.

☞ "JPLM is not accepting submissions at this time; however, I do encourage those seeking representation to read the 'Advice to Writers' essay on our website for some guidance on finding an agent."

HOW TO CONTACT Do not query this agency until they open their client list. Accepts simultaneous submissions.

RECENT SALES *TV* by Brian Brown, *The Movies That Changed Us* by Nick Clooney, *Strange, But True* by John Searles, *The Intelligencer* by Leslie Silbert, *In Her Shoes* and *The Guy Not Taken* by Jennifer Weiner.

THE PURCELL AGENCY

E-mail: tpaqueries@gmail.com. **Website:** www.thepurcellagency.com. **Contact:** Tina P. Schwartz. This is an agency for authors of children's and teen literature. Estab. 2012. Member of AAR. Signatory of WGA.

MEMBER AGENTS Tina P. Schwartz, Kim Blair McCollum, Mary Buza.

REPRESENTS Nonfiction, novels. **Considers these nonfiction areas:** juvenile nonfiction. **Considers these fiction areas:** juvenile, middle-grade, young adult.

☞ This agency also takes juvenile nonfiction for middle-grade and young adult markets. At this point, the agency is not considering fantasy, science fiction, or picture book submissions.

HOW TO CONTACT Check the website to see if agency is open at this time (as they can close submissions off).

RECENT SALES *I'm Not Her* by Cara Sue Achterberg, *Shyness: The Ultimate Teen Guide* by Bernardo J. Carducci and Lisa Kaiser, *Out of the Dragon's Mouth* by Joyce Burn Zeiss, *A Work of Art* by Melody Maysonet.

THE SUSAN RABINER LITERARY AGENCY, INC.

Website: www.rabinerlit.com. **Contact:** Susan Rabiner.

○ Prior to becoming an agent, Ms. Rabiner was editorial director of Basic Books. She is also the co-author of *Thinking Like Your Editor: How to Write Great Serious Nonfiction and Get it Published* (W.W. Norton).

MEMBER AGENTS Susan Rabiner, susan@rabiner.net (topical books written by fully credentialed academics, journalists, and recognized public intellectuals with the power to stimulate public debate on a broad range of issues—including the state of our economy, political discourse, history, science, and the arts); **Sydelle Kramer**, sydellek@rabiner.net, (represents a diverse group of academics, journalists, sportswriters, and memoirists); **Holly Bemiss**, hollyb@rabiner.net (clients include graphic novelists, journalists, memoirists, comedians, crafters, and entertainment writers).

☞ "Representing narrative nonfiction and big-idea books by scholars, public intellectuals, and established journalists. Actively seeks work that illuminates the past and the present in current affairs, history, the sciences, and the arts."

HOW TO CONTACT Please send all queries by e-mail. Note: "Because of the number of queries we receive, we cannot respond to every one. If your project fits the profile of the agency, we will be in touch within 2 weeks." Accepts simultaneous submissions. Obtains most new clients through recommendations from others.

TERMS Agent receives 15% commission on domestic sales; 20% commission on foreign sales. Offers written contract; 1-month notice must be given to terminate contract.

LYNNE RABINOFF AGENCY

72-11 Austin St., No. 201, Forest Hills NY 11375. **E-mail:** Lynne@lynnerabinoff.com. **Contact:** Lynne Rabinoff. Represents 50 clients.

○ Prior to becoming an agent, Ms. Rabinoff was in publishing and dealt with foreign rights.

REPRESENTS Considers these nonfiction areas: anthropology, archeology, autobiography, biography, business, cultural interests, current affairs, economics, ethnic, government, history, inspirational, law, memoirs, military, popular culture, politics, psychology, religious, science, technology, women's issues, women's studies.

☞ "This agency specializes in history, political issues, current affairs, and religion."

HOW TO CONTACT Query with SASE or by e-mail. Submit proposal package, synopsis, 1 sample chapter, author bio. Responds in 3 weeks to queries. Obtains most new clients through recommendations from others.

TERMS Agent receives 15% commission on domestic sales; 20% commission on foreign sales. Offers written contract; 60-day notice must be given to terminate contract. This agency charges for postage.

RECENT SALES *The Confrontation* by Walid Phares (Palgrave), *Flying Solo* by Robert Vaughn (Thomas Dunne), *Thugs* by Micah Halpern (Thomas Nelson), *Size Sexy* by Stella Ellis (Adams Media), *Cruel and Usual* by Nonie Darwish (Thomas Nelson), *Now They Call Me Infidel* by Nonie Darwish (Sentinel/Penguin), *34 Days* by Avid Issacharoff (Palgrave).

⊘◎ RED FOX LITERARY

129 Morro Ave., Shell Beach CA 93449. (805)459-3327. **E-mail:** info@redfoxliterary.com. **Website:** http://redfoxliterary.com. This agency specializes in books for children, looking for both authors and illustrators. Member of AAR. Signatory of WGA.

◯ Before co-founding Red Fox Literary with Ms. Grencik in 2011, Ms. Samoun was an in-house children's book editor for 10 years. Ms. Smith was formerly with Red Fox Literary.

MEMBER AGENTS Abigail Samoun, Karen Grencik, Danielle Smith, Stephanie Fretwell-Hill.

REPRESENTS Considers these fiction areas: juvenile, middle-grade, picture books, young adult.

HOW TO CONTACT Only accepts submissions by invitation, conference meetings, and referrals. A full list of book sales and clients (and illustrator portfolios) is available on the agency website.

RED SOFA LITERARY

P.O. Box 40482, St. Paul MN 55104. (651)224-6670. **E-mail:** dawn@redsofaliterary.com, jennie@redsofaliterary.com, laura@redsofaliterary.com, bree@redsofaliterary.com, amanda@redsofaliterary.com, stacey@redsofaliterary.com, erik@redsofaliterary.com. **Website:** http://redsofaliterary.com. **REPRESENTS** Nonfiction, novels, juvenile books. **Considers these nonfiction areas:** Americana, animals, anthropology, archeology, crafts, creative nonfiction, cultural interests, current affairs, dance, film,

gay/lesbian, government, health, history, hobbies, humor, investigative, juvenile nonfiction, popular culture, politics, recreation, satire, sociology, true crime, women's issues, women's studies, extreme sports. **Considers these fiction areas:** erotica, fantasy, feminist, gay, humor, juvenile, lesbian, literary, middle-grade, romance, science fiction, suspense, thriller, young adult.

HOW TO CONTACT Query by e-mail or mail with SASE. No attachments. Submit full proposal plus 3 sample chapters (or first 50 pages) and any other pertinent writing samples upon request by the specific agent. Accepts simultaneous submissions.

TERMS Agent receives 15% commission on domestic sales; 20% commission on foreign sales. Offers written contract.

RECENT SALES *Branded* by Eric Smith (Bloomsbury Spark), *Seeking Mansfield* by Kate Watson (Jolly Fish Press), *Behind the Books: How Debut Authors Navigate From the Idea to the End* by Chris Jones (University of Chicago Press), *Ten Years an Orc: A Decade in the World of Warcraft* by Tony Palumbi (Chicago Review Press), *Bad Bitch* by Christina Saunders (SMP Swerve).

TIPS "Always remember the benefits of building an author platform and the accessibility of accomplishing this task in today's industry. Most importantly, research the agents queried. Avoid contacting every literary agent about a book idea."

REES LITERARY AGENCY

14 Beacon St., Suite 710, Boston MA 02108. (617)227-9014. **Website:** http://reesagency.com. Estab. 1983. Member of AAR. Represents more than 100 clients.

MEMBER AGENTS **Ann Collette**, agent10702@aol.com (fiction interests include literary, upscale commercial women's, crime [including mystery, thriller and psychological suspense], upscale western, historical, military and war, horror; nonfiction interests include narrative, military and war, books on race and class, works set in Southeast Asia, biography, pop culture, books on film and opera, humor, and memoir); **Lorin Rees**, lorin@reesagency.com (literary fiction, memoirs, business books, self-help, science, history, psychology, and narrative nonfiction); **Rebecca Podos**, rebecca@reesagency.com (young adult and middle-grade fiction, particularly books about complex female relationships, beautifully written contemporary, genre novels with a strong focus on character, romance with more at stake than "will they/won't they," and LGBTQ books across all genres).

NEW AGENT SPOTLIGHT

ELISE ERICKSON
HAROLD OBER ASSOCIATES

www.haroldober.com
@eliseshaull

ABOUT ELISE: Elise Erickson graduated from St. Olaf College and the NYU Summer Publishing Institute in 2014, and spent several months interning at Penguin's New American Library imprint, Folio Literary Management, and Susanna Lea Associates before taking on her current position at Harold Ober Associates. She grew up in both Florida and Minnesota, but is quickly learning to love city life in New York. Elise is passionate about the role and responsibility of the literary agent, especially being an advocate for authors. In addition to actively building a client list of her own, she currently assists in selling the agency's TV, film, and subsidiary rights.

SHE IS SEEKING: Romance (all subgenres), women's fiction, paranormal, mystery (including clever cozy mysteries), thrillers, historical fiction, commercial literary fiction, and some young adult. She is particularly drawn to stories that contain a strong sense of place and female protagonists with unique, compelling voices. She is not looking for poetry, screenplays, picture books, horror, or self-help nonfiction.

HOW TO CONTACT: E-mail the first fifteen (or so) pages of your manuscript, a concise query letter, and a detailed synopsis to elise@haroldober.com.

REPRESENTS Novels, nonfiction. **Considers these nonfiction areas:** biography, business, film, history, humor, memoirs, military, popular culture, psychology, science, war. **Considers these fiction areas:** commercial, crime, historical, horror, literary, middle-grade, mystery, suspense, thriller, westerns, women's, young adult.
HOW TO CONTACT Consult website for each agent's submission guidelines, as they differ. Accepts simultaneous submissions. Obtains most new clients through recommendations from others, conferences, submissions.
TERMS Agent receives 15% commission on domestic sales; 20% commission on foreign sales.

RECENT SALES *The Marauders* by Tom Cooper, *The Gentleman's Guide to Vice and Virtue* by Mackenzi Lee, *Regret Nothing* by Sarah Nicolas, *Suffer Love* by Ashley Herring Blake, *Superbosses* by Sydney Finkelstein, *Idyll Threats* by Stephanie Gayle.

REGAL HOFFMANN & ASSOCIATES, LLC

242 W. 38th St., Floor 2, New York NY 10018. (212)684-7900. **Fax:** (212)684-7906. **E-mail:** submissions@regal-literary.com. **Website:** www.regal-literary.com. Member of AAR. Represents 70 clients.
MEMBER AGENTS Claire Anderson-Wheeler (nonfiction interests include memoirs and biographies, narrative histories, popular science, popular

psychology; adult fiction interests include primarily character-driven literary fiction; also seeks all genres of young adult and middle-grade fiction); **Markus Hoffmann** (international and literary fiction, crime, [pop] cultural studies, current affairs, economics, history, music, popular science, and travel literature); **Joseph Regal** (literary fiction, international thrillers, history, science, photography, music, culture, and whimsy).

REPRESENTS Considers these nonfiction areas: biography, creative nonfiction, current affairs, economics, history, memoirs, music, psychology, science, travel. **Considers these fiction areas:** literary, mainstream, middle-grade, thriller, young adult.

☞ "We represent works in a wide range of categories, with an emphasis on literary fiction, outstanding thriller and crime fiction, and serious narrative nonfiction." Actively seeking literary fiction and narrative nonfiction. Does not want romance, science fiction, poetry, or screenplays.

HOW TO CONTACT Query with SASE or via e-mail to submissions@rhaliterary.com. No phone calls. Submissions should consist of a one-page query letter detailing the book in question, as well as the qualifications of the author. For fiction, submissions may also include the first 10 pages of the novel or 1 short story from a collection. Responds if interested. Accepts simultaneous submissions. Responds in 8 weeks.

TERMS Agent receives 15% commission on domestic sales; 20% commission on foreign sales. "We charge no reading fees."

RECENT SALES *This Is How It Really Sounds* by Stuart Archer Cohen, *Autofocus* by Lauren Gibaldi, *We've Already Gone This Far* by Patrick Dacey, *A Fierce and Subtle Poison* by Samantha Mabry, *The Life of the World to Come* by Dan Cluchey, *Willful Disregard* by Lena Andersson, *The Sweetheart* by Angelina Mirabella.

TIPS "We are deeply committed to every aspect of our clients' careers, and are engaged in everything from the editorial work of developing a great book proposal or line editing a fiction ms to negotiating state-of-the-art book deals and working to promote and publicize the book when it's published."

⊘ THE AMY RENNERT AGENCY

1550 Tiburon Blvd., No. 302, Tiburon CA 94920. **E-mail:** queries@amyrennert.com. **Website:** www.pub-lishersmarketplace.com/members/amyrennert. **Contact:** Amy Rennert.

REPRESENTS Nonfiction, novels. **Considers these nonfiction areas:** biography, business, creative nonfiction, health, history, memoirs, money, sports. **Considers these fiction areas:** literary, mainstream, mystery.

☞ "The Amy Rennert Agency specializes in books that matter. We provide career management for established and first-time authors, and our breadth of experience in many genres enables us to meet the needs of a diverse clientele."

HOW TO CONTACT Amy Rennert is not currently accepting unsolicited submissions.

TIPS "Due to the high volume of submissions, it is not possible to respond to each and every one. Please understand that we are only able to respond to queries that we feel may be a good fit with our agency."

☺ THE RIGHTS FACTORY

P.O. Box 499, Station C, Toronto Ontario M6J 3P6 Canada. (416)966-5367. **E-mail:** sam@therightsfactory.com. **Website:** www.therightsfactory.com. "The Rights Factory is an international literary agency." Estab. 2004. Represents 150 clients.

MEMBER AGENTS Sam Hiyate (fiction, nonfiction, and graphic novels); **Kelvin Kong** (clients by referral only); **Ali McDonald** (young adult and children's literature of all kinds); **Olga Filina** (commercial fiction, historical fiction, mystery, romance; seeks nonfiction in the field of business, wellness, lifestyle, and memoir; also seeks young adult and middle-grade novels with memorable characters); **Cassandra Rogers** (literary fiction, commercial women's fiction, historical fiction; also seeks nonfiction on politics, history, science, and finance; enjoys humorous, heartbreaking, and inspiring memoir); **Lydia Moed** (science fiction and fantasy, historical fiction, diverse voices; seeks narrative nonfiction on a wide variety of topics, including history, popular science, biography, and travel); **Natalie Kimber** (literary and commercial fiction; also seeks creative nonfiction in categories such as memoir, cooking, pop culture, spirituality, and sustainability); **Harry Endrulat** (children's literature, especially author/illustrators and Canadian voices); **Haskell Nussbaum** (literature of all kinds).

REPRESENTS Nonfiction, novels, short story collections, novellas, juvenile books. **Considers these nonfiction areas:** biography, business, cooking, environment, foods, gardening, health, history, inspirational, juvenile nonfiction, memoirs, money, music, popular culture, politics, science, travel, women's issues, young adult. **Considers these fiction areas:** commercial, crime, family saga, fantasy, gay, hi-lo, historical, horror, juvenile, lesbian, literary, mainstream, middle-grade, multicultural, mystery, new adult, paranormal, picture books, romance, science fiction, short story collections, suspense, thriller, urban fantasy, women's, young adult.

☛ Does not want to receive plays, screenplays, textbooks.

HOW TO CONTACT There is a submission form on this agency's website. Accepts simultaneous submissions.

ANGELA RINALDI LITERARY AGENCY

P.O. Box 7875, Beverly Hills CA 90212-7875. (310)842-7665. **Fax:** (310)837-8143. **E-mail:** amr@rinaldiliterary.com. **Website:** www.rinaldiliterary.com. **Contact:** Angela Rinaldi. Member of AAR.

◒ Prior to opening her agency, Ms. Rinaldi was an editor at NAL/Signet, Pocket Books, and Bantam. She was also the manager of book development for *The Los Angeles Times*.

REPRESENTS Nonfiction, novels, TV and motion picture rights (for clients only). **Considers these nonfiction areas:** biography, business, cooking, current affairs, health, memoirs, parenting, psychology, self-help, women's issues, women's studies, narrative nonfiction, food narratives, wine, lifestyle, relationships, wellness, personal finance. **Considers these fiction areas:** commercial, historical, literary, mainstream, mystery, suspense, thriller, women's, contemporary, gothic, women's book club fiction.

☛ Actively seeking commercial and literary fiction, as well as nonfiction. "For fiction, we do not want to receive humor, CIA espionage, drug thrillers, techno-thrillers, category romances, science fiction, fantasy, horror/occult/paranormal, poetry, film scripts, magazine articles, or religion. For nonfiction, please do not send us magazine articles, celebrity bios, or tell-alls."

HOW TO CONTACT E-queries only. E-mail submissions should be sent to info@RinaldiLiterary.com. Include the word "Query" in the subject line. For fiction, please send a brief synopsis and paste the first 10 pages into an e-mail. Nonfiction queries should include a detailed cover letter, your credentials, platform information, as well as any publishing history. Tell us if you have a completed proposal. Accepts simultaneous submissions. Responds in 2-4 weeks.

TERMS Agent receives 15% commission on domestic sales; 25% commission on foreign sales. Offers written contract.

RLR ASSOCIATES, LTD.

Literary Department, 7 W. 51st St., New York NY 10019. **E-mail:** sgould@rlrassociates.net. **Website:** www.rlrassociates.net. **Contact:** Scott Gould. Member of AAR. Represents 50 clients.

REPRESENTS Nonfiction, novels. **Considers these nonfiction areas:** biography, creative nonfiction, foods, history, humor, popular culture, sports. **Considers these fiction areas:** commercial, literary, mainstream, middle-grade, picture books, romance, women's, young adult, genre.

☛ "We provide a lot of editorial assistance to our clients and have connections." Does not want to receive screenplays.

HOW TO CONTACT Query by either e-mail or snail mail. For fiction, send a query and 1-3 chapters (pasted in the body of the e-mail). For nonfiction, send query or proposal. Accepts simultaneous submissions. "If you do not hear from us within 3 months, please assume that your work is out of active consideration." Obtains most new clients through recommendations from others.

TERMS Agent receives 15% commission on domestic sales; 20% commission on foreign sales. Offers written contract.

RECENT SALES Clients include Shelby Foote, The Grief Recovery Institute, Don Wade, David Plowden, Nina Planck, Karyn Bosnak, Gerald Carbone, Jason Lethcoe, and Andy Crouch.

B.J. ROBBINS LITERARY AGENCY

5130 Bellaire Ave., North Hollywood CA 91607-2908. **E-mail:** Robbinsliterary@gmail.com. **Website:** www.publishersmarketplace.com/members/bjrobbins. **Contact:** (Ms.) B.J. Robbins. Estab. 1992. Member of AAR.

REPRESENTS Nonfiction, fiction. **Considers these nonfiction areas:** autobiography, biography, cultural interests, current affairs, ethnic, film, health, history, investigative, medicine, memoirs, multicultural, music, popular culture, psychology, science, sociology, sports, theater, travel, true crime, women's issues, women's studies. **Considers these fiction areas:** contemporary issues, crime, detective, ethnic, historical, literary, mainstream, multicultural, mystery, sports, suspense, thriller, women's.

☛ "We do not represent screenplays, plays, poetry, science fiction, horror, westerns, romance, techno-thrillers, religious tracts, dating books, or anything with the word 'unicorn' in the title."

HOW TO CONTACT E-query with no attachments. For fiction, you may include first 10 pages in the body of the e-mail. Accepts simultaneous submissions. Only responds to projects if interested. Obtains most new clients through conferences, referrals.

TERMS Agent receives 15% commission on domestic sales; 20% commission on foreign sales. Offers written contract; 3-month notice must be given to terminate contract.

RECENT SALES *Shoot for the Moon: The Perilous Voyage of Apollo 11* by James Donovan (Little, Brown), *Planet Earth 2050* by J. Maarten Troost (Holt), *Mongrels* by Stephen Graham Jones (William Morrow), *Blood Brothers: The Story of the Strange Friendship Between Sitting Bull and Buffalo Bill* by Deanne Stillman (Simon & Schuster), *Reliance Illinois* by Mary Volmer (Soho Press).

RODEEN LITERARY MANAGEMENT

3501 N. Southport, No. 497, Chicago IL 60657. **E-mail:** submissions@rodeenliterary.com. **Website:** www.rodeenliterary.com. **Contact:** Paul Rodeen. Estab. 2009. Member of AAR. Signatory of WGA.

○ Mr. Rodeen established Rodeen Literary Management in 2009 after 7 years of experience with the literary agency Sterling Lord Literistic, Inc.

REPRESENTS Nonfiction, novels, juvenile books, illustrations, graphic novels. **Considers these fiction areas:** juvenile, middle-grade, picture books, young adult, graphic novels, comics.

☛ Actively seeking "writers and illustrators of all genres of children's literature—including picture books, early readers, middle-grade fiction and nonfiction, graphic novels and comic books, as well as young adult fiction and nonfiction." This is primarily an agency devoted to children's books.

HOW TO CONTACT Unsolicited submissions are accepted by e-mail to submissions@rodeenliterary.

com. Cover letters with a synopsis and contact information should be included in the body of your e-mail. An initial submission of 50 pages from a novel or a longer work of nonfiction will suffice and should be pasted into the body of your e-mail. Electronic portfolios from illustrators are accepted, but please keep the images at 72 dpi; a link to your website or blog is also helpful. Electronic picture book dummies and picture book texts are accepted. Graphic novels and comic books are welcome. Accepts simultaneous submissions. You will receive an auto-generated response to confirm your submission, but please understand that further contact will be made only if we feel we can represent your work. Accepts simultaneous submissions.

LINDA ROGHAAR LITERARY AGENCY, LLC

133 High Point Dr., Amherst MA 01002. **E-mail:** linda@lindaroghaar.com. **E-mail:** contact@lindaroghaar.com. **Website:** www.lindaroghaar.com. **Contact:** Linda L. Roghaar. Member of AAR.

○ Prior to opening her agency, Ms. Roghaar worked in retail bookselling for 5 years and as a publishers' sales rep for 15 years.

☛ The Linda Roghaar Literary Agency represents authors with substantial messages and specializes in nonfiction. We sell to major, independent, and university presses. We are generalists, but we do not handle romance, horror, or science fiction.

HOW TO CONTACT "We prefer e-queries. Please put the word 'query' in the subject line, and do not include attachments." For fiction, paste the first 5 pages of your ms below the query. For queries by mail, please include a SASE. Accepts simultaneous submissions.

TERMS Agent receives 15% commission on domestic sales; negotiable commission on foreign sales. Offers written contract.

THE ROSENBERG GROUP

23 Lincoln Ave., Marblehead MA 01945. (781)990-1341. **Fax:** (781)990-1344. **Website:** www.rosenberggroup.com. **Contact:** Barbara Collins Rosenberg. Estab. 1998. Member of AAR. Recognized agent of the RWA. Represents 25 clients.

○ Prior to becoming an agent, Ms. Rosenberg was a senior editor for Harcourt.

REPRESENTS Nonfiction, novels, college textbooks. **Considers these nonfiction areas:** biography, current affairs, foods, music, popular culture, psychology, sci-

NEW AGENT SPOTLIGHT

ERIK HANE
RED SOFA LITERARY

www.redsofaliterary.com
@erikhane

ABOUT ERIK: Erik Hane graduated from Knox College and attended the Denver Publishing Institute after graduation. His first publishing job came soon after, as an editorial assistant and then assistant editor at Oxford University Press. He then moved to The Overlook Press as an acquiring editor, working on primarily upmarket nonfiction (history, biography, popular science), but was lucky enough to work on some novels as well.

HE IS SEEKING: Nonfiction in the areas of popular science, sports writing, popular culture/modern life, essays, and history. He loves seeing complex subjects written about in an engaging way for the non-expert, or energetic, incisive looks at topics not usually treated that way (looking at you, sports writers).

HOW TO CONTACT: Contact erik@redsofaliterary.com. Send a proposal that includes an overview of the project, a table of contents, a clear sense of who you are and why you are the one to write the book, comparable titles, and some sample writing.

ence, self-help, sports, women's issues, women's studies, women's health, wine/beverages. **Considers these fiction areas:** romance, women's, chick lit.

☞ Ms. Rosenberg is well-versed in the romance market (both category and single title). She is a frequent speaker at romance conferences. The Rosenberg Group is accepting new clients working in romance, women's fiction, and chick lit. Does not want to receive inspirational, time travel, futuristic, or paranormal.

HOW TO CONTACT Query via snail mail. Your query letter should not exceed 1 page in length. It should include the title of your work, the genre and/or sub-genre, the ms word count, and a brief description of the work. If you are writing category romance, please be certain to let her know the line for which your work is intended. Accepts simultaneous submissions. Obtains most new clients through recommendations from others, solicitations, conferences.

TERMS Agent receives 15% commission on domestic sales; 15% commission on foreign sales. Offers written contract; 1-month notice must be given to terminate contract. Charges maximum of $350/year for postage and photocopying.

RECENT SALES Sold 27 titles in the last year.

RITA ROSENKRANZ LITERARY AGENCY

440 West End Ave., #15D, New York NY 10024. (212)873-6333. **Website:** www.ritarosenkranzliteraryagency.com. **Contact:** Rita Rosenkranz. Member of AAR. Represents 35 clients.

◐ Prior to opening her agency, Ms. Rosenkranz worked as an editor at major New York publishing houses.

REPRESENTS Nonfiction. **Considers these nonfiction areas:** Americana, animals, anthropology, art, autobiography, biography, business, child guidance, computers, cooking, crafts, creative nonfiction, cultural interests, current affairs, dance, decorating, diet/nutrition, design, economics, education, ethnic, film, government, health, history, hobbies, how-to, humor, inspirational, interior design, language, law, literature, medicine, military, money, music, parenting, photography, popular culture, politics, psychology, religious, satire, science, self-help, sports, technology, theater, war, women's issues, women's studies.

☛ "This agency focuses on adult nonfiction, stresses strong editorial development and refinement before submitting to publishers, and brainstorms ideas with authors." Actively seeks authors who are well paired with their subject, either for professional or personal reasons.

HOW TO CONTACT Send query letter only (no proposal) via regular mail or e-mail. Submit proposal package with SASE only on request. No fax queries. Accepts simultaneous submissions. Responds in 2 weeks to queries. Obtains most new clients through directory listings, solicitations, conferences, word of mouth.

TERMS Agent receives 15% commission on domestic sales; 20% commission on foreign sales. Offers written contract, binding for 3 years; 3-month written notice must be given to terminate contract. Charges clients for photocopying. Makes referrals to editing services.

RECENT SALES *Mindshift: How Ordinary and Extraordinary People Have Transformed Their Lives Through Learning—And You Can Too* by Barbara A. Oakley (Tarcher), *On the Verge: Experience the Stillness of Presence, the Pulse of Potential, and the Power of Being Fully Alive* by Cara Bradley (New World Library), *Lost Science* by Kitty Ferguson (Sterling), *Power to the Poet* by Diane Luby Lane (Beyond Words/Atria).

TIPS "Identify the current competition for your project to make sure the project is valid. A strong cover letter is very important."

ANDY ROSS LITERARY AGENCY

767 Santa Ray Ave., Oakland CA 94610. (510)238-8965. **E-mail:** andyrossagency@hotmail.com. **Website:** www.andyrossagency.com. **Contact:** Andy Ross. Estab. 2008. Member of AAR.

REPRESENTS **Considers these nonfiction areas:** anthropology, autobiography, biography, child guidance, creative nonfiction, cultural interests, current affairs, education, environment, ethnic, government, history, language, law, literature, military, parenting, popular culture, politics, psychology, science, sociology, technology, war. **Considers these fiction areas:** commercial, juvenile, literary, young adult.

☛ "This agency specializes in general nonfiction, politics and current events, history, biography, journalism and contemporary culture, as well as literary, commercial, and young adult fiction." Actively seeking literary, commercial, and young adult fiction. Does not want to receive poetry.

HOW TO CONTACT Queries should be less than a half page. Please put the word "query" in the title header of the e-mail. In the first sentence, state the category of the project. Give a short description of the book and your qualifications for writing. Accepts simultaneous submissions. Responds in 1 week to queries.

TERMS Agent receives 15% commission on domestic sales; 20% commission on foreign sales or other deals made through a sub-agent. Offers standard written contract.

⊙ ROSS YOON AGENCY

1666 Connecticut Ave. NW, Suite 500, Washington DC 20009. (202)328-3282. **E-mail:** submissions@rossyoon.com. **Website:** www.rossyoon.com. **Contact:** Jennifer Manguera. This agency has a specialty representing nonfiction. Member of AAR.

MEMBER AGENTS Gail Ross, gail@rossyoon.com (represents important commercial nonfiction in a variety of areas; new projects must meet 2 criteria—it must make her daughters proud and offset their college educations); **Howard Yoon,** howard@rossyoon.com (specializes in narrative nonfiction, memoir, current events, history, science, cookbooks, and popular culture); **Anna Sproul-Latimer**, anna@rossyoon.com (nonfiction of all kinds—particularly working with clients who are driven by curiosity: exploring new worlds, uncovering hidden communities, and creating new connections with enthusiasm so infectious that national audiences have already begun to pay attention).

REPRESENTS Nonfiction.

NEW AGENT SPOTLIGHT

MARGARET SUTHERLAND BROWN
EMMA SWEENEY AGENCY, LLC

www.emmasweeneyagency.com

ABOUT MARGARET: Margaret Sutherland Brown brings a strong background in editorial to the Emma Sweeney Agency. She previously worked as an associate editor at Thomas Dunne Books/St. Martin's Press and as a freelance editor. She graduated from Wake Forest University with a bachelor of arts in English and minors in Spanish and journalism.

SHE IS SEEKING: She's particularly interested in commercial and literary fiction, mysteries and thrillers, narrative nonfiction, lifestyle, and cookbooks.

HOW TO CONTACT: Contact queries@emmasweeneyagency.com and put "Query for Emma: [Title]" in the subject line. Please begin your query with a succinct (and hopefully catchy) description of your plot or proposal. Always include a brief query letter telling how you heard about the agency, your previous writing credits, and a few lines about yourself. The agency cannot open any attachments unless specifically requested, and asks that you paste the first ten pages of your proposal or novel into the text of your e-mail.

"We are a Washington, DC-based literary agency specializing in serious nonfiction on a variety of topics. Our clients include CEOs, Pulitzer Prize-winning journalists, academics, politicos, and radio and TV personalities. We do not represent fiction, screenplays, poetry, young adult, or children's titles."

HOW TO CONTACT E-query submissions@rossyoon.com with a query letter briefly explaining your idea, media platform, and qualifications for writing on this topic. Or send a complete book proposal featuring an overview of your idea, author bio, media and marketing strategy, chapter outline, and 1-3 sample chapters. Please send these as attachments in .doc or .docx format. Accepts simultaneous submissions. Attempts to respond in 4-6 weeks to queries, but cannot guarantee a reply. Obtains most new clients through referrals from current clients.

TERMS Agent receives 15% commission on domestic sales; 20% commission on foreign sales. Reserves the right to bill clients for office expenses.

JANE ROTROSEN AGENCY, LLC

(212)593-4330. **Fax:** (212)935-6985. **Website:** www.janerotrosen.com. Estab. 1974. Member of AAR. Other memberships include Authors Guild. Represents more than 100 clients.

MEMBER AGENTS Jane Rotrosen Berkey (not taking on new clients); **Andrea Cirillo**, acirillo@janerotrosen.com (general fiction, suspense, and women's fiction); **Annelise Robey**, arobey@janerotrosen.com (women's fiction, suspense, mystery, literary fiction, and select nonfiction); **Meg Ruley**, mruley@janerotrosen.com (commercial fiction—including suspense, mysteries, romance, and general fiction); **Christina Hogrebe**, chogrebe@janerotrosen.com (young adult, new adult, book club fiction, romantic comedies, mystery, and suspense); **Amy Tannenbaum**, atannenbaum@janerotrosen.com (contemporary romance, psychological suspense, thrillers, new adult, as well as women's fiction that falls into that sweet spot between literary and commercial; also seeks memoir, narrative, and prescriptive nonfiction in the areas of health, business, pop culture, humor, and popular psychology); **Rebecca Scherer** rscherer@janerotrosen.com (women's fiction, mystery, suspense, thriller, romance, upmarket, and literary-leaning fiction); **Jessica Errera** (assistant).

REPRESENTS Nonfiction, novels. **Considers these nonfiction areas:** business, health, humor, memoirs, popular culture, psychology, narrative nonfiction. **Considers these fiction areas:** commercial, literary, mainstream, mystery, new adult, romance, suspense, thriller, women's, young adult.

> ☛ "Jane Rotrosen Agency is best known for representing writers of commercial fiction: thrillers, mystery, suspense, women's fiction, romance, historical novels, mainstream fiction, young adult, etc. We also work with authors of memoirs, narrative, and prescriptive nonfiction."

HOW TO CONTACT "Please e-mail the agent you think would best align with you and your work. Send a query letter that includes a concise description of your work, relevant biographical information, and any relevant publishing history. Also include a brief synopsis and the first 3 chapters of your novel or proposal for nonfiction. Paste all text in the body of your e-mail. We will not open e-mail attachments." Accepts simultaneous submissions. Obtains most new clients through recommendations from others.

TERMS Agent receives 15% commission on domestic sales; 20% commission on foreign sales. Offers written contract, binding for 3 years; two-month notice must be given to terminate contract. Charges clients for photocopying, express mail, overseas postage, book purchase.

◎ THE RUDY AGENCY

825 Wildlife Lane, Estes Park CO 80517. (970)577-8500. **Website:** http://rudyagency.com. **Contact:** Maryann Karinch. "We are a full-service agency, meaning that we partner with authors from proposal stage through implementation of a promotion plan (nonfiction) and provide guidance on ms development (nonfiction and fiction). We welcome both experienced, published authors and first-timers. We are a boutique agency; out clientele is limited to give proper attention to every client." Estab. 2004. Adheres to AAR canon of ethics. Represents 24 clients.

> ☐ Prior to becoming an agent, Ms. Karinch was, and continues to be, an author of nonfiction books—covering the subjects of health/medicine and human behavior. Prior to that, she was in public relations and marketing: areas of expertise she also applies in her practice as an agent.

MEMBER AGENTS Maryann Karinch, mak@rudyagency.com; **Fred Tribuzzo**, fred@rudyagency.com (fiction: thrillers, historical); **Jak Burke**, jak@rudyagency.com (children's and young adult); **Hilary Claggett**, claggett@rudyagency.com (selected nonfiction).

REPRESENTS Nonfiction, novels, short story collections, juvenile books, scholarly books, textbooks. **Considers these nonfiction areas:** Americana, anthropology, archeology, autobiography, biography, business, child guidance, computers, creative nonfiction, cultural interests, current affairs, diet/nutrition, economics, education, gay/lesbian, government, health, history, how-to, inspirational, juvenile nonfiction, law, literature, medicine, memoirs, military, money, music, parenting, popular culture, politics, psychology, science, self-help, sociology, sports, technology, theater, true crime, war, women's issues, women's studies, young adult. **Considers these fiction areas:** commercial, crime, historical, juvenile, literary, new adult, thriller.

> ☛ "We support authors from the proposal stage through promotion of the published work. We work in partnership with publishers to promote the published work and coach authors in their role in the marketing and public relations campaigns for the book." Actively seeking projects with social value, projects that open minds to new ideas and interesting lives, and projects that entertain through good storytelling. Does not want to receive poetry, screenplays, stage plays, art/photo books, novellas, religion books, or joke books.

HOW TO CONTACT "Query us. If we like the query, we will invite a complete proposal (or complete ms if writing fiction). No phone queries, please. We won't hang up on you, but it makes it easier if you send us a note first." Accepts simultaneous submissions. Responds in 8 weeks to mss. Obtains most new clients through recommendations from others, solicitations.

TERMS Agent receives 15% commission on domestic sales. Offers written contract, binding for 1 year.

RECENT SALES *Beethoven's Skull* by Tim Rayborn (Skyhorse), *Advocacy Journalism* by Larry Atkins (Prometheus), *Snipers* by Lena Sisco (Globe Pequot).

TIPS "Present yourself professionally. I tell people all the time: Subscribe to *Writer's Digest* (I do), because you will get good advice about how to approach an agent."

SADLER CHILDREN'S LITERARY

(815)209-6252. **E-mail:** submissions.sadlerliterary@gmail.com. **Website:** www.sadlerchildrensliterary.com. **Contact:** Jodell Sadler. "Sadler Children's Literary is an independent literary agency, serving aspiring authors and illustrators and branding careers through active media and marketing management in the field of children's literature." Member of AAR. Signatory of WGA.

REPRESENTS Nonfiction, novels, juvenile books. **Considers these nonfiction areas:** creative nonfiction, juvenile nonfiction, young adult. **Considers these fiction areas:** juvenile, middle-grade, picture books, young adult.

HOW TO CONTACT "We only take submissions from writers we've met through conferences, events, webinars, or other meeting opportunities. Your subject line should read 'CODE PROVIDED—(Genre), (Title), by (Author),' and specifically addressed to me. I prefer a short letter: hook (why my agency), pitch for you project, and bio (brief background and other categories you work in). All submissions should be in the body of the e-mail; no attachments. If you are submitting a picture book, send the entire text. If you are submitting young adult or middle-grade, submit the first 10 pages. If you are an illustrator or author-illustrator, I encourage you to contact me, and please send a link to your online portfolio. I only obtain clients through writing conferences, SCBWI, Writer's Digest, and KidLitCollege.com webinars and events." Accepts simultaneous submissions.

SALKIND LITERARY AGENCY

Part of Studio B, 62 Nassau Dr., Studio B, Great Neck NY 11021. (516)829-2102. **E-mail:** info@studiob.com. **Website:** www.studiob.com/salkindagency. **Contact:** Neil Salkind.

Prior to becoming an agent, Mr. Salkind authored numerous trade and textbooks.

MEMBER AGENTS Neil Salkind, neil@studiob.com (general nonfiction and textbooks); **Greg Aunapu,** greg@studiob.com (nonfiction interests include biography, history, narrative, memoir, true-crime, adventure/true story, business, finance, current affairs, technology, pop culture, psychology, how-to, self-help, science, travel, pets/animals, relationships, parenting); fiction interests include commercial fiction, historical, thrillers/suspense, mystery, detective, adventure, humor, science-fiction, fantasy); **Lynn Haller,** lynn@studiob.com (technical, business, travel, self-help, health, photography, design, cooking, art, craft, politics, essays, culture, history, textbooks).

REPRESENTS Considers these nonfiction areas: animals, art, biography, business, cooking, crafts, cultural interests, current affairs, design, health, history, how-to, memoirs, money, parenting, photography, popular culture, politics, psychology, science, self-help, technology, travel, true crime. **Considers these fiction areas:** adventure, commercial, detective, fantasy, historical, humor, mystery, science fiction, suspense, thriller.

Does not want "to receive nonfiction book proposals based on ideas where potential authors have not yet researched what has been published."

HOW TO CONTACT Query electronically. Accepts simultaneous submissions.

TERMS Agent receives 15% commission on domestic sales; 15% commission on foreign sales.

VICTORIA SANDERS & ASSOCIATES

440 Buck Rd., Stone Ridge NY 12484. (212)633-8811. **Fax:** (212)633-0525. **E-mail:** queriesvsa@gmail.com. **Website:** www.victoriasanders.com. **Contact:** Victoria Sanders. Estab. 1992. Member of AAR. Signatory of WGA. Represents 135 clients.

MEMBER AGENTS Victoria Sanders, Chris Kepner, Bernadette Baker-Baughman.

REPRESENTS Nonfiction, novels, juvenile books. **Considers these nonfiction areas:** autobiography, biography, cultural interests, current affairs, ethnic, film, gay/lesbian, government, history, humor, law, literature, music, popular culture, politics, psychology, satire, theater, translation, women's issues, women's studies. **Considers these fiction areas:** action, adventure, comic books, contemporary issues, crime, detective, ethnic, family saga, feminist, lesbian, literary, mainstream, middle-grade, mystery, new adult, picture books, thriller, young adult.

HOW TO CONTACT Query by e-mail only. "We will not respond to e-mails with attachments or attached files." Accepts simultaneous submissions.

TERMS Agent receives 15% commission on domestic sales; 20% commission on foreign/film sales. Offers written contract.

RECENT SALES Sold 20+ titles in the last year.

TIPS "Limit query to a letter (no calls) and give it your best shot. A good query is going to get a good response."

SCHIAVONE LITERARY AGENCY, INC.

236 Trails End, West Palm Beach FL 33413-2135. (561)966-9294. **Fax:** (561)966-9294. **E-mail:** profschia@aol.com. **Website:** www.publishersmarketplace.com/members/profschia; blog site: http://schiavoneliteraryagencyinc.blogspot.com. **Contact:** Dr. James Schiavone, CEO, corporate offices in Florida; Jennifer DuVall, president, New York office. Estab. 1996. Memberships include National Education Association. Represents 40+ clients.

○ Prior to opening his agency, Dr. Schiavone was a full professor of developmental skills at the City University of New York, as well as the author of 5 trade books and 3 textbooks. Ms. DuVall has many years of combined experience in office management and agenting.

MEMBER AGENTS James Schiavone, profschia@aol.com; **Jennifer DuVall**, jendu77@aol.com.

REPRESENTS Nonfiction, novels. **Considers these nonfiction areas:** biography, business, cooking, health, history, politics, science, sports, true crime. **Considers these fiction areas:** literary, mainstream, mystery, romance, suspense, thriller, young adult.

➤ This agency specializes in celebrity biography/autobiography and memoirs. Does not want to receive poetry.

HOW TO CONTACT "Send one-page e-mail queries only. Absolutely no attachments. Postal queries are not accepted. No phone calls. We do not consider poetry, short stories, anthologies, or children's books. Celebrity memoirs only. No scripts or screenplays. We handle dramatic, film and TV rights, options, and screenplays for books we have agented. We are not interested in work previously published in any format (e.g., self-published, online). E-mail queries may

be addressed to any of the agency's agents." Accepts simultaneous submissions. Responds in 2 weeks to queries. Responds in 6 weeks to mss. Obtains most new clients through referrals.

TERMS Agent receives 15% commission on domestic sales; 20% commission on foreign sales. Offers written contract. No fees.

TIPS "We prefer to work with established authors published by major houses in New York. We will consider marketable proposals from new/previously unpublished writers."

WENDY SCHMALZ AGENCY

402 Union St., #831, Hudson NY 12534. (518)672-7697. **E-mail:** wendy@schmalzagency.com. **Website:** www.schmalzagency.com. **Contact:** Wendy Schmalz. Estab. 2002. Member of AAR.

REPRESENTS Nonfiction, novels, juvenile books. **Considers these nonfiction areas:** biography, cultural interests, history, popular culture, young adult. Many nonfiction subjects are of interest to this agency. **Considers these fiction areas:** literary, mainstream, middle-grade, young adult.

➤ Not looking for picture books, science fiction, or fantasy.

HOW TO CONTACT Accepts only e-mail queries. Paste synopsis into the e-mail. Do not attach the ms or sample chapters or synopsis. Please do not send genre fiction or children's picture books. If you do not hear from this agency within 2 weeks, consider that a no. Accepts simultaneous submissions. Obtains clients through recommendations from others.

TERMS Agent receives 15% commission on domestic sales; 20% on foreign sales; 25% for Asian sales.

SERENDIPITY LITERARY AGENCY, LLC

305 Gates Ave., Brooklyn NY 11216. **E-mail:** rbrooks@serendipitylit.com; info@serendipitylit.com. **Website:** www.serendipitylit.com. **Contact:** Regina Brooks. Represents 50 clients.

○ Prior to becoming an agent, Ms. Brooks was an acquisitions editor for John Wiley & Sons, Inc. and McGraw-Hill Companies.

MEMBER AGENTS Regina Brooks; Dawn Michelle Hardy (nonfiction—including sports, pop culture, blog and trend, music, lifestyle, and social science); **Folade Bell** (literary and commercial women's fiction, young adult, literary mysteries and thrillers, historical fiction, African-American issues, gay/

NEW AGENT SPOTLIGHT

AMELIA APPEL
MCINTOSH & OTIS, INC.

www.mcintoshandotis.com
@ameliaappel

ABOUT AMELIA: Amelia Appel is a graduate of Hamilton College. Prior to joining McIntosh & Otis, Amelia interned at HSG Agency and Writers House. She joined McIntosh & Otis in 2014 as Elizabeth Winick Rubinstein's assistant and is currently seeking to build her own list as a junior agent.

SHE IS SEEKING: Primarily adult fiction with some young adult. For adult fiction, she is most interested in literary fiction, mystery, thriller, historical fiction, science fiction, fantasy, and horror. She likes projects with a smart, distinct voice, a fantastic setting to jump into, and/or a witty protagonist. For young adult in particular, she's interested in stories with a savvy protagonist and a slightly dark tone that deals with serious coming-of-age issues well.

HOW TO CONTACT: Contact aaquery@mcintoshandotis.com. For adult fiction submissions, send a query letter, synopsis, author bio, and the first three consecutive chapters (no more than thirty pages) of your novel. For adult nonfiction, send a query letter, proposal, outline, author bio, and three sample chapters (no more than thirty pages) of the manuscript. For children's and young adult, send a query letter, synopsis, and the first three consecutive chapters (not to exceed twenty-five pages) of the manuscript. "We ask that text be pasted in the body of the e-mail. E-mails containing attachments will not be opened and will be automatically deleted due to security reasons."

lesbian, Christian fiction, humor, and books that deeply explore other cultures; also seeks nonfiction that reads like fiction, including blog-to-book or pop culture); **Nadeen Gayle** (romance, memoir, pop culture, inspirational/religious, women's fiction, parenting, young adult, mystery, political thrillers, and all forms of nonfiction); **Chelcee Johns** (narrative nonfiction, investigative journalism, memoir, inspirational self-help, religion/spirituality, international, popular culture, current affairs; also seeks literary and commercial fiction).

REPRESENTS Considers these nonfiction areas: creative nonfiction, current affairs, inspirational, memoirs, music, parenting, popular culture, religious, self-help, spirituality, sports. **Considers these fiction areas:** commercial, gay, historical, lesbian, literary, middle-grade, mystery, romance, thriller, women's, young adult, Christian.

HOW TO CONTACT Check the website, as there are online submission forms for fiction, nonfiction, and juvenile. "Website will also state if we're temporarily closed to submissions to any areas." Accepts simultaneous submissions. Obtains most new clients through conferences, referrals.

TERMS Agent receives 15% commission on domestic sales; 20% commission on foreign sales. Offers written contract; 2-month notice must be given to terminate contract. Charges clients for office fees, which are taken from any advance.

TIPS "See the books *Writing Great Books for Young Adults* and *You Should Really Write a Book: How to Write Sell and Market Your Memoir.* We are looking for high-concept ideas with big hooks. If you get writer's block, try www.possibiliteas.co."

☼ SEVENTH AVENUE LITERARY AGENCY

2052-124th St., South Surrey British Columbia Canada. (604)538-7252. **Fax:** (604)538-7252. **E-mail:** info@seventhavenuelit.com. **Website:** www.seventhavenuelit.com. **Contact:** Robert Mackwood, director.

REPRESENTS Nonfiction. **Considers these nonfiction areas:** autobiography, biography, business, computers, economics, health, history, medicine, science, sports, technology, travel.

☞ Seventh Avenue Literary Agency is both a literary agency and personal management agency. (The agency was originally called Contemporary Management.)

HOW TO CONTACT Query with SASE. Submit outline, synopsis, 1 sample chapter (nonfiction), publishing history, author bio, table of contents with proposal, and query. Provide full contact information. Let us know the submission history. No fiction. Accepts simultaneous submissions. Obtains most new clients through recommendations from others, some solicitations.

TIPS "If you want your material returned, please include a SASE with adequate postage; otherwise, material will be recycled. (US stamps are not adequate; they do not work in Canada.)"

THE SEYMOUR AGENCY

Website: www.theseymouragency.com. Member of AAR, RWA, Authors Guild, HWA. Signatory of WGA.

☼ Ms. Resciniti was recently named "Agent of the Year" by the ACFW.

MEMBER AGENTS Nicole Resciniti, nicole@theseymouragency.com (accepts all genres of romance, young adult, middle-grade, new adult, suspense, thriller, mystery, science fiction, fantasy); **Julie Gwinn**, julie@theseymouragency.com (Christian and inspirational fiction and nonfiction, women's fiction [contemporary and historical], new adult, Southern fiction, literary fiction, and young adult); **Lane Heymont**, lane@theseymouragency.com (science fiction, fantasy, romance, nonfiction).

REPRESENTS Nonfiction, novels. **Considers these nonfiction areas:** business, health, how-to, Christian books, cookbooks, any well-written nonfiction that includes a proposal in standard format and 1 sample chapter. **Considers these fiction areas:** action, fantasy, inspirational, middle-grade, mystery, new adult, religious, romance, science fiction, suspense, thriller, young adult.

HOW TO CONTACT E-mail the query plus first 5 pages of the ms pasted into the e-mail. Accepts simultaneous submissions. Responds in 1 month to queries.

TERMS Agent receives 12-15% commission on domestic sales.

DENISE SHANNON LITERARY AGENCY, INC.

20 W. 22nd St., Suite 1603, New York NY 10010. **E-mail:** submissions@deniseshannonagency.com. **Website:** http://deniseshannonagency.com. **Contact:** Denise Shannon. Estab. 2002. Member of AAR.

☼ Prior to opening her agency, Ms. Shannon worked for 16 years with Georges Borchardt and International Creative Management.

REPRESENTS Nonfiction, novels. **Considers these nonfiction areas:** biography, business, health, narrative nonfiction, politics, journalism, social history. **Considers these fiction areas:** literary.

☞ "We are a boutique agency with a distinguished list of fiction and nonfiction authors."

HOW TO CONTACT "Queries may be submitted by post, accompanied by a SASE, or by e-mail to submissions@deniseshannonagency.com. Please include a description of the available book project and a brief bio, including details of any prior publications. We will reply and request more material if we are interested." Accepts simultaneous submissions.

RECENT SALES *Mister Monkey* by Francine Prose (Harper), *Hotel Solitaire* by Gary Shteyngart (Random House), *White Flights* by Jess Row (Graywolf Press), *The Underworld* by Kevin Canty (Norton), *A Simple Favor* by Darcey Bell (Harper), *The Gone Dead* by Chanelle Benz (Ecco).

TIPS "Please do not send queries regarding fiction projects until a complete ms is available for review.

We request that you inform us if you are submitting material simultaneously to other agencies."

⊘ KEN SHERMAN & ASSOCIATES

1275 N. Hayworth, No. 103, Los Angeles CA 90046. (310)273-8840. **Fax:** (310)271-2875. **Website:** www.kenshermanassociates.com. **Contact:** Ken Sherman.

○ Prior to opening his agency, Mr. Sherman was with The William Morris Agency, The Lantz Office, and Paul Kohner, Inc. He has taught The Business of Writing For Film and Television and The Book Worlds at UCLA and USC. He also lectures extensively at conferences and film festivals around the US. He is currently a Commissioner of Arts and Cultural Affairs in the City of West Hollywood and is on the International Advisory Board of the Christopher Isherwood Foundation.

REPRESENTS Nonfiction, novels, teleplays, life rights, film/TV rights to books, and life rights. **Considers these nonfiction areas:** agriculture, Americana, animals, anthropology, art, biography, business, child guidance, computers, cooking, crafts, current affairs, education, ethnic, film, gardening, gay/lesbian, government, health, history, horticulture, how-to, humor, interior design, language, memoirs, military, money, multicultural, music, New Age, philosophy, photography, popular culture, psychology, recreation, regional, religious, science, self-help, sex, sociology, software, spirituality, sports, translation, travel, true crime, women's issues, young adult, creative nonfiction. **Considers these fiction areas:** action, adventure, commercial, crime, detective, family saga, gay, literary, mainstream, middle-grade, mystery, police, romance, science fiction, suspense, thriller, women's, young adult.

HOW TO CONTACT Contact by referral only. Responds in 1 month to mss. Obtains most new clients through recommendations from others.

WENDY SHERMAN ASSOCIATES, INC.

27 W. 24th St., Suite 700B, New York NY 10010. (212)279-9027. **E-mail:** submissions@wsherman.com. **Website:** www.wsherman.com. **Contact:** Wendy Sherman. Member of AAR.

○ Prior to opening the agency, Ms. Sherman served as vice president, executive director, associate publisher, subsidiary rights director, and sales and marketing director for major publishers.

MEMBER AGENTS Wendy Sherman (women's fiction that hits that sweet spot between literary and mainstream, Southern voices, historical dramas, suspense with a well-developed protagonist, and writing that illuminates the multicultural experience; enjoys anything related to food, dogs, mothers, and daughters).

REPRESENTS Nonfiction, novels. **Considers these nonfiction areas:** creative nonfiction, foods, humor, memoirs, parenting, popular culture, psychology, self-help, narrative nonfiction. **Considers these fiction areas:** mainstream.

☞ "We specialize in developing new writers, as well as working with more established writers. My experience as a publisher has proven to be a great asset to my clients."

HOW TO CONTACT Query via e-mail only. "We ask that you include your last name, title, and the name of the agent you are submitting to in the subject line. For fiction, please include a query letter and your first 10 pages pasted in the body of the e-mail. We will not open attachments unless they have been requested. For nonfiction, please include your query letter and author bio. Due to the large number of e-mail submissions that we receive, we can only reply to e-mail queries in the affirmative. We respectfully ask that you do not send queries to our individual e-mail addresses." Accepts simultaneous submissions. Obtains most new clients through recommendations from other writers.

TERMS Agent receives standard 15% commission. Offers written contract.

RECENT SALES *All is Not Forgotten* by Wendy Walker, *The Charm Bracelet* by Viol Shipman, *The Silence of Bonaventure Arrow* by Rita Leganski, *Together Tea* by Marjan Kamali, *A Long Long Time Ago and Essentially True* by Brigid Pasulka, *Lunch in Paris* by Elizabeth Bard, *The Rules of Inheritance* by Claire Bidwell Smith.

TIPS "Do your homework. Be as prepared as possible. Read the books that will help you present yourself and your work with polish. You want your submission to stand out."

☯ BEVERLEY SLOPEN LITERARY AGENCY

131 Bloor St. W., Suite 711, Toronto Ontario M5S 1S3 Canada. (416)964-9598. **E-mail:** beverly@slopenagency.ca. **Website:** www.slopenagency.ca. **Contact:** Beverley Slopen. Represents 70 clients.

○ Prior to opening her agency, Ms. Slopen worked in publishing and as a journalist.

Considers these nonfiction areas: anthropology, archeology, autobiography, biography, business, creative nonfiction, current affairs, economics, investigative, psychology, sociology, true crime. **Considers these fiction areas:** commercial, literary, mystery, suspense.

☛ "This agency has a strong bent toward Canadian writers." Actively seeking serious nonfiction that is accessible and appealing to the general reader. Does not want to receive fantasy, science fiction, or children's books.

HOW TO CONTACT Query by e-mail. Returns materials only with SASE (Canadian postage only). To submit a work for consideration, e-mail a short query letter and a few sample pages. Submit only 1 work at a time. "If we want to see more, we will contact the writer by phone or e-mail." Accepts simultaneous submissions. Responds in 1 month to queries only if interested.

RECENT SALES *Solar Dance* by Modris Eksteins (Knopf Canada, Harvard University Press, US), *The Novels* by Terry Fallis, *God's Brain* by Lionel Tiger and Michael McGuire (Prometheus Books), *What They Wanted* by Donna Morrissey (Penguin Canada, Premium/DTV Germany).

TIPS "Please do not send unsolicited mss."

SPECTRUM LITERARY AGENCY

320 Central Park W., Suite 1-D, New York NY 10025. **Website:** www.spectrumliteraryagency.com. **Contact:** Eleanor Wood, president. Estab. 1976. Member of SFWA. Represents 90 clients.

MEMBER AGENTS Eleanor Wood (referrals only; seeks science fiction, fantasy, suspense, as well as select nonfiction); Justin Bell (science fiction, mysteries, and select nonfiction).

REPRESENTS Novels. **Considers these fiction areas:** commercial, fantasy, mystery, science fiction, suspense.

HOW TO CONTACT Unsolicited mss are not accepted. Send snail mail query with a SASE. "The letter should describe your book briefly and include publishing credits and background information or qualifications relating to your work, and the first 10 pages of your work. Our response time is generally 2-3 months."

TERMS Agent receives 15% commission on domestic sales. Deducts for photocopying and book orders.

TIPS "Spectrum's policy is to read only book-length mss that we have specifically asked to see. Unsolicited mss are not accepted. Your query letter should describe your book briefly and include publishing credits and background information or qualifications relating to your work, if any."

SPEILBURG LITERARY AGENCY

E-mail: speilburgliterary@gmail.com. **Website:** http://speilburgliterary.com. **Contact:** Alice Speilburg. Estab. 2012. Member of SCBWI, MWA, RWA.

○ Ms. Speilburg previously held publishing positions at John Wiley & Sons and Howard Morhaim Literary Agency.

REPRESENTS Nonfiction, novels. **Considers these nonfiction areas:** biography, foods, health, history, investigative, music, popular culture, science, travel, women's issues, women's studies. **Considers these fiction areas:** historical, literary, mainstream, middle-grade, mystery, police, science fiction, thriller, women's, young adult.

HOW TO CONTACT If you are interested in submitting your ms or proposal for consideration, please e-mail a query letter along with either 3 sample chapters for fiction, or a table of contents and proposal for nonfiction. Accepts simultaneous submissions.

SPENCERHILL ASSOCIATES

8131 Lakewood Main St., Building M, Suite 205, Lakewood Ranch FL 34202. (941)907-3700. **E-mail:** submission@spencerhillassociates.com. **Website:** www.spencerhillassociates.com. **Contact:** Karen Solem, Nalini Akolekar, Amanda Leuck, Sandy Harding. Member of AAR.

○ Prior to becoming an agent, Ms. Solem was editor-in-chief at HarperCollins and an associate publisher.

MEMBER AGENTS Karen Solem, Nalini Akolekar, Amanda Leuck, Sandy Harding.

REPRESENTS Novels. **Considers these fiction areas:** commercial, erotica, literary, mainstream, mystery, paranormal, romance, thriller.

☛ "We handle mostly commercial women's fiction, historical novels, romance (historical, contemporary, paranormal, urban fantasy), thrillers, and mysteries. We also represent Christian fiction—no Christian nonfiction."

No nonfiction, poetry, science fiction, children's picture books, or scripts.

HOW TO CONTACT "We accept electronic submissions and are no longer accepting paper queries. Please send us a query letter in the body of an e-mail, pitch us your project, and tell us about yourself: Do you have prior publishing credits? Attach the first 3 chapters and synopsis, preferably in .doc, .rtf or .txt format to your e-mail. Send all queries to submission@spencerhillassociates.com. We do not have a preference for exclusive submissions, but do appreciate knowing if the submission is simultaneous. We receive thousands of submissions a year, and each query receives our attention. Unfortunately, we are unable to respond to each query individually. If we are interested in your work, we will contact you within 12 weeks." Accepts simultaneous submissions.

TERMS Agent receives 15% commission on domestic sales; 20% commission on foreign sales. Offers written contract; 3-month notice must be given to terminate contract.

RECENT SALES A full list of sales and clients is available on the agency website.

THE SPIELER AGENCY

27 W. 20 St., Suite 305, New York NY 10011. **E-mail:** thespieleragency@gmail.com. **Website:** http://thespieleragency.com. **Contact:** Joe Spieler. Represents 160 clients.

○ Prior to opening his agency, Mr. Spieler was a magazine editor.

MEMBER AGENTS Victoria Shoemaker, victoria@thespieleragency.com (environment and natural history, popular culture, memoir, photography and film, literary fiction, poetry, food/cooking); **John Thornton**, john@thespieleragency.com (nonfiction); **Joe Spieler**, joe@thespieleragency.com (nonfiction and fiction and books for children and young adults); **Helen Sweetland**, helen@TheSpielerAgency.com (children's—from board books through young adult fiction; also seeks adult general interest nonfiction, including nature, green living, gardening, architecture, interior design, health, and popular science). **REPRESENTS** Nonfiction, novels, juvenile books. **Considers these nonfiction areas:** architecture, biography, cooking, environment, film, foods, gardening, health, history, memoirs, photography, popular culture, science, sociology, spirituality. **Considers**

these fiction areas: literary, middle-grade, New Age, picture books, thriller, young adult.

HOW TO CONTACT "Before submitting projects to the Spieler Agency, check the listings of our individual agents and see if any particular agent shows a general interest in your subject (e.g., history, memoir, young adult, etc.). Please send all queries either by e-mail or regular mail. If you query us by regular mail, we can only reply to you if you include a SASE." Accepts simultaneous submissions. Cannot guarantee a personal response to all queries. Obtains most new clients through recommendations, listing in *Guide to Literary Agents*.

TERMS Agent receives 15% commission on domestic sales. Charges clients for messenger bills, photocopying, postage.

WRITERS CONFERENCES London Book Fair.

TIPS "Check www.publishersmarketplace.com/members/spielerlit."

PHILIP G. SPITZER LITERARY AGENCY, INC

50 Talmage Farm Lane, East Hampton NY 11937. (631)329-3650. **Fax:** (631)329-3651. **E-mail:** lukas.ortiz@spitzeragency.com, spitzer516@aol.com, kim.lombardini@spitzeragency.com. **Website:** www.spitzeragency.com. **Contact:** Lukas Ortiz. Estab. 1969. Member of AAR.

○ Prior to opening his agency, Mr. Spitzer served at New York University Press, McGraw-Hill, and the John Cushman Associates Literary Agency.

MEMBER AGENTS Philip G. Spitzer, Lukas Ortiz. **REPRESENTS** Nonfiction, novels. **Considers these nonfiction areas:** biography, current affairs, history, politics, sports, travel. **Considers these fiction areas:** juvenile, literary, mainstream, suspense, thriller.

☞ This agency specializes in mystery/suspense, literary fiction, sports, and general nonfiction (no how-to).

HOW TO CONTACT E-mail a query containing a pitch and brief biography. Include 2 sample chapters pasted into the e-mail. Be aware that this agency openly says their client list is quite full. Accepts simultaneous submissions. Obtains most new clients through recommendations from others.

TERMS Agent receives 15% commission on domestic sales; 20% commission on foreign sales. Charges clients for photocopying.

RECENT SALES *Creole Belle* by James Lee Burke (Simon & Schuster), *Never Tell* by Alafair Burke (HarperCollins), *Townie* by Andre Dubus III (Norton), *The Black Box* by Michael Connelly (Little, Brown & Co), *Headstone* Ken Bruen (Mysterious Press/Grove-Atlantic).

NANCY STAUFFER ASSOCIATES

P.O. Box 1203, Darien CT 06820. (203)202-2500. E-mail: nancy@staufferliterary.com. **Website:** www.publishersmarketplace.com/members/nstauffer. **Contact:** Nancy Stauffer Cahoon. Nancy Stauffer Associates is a boutique agency representing a small, select group of authors of the highest quality literary fiction and literary narrative nonfiction. Member of The Authors Guild.

○ "Over the course of my more than 20-year career, I've held positions in the editorial, marketing, business, and rights departments of *The New York Times*, McGraw-Hill, and Doubleday."

REPRESENTS Considers these fiction areas: literary.

HOW TO CONTACT Accepts simultaneous submissions. Obtains most new clients through referrals from existing clients.

TERMS Agent receives 15% commission on domestic sales; 20% commission on foreign sales.

RECENT SALES *Thunder Boy Jr.* by Sherman Alexie, *Our Souls at Night* by Kent Haruf, *Bone Fire* by Mark Spragg.

STERNIG & BYRNE LITERARY AGENCY

2370 S. 107th St., Apt. 4, Milwaukee WI 53227. (414)328-8034. **E-mail:** jackbyrne@hotmail.com. **Website:** www.sff.net/people/jackbyrne. **Contact:** Jack Byrne. Memberships include SFWA, MWA.

REPRESENTS Novels. **Considers these fiction areas:** fantasy, horror, mystery, science fiction, suspense.

☛ "Our client list is comfortably full, and our current needs are therefore quite limited." Actively seeking science fiction, fantasy, and mystery by established writers. Does not want to receive romance, poetry, textbooks, or highly specialized nonfiction.

HOW TO CONTACT Prefers e-mail queries (no attachments); hard copy queries also acceptable (with a SASE).

TIPS "Don't send first drafts. Have a professional presentation (including a cover letter) and know your field. Read what's been done—good and bad."

STIMOLA LITERARY STUDIO

308 Livingston Court, Edgewater NJ 07020. **E-mail:** info@stimolaliterarystudio.com. **Website:** www.stimolaliterarystudio.com. **Contact:** Rosemary B. Stimola. "A full-service literary agency devoted to representing authors and author/illustrators of fiction and nonfiction, pre-school through young adult, who bring unique and substantive contributions to the industry." Estab. 1997. Member of AAR. Represents 45 clients.

○ Agency is owned and operated by a former educator and children's bookseller with a Ph.D in linguistics.

MEMBER AGENTS Rosemary B. Stimola.

REPRESENTS Juvenile books. **Considers these nonfiction areas:** cooking. **Considers these fiction areas:** young adult.

☛ Actively seeking remarkable middle-grade, young adult, and debut picture book author/illustrators. No institutional books.

HOW TO CONTACT Query via e-mail. Author/illustrators of picture books may attach text and sample art. A PDF dummy is preferred. Accepts simultaneous submissions. Responds in 3 weeks to queries if interested. Responds in 2 months to requested mss. While unsolicited queries are welcome, most clients come through editor, agent, and client referrals.

TERMS Agent receives 15% commission on domestic sales; 20% (if subagents are employed) commission on foreign sales. Offers written contract, binding for all children's projects. 60 days notice must be given to terminate contract.

TIPS Agent is hands-on, no-nonsense. May request revisions. Does not line edit but may offer suggestions for improvement before submission.

STONESONG

270 W. 39th St., No. 201, New York NY 10018. (212)929-4600. **Fax:** (212)486-9123. **E-mail:** editors@stonesong.com. **E-mail:** submissions@stonesong.com. **Website:** http://stonesong.com. Member of AAR. Signatory of WGA.

MEMBER AGENTS Alison Fargis, Ellen Scordato, Judy Linden, Emmanuelle Morgen, Leila Campoli (business, science, technology, and self improvement); Maria Ribas (cookbooks, self-help, health, diet, home, parenting, and humor, all from authors with demonstrable platforms; she's also interested in narrative nonfiction and select memoir).

NEW AGENT SPOTLIGHT

KATIE ZANECCHIA
ROSS YOON LITERARY AGENCY

www.rossyoon.com
@klz4k

ABOUT KATIE: Katie Zanecchia, Ross Yoon's literary agent in New York, has worked at the intersection of content, creativity, and advocacy for her entire career—from literary magazines and major publishers to arts-based non-profits. She began her career at Writers House, where she helped create their first digital rights department. Recently, she's helped build and celebrate creative communities at CreativeMornings and Girls Write Now, where she's experienced the transformative power of the written word firsthand. She graduated from the Columbia Publishing Course and has a bachelor of arts in comparative literature from the University of Virginia.

SHE IS SEEKING: Adult narrative nonfiction that catalyzes social change, challenges the status quo, gives voice to the underrepresented, and inspires improvement of all kinds—whether it's through the lens of women's rights and feminism, arts and design, technology, politics, social science, memoir, or pop culture.

HOW TO CONTACT: E-mail a query letter, proposal, and sample chapter to katie@rossyoon.com. "I read every query and will respond to projects I'm interested in within six weeks (if not sooner). No snail mail, please."

REPRESENTS Nonfiction, novels, juvenile books. **Considers these nonfiction areas:** architecture, art, biography, business, cooking, crafts, creative nonfiction, cultural interests, current affairs, dance, decorating, diet/nutrition, design, economics, foods, gay/lesbian, health, history, hobbies, how-to, humor, interior design, investigative, literature, memoirs, money, music, New Age, parenting, photography, popular culture, politics, psychology, science, self-help, sociology, spirituality, sports, technology, women's issues, young adult.

☞ Does not represent plays, screenplays, picture books, or poetry.

HOW TO CONTACT Accepts electronic queries for fiction and nonfiction. Submit query addressed to 1 agent. Include first chapter or first 10 pages of ms. Accepts simultaneous submissions.
RECENT SALES *Revolutionary* by Alex Myers, *Rebel* by Amy Tintera, *Dangerous Curves Ahead* by Sugar Jamison, *Sunday Suppers* by Karen Mordechai, *Find Momo* by Andrew Knapp, *Smitten Kitchen* by Deb Perelman.

STRACHAN LITERARY AGENCY

P.O. Box 2091, Annapolis MD 21404. **E-mail:** query@strachanlit.com. **Website:** www.strachanlit.com. **Contact:** Laura Strachan. Estab. 1998.

Prior to becoming an agent, Ms. Strachan was (and still is) an attorney.

REPRESENTS Nonfiction, novels. **Considers these nonfiction areas:** creative nonfiction, narrative nonfiction. **Considers these fiction areas:** literary, short story collections, translation, young adult.

☛ "This agency specializes in literary fiction and narrative nonfiction."

HOW TO CONTACT E-mail queries only with brief synopsis and bio; no attachments or samples unless requested. Accepts simultaneous submissions.

RECENT SALES *The Golden Bristled Boar* (UVA Press), *Misdirected* (TriangleSquare/Seven Stories), *Choosing a Good Life* (Hazelden), *Café Oc* (Shanti Arts), *Café Neandertal* (Counterpoint).

ROBIN STRAUS AGENCY, INC.

229 E. 79th St., Suite 5A, New York NY 10075. (212)472-3282. **Fax:** (212)472-3833. **E-mail:** info@robinstrausagency.com. **Website:** www.robinstrausagency.com. **Contact:** Ms. Robin Straus. Estab. 1983. Member of AAR.

Prior to becoming an agent, Robin Straus served as a subsidiary rights manager at Random House and Doubleday. She began her career in the editorial department of Little, Brown.

REPRESENTS Considers these nonfiction areas: biography, cooking, creative nonfiction, current affairs, history, memoirs, parenting, popular culture, psychology, mainstream science. **Considers these fiction areas:** commercial, literary, mainstream, women's.

☛ Does *not* represent juvenile, young adult, science fiction, fantasy, horror, romance, westerns, poetry, or screenplays.

HOW TO CONTACT E-query or query via snail mail with SASE. "Send us a query letter with contact information, an autobiographical summary, a brief synopsis or description of your book project, submission history, and information on competition. If you wish, you may also include the opening chapter of your ms (pasted). While we do our best to reply to all queries, you can assume that if you haven't heard from us after 6 weeks, we are not interested." Accepts simultaneous submissions.

TERMS Agent receives 15% commission on domestic sales; 20% commission on foreign sales. Offers written contract.

THE STRINGER LITERARY AGENCY LLC

P.O. Box 770365, Naples FL 34107. **E-mail:** mstringer@stringerlit.com. **Website:** www.stringerlit.com. **Contact:** Marlene Stringer. This agency focuses on commercial fiction for adults and teens. Estab. 2008; previously an agent with Barbara Bova Literary Agency. Member of AAR, RWA, MWA, ITW, SBCWI. Signatory of WGA. Represents 50 clients.

REPRESENTS Fiction. **Considers these fiction areas:** commercial, crime, detective, fantasy, historical, mainstream, multicultural, mystery, new adult, paranormal, police, romance, science fiction, suspense, thriller, urban fantasy, women's, young adult.

☛ This agency specializes in fiction. "We are an editorial agency and work with clients to make their mss the best they can be in preparation for submission. We focus on career planning and help our clients reach their publishing goals. Because we are so hands-on, we limit the size of our list; however, we are always looking for exceptional voices and stories that demand we read to the end. You never know where the next great story is coming from." This agency is seeking thrillers, crime fiction (not true crime), mystery, women's fiction, single-title and category romance, fantasy (all subgenres), earth-based science fiction (no space opera, aliens, etc.), and young adult. Does not want to receive picture books, middle-grade, plays, short stories, or poetry. This is not the agency for inspirational romance or erotica. The agency is not seeking nonfiction as of this time (2016).

HOW TO CONTACT Electronic submissions through website submission form only. Please make sure your ms is as good as it can be before you submit. Accepts simultaneous submissions. "We strive to respond quickly, but current clients' work always comes first."

RECENT SALES *The Conqueror's Wife* by Stephanie Thornton, *When I'm Gone* by Emily Bleeker, *Magic Bitter, Magic Sweet* by Charlie N. Holmberg, *Belle Chasse* by Suzanne Johnson, *Chapel of Ease* by Alex Bledsoe, *Wilds of the Bayou* by Susannah Sandlin, *Summit Lake* by Charlie Donlea.

TIPS "If your ms falls between categories, or you are not sure of the category, query and we'll let you know if we'd like to take a look. We strive to respond as quickly as possible. If you have not received a response in the time period indicated on website, please re-query."

THE STROTHMAN AGENCY, LLC

63 E. 9th St., 10X, New York NY 10003. **E-mail:** info@strothmanagency.com. **Website:** www.strothmanagency.com. **Contact:** Wendy Strothman, Lauren MacLeod. Member of AAR, Authors Guild. Represents 50 clients.

○ Prior to becoming an agent, Ms. Strothman was head of Beacon Press (1983-1995) and executive vice president of Houghton Mifflin's Trade & Reference Division (1996-2002).

MEMBER AGENTS Wendy Strothman (history, narrative nonfiction, narrative journalism, science and nature, and current affairs); **Lauren MacLeod** (young adult fiction and nonfiction, middle-grade novels, highly polished literary fiction, and narrative nonfiction [particularly food writing, science, pop culture and history]).

REPRESENTS Nonfiction, novels, juvenile books. **Considers these nonfiction areas:** business, current affairs, economics, environment, foods, history, language, popular culture, science. **Considers these fiction areas:** literary, middle-grade, young adult.

☛ "The Strothman Agency seeks out scholars, journalists, and other acknowledged and emerging experts in their fields. We specialize in history, science, narrative journalism, nature and the environment, current affairs, narrative nonfiction, business and economics, young adult fiction and nonfiction, and middle-grade fiction and nonfiction. Browse the 'Recent News' on our website to get an idea of the types of books that we represent. We are not signing up projects in romance, science fiction, picture books, or poetry." Does not want to receive adult fiction or self-help.

HOW TO CONTACT Accepts queries only via e-mail, through strothmanagency@gmail.com. See submission guidelines online. Accepts simultaneous submissions. "All e-mails received will be responded to with an auto-reply. If we have not replied to your query within 6 weeks, we do not feel that it is right for us." Accepts simultaneous submissions. Obtains most new clients through recommendations from others.

TERMS Agent receives 15% commission on domestic sales; 20% commission on foreign sales. Offers written contract; 30-day notice must be given to terminate contract.

THE STUART AGENCY

260 W. 52 St., #25C, New York NY 10019. (212)586-2711. **E-mail:** andrew@stuartagency.com. **Website:** http://stuartagency.com. **Contact:** Andrew Stuart. The Stuart Agency is a full-service literary agency representing a wide range of high-quality nonfiction and fiction, from Pulitzer Prize winners and entertainment figures to journalists, public intellectuals, academics, and novelists. Estab. 2002.

○ Prior to his current position, Mr. Stuart was an agent with Literary Group International for 5 years. Prior to becoming an agent, he was an editor at Random House and Simon & Schuster.

MEMBER AGENTS Andrew Stuart (history, science, narrative nonfiction, business, current events, memoir, psychology, sports, literary fiction); **Christopher Rhodes,** christopher@stuartagency.com (literary and upmarket fiction [including thriller and horror], connected stories/essays [humorous and serious], memoir, creative/narrative nonfiction, history, religion, pop culture, and art/design), **Rob Kirkpatrick,** rob@stuartagency.com (memoir, biography, sports, music, pop culture, current events, history, and pop science).

REPRESENTS Nonfiction, novels. **Considers these nonfiction areas:** art, business, creative nonfiction, current affairs, history, memoirs, popular culture, psychology, religious, science, sports. **Considers these fiction areas:** horror, literary, thriller.

HOW TO CONTACT Query via online submission form on the agency website. Accepts simultaneous submissions.

STEPHANIE TADE LITERARY AGENCY

P.O. Box 235, Durham PA 18039. (610)346-8667. **Website:** http://stephanietadeagency.com/. **Contact:** Stephanie Tade.

○ Prior to becoming an agent, Ms. Tade was an executive editor at Rodale Press. She was also an agent with the Jane Rotrosen Agency.

REPRESENTS Nonfiction, fiction.

☛ Seeks prescriptive and narrative nonfiction, specializing in physical, emotional, psychological, and spiritual wellness, as well as select commercial fiction.

HOW TO CONTACT Query by e-mail, or mail with SASE. "When you write to the agency, please include information about your proposed book, your publishing history, and any media or online platform you have developed." Accepts simultaneous submissions.

TALCOTT NOTCH LITERARY

31 Cherry St., Suite 104, Milford CT 06460. (203)876-4959. **Fax:** (203)876-9517. **E-mail:** editorial@talcottnotch.net. **Website:** www.talcottnotch.net. **Contact:** Gina Panettieri, president. Represents 150 clients.

○ Prior to becoming an agent, Ms. Panettieri was a freelance writer and editor. Ms. Munier was director of acquisitions for Adams Media Corporation and had previously worked for Disney. Ms. Dugas and Ms. Sulaiman had both completed internships with Sourcebooks prior to joining Talcott Notch.

MEMBER AGENTS Gina Panettieri, gpanettieri@talcottnotch.net (history, business, self-help, science, gardening, cookbooks, crafts, parenting, memoir, true crime, travel, young adult, middle-grade, women's fiction, paranormal, urban fantasy, horror, science fiction, historical, mystery, thrillers and suspense); **Paula Munier**, pmunier@talcottnotch.net (mystery, thriller, science fiction, fantasy, romance, young adult, memoir, humor, pop culture, health and wellness, cooking, self-help, pop psych, New Age, inspirational, technology, science, and writing); **Rachael Dugas**, rdugas@talcottnotch.net (young adult, middle-grade, romance, and women's fiction); **Saba Sulaiman**, ssulaiman@talcottnotch.net (upmarket literary and commercial fiction, romance [all subgenres except paranormal], character-driven psychological thrillers, cozy mysteries, memoir, young adult [except paranormal and science fiction], middle-grade, and nonfiction humor).

REPRESENTS Nonfiction, novels, juvenile books. **Considers these nonfiction areas:** business, cooking, crafts, gardening, health, history, humor, inspirational, memoirs, parenting, popular culture, psychology, science, self-help, technology, travel, true crime. **Considers these fiction areas:** commercial, fantasy, historical, horror, literary, mainstream, middle-grade, mystery, New Age, paranormal, romance, science fiction, suspense, thriller, urban fantasy, women's, young adult.

HOW TO CONTACT Query via e-mail (preferred) with first 10 pages of the ms pasted within the body of the e-mail, not as an attachment. Accepts simultaneous submissions. Responds in 2 weeks to queries. Responds in 6-10 weeks to mss.

TERMS Agent receives 15% commission on domestic sales; 20% commission on foreign sales. Offers written contract, binding for 1 year.

RECENT SALES *Tier One* by Brian Andrews and Jeffrey Wilson (Thomas & Mercer), *Firestorm* by Nancy Holzner (Berkley Ace Science Fiction), *The New Jersey Mob* by Scott Deitche (Rowman and Littlefield).

TIPS "Know your market and how to reach them. A strong platform is essential in your book proposal. Can you effectively use social media? Are you a strong networker? Are you familiar with the book bloggers in your genre? Are you involved with the interest-specific groups that can help you? What can you do to break through the 'noise' and help present your book to your readers? Check our website for more tips and information on this topic."

THOMPSON LITERARY AGENCY

115 W. 29th St., Third Floor, New York NY 10001. (347)281-7685. **E-mail:** info@thompsonliterary.com; meg@thompsonliterary.com, submissions@thompsonliterary.com. **Website:** http://thompsonliterary.com. **Contact:** Meg Thompson. Estab. 2014. Member of AAR. Signatory of WGA.

○ Before her current position, Ms. Thompson was with LJK Literary and the Einstein Thompson Agency.

MEMBER AGENTS Meg Thompson; Cindy Uh (senior agent), (picture book, middle-grade, and young adult submissions [including nonfiction queries]; she loves compelling characters and distinct voices, and more diversity of all types is welcome); **John Thorn** (affiliate agent); **Sandy Hodgman** (director of foreign rights).

REPRESENTS Nonfiction, novels, juvenile books. **Considers these nonfiction areas:** autobiography, biography, business, cooking, crafts, creative nonfiction, diet/nutrition, design, education, foods, health, history, how-to, humor, inspirational, interior design, juvenile nonfiction, memoirs, multicultural, popular culture, politics, science, self-help, sports, travel, women's issues, women's studies, young adult. **Considers these fiction areas:** commercial, historical, juvenile, literary, middle-grade, picture books, women's, young adult.

☛ The agency is always on the lookout for both commercial and literary fiction, as well as young adult and children's books. "Nonfiction, however, is our specialty, and our interests include biography, memoir, music, popular science, politics, blog-to-book projects, cookbooks, sports, health and wellness, fashion, art, and popular culture. Please note that we do not accept submissions for poetry collections or screenplays, and we only consider picture books by established illustrators."

HOW TO CONTACT "For fiction: Please send a query letter, including any salient biographical information or previous publications, and attach the first 25 pages of your ms. For nonfiction: Please send a query letter and a full proposal, including biographical information, previous publications, credentials that qualify you to write your book, marketing information, and sample material. You should address your query to whichever agent you think is best suited for your project." Accepts simultaneous submissions. Responds in 6 weeks if interested.

THREE SEAS LITERARY AGENCY

P.O. Box 8571, Madison WI 53708. (608)834-9317. **E-mail:** queries@threeseaslit.com. **Website:** http://threeseasagency.com. **Contact:** Michelle Grajkowski, Cori Deyoe. Estab. 2000. Member of AAR, RWA, SCBWI. Represents 55 clients.

◐ Since its inception, Three Seas has sold more than 500 titles worldwide. Ms. Grajkowski's authors have appeared on all the major lists including *The New York Times*, *USA Today* and *Publishers Weekly*. Prior to joining the agency in 2006, Ms. Deyoe was a multi-published author. She represents a wide range of authors and has sold many projects at auction.

MEMBER AGENTS Michelle Grajkowski (romance, women's fiction, young adult and middle-grade fiction, select nonfiction); **Cori Deyoe** (romance [all types], women's fiction, young adult, middle-grade, picture books, thrillers, mysteries, and select nonfiction); **Linda Scalissi** (women's fiction, thrillers, young adult, mysteries and romance).

REPRESENTS Nonfiction, novels. **Considers these fiction areas:** middle-grade, mystery, picture books, romance, thriller, women's, young adult.

☛ "Currently, we are looking for fantastic authors with a voice of their own." Three Seas does not represent poetry or screenplays.

HOW TO CONTACT E-mail queries only; no attachments, unless requested by agents. For fiction, please e-mail the first chapter and synopsis along with a cover letter. Also, be sure to include the genre and the number of words in your ms, as well as pertinent writing experience in your query letter. For nonfiction, e-mail a complete proposal, including a query letter and your first chapter. For picture books, query with complete text. Accepts simultaneous submissions. Obtains most new clients through recommendations from others, conferences.

TERMS Agent receives 15% commission on domestic sales; 20% commission on foreign sales. Offers written contract.

◐ TRANSATLANTIC LITERARY AGENCY

2 Bloor St. E, Suite 3500, Toronto Ontario M4W 1A8 Canada. (416)488-9214. **E-mail:** info@transatlanticagency.com. **Website:** http://transatlanticagency.com. "The Transatlantic Agency represents adult and children's authors of all genres, including illustrators. We do not handle stage plays, musicals, or screenplays." Please review the agency website and guidelines carefully before making any inquiries, as each agent has her own particular submission guidelines.

MEMBER AGENTS Trena White (upmarket/accessible nonfiction in the categories of current affairs, business, culture, politics, technology, and the environment); **Amy Tompkins** (literary fiction, historical fiction, women's fiction [including smart romance], narrative nonfiction, and quirky or original how-to books; also seeks early readers, middle-grade, young adult, and new adult); **Stephanie Sinclair** (literary fiction, upmarket women's and commercial fiction, literary thriller and suspense, young adult crossover, narrative nonfiction, memoir, investigative journalism, and true crime); **Samantha Haywood** (literary fiction and upmarket commercial fiction—specifically literary thrillers and upmarket mystery; also seeks historical fiction, smart contemporary fiction, upmarket women's fiction, and cross-over novels; enjoys narrative nonfiction, including investigative journalism, politics, women's issues, memoirs, environmental issues, historical narratives, sexuality, true crime; graphic novels [fiction and nonfiction, preferably full length], story collections, memoirs, biographies, travel narratives); **Jesse Finkelstein** (nonfiction in the categories of current affairs, business, culture, politics, technology, religion, and the environment); **Marie Campbell** (middle-grade); **Shaun Bradley** (referrals only; adult literary fiction and narrative nonfiction, primarily science and investigative journalism); **Sandra Bishop** (biography, memoir; also seeks positive or humorous how-to books on advice/relationships, mind/body, religion, healthy living, finances, life hacks, traveling, living a better life); **Fiona Kenshole** (children's and young adult; only accepting submissions from referrals or conferences she attends as faculty); **Lynn Bennett** (not accepting submissions or new clients); **David Bennett**.

REPRESENTS Nonfiction, novels, juvenile books.

➤ "In both children's and adult literature, we market directly into the US, the United Kingdom, and Canada." Represents adult and children's authors of all genres, including illustrators. Does not want to receive picture books, musicals, screenplays, or stage plays.

HOW TO CONTACT Always refer to the website, as guidelines will change, and only various agents are open to new clients at any given time. Obtains most new clients through recommendations from others.

TERMS Agent receives 15% commission on domestic sales; 20% commission on foreign sales. Offers written contract; 45-day notice must be given to terminate contract. This agency charges for photocopying and postage when it exceeds $100.

RECENT SALES Sold 250 titles in the past year.

TRIADA US LITERARY AGENCY, INC.

P.O. Box 561, Sewickley PA 15143 USA. (412)401-3376. **E-mail:** uwe@triadaus.com; brent@triadaus.com; laura@triadaus.com; mallory@triadaus.com. **Website:** www.triadaus.com. **Contact:** Dr. Uwe Stender. Estab. 2004. Member of AAR.

MEMBER AGENTS Uwe Stender, Brent Taylor, Laura Crockett, Mallory Brown.

REPRESENTS Nonfiction, novels, juvenile books. **Considers these nonfiction areas:** biography, business, cooking, crafts, current affairs, diet/nutrition, economics, education, environment, foods, gardening, health, history, how-to, memoirs, music, parenting, popular culture, politics, science, self-help, sports, true crime, young adult. **Considers these fiction areas:** action, adventure, contemporary issues, crime, detective, ethnic, fantasy, gay, historical, horror, juve-

nile, literary, mainstream, middle-grade, multicultural, mystery, new adult, occult, police, romance, suspense, thriller, urban fantasy, women's, young adult.

➤ "We are looking for great writing and story platforms. Our response time is fairly unique. We recognize that neither we nor the authors have time to waste, so we guarantee a 5-day response time. We usually respond within 24 hours." Actively looking for both fiction and nonfiction in all areas.

HOW TO CONTACT E-mail queries preferred. Accepts simultaneous submissions. Obtains most new clients through recommendations from others, conferences.

TERMS Agent receives 15% commission on domestic sales; 20% commission on foreign sales. Offers written contract; 30-day notice must be given to terminate contract.

RECENT SALES *Gettysburg Rebels* by Tom McMillan (Regency), *Who's That Girl* by Blair Thornburgh (Harper Collins Children's), *Perfect Ten* by L.Philips (Viking Children's), *You're Welcome Universe* by Whitney Gardner (Knopf Children's), *Timekeeper* by Tara Sim (Sky Pony).

TIPS "We comment on all requested mss that we reject."

TRIDENT MEDIA GROUP

41 Madison Ave., 36th Floor, New York NY 10010. (212)333-1511. **Website:** www.tridentmediagroup. com. Member of AAR.

MEMBER AGENTS Kimberly Whalen, ws.assistant@tridentmediagroup (commercial fiction and nonfiction—including women's fiction, romance, suspense, and paranormal; also seeks pop culture); **Alyssa Eisner Henkin** (picture books through young adult fiction—in the genres of mysteries, period pieces, contemporary school-settings, issues of social justice, family sagas, eerie magical realism, and retellings of classics); **Scott Miller**, smiller@tridentmediagroup.com (commercial fiction—including thrillers, crime fiction, women's, book club fiction, middle-grade, young adult; nonfiction interests include military, celebrity and pop culture, narrative, sports, prescriptive, and current events); **Melissa Flashman**, mflashman@tridentmediagroup. com (nonfiction interests include pop culture, memoir, wellness, popular science, business and economics, technology; fiction interests include adult and

NEW AGENT SPOTLIGHT

SARAH BUSH
TRIDENT MEDIA GROUP

www.tridentmediagroup.com

ABOUT SARAH: Sarah Bush's love of books was the driving force that brought her to New York City to pursue a master of arts in literature. After that, she decided that the best way to build a career in books was as a literary agent. She sought out Trident, because she believed that it was the preeminent literary agency. Sarah began her career as an assistant, managing the business of two agents at Trident. She was then promoted to the position of audio agent and negotiated deals with audio publishers for Trident authors. Her next promotion was as a sales agent in Trident's unique foreign rights department. In this position, Sarah contacted editors at publishers around the globe to offer the works of Trident authors and negotiate deals on their behalf. With this diverse experience, Sarah is ready to become a leading literary agent at Trident.

SHE IS SEEKING: She is solely looking for women's fiction—both commercial and upmarket. She seeks stories that are character driven, that make you think and feel. Sarah wants to take her experience and drive and match that with "stories that use a fresh voice to explore different aspects of the female experience: emotionally complex, with insights, laughter, and sometimes tears."

HOW TO CONTACT: To contact Sarah, use Trident's website submission form and follow the instructions.

young adult, literary and commercial); **Don Fehr**, dfehr@tridentmediagroup.com (literary and commercial fiction, young adult fiction, narrative nonfiction, memoirs, travel, science, and health); **John Silbersack**, silbersack.assistant@tridentmediagroup.com (literary fiction, crime fiction, science fiction, fantasy, children's, thrillers/suspense; nonfiction interests include narrative nonfiction, science, history, biography, current events, memoirs, finance, pop culture); **Erica Spellman-Silverman; Ellen Levine**, levine.assistant@tridentmediagroup.com (popular commercial fiction; also seeks compelling nonfiction—including memoir, popular culture, narrative nonfiction, history, politics, biography, science, and the odd quirky book); **Mark Gottlieb** (science fiction, fantasy, young adult, graphic novels, historical, middle-grade, mystery, romance, suspense, thrillers; nonfiction interests include business, finance, history, religious, health, cookbooks, sports, African-American, biography, memoir, travel, mind/body/spirit, narrative nonfiction, science, technology); **Alexander Slater**, aslater@tridentmediagroup.com (children's, middle-grade, young adult); **Amanda O'Connor**, aoconnor@tridentmediagroup.com; **Alexa Stark**, astark@tridentmediagroup.com (literary fiction, upmarket commercial fiction, young adult, memoir, narrative nonfiction, popular science, cultural criticism, and women's issues); **Katie Bush** (women's fiction).

REPRESENTS Considers these nonfiction areas: biography, business, cooking, creative nonfiction, current affairs, economics, health, history, memoirs, military, popular culture, politics, religious, science, sports, technology, travel, women's issues, young adult, middle-grade. **Considers these fiction areas:** commercial, crime, fantasy, historical, juvenile, literary, middle-grade, mystery, new adult, paranormal, picture books, romance, science fiction, suspense, thriller, women's, young adult.

☞ Actively seeking new or established authors in a variety of fiction and nonfiction genres.

HOW TO CONTACT Submit through the agency's online submission form on the website. Query only 1 agent at a time. If you e-query, include no attachments. Accepts simultaneous submissions.

RECENT SALES *Fish Wielder* by J.R.R.R. (Jim) Hardison, *How to Steal the Mona Lisa (And Six Other World-Famous Treasures)* by Taylor Bayouth.

TIPS "If you have any questions, please check our FAQ page online before e-mailing us."

UNION LITERARY

30 Vandam St., Suite 5A, New York NY 10013. (212)255-2112. **E-mail:** info@unionliterary.com, submissions@unionliterary.com. **Website:** http://union literary.com. "Union Literary is a full-service boutique agency specializing in literary fiction, popular fiction, narrative nonfiction, memoir, social history, business and general big idea books, popular science, cookbooks, and food writing. We excel at project development, hands-on editing, and placing our projects with domestic and foreign publishers, film, and TV companies." Member of AAR. Signatory of WGA.

☐ "Prior to becoming an agent, Ms. Keating was senior editor at HarperCollins, and also the humanities assistant at Stanford University Press.

MEMBER AGENTS Trena Keating, tk@unionliterary.com (fiction and nonfiction—specifically a literary novel with an exotic setting, a kidlit journey or transformation novel, a distinctly modern novel with a female protagonist, a creepy page-turner, a quest memoir that addresses larger issues, nonfiction based on primary research or a unique niche, a great essayist, and a voicy writer who is a great storyteller or makes her laugh); **Sally Wofford-Girand**, swg@unionliterary.com (history, memoir, women's issues, cultural studies, gripping literary fiction); **Jenni Ferrari-Adler**, jenni@unionliterary.com (cookbook/food, young adult and middle-grade, narrative nonfiction); **Christina Clifford**, christina@unionliterary.com (literary fiction, international fiction, narrative nonfiction, specifically historical biography, memoir, business, and science); **Shaun Dolan,** sd@unionliterary.com (muscular and lyrical literary fiction, narrative nonfiction, memoir, pop culture, and sports narratives).

☞ "Union Literary is a full-service boutique agency specializing in literary fiction, popular fiction, narrative nonfiction, memoir, social history, business, general big idea books, popular science, cookbooks and food writing." The agency does not represent romance, poetry, science fiction or illustrated books.

HOW TO CONTACT Nonfiction submissions should include a query letter, proposal, and sample chapter. Fiction submissions should include a query letter, synopsis, and either sample pages or full ms. "Due to the high volume of submissions we receive, we will only be in contact regarding projects that feel like a match for the respective agent." Accepts simultaneous submissions. Accepts simultaneous submissions. Responds in 1 month.

RECENT SALES *The Sunlit Night* by Rebecca Dinerstein, *Dept. of Speculation* by Jenny Offill, *Mrs. Houdini* by Victoria Kelly.

THE UNTER AGENCY

23 W. 73rd St., Suite 100, New York NY 10023. (212)401-4068. **E-mail:** Jennifer@theunteragency.com. **Website:** www.theunteragency.com. **Contact:** Jennifer Unter. Estab. 2008. Member of AAR. Signatory of WGA.

☐ Ms. Unter began her book publishing career in the editorial department at Henry Holt & Co. She later worked at the Karpfinger Agency while she attended law school. She then became an associate at the entertainment firm of Cowan, DeBaets, Abrahams & Sheppard, where she practiced primarily in the areas of publishing and copyright law.

REPRESENTS Nonfiction, novels, short story collections, juvenile books. **Considers these nonfiction areas:** animals, art, autobiography, biography, cooking, creative nonfiction, current affairs, diet/nutrition, environment, foods, health, history, how-to, humor, juvenile nonfiction, law, memoirs, popular culture, politics, spirituality, sports, travel, true crime, women's issues, young adult, nature subjects. **Considers these fiction areas:** action, adventure, cartoon, commercial, family saga, inspirational, juvenile, mainstream, middle-grade, mystery, paranormal, picture books, thriller, women's, young adult.

☛ This agency specializes in children's and nonfiction, but also takes quality adult fiction.

HOW TO CONTACT Send an e-query. There is also an online submission form. If you do not hear back from this agency within 3 months, consider that a no. Accepts simultaneous submissions.

RECENT SALES A full list of recent sales/titles is available on the agency website.

UPSTART CROW LITERARY

244 Fifth Ave., 11th Floor, New York NY 10001. E-mail: danielle.submission@gmail.com. **Website:** www.upstartcrowliterary.com. **Contact:** Danielle Chiotti, Alexandra Penfold. Estab. 2009. Member of AAR. Signatory of WGA.

MEMBER AGENTS Michael Stearns (not accepting submissions); **Danielle Chiotti** (all genres of young adult and middle-grade fiction, adult upmarket commercial fiction [not considering romance, mystery/suspense/thriller, science fiction, horror, or erotica]; also seeks nonfiction in the areas of narrative/memoir, lifestyle, relationships, humor, current events, food, wine, and cooking); **Ted Malawer** (not accepting submissions); **Alexandra Penfold** (not accepting submissions).

REPRESENTS Considers these nonfiction areas: cooking, current affairs, foods, humor, memoirs. **Considers these fiction areas:** commercial, mainstream, middle-grade, picture books, young adult.

HOW TO CONTACT Submit a query and 20 pages of your ms pasted into an e-mail. Accepts simultaneous submissions.

VENTURE LITERARY

2683 Via de la Valle, G-714, Del Mar CA 92014. (619)807-1887. **Fax:** (772)365-8321. **E-mail:** submissions@ventureliterary.com. **Website:** www.ventureliterary.com. **Contact:** Frank R. Scatoni. "We are accepting queries in all genres except: fantasy, science fiction, romance, children's picture books, and westerns."

☐ Prior to becoming an agent, Mr. Scatoni worked as an editor at Simon & Schuster.
MEMBER AGENTS Frank R. Scatoni, Greg Dinkin.
REPRESENTS Nonfiction, novels, graphic novels, narratives. **Considers these nonfiction areas:** anthropology, biography, business, cultural interests, current affairs, dance, economics, environment, ethnic, government, history, investigative, law, memoirs, military, money, multicultural, music, popular culture, politics, psychology, science, sports, technology, true crime, women's issues, women's studies. **Considers these fiction areas:** action, adventure, crime, detective, historical, literary, mainstream, mystery, police, sports, suspense, thriller, women's.

☛ "We specialize in nonfiction and fiction projects that coincide with our interests—history, sports, business, philanthropy, pop culture, and any narrative that fascinates us. We are accepting queries in all genres except fantasy, science fiction, romance, children's picture books, and western."

HOW TO CONTACT Considers e-mail queries only. No unsolicited mss and no snail mail whatsoever. Usually responds within 1 month. See website for complete submission guidelines. Obtains most new clients through recommendations from others. Obtains most new clients through recommendations from others.

TERMS Agent receives 15% commission on domestic sales; 20% commission on foreign sales. Offers written contract.

VERITAS LITERARY AGENCY

601 Van Ness Ave., Opera Plaza, Suite E, San Francisco CA 94102. (415)647-6964. **Fax:** (415)647-6965. **E-mail:** submissions@veritasliterary.com. **Website:** www.veritasliterary.com. **Contact:** Katherine Boyle. Member of AAR, Authors Guild, SCBWI.

MEMBER AGENTS Katherine Boyle, katherine@veritasliterary.com (literary fiction, middle-grade, young adult, narrative nonfiction, memoir, historical fiction, crime, suspense, history, pop culture, popular science, business/career); **Michael Carr**, michael@veritasliterary.com (historical fiction, women's fiction, science fiction, fantasy, nonfiction), **Chiara Rosati**, chiara@veritasliterary.com (literary fiction, middle-grade, young adult, new adult, women's studies, narrative nonfiction).

NEW AGENT SPOTLIGHT

LATOYA C. SMITH
L. PERKINS AGENCY

www.lperkinsagency.com
@glameditor_girl

ABOUT LATOYA: Before joining the L. Perkins Agency, Latoya C. Smith was an editor for thirteen years working at publishing houses such as Kensington Publishing, Hachette Book Group, and Samhain Publishing. Born and raised in Brooklyn, Latoya started her editorial career as an administrative assistant to *New York Times* best-selling author Teri Woods, while pursuing her B.A. at Temple University. In 2006, Latoya joined Grand Central Publishing, an imprint at Hachette Book Group, where she acquired a variety of titles from hardcover fiction and nonfiction, to digital romance and erotica. In 2014, Latoya was named executive editor at Samhain Publishing, where she acquired romance as well as erotic fiction. She was also the winner of the 2012 RWA Golden Apple for Editor of the Year.

SHE IS SEEKING: Latoya is seeking romance, erotica, erotic fiction, women's fiction, women's thrillers, LGBTQ romance, and LGBTQ erotic fiction. She also seeks nonfiction books in the categories of advice, how-to, and memoir. Latoya tends to shy away from young adult, science fiction, fantasy, historical, steampunk, and urban fantasy.

HOW TO CONTACT: E-mail a query letter containing the following to latoya@lperkinsagency.com: a brief synopsis, your bio, and the first five pages from your novel or book proposal. Send all material in the body of your e-mail.

REPRESENTS Nonfiction, novels. **Considers these nonfiction areas:** business, history, memoirs, popular culture, women's issues. **Considers these fiction areas:** commercial, crime, fantasy, historical, literary, middle-grade, new adult, science fiction, suspense, women's, young adult.

HOW TO CONTACT This agency accepts short queries or proposals via e-mail only. "Fiction submissions: Please include a cover letter listing previously published work, a one-page query and the first 5 pages in the body of the e-mail (not as an attachment). Nonfiction submissions: If you are sending a proposal, please include an author biography, an overview, a chapter-by-chapter summary, and an analysis of competitive titles. We do our best to review all queries within 4-6 weeks; however, if you have not heard from us in 12 weeks, consider that a no." Accepts simultaneous submissions. If you have not heard from this agency in 12 weeks, consider that a no.

WALES LITERARY AGENCY, INC.

1508 Tenth Ave. E, #401, Seattle WA 98102. (206)284-7114. **E-mail:** waleslit@waleslit.com. **Website:** www.

waleslit.com. **Contact:** Elizabeth Wales, Neal Swain. Estab. 1990. Member of ΛΛR, Λuthors Guild.

○ Prior to becoming an agent, Ms. Wales worked at Oxford University Press and Viking Penguin.

MEMBER AGENTS Elizabeth Wales, Neal Swain.

REPRESENTS Nonfiction, novels.

☛ This agency specializes in quality mainstream fiction and narrative nonfiction. Does not handle screenplays, children's picture books, genre fiction, or most category nonfiction (such as self-help or how-to books).

HOW TO CONTACT E-query with no attachments. Accepts simultaneous submissions. Responds in 2 weeks to queries, 2 months to mss.

TERMS Agent receives 15% commission on domestic sales; 20% commission on foreign sales. Offers written contract.

RECENT SALES *Mozart's Starling* by Lyanda Lynn Haupt (Little, Brown), *The Witness Tree Lynda Mapes* (Bloomsbury USA), *Discovering America's Native Bees* by Paige Embry (Timber Press), *Still Time* by Jean Hegland (Arcade).

TIPS "We are especially interested in work that espouses a progressive cultural or political view, projects a new voice, or simply shares an important, compelling story. We also encourage writers living in the Pacific Northwest, West Coast, Alaska, and Pacific Rim countries, and writers from historically underrepresented groups (such as gay and lesbian writers and writers of color) to submit work (but we do not discourage writers outside these areas). Most importantly, whether in fiction or nonfiction, the agency is looking for talented storytellers."

WAXMAN LEAVELL LITERARY AGENCY, INC.

443 Park Ave. S, Suite 1004, New York NY 10016. (212)675-5556. **Fax:** (212)675-1381. **Website:** www.waxmanleavell.com.

MEMBER AGENTS Scott Waxman (history, biography, health and science, adventure, business, inspirational sports); **Byrd Leavell** (narrative nonfiction, sports, humor, and select commercial fiction); **Holly Root** (middle-grade, young adult, women's fiction [commercial and upmarket], urban fantasy, romance, select nonfiction); **Larry Kirschbaum** (fiction and nonfiction; also represents select self-published breakout books); **Rachel Vogel** (subject-driven narratives, memoirs and biography, journalism, popular culture, and the occasional humor/gift book; also seeks selective fiction); **Julie Stevenson** (literary fiction, atmospheric thrillers, suspense-driven work); **Taylor Haggerty** (young adult, historical, contemporary and historical romance, middle-grade, women's, new adult); **Cassie Hanjian** (new adult novels, plot-driven commercial and upmarket women's fiction, historical fiction, psychological suspense, cozy mysteries, and contemporary romance; nonfiction interests include mind/body/spirit, self-help, health and wellness, inspirational memoir, food/wine (narrative and prescriptive), and a limited number of accessible cookbooks); **Fleetwood Robbins** (fantasy and speculative fiction—all subgenres); **Molly O'Neill** (middle-grade and young adult fiction, picture book author/illustrators, and selective narrative nonfiction [including kidlit, pop science, pop culture, lifestyle, food, and travel projects by authors with established platforms]).

REPRESENTS Nonfiction, novels. **Considers these nonfiction areas:** biography, business, foods, health, history, humor, inspirational, memoirs, popular culture, science, sports, adventure. **Considers these fiction areas:** fantasy, historical, literary, mainstream, middle-grade, mystery, paranormal, romance, science fiction, suspense, thriller, urban fantasy, women's, young adult.

HOW TO CONTACT To submit a project, please send a query letter only via e-mail to 1 of the e-mail addresses included on the website. Do not send attachments, though for fiction you may include 5-10 pages of your ms in the body of your e-mail. "Due to the high volume of submissions, agents will reach out to you directly if interested. The typical time range for consideration is 6-8 weeks." Accepts simultaneous submissions.

CK WEBBER ASSOCIATES, LITERARY MANAGEMENT

E-mail: carlie@ckwebber.com. **Website:** http://ckwebber.com. **Contact:** Carlie Webber. CK Webber Associates is a literary agency open to commercial fiction and high-interest nonfiction. Our mission is to develop long-term careers for writers in a variety of genres. Our prime directive is outstanding fiduciary and editorial services for our clients. Member of AAR. Signatory of WGA.

○ Ms. Webber's professional publishing experience includes an internship at Writers House and work with the Publish or Perish Agency/ New England Publishing Associates and the Jane Rotrosen Agency.

REPRESENTS Nonfiction, novels. **Considers these nonfiction areas:** memoirs. **Considers these fiction areas:** fantasy, literary, mainstream, middle-grade, mystery, new adult, romance, science fiction, suspense, thriller, women's, young adult.

- "We are currently not accepting: picture books, easy readers, poetry, scripts, and curriculum nonfiction."

HOW TO CONTACT To submit your work for consideration, please send a query letter, synopsis, and the first 30 pages (or 3 chapters) of your work, whichever is more, to carlie@ckwebber.com and put the word "Query" in the subject line of your e-mail. You may include your materials either in the body of your e-mail or as a Word or PDF attachment. Blank e-mails that include an attachment will be deleted unread. We only accept queries via e-mail. Accepts simultaneous submissions.

THE WEINGEL-FIDEL AGENCY

310 E. 46th St., 21E, New York NY 10017. (212)599-2959. **Contact:** Loretta Weingel-Fidel.

- Prior to opening her agency, Ms. Weingel-Fidel was a psychoeducational diagnostician.

REPRESENTS Nonfiction, novels. **Considers these nonfiction areas:** art, autobiography, biography, dance, memoirs, music, psychology, science, sociology, technology, women's issues, women's studies, investigative journalism. **Considers these fiction areas:** literary, mainstream.

- This agency specializes in commercial and literary fiction and nonfiction. Does not want to receive childrens books, self-help, science fiction, or fantasy.

HOW TO CONTACT Accepts writers by referral only. *No unsolicited mss.* Accepts simultaneous submissions.

TIPS "A very small, selective list enables me to work very closely with my clients to develop and nurture talent. I only take on projects and writers about which I am extremely enthusiastic."

⊙ WELLS ARMS LITERARY

E-mail: info@wellsarms.com. **Website:** www.wellsarms.com. **Contact:** Victoria Wells Arms. Wells Arms Literary represents children's book authors

and illustrators to the trade children's book market. Estab. 2013. Member of SCBWI. Represents 25 clients.

- Ms. Arms's career began as an editor at Dial Books for Young Readers, then G. P. Putnam's Sons, and then as the founding editorial director and associate publisher of Bloomsbury USA's Children's Division.

REPRESENTS Nonfiction fiction, juvenile books, illustrators. **Considers these nonfiction areas:** juvenile nonfiction. **Considers these fiction areas:** juvenile, middle-grade, picture books, young adult.

- We focus on books for young readers of all ages: board books, picture books, readers, chapter books, middle-grade, and young adult fiction. We do not represent to the textbook, magazine, adult romance, or fine art markets.

HOW TO CONTACT E-query. Put "query" and your title in your e-mail subject line. No attachments. Accepts simultaneous submissions. "We try to respond in a month's time."

WERNICK & PRATT AGENCY

E-mail: info@wernickpratt.com. **Website:** www.wernickpratt.com. **Contact:** Marcia Wernick, Linda Pratt, Emily Mitchell. "Wernick & Pratt Agency provides each client with personal attention and the highest quality of advice and service that has been the hallmark of our reputations in the industry. We have the resources and accumulated knowledge to assist clients in all aspects of their creative lives, including editorial input, contract negotiations, and subsidiary rights management. Our goal is to represent and manage the careers of our clients so they may achieve industry-wide and international recognition, as well as the highest level of financial potential." Member of AAR, SCBWI. Signatory of WGA.

- Prior to co-founding Wernick & Pratt Agency, Ms. Wernick worked at the Sheldon Fogelman Agency in subsidiary rights, advancing to director of subsidiary rights; Ms. Pratt also worked at the Sheldon Fogelman Agency.

MEMBER AGENTS Marcia Wernick, Linda Pratt, Emily Mitchell.

- "Wernick & Pratt Agency specializes in children's books of all genres, from picture books through young adult literature and everything in between. We represent both authors and illustrators. We do not represent authors of adult books." Actively seeking people who both write and illustrate in the picture book genre, humorous young chapter books with strong voice, and middle-grade and young adults novels in both the literary and commercial realms. No picture book mss of more than 750 words or mood pieces. Does not want work specifically targeted to the educational market, fiction about the American Revolution, Civil War, or World War II unless it is told from a very unique perspective.

HOW TO CONTACT Submit via e-mail only to submissions@wernickpratt.com. "Please indicate to which agent you are submitting." Detailed submission guidelines available on website. "Submissions will only be responded to further if we are interested in them. If you do not hear from us within 6 weeks of your submission, it should be considered declined."

WESTWOOD CREATIVE ARTISTS, LTD.

94 Harbord St., Toronto Ontario M5S 1G6 Canada. (416)964-3302. **E-mail:** wca_office@wcaltd.com. **Website:** www.wcaltd.com. Represents 350+ clients. **MEMBER AGENTS** Jack Babad; Liz Culotti (foreign contracts and permissions); **Carolyn Ford** (literary fiction, commerical, women's/literary crossover, thrillers, serious narrative nonfiction, pop culture); **Jackie Kaiser** (president and CEO); **Michael A. Levine; Linda McKnight; Hilary McMahon** (fiction, nonfiction, children's); **John Pearce** (fiction and nonfiction); **Meg Tobin-O'Drowsky; Bruce Westwood**. **REPRESENTS** Nonfiction, novels. **Considers these nonfiction areas:** biography, current affairs, history, parenting, science, journalism, practical nonfiction. **Considers these fiction areas:** commercial, juvenile, literary, thriller, women's, young adult.

> "We take on children's and young adult writers very selectively. The agents bring their diverse interests to their client lists, but are generally looking for authors with a mastery of language, as well as a passionate, expert, or original perspective on their subject. Please note that WCA does not represent screenwriters, and our agents are not currently seeking poetry or children's picture book submissions."

HOW TO CONTACT E-query only. Include credentials, synopsis, and no more than 10 pages. No attachments. Accepts simultaneous submissions.

RECENT SALES *Ellen in Pieces* by Caroline Adderson (HarperCollins), *Paper Swan* by Ann Y.K. Choi (Simon & Schuster), *Hope Makes Love* by Trevor Cole (Cormorant).

TIPS "We prefer to receive exclusive submissions and request that you do not query more than 1 agent at [our] agency simultaneously. It's often best if you approach WCA after you have accumulated some publishing credits."

WHIMSY LITERARY AGENCY, LLC

49 N. Eighth St., 6G, Brooklyn NY 11249. (212)674-7162. **E-mail:** whimsynyc@aol.com. **Website:** http://whimsyliteraryagency.com/. **Contact:** Jackie Meyer. Whimsy Literary Agency, LLC, specializes in nonfiction books and authors that educate, entertain, and inspire people. Represents 30 clients.

> Prior to becoming an agent, Ms. Meyer was a VP at Warner Books for 20 years.

MEMBER AGENTS Jackie Meyer, Lenore Skomal. **REPRESENTS** Nonfiction, novels. **Considers these nonfiction areas:** art, autobiography, biography, business, child guidance, cooking, design, education, health, history, how-to, humor, inspirational, interior design, literature, memoirs, money, New Age, popular culture, psychology, self-help, women's issues. **Considers these fiction areas:** commercial, glitz, inspirational, mainstream, metaphysical, New Age, paranormal, psychic.

> "Whimsy looks for projects that are concept- and platform-driven. We seek books that educate, inspire, and entertain." Actively seeking experts in their field with integrated established platforms.

HOW TO CONTACT Send your proposal via e-mail to whimsynyc@aol.com. Include your media platform and table of contents with full description of each chapter. "Note to first-time authors: We appreciate proposals that are professional and complete. Please consult the many fine books available on writing book proposals. We are not considering poetry or screenplays. Due to the volume of queries and submissions, we are unable to respond unless they are of interest to us." Accepts simultaneous submissions. *Does not accept unsolicited mss.* Obtains most new clients through recommendations from others, solicitations. **TERMS** Agent receives 15% commission on domestic sales; 20% commission on foreign sales. Offers written contract.

⊘ WILLIAM MORRIS ENDEAVOR ENTERTAINMENT

1325 Avenue of the Americas, New York NY 10019. (212)586-5100. **Fax:** (212)246-3583. **Website:** www. wma.com. **Contact:** Literary department coordinator. Member of AAR.

REPRESENTS Novels.

HOW TO CONTACT This agency is generally closed to unsolicited literary submissions. Meet an agent at a conference, or query through a referral.

WOLF LITERARY SERVICES, LLC

Website: http://wolflit.com. "Wolf Literary Services LLC is a full-service literary agency specializing in dynamic, quirky books written for all ages. As an agency, we have a deep respect for the place where 'low' art meets high art. We like a good story, regardless of genre." Estab. 2008. Member of AAR. Signatory of WGA.

MEMBER AGENTS Kirsten Wolf (no queries); **Kate Johnson** (literary fiction [particularly character-driven stories], psychological investigations, modern-day fables, international tales, magical realism, and historical fiction; nonfiction interests include food, feminism, parenting, art, travel, and the environment; she loves working with journalists); **Allison Devereux** (literary and upmarket commercial fiction; nonfiction interests include examinations of contemporary culture, pop science, modern feminist perspectives, humor, blog-to-book, and narrative nonfiction that uses a particular niche topic to explore larger truths about our culture).

REPRESENTS Considers these nonfiction areas: art, creative nonfiction, environment, foods, history, humor, memoirs, parenting, science, travel, women's issues. **Considers these fiction areas:** commercial, historical, literary, magical realism.

HOW TO CONTACT To submit a project, please send a query letter along with a 50-page writing sample (for fiction) or a detailed proposal (for nonfiction) to queries@wolflit.com. Samples may be submitted as an attachment or embedded in the body of the e-mail. Accepts simultaneous submissions.

RECENT SALES *A Criminal Magic* by Lee Kelly (Saga Press/Simon & Schuster), *Shallow Graves* by Kali Wallace (Katherine Tegen Books/HarperCollins), *A Hard and Heavy Thing* by Matthew J. Hefti (Tyrus Books).

WOLFSON LITERARY AGENCY

P.O. Box 266, New York NY 10276. **E-mail:** query@ wolfsonliterary.com. **Website:** www.wolfsonliterary. com. **Contact:** Michelle Wolfson. Estab. 2007. Adheres to AAR canon of ethics.

◖ Prior to forming her own agency in December 2007, Ms. Wolfson spent 2 years with Artists & Artisans, Inc., and 2 years with Ralph Vicinanza, Ltd.

REPRESENTS Nonfiction, fiction. **Considers these nonfiction areas:** creative nonfiction, health, humor, medicine, parenting, popular culture, relationships. **Considers these fiction areas:** mainstream, mystery, new adult, romance, suspense, thriller, women's, young adult.

⊶ Actively seeking young adult, mainstream fiction, mysteries, thrillers, suspense, women's fiction, romance. Fiction interests include fun, practical advice books in any area, but particularly those that are of interest to women. Also seeks books on relationships, parenting, health/medical, humor, pop culture, and narrative nonfiction.

HOW TO CONTACT E-queries only. Accepts simultaneous submissions. Responds only if interested. Positive response is generally given within 2-4 weeks. Obtains most new clients through queries or recommendations from others.

TERMS Agent receives 15% commission on domestic sales; receives 25% commission on foreign sales. Offers written contract; 30-day notice must be given to terminate contract.

TIPS "Be persistent."

◎ WORDSERVE LITERARY GROUP

7061 S. University Blvd., Suite 307, Centennial CO 80122. **E-mail:** admin@wordserveliterary.com. **Website:** www.wordserveliterary.com. **Contact:** Greg Johnson. WordServe Literary Group was founded in 2003 by veteran literary agent Greg Johnson. After more than a decade in serving authors, the agency has represented more than 700 books in every fiction category and nonfiction genre. "We specialize in serving authors of faith in all of their creative endeavors, as well as select titles and genres in the general market." Represents 100 clients.

◖ Prior to becoming an agent in 1994, Mr. Johnson was a magazine editor and freelance writer of more than 20 books and 200 articles.

MEMBER AGENTS Greg Johnson, Nick Harrison, Sarah Freese.

REPRESENTS Nonfiction, novels. **Considers these nonfiction areas:** biography, current affairs, diet/nu-

NEW AGENT SPOTLIGHT

SUZY EVANS
SANDRA DIJKSTRA LITERARY AGENCY

www.dijkstraagency.com
@thehistorychef

ABOUT SUZY: Suzy Evans is an attorney, author, and agent who holds a PhD in history from University of California, Berkeley. Her most recent books include *Machiavelli for Moms* (Simon & Schuster) and *Forgotten Crimes*. She is also a ghostwriter for a best-selling author with more than 15 million copies in print. Her first children's book will be published by HarperCollins in 2018.

SHE IS SEEKING: General fiction, suspense/thriller, juvenile fiction, biography, business/investing, history, health, travel, lifestyle, cookbooks, middle-grade, young adult, sports, and science. "In the adult market, I'm particularly on the hunt for great serious nonfiction, especially by established historians who are looking to make the transition from an academic to trade readership, as well as journalists who have something truly unique and significant to say. I'm also on the lookout for smart parenting books with useful, original, unexpected hooks that fill a gap in the market (bonus points for humor). On the children's front, I have a great love of middle-grade and am particularly on the hunt for engaging, original nonfiction that pops off the page and makes kids excited about learning. I also have a huge soft spot for contemporary young adult fiction that tackles difficult issues in bold, daring ways and with inventive formats that can be brought into the classroom to stimulate meaningful discussion and debate.

HOW TO CONTACT: Contact suzy@dijkstraagency.com. For fiction, please send a synopsis and the first chapter of your polished manuscript pasted below your query. For nonfiction, send your query and first chapter with a concise author bio. Response time varies from a few minutes to a few weeks.

---

trition, history, inspirational, memoirs, military, parenting, religious, self-help, women's issues. **Considers these fiction areas:** historical, inspirational, literary, mainstream, spiritual, suspense, thriller, women's, young adult.

Actively seeking materials with a faith-based angle. No gift books, poetry, short stories, screenplays, graphic novels, children's picture books, science fiction, or fantasy. Please do not send mss that are more than 120,000 words.

HOW TO CONTACT E-query admin@word-serveliterary.com. In the subject line, include the word "query." All queries should include the following 3 elements: a pitch for the book, information about you and your platform (for nonfiction) or writing background (for fiction), and the first 5 (or so) pages of the ms pasted into the e-mail. View our website for full guidelines. Accepts simultaneous submissions. Response within 60 days. Obtains most new clients through recommendations from others.

TIPS "We are looking for good proposals, great writing, and authors willing to market their books, as appropriate. Also, we're only looking for projects with a faith element bent. See the website before submitting."

WRITERS HOUSE

21 W. 26th St., New York NY 10010. (212)685-2400. **Fax:** (212)685-1781. **Website:** www.writershouse.com. Estab. 1973. Member of AAR.

MEMBER AGENTS Amy Berkower, Stephen Barr, Susan Cohen, Dan Conaway, Lisa DiMona, Susan Ginsburg, Susan Golomb, Merrilee Heifetz, Brianne Johnson, Daniel Lazar, Simon Lipskar, Steven Malk, Jodi Reamer, Esq., Robin Rue, Rebecca Sherman, Geri Thoma, Albert Zuckerman, Alec Shane, Stacy Testa, Victoria Doherty-Munro, Beth Miller, Andrea Morrison, Soumeya Roberts.

REPRESENTS Nonfiction, novels. **Considers these nonfiction areas:** biography, business, cooking, economics, history, how-to, juvenile nonfiction, memoirs, parenting, psychology, science, self-help. **Considers these fiction areas:** commercial, fantasy, juvenile, literary, mainstream, middle-grade, picture books, science fiction, women's, young adult.

⌐ This agency specializes in all types of popular fiction and nonfiction, for both adult and juvenile books, as well as illustrators. Does not want to receive scholarly, professional, poetry, plays, or screenplays.

HOW TO CONTACT Individual agent e-mail addresses are available on the website. "Please e-mail us a query letter, which includes your credentials, an explanation of what makes your book unique and special, and a synopsis. Some agents within our agency have different requirements. Please consult their individual Publishers Marketplace profile for additional details. We respond to all queries, generally within 8 weeks." If you prefer to submit my mail, address it to an individual agent, and please include a SASE for our reply. (If submitting to Steven Malk: Writers House, 7660 Fay Ave., #338H, La Jolla, CA 92037.) Accepts simultaneous submissions. Obtains most new clients through recommendations from authors and editors.

TERMS Agent receives 15% commission on domestic sales; 20% commission on foreign sales. Offers written contract, binding for 1 year. Agency charges fees for copying mss/proposals and overseas airmail of books.

TIPS "Do not send mss. Write a compelling letter. If you do, we'll ask to see your work. Follow submission guidelines and please do not simultaneously submit your work to more than 1 Writers House agent."

WRITERS' REPRESENTATIVES, LLC

116 W. 14th St., 11th Floor, New York NY 10011-7305. **E-mail:** transom@writersreps.com. **Website:** www.writersreps.com. Represents 100 clients.

◖ Prior to becoming an agent, Ms. Chu was a lawyer; Mr. Hartley worked at Simon & Schuster, Harper & Row, and Cornell University Press.

MEMBER AGENTS Lynn Chu, Glen Hartley.

REPRESENTS Nonfiction, novels, poetry books. **Considers these nonfiction areas:** biography, business, cooking, current affairs, economics, history, humor, law, memoirs, philosophy, politics, science, self-help, reference, literature, personal finance, criticism. **Considers these fiction areas:** literary, mystery, thriller.

⌐ Seeking serious nonfiction and quality fiction. No motion picture or TV screenplays. "We generally will not consider science fiction, children's, or young adult fiction unless it aspires to serious literature."

HOW TO CONTACT Query with SASE or by e-mail. Send ms, full CV, list of previously published works, and a table of contents. Advise on submission if the projects has been sent to other agents and if it was previously submitted to publishers. Accepts simultaneous submissions.

JASON YARN LITERARY AGENCY

3544 Broadway, No. 68, New York NY 10031. **E-mail:** jason@jasonyarnliteraryagency.com. **Website:** www.jasonyarnliteraryagency.com. Member of AAR. Signatory of WGA.

REPRESENTS Nonfiction, fiction. **Considers these nonfiction areas:** creative nonfiction, current affairs, foods, history, science. **Considers these fiction areas:** commercial, fantasy, literary, middle-grade, science fiction, suspense, thriller, young adult, graphic novels, comics.

HOW TO CONTACT Please e-mail your query to jason@jasonyarnliteraryagency.com with the word "Query" in the subject line, and please paste the first 10 pages of your ms or proposal into the text of your e-mail. Do not send any attachments. "Visit the 'About' page [on our website] for information on what we are interested in, and please note that JYLA does not accept queries for film, TV, or stage scripts." Accepts simultaneous submissions.

KAREN GANTZ ZAHLER LITERARY MANAGEMENT AND ATTORNEY AT LAW

(212)734-3619. **E-mail:** karen@karengantzlit.com. **Website:** www.karengantzlit.com. **Contact:** Karen Gantz Zahler.

◯ Prior to her current position, Ms. Gantz Zahler practiced law at 2 law firms and wrote 2 cookbooks: *Taste of New York* (Addison-Wesley) and *Superchefs* (John Wiley & Sons). She also participated in a Presidential Advisory Committee on Intellectual Property, US Department of Commerce.

REPRESENTS Nonfiction.

HOW TO CONTACT Accepting queries and summaries by e-mail only. Check the website for complete submission information (karengantzlit.com/submission.html), because it is intricate and specific. Accepts simultaneous submissions. Responds in 4-8 weeks to queries.

RECENT SALES *Nevertheless* by Alec Baldwin (Harper), *The Magic of Math: Solving for X and Figuring Out Why* by Arthur Benjamin (Basic Books), *The*

Nixon Effect: How His Presidency has Changed American Politics by Douglas Schoen (Encounter Books).

HELEN ZIMMERMANN LITERARY AGENCY

E-mail: submit@zimmagency.com. **Website:** www.zimmermannliterary.com. **Contact:** Helen Zimmermann. Estab. 2003.

◯ Prior to opening her agency, Ms. Zimmermann was the director of advertising and promotion at Random House and the events coordinator at an independent bookstore.

REPRESENTS Nonfiction, fiction. **Considers these nonfiction areas:** diet/nutrition, health, memoirs, music, sports, women's issues, relationships. **Considers these fiction areas:** literary, mainstream.

☛ "I am currently concentrating my nonfiction efforts in health and wellness, relationships, popular culture, women's issues, lifestyle, sports, and music. I am also drawn to memoirs that speak to a larger social or historical circumstance, or introduce me to a new phenomenon. And I am always looking for a work of fiction that will keep me up at night!"

HOW TO CONTACT Accepts e-mail queries only. "For nonfiction queries, initial contact should just be a pitch letter. For fiction queries, I prefer a summary, your bio, and the first chapter as text in the e-mail (not as an attachment). If I express interest, I will need to see a full proposal for nonfiction and the remainder of the ms for fiction." Accepts simultaneous submissions. Responds in 2 weeks to queries, only if interested. Obtains most new clients through recommendations from others, solicitations.

WRITERS CONFERENCES

Attending a writers conference that includes agents gives you the opportunity to learn more about what agents do and to show an agent your work. Ideally, a conference should include a panel or two with a number of agents to give writers a sense of the variety of personalities and tastes of different agents.

Not all agents are alike: Some are more personable, and sometimes you simply click better with one agent versus another. When only one agent attends a conference, there is a tendency for every writer at that conference to think, "Ah, this is the agent I've been looking for!" When the number of agents attending is larger, you have a wider group from which to choose, and you may have less competition for the agent's time.

Besides including panels of agents discussing what representation means and how to go about securing it, many of these gatherings also include time—either scheduled or impromptu—to meet briefly with an agent to discuss your work.

If they're impressed with what they see and hear about your work, they will invite you to submit a query, a proposal, a few sample chapters, or possibly your entire ms. Some conferences even arrange for agents to review mss in advance and schedule one-on-one sessions during which you can receive specific feedback or advice regarding your work. Such meetings often cost a small fee, but the input you receive is usually worth the price.

Ask writers who attend conferences and they'll tell you that, at the very least, you'll walk away with new knowledge about the industry. At the very best, you'll receive an invitation to send an agent your material!

Many writers try to make it to at least one conference a year, but cost and location can count as much as subject matter when determining which one to attend. There are conferences in almost every state and province that can provide answers to your questions about writing and the publishing industry. Conferences also connect you with a community of other writers. Such connections help you learn about the pros and cons of different agents, and they can also give you a renewed sense of purpose and direction in your own writing.

SUBHEADS

Each listing is divided into subheads to make locating specific information easier. In the first section, you'll find contact information for conference contacts. You'll also learn conference dates, specific focus, and the average number of attendees. Finally, names of agents who will be speaking or have spoken in the past are listed along with details about their availability during the conference. Calling or e-mailing a conference director to verify the names of agents in attendance is always a good idea.

COSTS: Looking at the price of events, plus room and board, may help writers on a tight budget narrow their choices.

ACCOMMODATIONS: Here conferences list overnight accommodations and travel information. Often conferences held in hotels will reserve rooms at a discount rate and may provide a shuttle bus to and from the local airport.

ADDITIONAL INFORMATION: This section includes information on conference-sponsored contests, individual meetings, the availability of brochures, and more.

ABROAD WRITERS CONFERENCES

17363 Sutter Creek Rd., (209)296-4052. **E-mail:** abroadwriters@yahoo.com; nancy@abroadwritersconference.com. **Website:** abroadwritersconference.com. "Abroad Writers Conferences are devoted to introducing our participants to world views here in the United States and abroad. Throughout the world we invite authors to give readings and to participate on panels. Our discussion groups touch upon a wide range of topics. Our objective is to broaden our cultural and scientific perspectives of the world through discourse and writing." Conferences are held throughout the year in various places worldwide. See website for scheduling details. Conference duration: 7-10 days. "Instead of being lost in a crowd at a large conference, Abroad Writers' Conference prides itself on holding small group meetings where participants have personal contact with everyone. Stimulating talks, interviews, readings, Q&As, writing workshops, film screenings, private consultations, and social gatherings all take place within 7-10 days. Abroad Writers' Conference promises you true networking opportunities and full detailed feedback on your writing submissions."

COSTS See website for pricing details.

ADDITIONAL INFORMATION Agents participate in conferences. Application is online at website.

ALASKA WRITERS CONFERENCE

Alaska Writers Guild, P.O. Box 670014, Chugiak AK 99567. **E-mail:** alaskawritersguild.awg@gmail.com. **Website:** alaskawritersguild.com. Annual event held in the fall—usually September. Duration: 2 days. There are many workshops and instructional tracks of courses. This event sometimes teams up with SCBWI and Alaska Pacific University to offer courses at the event. Literary agents are in attendance each year to hear pitches and meet writers.

ALGONKIAN FIVE DAY NOVEL CAMP

2020 Pennsylvania Ave. NW, Suite 443, Washington DC 20006. **E-mail:** info@algonkianconferences.com. **Website:** http://algonkianconferences.com/index.htm. Conference duration: 5 days. Average attendance: 12 students maximum per workshop. "During 45+ hours of actual workshop time, students will engage in those rigorous exercises necessary to produce a publishable ms. Genres we work with include general commercial fiction, literary fiction, serious and light women's fiction, mystery/cozy/thriller, science fiction, fantasy, young adult, memoir, and narrative nonfiction. The 3 areas of workshop emphasis will be premise, platform, and execution.

AMERICAN CHRISTIAN WRITERS CONFERENCES

P.O. Box 110390, Nashville TN 37222-0390. (800)219-7483, (800)21-WRITE. **E-mail:** ACWriters@aol.com. **Website:** www.ACWriters.com. **Contact:** Reg Forder, director. Estab. 1981. ACW hosts a dozen annual two-day writers conferences and mentoring retreats across America. These are taught by editors and professional freelance writers. These events provide excellent instruction, networking opportunities, and valuable one-on-one time with editors. Annual conferences promoting all forms of Christian writing (fiction, nonfiction, scriptwriting). Conferences are held between March and November during each year.

COSTS Costs vary based on conference. Prices also depend on whether it is a conference or a mentoring retreat.

ACCOMMODATIONS Special rates are available at the host hotel (usually a major chain like Holiday Inn).

ADDITIONAL INFORMATION E-mail or call for conference brochures.

ANTIOCH WRITERS' WORKSHOP

c/o Antioch University Midwest, 900 Dayton St., Yellow Springs OH 45387. (937)769-1803. **E-mail:** info@antiochwritersworkshop.com. **Website:** www.antiochwritersworkshop.com. **Contact:** Sharon Short, director. Estab. 1986. Average attendance: 80. Programs are offered year-round; see the website for details. The dates of the 2016 conference are July 9-16. Workshop concentration: fiction, poetry, personal essay, memoir. Workshop located at Antioch University Midwest in the Village of Yellow Springs. Literary agents attend. Writers of all levels (beginner to advanced) of fiction, memoir, personal essay, and poetry are warmly welcomed to discover their next steps on their writing paths—whether that's developing craft or preparing to submit for publication. An agent and an editor will be speaking and available for meetings with attendees.

ACCOMMODATIONS Accommodations are available at local hotels.

ADDITIONAL INFORMATION The easiest way to contact this event is through the online website contact form.

ASJA ANNUAL WRITERS CONFERENCE

American Society of Journalists and Authors, 355 Lexington Ave., 15th Floor, New York NY 10017. (212)997-0947. **E-mail:** asjaoffice@asja.org, director@asja.org. **Website:** www.asjaconferences.org. **Contact:** Alexandra Owens, executive director. Estab. 1971. Annual conference held in New York City each spring. Conference duration: 2-3 days. Average attendance: 600. Covers nonfiction. Held at the Roosevelt Hotel in New York. Speakers have included Kitty Kelley, Jennifer Finney Boylan, Daniel Jones, D.T. Max, and more.

COSTS In the range of $300/day, depending on when you sign up. Check website for details.

ACCOMMODATIONS Venue hotel has block of rooms at discounted conference rate.

ADDITIONAL INFORMATION Conference program online by mid-January. Registration is online only. Sign up for e-mail updates online.

ATLANTA WRITERS CONFERENCE

Atlanta Writers Club, Westin Atlanta Airport Hotel, 4736 Best Rd., Atlanta GA 30337. **E-mail:** awconference@gmail.com. **E mail:** gjweinstein@yahoo.com. **Website:** www.atlantawritersconference.com. **Contact:** George Weinstein. Estab. 2008. The Atlanta Writers Conference happens twice a year (May and October/November) with 10 agents and publishing editors attending each event. These agents and editors critique ms samples and query letters, and also respond to pitches. There also is a self-editing workshop with editor Angela James and instructional sessions with local authors as well as separate Q&A panels with the editors and agents. The first 2016 event is May 6-7.

COSTS Ms critiques are $160 each. Pitches on Saturday are $60 each. The query letter critique on Friday is $60 (you may register for only 1 spot). Other workshops and panels may also cost extra—check the website. The conference "All Activities" option (which includes 2 ms critiques, 2 pitches, and 1 of each remaining activity) is $560.

ACCOMMODATIONS Westin Airport Atlanta Hotel.

ADDITIONAL INFORMATION There is a free shuttle that runs between the airport and the hotel.

BALTIMORE WRITERS' CONFERENCE

English Department, Liberal Arts Bldg., Towson University, 8000 York Rd., Towson MD 21252. (410)704-3695. **E-mail:** prwr@towson.edu. **Website:** baltimorewritersconference.org. Estab. 1994. "Annual conference held in November at Towson University. Conference duration: 1 day. Average attendance: 150-200. Covers all areas of writing and getting published. Held at Towson University. Session topics include fiction, nonfiction, poetry, magazine, journals, agents, and publishers. Sign up the day of the conference for quick critiques to improve your stories, essays, and poems."

ACCOMMODATIONS Hotels are close by, if required.

ADDITIONAL INFORMATION Writers may register through the BWA website. Send inquiries via e-mail.

BAY TO OCEAN WRITERS CONFERENCE

P.O. Box 1773, Easton MD 21601. (410)482-6337. **E-mail:** info@baytoocean.com. **Website:** www.baytoocean.com. Estab. 1998. Annual conference held the second Saturday in March. Average attendance: 200. Approximately 30 speakers conduct workshops on publishing, agents, editing, marketing, craft, the Internet, poetry, fiction, nonfiction, and freelance writing. The location is Chesapeake College, Rt. 213 and Rt. 50, Wye Mills, on Maryland's historic eastern shore. Accessible to individuals with disabilities.

COSTS Adults $115, students $55. A paid ms review is also available—details on website. Includes continental breakfast and networking lunch.

ADDITIONAL INFORMATION Registration is on website. Pre-registration is required; no registration at door. Conference usually sells out 1 month in advance. Conference is for all levels of writers.

BIG SUR WRITING WORKSHOP

Henry Miller Library, Hwy. 1, Big Sur CA 93920. (831)667-2574. **E-mail:** writing@henrymiller.org. **Website:** http://bigsurwriting.wordpress.com. Annual workshops focusing on children's and young adult writing (picture books, middle-grade, and young adult). 2016 dates: March 4-6. Workshop held in Big Sur Lodge in Pfeiffer State Park. Cost of workshop includes meals, lodging, workshop, Saturday evening reception. This event is helmed by the literary agents of the Andrea Brown Literary Agency, which is the most successful agency nationwide in selling children's books. All attendees meet with at least 2 faculty members, and their work is critiqued.

BLUE RIDGE MOUNTAINS CHRISTIAN WRITERS CONFERENCE

(800)588-7222. **E-mail:** alton@altongansky.com. **Website:** www.brmcwc.com. Annual conference held in May. Conference duration: Sunday through lunch on Thursday. Average attendance: 350. The conference is a training and networking event for both seasoned and aspiring writers that allows attendees to interact with editors, agents, professional writers, and readers. Workshops and continuing classes in a variety of creative categories are offered.

COSTS $325 for the conference; meal package is $145 per person (12 meals beginning with dinner Sunday and ending with lunch on Thursday). $350 conference fee for those not staying on campus. Room rates vary from $60-70 per night.

ADDITIONAL INFORMATION For a PDF of the complete BRMCWC schedule (typically posted in April), visit the website.

BOOKS-IN-PROGRESS CONFERENCE

Carnegie Center for Literacy and Learning, 251 W. Second St., Lexington KY 40507. (859)254-4175. **E-mail:** lwhitaker@carnegiecenterlex.org. **Website:** www.carnegiecenterlex.org. **Contact:** Laura Whitaker. Estab. 2010. This is an annual writing conference at the Carnegie Center for Literacy and Learning in Lexington. It typically happens in June. "Each conference will offer writing and publishing workshops and includes a keynote presentation." Literary agents are flown in to meet with writers and hear pitches. Website is updated several months prior to each annual event.

ACCOMMODATIONS Several area hotels are nearby.

◐ BREAD LOAF IN SICILY WRITERS' CONFERENCE

Middlebury College, Middlebury VT 05753. (802)443-5286. **Fax:** (802)443-2087. **E-mail:** blwc@middlebury.edu. **Website:** www.middlebury.edu/bread-loaf-conferences/blSicily. Estab. 2011. Annual conference held in September in Erice, Sicily (western coast of the island). Conference duration: 7 days. Offers workshops for fiction, nonfiction, and poetry. Agents and editors will be in attendance. 2016 dates: September 18-24. Average attendance: 32.

COSTS The fee (contributor, $2,930) includes the conference program, transfer to and from Palermo Airport, 6 nights of lodging, 3 meals daily (except for Wednesday), wine reception at the readings, and an excursion to the ancient ruins of Segesta. The charge for an additional person is $1,750. There is a $15 application fee and a $300 deposit.

ACCOMMODATIONS Accommodations are single rooms with private bath. Breakfast and lunch are served at the hotel and dinner is available at select Erice restaurants. A double room is possible for those who would like to be accompanied by a spouse or significant other.

ADDITIONAL INFORMATION Application period is from November through March. Rolling admissions. Space is limited.

BREAD LOAF ORION ENVIRONMENTAL WRITERS' CONFERENCE

Middlebury College, Middlebury VT 05753. (802)443-5286. **Fax:** (802)443-2087. **E-mail:** blwc@middlebury.edu. **Website:** www.middlebury.edu/bread-loaf-conferences/BLOrion. Estab. 2014. Annual specialized conference held in June. Conference duration: 7 days. Offers workshops for fiction, nonfiction, and poetry. Agents and editors will be in attendance. 2016 dates: June 3-9. Average attendance: 60. Application period is from November through March. Rolling admissions. Space is limited.

ACCOMMODATIONS Mountain campus of Middlebury College in Vermont.

ADDITIONAL INFORMATION The event is designed to hone the skills of people interested in producing literary writing about the environment and the natural world. The conference is cosponsored by the Bread Loaf Writers' Conference and Middlebury College's Environmental Studies Program.

BREAD LOAF WRITERS' CONFERENCE

Middlebury College, Middlebury VT 05753. (802)443-5286. **Fax:** (802)443-2087. **E-mail:** blwc@middlebury.edu. **Website:** www.middlebury.edu/bread-loaf-conferences/bl_writers. Estab. 1926. Annual conference held in late August. Conference duration: 10 days. Offers workshops for fiction, nonfiction, and poetry. Agents and editors will be in attendance.

ACCOMMODATIONS Bread Loaf Campus in Ripton, Vermont.

ADDITIONAL INFORMATION 2016 Conference Dates: August 10-20. Location: Bread Loaf campus of

Middlebury College in Vermont. Average attendance: 230. There is a $15 application fee.

CALIFORNIA CRIME WRITERS CONFERENCE

Co-sponsored by Sisters in Crime Los Angeles and the Southern California Chapter of Mystery Writers of America, **E-mail:** sistersincrimela@gmail.com. **Website:** www.ccwconference.org. Estab. 1995. Biennial. Previous conference dates have been early June. Average attendance: 200. Two-day conference on mystery and crime writing. Offers craft, forensic, industry news, marketing, and career-buildings sessions also has 2 keynote speakers, author panels, editor panels, agent panels, and several book signings. Past keynote speakers were Charlaine Harris and Anne Perry. Breakfast and lunch both days included.

ADDITIONAL INFORMATION Conference information, as well as other details, is available at www.ccwconference.org.

CAPE COD WRITERS CENTER ANNUAL CONFERENCE

P.O. Box 408, Osterville MA 02655. **E-mail:** writers@capecodwriterscenter.org. **Website:** www.capecod writerscenter.org. **Contact:** Nancy Rubin Stuart, executive director. Duration: 3 days; held during first week in August. Offers workshops in fiction, commercial fiction, nonfiction, poetry, writing for children, memoir, pitching your book, screenwriting, digital communications, and getting published. There are ms evaluation and mentoring sessions with faculty.

COSTS Costs vary, depending on the number of courses selected.

ACCOMMODATIONS Held at Resort and Conference Center of Hyannis, Hyannis, Massachusetts. Pricing varies.

CELEBRATION OF SOUTHERN LITERATURE

Southern Lit Alliance, 3069 S. Broad St., Suite 2, Chattanooga TN 37408-3056. (423)267-1218. **Fax:** (866)483-6831. **E-mail:** srobinson@southernlitalliance.org. **Website:** www.southernlitalliance.org. **Contact:** Susan Robinson. "The Celebration of Southern Literature stands out because of its unique collaboration with the Fellowship of Southern Writers, an organization founded by towering literary figures like Eudora Welty, Cleanth Brooks, Walker Percy, and Robert Penn Warren to recognize and encourage literature in the South. The

2015 celebration marked 26 years since the Fellowship selected Chattanooga for its headquarters and chose to collaborate with the Celebration of Southern Literature. The Fellowship awards 11 literary prizes and induct new members, making this event the place to discover up-and-coming voices in Southern literature. The Southern Lit Alliance's Celebration of Southern Literature attracts more than 1,000 readers and writers from all over the US. It strives to maintain an informal atmosphere where conversations will thrive, inspired by a common passion for the written word. The Southern Lit Alliance (formerly The Arts & Education Council) started as one of 12 pilot agencies founded by a Ford Foundation grant in 1952. The Alliance is the only organization of the 12 still in existence. The Southern Lit Alliance celebrates southern writers and readers through community education and innovative literary arts experiences."

CHICAGO WRITERS CONFERENCE

E-mail: mare@chicagowritersconference.org. **Website:** chicagowritersconference.org. **Contact:** Mare Swallow. Estab. 2011. This conference happens every year in the fall (typically September or October). Find them on Twitter at @ChiWritersConf. The conference brings together a variety of publishing professionals (agents, editors, authors) and brings together several Chicago literary, writing, and bookselling groups. The conference often sells out. Past speakers have included *New York Times* best-selling author Sara Paretsky, children's author Allan Woodrow, young adult author Erica O'Rourke, novelist Eric Charles May, and novelist Loretta Nyhan.

CHRISTOPHER NEWPORT UNIVERSITY WRITERS' CONFERENCE & WRITING CONTEST

(757)269-4368. **E-mail:** eleanor.taylor@cnu.edu. **Website:** writers.cnu.edu. Estab. 1981. 2016 conference held in May. This is a working conference. Presentations made by editors, agents, fiction writers, poets, and more. Breakout sessions in fiction, nonfiction, poetry, juvenile fiction, and publishing. Previous panels included "Publishing," "Proposal Writing," and "Internet Research."

ACCOMMODATIONS Provides list of area hotels.

ADDITIONAL INFORMATION 2016 conference dates were May 6-7.

CLARION WEST WRITERS WORKSHOP

P.O. Box 31264, Seattle WA 98103-1264. (206)322-9083. **E-mail:** info@clarionwest.org. **Website:** www.clarionwest.org. "Contact us through our webform." **Contact:** Nelle Graham, workshop director. Clarion West is an intensive six-week workshop for writers preparing for professional careers in science fiction and fantasy, held annually in Seattle. Usually goes from mid-June through end of July. Conference duration: 6 weeks. Average attendance: 18. Held near the University of Washington. Deadline for applications is March 1. Instructors are well-known writers and editors in the field.

COSTS $3,800 (for tuition, housing, most meals). Limited scholarships are available based on financial need.

ACCOMMODATIONS Workshop tuition, dormitory housing, and most meals: $3,800. Students stay onsite in workshop housing at one of the University of Washington's sorority houses. "Students write their own stories every week while preparing critiques of all the other students' work for classroom sessions. This gives participants a more focused, professional approach to their writing. The core of the workshop remains about speculative fiction and short stories (not novels)." Conference information available in fall. For brochure/guidelines send a SASE, visit website, e-mail, or call. Students must submit 20-30 pages of ms with four-page biography and $50 fee ($30 if received prior to February 10) for applications sent by mail or e-mail to qualify for admission.

ADDITIONAL INFORMATION This is a critique-based workshop. Students are encouraged to write a story every week; the critique of student material produced at the workshop forms the principal activity of the workshop. Students and instructors critique mss as a group. Visit the website for updates and complete details.

CLARKSVILLE WRITERS CONFERENCE

1123 Madison St., Clarksville TN 37040. (931)551-8870. **E-mail:** artsandheritage@cdelightband.net, burawac@apsu.edu. **E-mail:** artsandheritage@cdelightband.net, burawac@apsu.edu. **Website:** www.artsandheritage.us/writers. **Contact:** Ellen Kanervo. Annual conference held in the summer at Austin Peay State University. The conference features a variety of presentations on fiction, nonfiction, and more. Past presenting authors include Tom Franklin, Frye Gail-lard, William Gay, Susan Gregg Gilmore, Will Campbell, John Seigenthaler Sr., Alice Randall, George Singleton, Alanna Nash, and Robert Hicks. Our presentations and workshops are valuable to writers and interesting to readers.

COSTS Costs available online; prices vary depending on how long attendees stay and if they attend the banquet dinner.

ADDITIONAL INFORMATION Multiple literary agents are flown in to the event every year to meet with writers and take pitches.

COMMUNITY OF WRITERS AT SQUAW VALLEY

Community of Writers at Squaw Valley, P.O. Box 1416, Nevada City CA 95959-1416. (530)470-8440. **E-mail:** info@communityofwriters.org. **Website:** www.communityofwriters.org. **Contact:** Brett Hall Jones, executive director. Estab. 1969.

COSTS Tuition is $1,075, which includes 6 dinners. Limited financial aid is available.

ACCOMMODATIONS The Community of Writers rents houses and condominiums in the Valley for participants to live in during the week of the conference. Single room (1 participant): $700/week. Double room (twin beds, with room shared by conference participant of the same sex): $465/week. Multiple room (bunk beds, room shared with 2 or more participants of the same sex): $295/week. All rooms subject to availability; early requests are recommended. Can arrange airport shuttle pick-ups for a fee.

ADDITIONAL INFORMATION More information is online at www.communityofwriters.org/workshops/writers-workshops.

CRESTED BUTTE WRITERS CONFERENCE

P.O. Box 1361, Crested Butte CO 81224. **E-mail:** coordinator@conf.crestedbuttewriters.org. **Website:** www.crestedbuttewriters.org/conf.php. **Contact:** Barbara Crawford or Theresa Rizzo, co-coordinators. Estab. 2006. Annual conference held in June. Previous faculty members have included numerous literary agents as well as some Writer's Digest Books staffers. There was no event in 2015, but there could be future summer conferences. Check the website.

COSTS Previous prices: $330 nonmembers; $300 members; $297 early bird; The Sandy Writing Contest finalist $280; and groups of 5 or more $280.

ACCOMMODATIONS The conference is held at The Elevation Hotel, located at the Crested Butte Mountain Resort at the base of the ski mountain. The quaint historic town lies nestled in a stunning mountain valley 3 short miles from the resort area of Mt. Crested Butte. A free bus runs frequently between the 2 towns. The closest airport is 30 miles away in Gunnison. The conference website lists 3 lodging options besides rooms at the event facility. All condos, motels, and hotel options offer special conference rates. No special travel arrangements are made through the conference; however, information for car rental from Gunnison airport or the Alpine Express shuttle is listed on the online conference FAQ page.

ADDITIONAL INFORMATION "Our conference workshops address a wide variety of writing craft and business. Our most popular workshop is our "First Pages Reading"—with a twist. Agents and editors read opening pages volunteered by attendees, with a few best-selling authors' openings mixed in. Writers may request additional conference information by e-mail."

DESERT DREAMS CONFERENCE: REALIZING THE DREAM

P.O. Box 27407, Tempe AZ 85285. **E-mail:** desertdreams@desertroserwa.org; desertdreamsconference@gmail.com. **Website:** desertroserwa.org/desertdreams. **Contact:** Conference coordinator. Estab. 1986. Conference held every 2 years (even years). 2016 dates: April 7-10. Average attendance: 250. The Desert Dreams conference provides authors of all skill levels, from beginner to multi-published, with the tools necessary to take their writing to the next level. Sessions will include general writing, career development, genre-specific, agent/publisher spotlights, as well as an agent/editor panel. There will also be one-on-one appointments with editors or agents, a book signing, and keynote addresses.

ADDITIONAL INFORMATION Agents and editors participate in conference.

DETROIT WORKING WRITERS ANNUAL WRITERS CONFERENCE

Detroit Working Writers, Box 82395, Rochester MI 48308. **E-mail:** conference@detworkingwriters.org. **Website:** dww-writers-conference.org. Estab. 1961. 2016 dates: May 21. Location: MSU Management Education Center, Troy, Michigan. Conference is 1 day, with breakfast, luncheon and keynote speaker, 4 breakout sessions, and 3 choices of workshop sessions. Much more info is available online. Detroit Working Writers was founded on June 5, 1900, as the Detroit Press Club, Detroit's first press club. Today, more than a century later, it is a 501(c)(6) organization, and Michigan's oldest writers' organization. There are 5 writing competitions with cash prizes in different categories: young adult/new adult, creative nonfiction, poetry, children's, and adult fiction. Registration and competition entry begins each January, online.

COSTS Costs vary, depending on early bird registration and membership status within the organization.

ERMA BOMBECK WRITERS' WORKSHOP

University of Dayton, 300 College Park, Dayton OH 45469. **E-mail:** erma@udayton.edu. **Website:** humorwriters.org. **Contact:** Teri Rizvi. This is a specialized writing conference for writers of humor (books, articles, essays, blogs, film/TV). It happens every 2 years. The 2016 conference dates were March 31 through April 2. The Bombeck Workshop is the only one in the country devoted to both humor and human interest writing. Through the workshop, the University of Dayton and the Bombeck family honor one of America's most celebrated storytellers and humorists. Over the past decade, the workshop has attracted such household names as Dave Barry, Art Buchwald, Phil Donahue, Nancy Cartwright, Don Novello, Garrison Keillor, Gail Collins, Connie Schultz, Adriana Trigiani, and Alan Zweibel. The workshop draws approximately 350 writers from around the country and typically sells out very quickly, so don't wait once registration opens.

ADDITIONAL INFORMATION Connect with the event on Twitter @ebww.

FLORIDA CHRISTIAN WRITERS CONFERENCE

Word Weavers International, Inc., 530 Lake Kathryn Circle, Casselberry FL 32707. (386)295-3902. **E-mail:** FloridaCWC@aol.com. **Website:** floridacwc.net. **Contact:** Eva Marie Everson & Mark T. Hancock. Estab. 1988. Annual conference during the last Wednesday of February to the first Sunday in March at Lake Yale Conference Center, Leesburg, Florida. Workshops/classes geared toward all levels, from beginners to published authors. Open to students. FCWC offers 6 keynote addresses, 8 continuing classes, and a number of three-hour workshops, one-hour workshops, and after hours workshops. FCWC brings in the finest the industry as to offer in editors, agents, freelancers, and marketing/media experts. Additionally, FCWC provides a book proposal studio and a pitch studio. For those flying in to Orlando or Sanford, FCWC provides a shuttle from and to the conference center. Accommodations for both single- and double-room occupancy. Meals provided. The awards banquet is Saturday night. Advanced critique services offered. Scholarships offered. For more information or to register, go to the conference website.

COSTS Ranges: $275 (daily rate—in advance, includes lunch and dinner; specify days); $1,495 (full attendee and participating spouse/family member in same room).

ACCOMMODATIONS Private rooms and double-occupancy.

FLORIDA ROMANCE WRIITERS FUN IN THE SUN CONFERENCE

Florida Romance Writers, P.O. Box 550562, Fort Lauderdale FL 33355. **E-mail:** FRWfuninthesun@yahoo.com. **Website:** frwfuninthesunmain.blogspot.com. Estab. 1986. "Fun in the Sun 2017" happens February 16-20, 2017. Conference with the Florida Romance Writers and *New York Times* best-selling author and keynote speaker Julia Quinn, a slue of talented writers, and wonderful industry professionals. Inspiring workshops and panels will keep your muse buzzing with plot twists. For those with a well behaved muse who continues to do her job, schedule an appointment with our guests: Nalini Akolekar with Spencerhill Associates, Ltd., Beth Campbell with Bookends, LLC, Leah Hultenschmidt with Grand Central Publishing, Rhonda Penders with The Wild Rose Press, Peter Senftleben with Kensington Books, or Deb Werksman with Sourcebooks. Also, take advantage of the opportunities to build a website and create a marketing plan while at sea. Space is limited.

GREEN MOUNTAIN WRITERS CONFERENCE

47 Hazel St., Rutland VT 05701. (802)236-6133. **E-mail:** ydaley@sbcglobal.net. **E-mail:** yvonnedaley@me.com. **Website:** www.vermontwriters.com. **Contact:** Yvonne Daley, director. Estab. 1998. "Annual conference held in the summer. Covers fiction, creative nonfiction, poetry, young adult fiction, journalism, nature writing, essay, memoir, personal narrative, and biography. Held at The Mountain Top Inn and Resort, a lakeside inn located in Chittenden, Vermont. Speakers have included Grace Paley, Ruth Stone,

Howard Frank Mosher, Chris Bohjalian, Yvonne Daley, David Huddle, David Budbill, Jeffrey Lent, Verandah Porche, Tom Smith, and Chuck Clarino."

COSTS $575 before April 15; $625 before May 15; $650 before June 1. Partial scholarships are available.

ACCOMMODATIONS Dramatically reduced rates at The Mountain Top Inn and Resort for attendees. Close to other area hotels in Rutland County, Vermont.

ADDITIONAL INFORMATION Participants' mss can be read and commented on at a cost. Sponsors contests. Conference publishes a literary magazine featuring work of participants. Brochures available on website or e-mail. "We offer the opportunity to learn from some of the nation's best writers at a small, supportive conference in a lakeside setting that allows one-to-one feedback. Participants often continue to correspond and share work after conferences."

HAMPTON ROADS WRITERS CONFERENCE

P.O. Box 56228, Virginia Beach VA 23456. **E-mail:** hrwriters@cox.net. **Website:** www.hamptonroads writers.org. Annual conference usually held in September. Workshops cover fiction, nonfiction, memoir, poetry, and the business of getting published. A bookshop, 3 free contests with cash prizes, free evening networking social, and many networking opportunities will be available. Multiple literary agents are in attendance each year to meet with writers and hear 10-minute pitches. Much more information available on the website.

COSTS Costs vary. There are discounts for members, for early bird registration, for students, and more.

HOUSTON WRITERS GUILD CONFERENCE

P.O. Box 42255, Houston TX 77242. (281)736-7168. **E-mail:** HoustonWritersGuild@Hotmail.com. **Website:** houstonwritersguild.org. 2016 dates: April 29 through May 1. This annual conference, organized by the Houston Writers Guild, happens in the spring, and has concurrent sessions and tracks on the craft and business of writing. Each year, multiple agents are in attendance taking pitches from writers. The 2016 special guest speaker was Jamie Ford.

COSTS Costs are different for members and non-members. Costs depend on how many days and events you sign up for.

ADDITIONAL INFORMATION There is a writing contest at the event. There is also a for-pay pre-conference workshop the day before the conference.

IDAHO WRITERS LEAGUE WRITERS' CONFERENCE

601 W. 75 S., Blackfoot ID 83221-6153. (208)684-4200. **Website:** www.idahowritersleague.org. Estab. 1940. Annual floating conference, usually held in September. This conference has at least 1 agent in attendance every year, along with other writers and presenters. **COSTS** Pricing varies. Check website for more information. The location within Idaho changes each year.

● INTERNATIONAL WOMEN'S FICTION FESTIVAL

Via Cappuccini 8E, Matera 75100 Italy. (39)0835-312044. **Fax:** (39)0835-312093. **E-mail:** e.jennings@womensfictionfestival.com. **Website:** www.womensfictionfestival.com. **Contact:** Elizabeth Jennings. Estab. 2004. Annual conference usually held in September. Average attendance: 100. International writers' conference with a strong focus on fiction and a strong focus on marketing to international markets. Numerous literary agents and editors (both American and international) are in attendance—both from the United States and Europe.
COSTS Registration costs vary. Check website for full details.
ACCOMMODATIONS Le Monacelle, a restored 17th century convent, is a nearby hotel. Conference travel agency will find reasonably priced accommodation. A paid shuttle is available from the Bari Airport to the hotel in Matera.

JACKSON HOLE WRITERS CONFERENCE

P.O. Box 1974, Jackson WY 83001. (307)413-3332. **E-mail:** connie@blackhen.com. **Website:** jacksonholewritersconference.com. Estab. 1991. Annual conference. 2016 dates: June 23-25. Conference duration: 3-4 days. Average attendance: 110. Covers fiction, creative nonfiction, and young adult. Offers ms critiques from authors, agents, and editors. Agents in attendance will take pitches from writers. Paid ms critique programs are available.
ADDITIONAL INFORMATION Held at the Center for the Arts in Jackson, Wyoming, and online.

JAMES RIVER WRITERS CONFERENCE

2319 E. Broad St., Richmond VA 23223. (804)433-3790. **Fax:** (804)291-1466. **E-mail:** info@jamesriverwriters.com; fallconference@jamesriverwriters.com. **Website:** www.jamesriverwriters.com. Estab. 2003. Annual conference held in October. The event has master classes, agent pitching, editor pitching, critiques, sessions, panels, and more. Previous attending agents have included Kimiko Nakamura, Kaylee Davis, Peter Knapp, and more.
COSTS Check website for updated pricing.

KACHEMAK BAY WRITERS' CONFERENCE

Kenai Peninsula College, Kachemak Bay Campus, 533 E. Pioneer Ave., Homer AK 99603. (907)235-7743. **E-mail:** iconf@uaa.alaska.edu. **Website:** writersconf.kpc.alaska.edu. Annual writers conference held in June. 2016 dates: June 10-14. The 2016 keynote speaker was Natasha Tretheway. Sponsored by Kachemak Bay Campus, Kenai Peninsula College/UAA. This nationally recognized writing conference features workshops, readings, and panel presentations in fiction, poetry, nonfiction, and the business of writing. There are "open mic" sessions for conference registrants, evening readings open to the public, agent/editor consultations, and more.
COSTS See the website. Some scholarships available.
ACCOMMODATIONS Homer is 225 miles south of Anchorage on the southern tip of the Kenai Peninsula and the shores of Kachemak Bay. There are multiple hotels in the area.

KENTUCKY WOMEN WRITERS CONFERENCE

University of Kentucky College of Arts & Sciences, 232 E. Maxwell St., Lexington KY 40506. (859)257-2874. **E-mail:** kentuckywomenwriters@gmail.com. **Website:** www.kentuckywomenwriters.org. **Contact:** Julie Wrinn, director. Estab. 1979. Conference held in second or third weekend of September. The location is the Carnegie Center for Literacy in Lexington, Kentucky. Conference duration: 2 days. Average attendance: 150-200. Conference covers poetry, fiction, creative nonfiction, and playwriting. Writing workshops, panels, and readings featuring contemporary women writers.
COSTS $200 for general admission and a workshop; $125 for admission with no workshop. Check website for most current pricing.
ADDITIONAL INFORMATION Sponsors prizes in poetry ($200), fiction ($200), nonfiction ($200), playwriting ($500), and spoken word ($500). Winners also invited to read during the conference. Pre-registration opens May 1.

KENTUCKY WRITERS CONFERENCE

Southern Kentucky Book Fest, Knicely Conference Center, 2355 Nashville Rd., Bowling Green KY 42101. (270)745-4502. **E-mail:** sara.volpi@wku.edu]. **Website:** www.sokybookfest.org/kywritersconf. **Contact:** Sara Volpi. This event is entirely free to the public. 2016 date: April 23. Duration: 1 day. Precedes the Southern Kentucky Book Fest the next day. Authors who will be participating in the book fest on Saturday will give attendees at the writers' conference the benefit of their wisdom on Friday. Free workshops on a variety of writing topics will be presented during this day-long event. Sessions run for 75 minutes, and the day begins at 9 a.m. and ends at 3:30 p.m. The conference is open to anyone who would like to attend, including high school students, college students, teachers, and the general public.

KILLER NASHVILLE

P.O. Box 680759, Franklin TN 37068-0686. (615)599-4032. **E-mail:** contact@killernashville.com. **Website:** www.killernashville.com. Estab. 2006. Annual event held the late summer or fall. Conference duration: 3 days. Average attendance: 400+. The event draws in literary agents seeking thrillers as well as some of the industry's top thriller authors. Conference designed for writers and fans of mysteries and thrillers, including fiction and nonfiction authors, playwrights, and screenwriters. There are many opportunities for authors to sign books. Killer Nashville's past writers conferences have had sessions, guests of honor, agent/editor roundtables, distinct session tracks (general writing, genre specific writing, publishing, publicity, promotion, forensics), breakout sessions for intense study, special sessions, ms critiques (fiction, nonfiction, short story, screenplay, marketing, query), realistic mock crime scene for guests to solve, networking with best-selling authors, agents, editors, publishers, attorneys, publicists, representatives from law and emergency services, mystery games, authors' bar, wine tasting event, 2 cocktail receptions, guest of honor dinner and awards program, prizes, free giveaways, free book signings, and more.

COSTS Costs are $128-210 for basic registration. Add-on costs available for other items.

ADDITIONAL INFORMATION Additional information about registration is provided online.

LA JOLLA WRITERS CONFERENCE

P.O. Box 178122, San Diego CA 92177. **E-mail:** akuritz@san.rr.com. **Website:** www.lajollawritersconference.com. **Contact:** Jared Kuritz, director. Estab. 2001. Annual conference held in November. 2016 dates: November 11-13. Conference duration: 3 days. Average attendance: 200. The LJWC covers all genres and both fiction and nonfiction as well as the business of writing. "We take particular pride in educating our attendees on the business aspect of the book industry and have agents, editors, publishers, publicists, and distributors teach classes. There is unprecedented access to faculty at the LJWC. Our conference offers lecture sessions that run for 50 minutes, and workshops that run for 110 minutes. Each block period is dedicated to either workshop or lecture-style classes, with 6-8 classes on various topics available each block. For most workshop classes, you are encouraged to bring written work for review. Literary agents from prestigious agencies have participated in the past, teaching workshops in which they are familiarized with attendee work. Late night and early bird sessions are also available. The conference creates a strong sense of community, and it has seen many of its attendees successfully published."

COSTS $395 for full 2016 conference registration (doesn't include lodging or breakfast). Conference limited to 200 attendees.

LAS VEGAS WRITERS CONFERENCE

Henderson Writers' Group, P.O. Box 92032, Henderson NV 89009. (702)564-2488; (866)869-7842. **E-mail:** lasvegaswritersconference@gmail.com. **Website:** www.lasvegaswritersconference.com. Annual event. 2016 dates: April 28-30. Conference duration: 3 days. Average attendance: 150 maximum. "Join writing professionals, agents, industry experts, and your colleagues for 3 days in Las Vegas as they share their knowledge on all aspects of the writer's craft. While there are formal pitch sessions, panels, workshops, and seminars, the faculty is also available throughout the conference for informal discussions and advice. Workshops, seminars, and expert panels cover topics in both fiction and nonfiction, screenwriting, marketing, indie publishing, and the craft of writing itself. There will be many Q&A panels for attendees to ask the experts questions." Site: Sam's Town Hotel and Gambling Hall in Las Vegas (Henderson, Nevada). The 2016 keynote was Larry Brooks.

COSTS Costs vary depending on the package. See the website. There are early bird rates as well as deep discounts for Clark County high school students.

ADDITIONAL INFORMATION Sponsors contest. Agents and editors participate in conference.

LAS VEGAS WRITING WORKSHOP

Writing Day Workshops. **E-mail:** writingdayworkshops@gmail.com. **Website:** www.lasvegaswritingworkshop.com. Estab. 2016. One-day conference. 2016 date: November 19. Presentations on publishing options today, literary agents and queries, marketing and promotion, first pages, and how to make a living as a writer. Several literary agents are in attendance to meet with writers and take pitches. See the website for the names of the attending agents.

COSTS $149 basic registration; add-on costs include query critiques and consultations/pitches.

ACCOMMODATIONS The event venue has hotel rooms available. The 2016 venue is the Embassy Suites.

ADDITIONAL INFORMATION Multiple writers have come out of a Writing Day Workshops event with a literary agent to show for it.

MIDWEST WRITERS WORKSHOP

Ball State University, Department of English, Muncie IN 47306. (765)282-1055. **E-mail:** midwestwriters@yahoo.com. **Website:** www.midwestwriters.org. **Contact:** Jama Kehoe Bigger, director. Annual workshop held in July in east central Indiana. Writer workshops geared toward writers of all levels, including craft and business sessions. Topics include most genres. Faculty/speakers have included Joyce Carol Oates, George Plimpton, Clive Cussler, Haven Kimmel, William Kent Krueger, William Zinsser, John Gilstrap, Lee Martin, Jane Friedman, Chuck Sambuchino, and numerous bestselling mystery, literary fiction, young adult, and children's authors. Workshop also includes agent pitch sessions, ms evaluation, and query letter critiques. Registration tentatively limited to 240.

COSTS $155-400. Most meals included.

ADDITIONAL INFORMATION Offers scholarships. See website for more information.

MISSOURI WRITERS' GUILD CONFERENCE

St. Louis MO **E-mail:** mwgconferenceinfo@gmail.com. **Website:** www.missouriwritersguild.org. **Contact:** Tricia Sanders, vice president/conference chairman. Writer and illustrator workshops geared to all levels. **Open to students.** Conference "gives writers the opportunity to hear outstanding speakers and to receive information on marketing, research, and writing techniques." Agents, editors, and published authors in attendance. 2016 dates were April 29-May 1. 2016 keynote speakers include Rachel R. Russell and Pamela Grout. The keynote speaker in 2014 was Writer's Digest Books editor Chuck Sambuchino.

ADDITIONAL INFORMATION The primary contact individual changes every year, because the conference chair changes every year. See the website for contact info.

MONTROSE CHRISTIAN WRITERS' CONFERENCE

218 Locust St., Montrose PA 10001. (570)278-1001. **Fax:** (570)278-3061. **E-mail:** mbc@montrosebible.org. **Website:** www.montrosebible.org. Estab. 1990. "Annual conference held in July. Offers workshops, editorial appointments, and professional critiques. We try to meet writing needs, for beginners and advanced, covering fiction, poetry, and writing for children. It is small enough to allow personal interaction between attendees and faculty. Speakers have included William Petersen, Mona Hodgson, Jim Fletcher, and Terri Gibbs." Held in Montrose.

COSTS Tuition is $180.

ACCOMMODATIONS Will meet planes in Binghamton, New York, and Scranton, Pennsylvania. On-site accommodations: room and board $340-475/conference, including food. RV court available.

ADDITIONAL INFORMATION Writers can send work ahead of time and have it critiqued for a small fee. The attendees are usually church-related. The writing has a Christian emphasis. Conference information available in April. For brochure, visit website, e-mail, or call. Accepts inquiries by phone or e-mail.

MOONLIGHT AND MAGNOLIAS WRITERS CONFERENCE

Georgia Romance Writers, 3741 Casteel Park Dr., Marietta GA 30064. **Website:** www.georgiaromancewriters.org/mm-conference. Estab. 1982. Georgia Romance Writers Annual Conference. 2016 dates: September 29 through October 2. "Conference focuses on writing of women's fiction with emphasis on romance. Includes agents and editors from major publishing houses. Previous workshops have included beginning writer sessions, research topics, writing basics, and professional issues for the published author. There are also specialty sessions on writing young adult, multicultural, paranormal, and regency. Speakers have included experts in law enforcement, screenwriting, and research. Literary raffle and advertised speaker and GRW member autographing open to the public. Please note the Maggies are now 100% electronic. Published authors make up first round, editors judge final."

MUSE AND THE MARKETPLACE

Grub Street, 162 Boylston St., Fifth Floor, Boston MA 02116. (617)695-0075. **E-mail:** info@grubstreet.org. **Website:** http://museandthemarketplace.com. The conferences are held in the late spring, such as early May. (2016 dates were April 29 through May 1.) Conference duration: 3 days. Average attendance: 400. Dozens of agents are in attendance to meet writers and take pitches. The conference has workshops on all aspects of writing.

ACCOMMODATIONS Boston Park Plaza Hotel.

NAPA VALLEY WRITERS' CONFERENCE

Napa Valley College, 1088 College Ave., St. Helena CA 94574. (707)967-2900. **E-mail:** writecon@napa valley.edu. **Website:** www.napawritersconference.org. **Contact:** Andrea Bewick, managing director. Estab. 1981. Established 1981. Annual weeklong event. 2016 dates: July 24 through July 29. Location: Upper Valley Campus in the historic town of St. Helena, 25 miles north of Napa in the heart of the valley's wine growing community. Average attendance: 48 in poetry and 48 in fiction. "Serious writers of all backgrounds and experience are welcome to apply." Offers poets and fiction writers workshops, lectures, faculty readings at Napa Valley wineries, and one-on-one faculty counseling. "Poetry session provides the opportunity to work both on generating new poems and on revising previously written ones."

COSTS $975; $25 application fee.

NATIONAL WRITERS ASSOCIATION FOUNDATION CONFERENCE

10940 S. Parker Rd., No. 508, Parker CO 80138. (303)841-0246. **E-mail:** natlwritersassn@hotmail.com. **Website:** www.nationalwriters.com. **Contact:** Sandy Whelchel, executive director. Estab. 1926. Annual conference held the second week of June in Denver. Conference duration: 1 day. Average attendance: 100. Focuses on general writing and marketing.

ADDITIONAL INFORMATION Awards for previous contests will be presented at the conference. Brochures/guidelines are online, or send a SASE.

NETWO WRITERS CONFERENCE

Northeast Texas Writers Organization, P.O. Box 411, Winfield TX 75493. (469)867-2624 or Paul at (903)573-6084. **E-mail:** jimcallan@winnsboro.com. **Website:** www.netwo.org. Estab. 1987. Annual conference held in April. (2016 dates were April 22-23.) Conference duration: 2 days. Presenters include agents, writers, editors, and publishers. Agents in attendance will take pitches from writers. The conference features a writing contest, pitch sessions, critiques from professionals, as well as dozens of workshops and presentations.

COSTS $90 for members before February 29, and $100 after. $112.50 for non-members before February 29, and $125 after.

ACCOMMODATIONS "On the website, we have posted information on lodging.The conference is held at the Titus County Civic Center in Mt. Pleasant, Texas."

ADDITIONAL INFORMATION Conference is cosponsored by the Texas Commission on the Arts. See website for current updates.

NEW JERSEY ROMANCE WRITERS PUT YOUR HEART IN A BOOK CONFERENCE

P.O. Box 513, Plainsboro NJ 08536. **Website:** www.njromancewriters.org/conference.html. Estab. 1984. Annual conference held in October. Average attendance: 500. Workshops are offered on various topics for all writers of romance, from beginner to advanced. Speakers have included Nora Roberts, Kathleen Woodiwiss, Patricia Gaffney, Jill Barnett, and Kay Hooper. Appointments are offered with editors/agents.

NORTH CAROLINA WRITERS' NETWORK FALL CONFERENCE

P.O. Box 21591, Winston-Salem NC 27120. (336)293-8844. **E-mail:** mail@ncwriters.org. **Website:** www.ncwriters.org. Estab. 1985. Annual conference held in November in different state venues. Average attendance: 250. This organization hosts 2 conferences: 1 in the spring and 1 in the fall. Each conference is a weekend full of workshops, panels, book signings, and readings (including open mic). There will be a keynote speaker, a variety of sessions on the craft and business of writing, and opportunities to meet with agents and editors.

COSTS Approximately $250 (includes 4 meals).

ACCOMMODATIONS Special rates are usually available at the conference hotel, but conferees must make their own reservations.

NORTHERN COLORADO WRITERS CONFERENCE

2107 Thunderstone Court, Fort Collins CO 80525. (970)556-0908. **E-mail:** kerrie@northerncolorado writers.com. **Website:** www.northerncoloradowriters. com. Estab. 2006. Annual conference held in March in Fort Collins. 2016 dates: April 22-23. Conference duration: 2-3 days. The conference features a variety of speakers, agents, and editors. There are workshops and presentations on fiction, nonfiction, screenwriting, children's books, marketing, magazine writing, staying inspired, and more. Previous agents who have attended and taken pitches from writers include Jessica Regel, Kristen Nelson, Rachelle Gardner, Andrea Brown, Ken Sherman, Jessica Faust, Gordon Warnock, and Taylor Martindale. Each conference features more than 30 workshops from which to choose from. Previous keynotes include Chuck Sambuchino, Andrew McCarthy, and Stephen J. Cannell.

COSTS $250-550+, depending on what package the attendee selects, whether you're a member or non-member, and whether you're renewing your NCW membership.

NORWESCON

100 Andover Park W. PMB 150-165, Tukwila WA 98188. (425)243-4692. **E-mail:** info@norwescon.org. **Website:** www.norwescon.org. Estab. 1978. Annual conference held on Easter weekend. Average attendance: 2,800-3,000. General convention (with multiple tracks) focusing on science fiction and fantasy literature with wide coverage of other media. Tracks cover science, sociocultural, literary, publishing, editing, writing, art, and other media of a science fiction and fantasy orientation. Literary agents will be speaking and available for meetings with attendees.

ACCOMMODATIONS Conference is held at the Doubletree Hotel Seattle Airport.

ODYSSEY FANTASY WRITING WORKSHOP

P.O. Box 75, Mont Vernon NH 03057. (603)673-6234. **E-mail:** jcavelos@sff.net. **Website:** www.odyssey workshop.org. **Contact:** Jeanne Cavelos. Saint Anselm College, 100 Saint Anselm Dr., Manchester, New Hampshire, 03102. Estab. 1996. Annual workshop held in June (through July). Conference duration: 6 weeks. Average attendance: 15. This is a workshop for fantasy, science fiction, and horror writers that combines an intensive learning and writing experience with in-depth feedback on students' mss. Held on the campus of Saint Anselm College in Manchester, New Hampshire. Speakers have included George R.R. Martin, Elizabeth Hand, Jane Yolen, Harlan Ellison, Melissa Scott, and Dan Simmons.

COSTS In 2016: $2,025 tuition, $850 housing (double room), $1,700 housing (single room), $40 application fee, $600 food (approximate), $700 optional processing fee to receive college credit.

ADDITIONAL INFORMATION Students must apply and include a writing sample. Application deadline: April 8. Students' works are critiqued throughout the 6 weeks. Workshop information available in October. For brochure/guidelines, send SASE, e-mail, visit website, or call.

OKLAHOMA WRITERS' FEDERATION, INC. ANNUAL CONFERENCE

9800 South Hwy. 137, Miami OK 74354. **Website:** www.owfi.org. Annual conference held just outside Oklahoma City. Held first weekend in May each year. Writer workshops geared toward all levels. The goal of the conference is to create good stories with strong bones. We will be exploring cultural writing and cultural sensitivity in writing. Several literary agents are in attendance each year to meet with writers and hear pitches.

COSTS Costs vary depending on when registrants sign up. Cost includes awards banquet and famous author banquet. Three extra sessions are available for an extra fee. Visit the event website for a complete faculty list and conference information

OREGON CHRISTIAN WRITERS SUMMER CONFERENCE

Red Lion Hotel on the River, 909 N. Hayden Island Dr., Portland OR 97217. **E-mail:** summerconf@ oregonchristianwriters.org. **Website:** www.oregon christianwriters.org. **Contact:** Lindy Jacobs, OCW Summer Conference director. Estab. 1989. Held annually in August at the Red Lion Hotel on the River, a full-service hotel. Conference duration: 4 days. 2016 dates: August 15-18. Average attendance: 225 (175 writers, 50 faculty). Top national editors, agents, and authors in the field of Christian publishing teach 12 intensive coaching classes and 30 workshops plus critique sessions. Published authors as well as emerging writers have opportunities to improve their craft, get feedback through ms reviews, meet one-on-one with editors and agents, and have half-hour mentoring appointments with published authors. Classes include fiction, nonfiction, memoir, young adult, poetry, magazine articles, devotional writing, children's books, and marketing. Daily general sessions include worship and an inspirational keynote address. Each year contacts made during the OCW summer conference lead to publishing contracts. The 2016 conference theme was "Vision and Voice," based on Psalm 19:14. 2016 Keynote speakers: James Scott Bell and Angela Hunt. Past agents in attendance include Chip MacGregor of MacGregor Literary, Nick Harrison of WordServe Agency, Sally Apokedak of Les Stobbe Agency, Bill Jensen of William K. Jensen Literary, Karen Ball of the Steve Laube Agency, and more. Past editors in attendance include personnel from Revell, Bethany/Chosen, HarperCollins, LIVE, Grace Publishing, Focus on the Family Clubhouse, The Upper Room, Bible Advocate, and *Splickety Magazine.*

COSTS $525 for OCW members; $560 for nonmembers. Registration fee includes all classes, workshops, and 2 lunches and 3 dinners. Lodging additional. Full-time registered registrants may also pre-submit 3 proposals for review by an editor (or agent) through the conference, plus sign up for a half-hour mentoring appointment with an author.

ACCOMMODATIONS Conference is held at the Red Lion on the River Hotel. Conferees wishing to stay at the hotel must make a reservation through the hotel. A block of rooms has been reserved at the hotel at a special rate for conferees and held until mid-July. The hotel reservation link will be posted on the website in late spring. Shuttle bus transportation will be provided by the hotel for conferees from Portland Airport (PDX) to the hotel, which is 20 minutes away.

ADDITIONAL INFORMATION Conference details will be posted online beginning in January. All attendees are welcome to attend the Cascade Awards ceremony, which takes place Wednesday evening during the conference. For more information about the Cascade Writing Contest, please check the website.

OZARK CREATIVE WRITERS, INC. CONFERENCE

P.O. Box 9076, Fayetteville AR 72703. **E-mail:** ozarkcreativewriters1@gmail.com. **Website:** www.ozarkcreativewriters.org. The annual event is held in Oc-

tober at the Inn of the Ozarks, in the resort town of Eureka Springs, Arkansas. The event has approximately 200 attend each year; many also enter the creative writing competitions. Open to professional and amateur writers, workshops are geared to all levels and all forms of the creative process and literary arts. Sessions sometimes include songwriting, with presentations by best-selling authors, editors, and agents. The OCW Conference promotes writing by offering writing competitions in all genres.

PENNWRITERS CONFERENCE

5706 Sonoma Ridge, Missouri City TX 77459. **E-mail:** conferenceco@pennwriters.org, info@pennwriters.org. **Website:** http://pennwriters.org/conference. Estab. 1987. The Mission of Pennwriters Inc. is to help writers of all levels, from the novice to the award-winning and multi-published, improve and succeed in their craft. The annual Pennwriters conference is held every year in May in Pennsylvania, switching between locations—Lancaster in even years and Pittsburgh in odd years. 2016 event dates: May 20-22 in Lancaster. Literary agents are in attendance meeting with writers.

ACCOMMODATIONS Costs vary. Pennwriters members in good standing get a slightly reduced rate.

ADDITIONAL INFORMATION Sponsors contest. Published authors judge fiction in various categories. Agent/editor appointments are available on a first-come, first serve basis.

PHILADELPHIA WRITERS' CONFERENCE

P.O. Box 7171, Elkins Park PA 19027-0171. (215)619-7422. **E-mail:** info@pwcwriters.org. **E-mail:** info@pwcwriters.org. **Website:** www.pwcwriters.org. Estab. 1949. Annual. Conference held in June. Average attendance: 160-200. Conference covers many forms of writing: novel, short story, genre fiction, nonfiction book, magazine writing, blogging, juvenile, poetry.

ACCOMMODATIONS Wyndham Hotel (formerly the Holiday Inn), Independence Mall, Fourth and Arch streets, Philadelphia, PA 19106-2170. Hotel offers discount for early registration.

ADDITIONAL INFORMATION Accepts inquiries by e-mail. Agents and editors attend the conference. Many questions are answered online.

PIKES PEAK WRITERS CONFERENCE

Pikes Peak Writers, P.O. Box 64273, Colorado Springs CO 80962. (719)244-6220. **Website:** www.pikespeak

writers.com/ppwc. Estab. 1993. Annual conference held in April. 2016 dates: April 15-17. Conference duration: 3 days. Average attendance: 300. Workshops, presentations, and panels focus on writing and publishing. Attention is paid to both mainstream and genre fiction (romance, science fiction, fantasy, suspense/thrillers, action/adventure, mysteries, children's, young adult). Agents and editors are available for meetings with attendees on Saturday. 2016 speakers included Jeff Lindsay, Rachel Caine, and Kevin J. Anderson.

COSTS $395-465 (includes all 7 meals).

ACCOMMODATIONS Marriott Colorado Springs holds a block of rooms at a special rate for attendees until late March.

ADDITIONAL INFORMATION Readings with critiques are available on Friday afternoon. Registration forms are online; brochures are available in January. Send inquiries via e-mail.

PNWA SUMMER WRITERS CONFERENCE

317 NW Gilman Blvd., Suite 8, Issaquah WA 98027. (425)673-2665. **E-mail:** pnwa@pnwa.org. **Website:** www.pnwa.org. Estab. 1955. Annual conference held in July. Conference duration: 4 days. Average attendance: 400. Attendees have the chance to meet agents and editors, learn craft from authors, and uncover marketing secrets. Speakers have included J.A. Jance, Sheree Bykofsky, Kimberley Cameron, Jennie Dunham, Donald Maass, Jandy Nelson, Chuck Sambuchino, Robert Dugoni, and Terry Brooks.

ROMANCE WRITERS OF AMERICA NATIONAL CONFERENCE

14615 Benfer Rd., Houston TX 77069. (832)717-5200. **Fax:** (832)717-5201. **E-mail:** info@rwa.org. **Website:** www.rwa.org/conference. Estab. 1981. Annual conference held in July. (2016 conference: July 13-16 in San Diego.) Average attendance: 2,000. Features more than 100 workshops on writing, researching, and the business side of being a working writer. Publishing professionals attend and accept appointments. The keynote speaker is a renowned romance writer. "Romance Writers of America (RWA) is a nonprofit trade association, with a membership of more than 10,000 romance writers and related industry professionals, whose mission is to advance the professional interests of career-focused romance writers through networking and advocacy."

COSTS $450-675 depending on your membership status, as well as when you register.

ADDITIONAL INFORMATION Annual RTA awards are presented for romance authors. Annual Golden Heart awards are presented for unpublished writers. Numerous literary agents are in attendance to meet with writers and hear book pitches.

RT BOOKLOVERS CONVENTION

81 Willoughby St., Suite 701, Brooklyn NY 11201. **E-mail:** tere@rtconvention.com. **Website:** www.rtconvention.com. **Contact:** Tere Michaels. Annual conference with a varying location. 2016 details: April 12-17 in Las Vegas. Features 200 workshops, agent and editor appointments, a Giant Book Fair, and more. More than 1,000 authors will be at the 2016 event.

COSTS $489 normal registration; $425 for industry professionals (agents, editors). Special discounted rate for readers ($449). Many other pricing options available. See website.

ACCOMMODATIONS Rooms available at the event convention hotel.

SALT CAY WRITERS RETREAT

Salt Cay Bahamas. (732)267-6449. **E-mail:** admin@ saltcaywritersretreat.com. **Website:** www.saltcay writersretreat.com. **Contact:** Karen Dionne and Christopher Graham. Five-day retreat held in the Bahamas in May. "The Salt Cay Writers Retreat is particularly suited for novelists (especially those writing literary, upmarket commercial fiction, or genre novelists wanting to write a breakout book), memoirists, and narrative nonfiction writers. However, any author (published or not-yet-published) who wishes to take their writing to the next level is welcome to apply." Speakers have included or will include editors Chuck Adams (Algonquin Books) and Amy Einhorn (Amy Einhorn Books); agents Jeff Kleinman, Michelle Brower, Erin Niumata, and Erin Harris (all of Folio Literary Management); and authors Robert Goolrick and Jacquelyn Mitchard.

COSTS $2,450 if you register on/before May 1; $2,950 after.

ACCOMMODATIONS Comfort Suites, Paradise Island, Nassau, Bahamas.

SAN DIEGO STATE UNIVERSITY WRITERS' CONFERENCE

SDSU College of Extended Studies, 5250 Campanile Dr., San Diego State University, San Diego CA 92182.

(619)594-3946. **Fax:** (619)594-8566. **E-mail:** sdsuwrit ersconference@mail.sdsu.edu. **Website:** ces.sdsu.edu/ writers. Estab. 1984. Annual conference held in January. Conference duration: 2.5 days. Average attendance: 350. Covers fiction, nonfiction, scriptwriting, and e-books. Held at the San Diego Marriott Mission Valley Hotel. Each year, the conference offers a variety of workshops for beginners and advanced writers. This conference allows the individual writer to choose which workshop best suits her needs. In addition to the workshops, editor reading appointments and agent/editor consultation appointments are provided so attendees may meet with editors and agents one-on-one to discuss specific questions. A reception is offered Saturday immediately following the workshops, offering attendees the opportunity to socialize with the faculty in a relaxed atmosphere.

COSTS Approximately $495-549. Extra costs for consultations.

ACCOMMODATIONS Attendees must make their own travel arrangements. A conference rate for attendees is available at the event hotel.

SAN FRANCISCO WRITERS CONFERENCE

1029 Jones St., San Francisco CA 94109. (415)673-0939. **E-mail:** barbara@sfwriters.org; sfwriterscon@ aol.com.. **Website:** www.sfwriters.org. **Contact:** Barbara Santos, marketing director. Estab. 2003. 2016 dates: February 11-14. Annual conference held President's Day weekend in February. Average attendance: 700. More than 100 top authors, respected literary agents, and major publishing houses are at the event so attendees can make face-to-face contact with all the right people. Writers of nonfiction, fiction, poetry, and specialty writing (children's books, cookbooks, travel, etc.) will all benefit from the event. There are important sessions on marketing, self-publishing, technology, and trends in the publishing industry. Plus, there's an optional four-hour session called "Speed Dating for Agents" where attendees can meet with 20+ agents. Speakers have included Jennifer Crusie, R.L. Stine, Richard Paul Evans, Jamie Raab, Mary Roach, Jane Smiley, Debbie Macomber, Jane Friedman, Chuck Sambuchino, Clive Cussler, Guy Kawasaki, Lisa See, Steve Berry, and Jacquelyn Mitchard. More than 20 agents and editors participate each year, many of whom will be available for meetings with attendees."

COSTS Check the website for pricing. Pricing starts at $725 (as of the 2016 event) depending on when you signed up and early bird registration, etc.

ACCOMMODATIONS The Intercontinental Mark Hopkins Hotel is a historic landmark at the top of Nob Hill in San Francisco. The hotel is located so that everyone arriving at the Oakland or San Francisco airport can take BART to either the Embarcadero or Powell street exits, then walk or take a cable car or taxi directly to the hotel.

ADDITIONAL INFORMATION "Present yourself in a professional manner and the contacts you will make will be invaluable to your writing career. Fliers, details, and registration information are online."

SAN FRANCISCO WRITING FOR CHANGE CONFERENCE

San Francisco Writers Conference, 1029 Jones St., San Francisco CA 94109. (415)673-0939. **E-mail:** barbara@sfwriters.org. **Website:** www.sfwritingforchange. org. **Contact:** Barbara Santos, marketing director; Michael Larsen, co-director. Estab. 2004. Annual conference held in the fall. 2016 date: September 10, at Unitarian Universalist Center in San Francisco. Average attendance: 100. Early discounts available. Includes panels, workshops, keynote address, lunch, and editor consultations.

COSTS $199. Early registration discounts available. Please visit the website.

ACCOMMODATIONS Check website for event details, accommodations, directions, and parking.

ADDITIONAL INFORMATION "The limited number of attendees (150 or fewer) and excellent presenter-to-attendee ratio make this a highly effective and productive conference. The presenters are major names in the publishing business, but take personal interest in the projects discovered at this event each year." Guidelines available on website.

SCBWI; ANNUAL CONFERENCES ON WRITING AND ILLUSTRATING FOR CHILDREN

8271 Beverly Blvd., Los Angeles CA 90048. **E-mail:** scbwi@scbwi.org. **Website:** www.scbwi.org. **Contact:** Lin Oliver, conference director. The two events are writer and illustrator workshops geared toward all levels. **Open to students.** Covers all aspects of children's book and magazine publishing—the novel, illustration techniques, marketing, etc. Annual conferences held in the summer in Los Angeles and in New York in the winter. Cost of conference includes all 4 days and 1 banquet meal. Write for more information or visit website.

⊙ SCBWI—CANADA EAST

Canada. **E-mail:** canadaeast@scbwi.org; almafullerton@almafullerton.com. **Website:** www.canadaeast.scbwi.org. **Contact:** Alma Fullerton, regional advisor. Writer and illustrator events geared toward all levels. Usually offers 1 event in spring and another in the fall. Check website "Events" page for all updated information.

SCBWI—MIDATLANTIC; ANNUAL FALL CONFERENCE

P.O. Box 3215, Reston VA 20195. **E-mail:** scbwimidatlantic@gmail.com. **Website:** midatlantic.scbwi.org. For updates and details, visit website. Registration limited to 275. Conference fills quickly. Includes continental breakfast and boxed lunch. Optional craft-focused workshops and individual consultations with conference faculty are available for additional fees.

SCBWI—NORTHERN OHIO; ANNUAL CONFERENCE

225 N. Willow St., Kent OH 44240-2561. **E-mail:** vselvaggio@windstream.net. **Website:** ohionorth.scbwi.org. **Contact:** Victoria A. Selvaggio, regional advisor. Northern Ohio's conference is crafted for all levels of writers and illustrators of children's literature. Annual event held in the fall. "Our annual event will be held at the Sheraton Cleveland Airport Hotel. Conference costs will be posted on our website with registration information. SCBWI members receive a discount. Additional fees apply for late registration, critiques, or portfolio reviews. Cost includes the following: an optional Friday evening opening banquet from 6-10 p.m. with a keynote speaker; Saturday event from 8:30 a.m. to 5 p.m., which features a breakfast snack; the full-day conference with headliner presentations, general sessions, breakout workshops, lunch, panel discussion, bookstore, and an autograph session. The Illustrator Showcase is open to all attendees at no additional cost. Grand door prize, drawn at the end of the day Saturday, is free admission to the following year's conference. Further information, including headliner speakers will be posted on our website."

SCIENCE FICTION WRITERS WORKSHOP

English Department/University of Kansas, Wesoce Hall, 1445 Jayhawk Blvd., Room 3001, Lawrence KS 66045-7590. (785)864-2508. **E-mail:** cmckit@ku.edu. **Website:** www.sfcenter.ku.edu/sfworkshop.htm. Estab. 1985. Annual workshop held in June. The workshop is "small, informal, and aimed at writers on the edge of publication or regular publication." This is an event for writing and marketing science fiction and fantasy. Workshop sessions operate informally in a university housing lounge on the University of Kansas campus where most participants also reside. Established in 1985 by James Gunn and currently led by Christopher McKitterick, with guest authors joining for the second week. Writer and editor instructors have included Lou Anders, Bradley Denton, James Gunn, Kij Johnson, John Ordover, Frederik Pohl, Pamela Sargent, and George Zebrowski. Each year the winners of the Campbell and Sturgeon Memorial awards participate in 1 or more days of the workshop.

COSTS $600, exclusive of meals and housing.

ACCOMMODATIONS Housing information is available online. Several airport shuttle services offer reasonable transportation from the Kansas City International Airport to Lawrence, Kansas.

ADDITIONAL INFORMATION Admission to the workshop is by submission of an acceptable story, usually by May. Two additional stories are submitted by the middle of June. These 3 stories are distributed to other participants for critiquing and are the basis for the first week of the workshop. One story is rewritten for the second week, when students also work with guest authors. See website for guidelines. This workshop is intended for writers who have just started to sell their work or need that extra bit of understanding or skill to become a published writer.

SEWANEE WRITERS' CONFERENCE

735 University Ave., 119 Gailor Hall, Stamler Center, Sewanee TN 37383-1000. (931)598-1654. **E-mail:** swc@sewanee.edu. **Website:** www.sewaneewriters.org. **Contact:** Adam Latham. Estab. 1990. Annual conference. 2016 dates: July 19-31. Average attendance: 150. "The University of the South will host the 27th session of the Sewanee Writers' Conference. Thanks to the generosity of the Walter E. Dakin Memorial Fund, supported by the estate of the late Tennessee Williams, the conference will gather a distinguished faculty to provide instruction and criticism through workshops and craft

lectures in poetry, fiction, and playwriting. During an intense 12-day period, participants will read and critique workshop mss under the leadership of some of our country's finest fiction writers, poets, and playwrights. Faculty members and fellows give scheduled readings, senior faculty members offer craft lectures, and open-mic readings are available. Additional writers, along with a host of writing professionals, visit to give readings, participate in panel discussions, and answer questions from the audience. Receptions and mealtimes offer ample social opportunities. 2016 faculty included fiction writers Richard Bausch, John Casey, Tony Earley, Randall Kenan, Jill McCorkle, Alice McDermott, Erin McGraw, Christine Schutt, Allen Wier, and Steve Yarbrough. Attending poets included Daniel Anderson, B.H. Fairchild, Robert Hass, Mark Jarman, Maurice Manning, Marilyn Nelson, A.E. Stallings, and Sidney Wade. Naomi Iizuka and Dan O'Brien led the playwriting workshop. Charles Martin, A.E. Stallings, and N.S. Thompson offered a supplemental poetry translation workshop. Adrianne Harun, Andrew Hudgins, Charles Martin, and Wyatt Prunty will read from their work."

COSTS $1,100 for tuition; $800 for room, board, and activity costs.

ACCOMMODATIONS Participants are housed in single rooms in university dormitories. Bathrooms are shared by small groups.

SLEUTHFEST

MWA Florida Chapter. **E-mail:** sleuthfestinfo@yahoo.com. **Website:** www.sleuthfest.com. Annual conference held in February or March, at the Deerfield Beach Hilton, Florida. 2016 dates: February 25-28. Conference duration: 4 days. The event features hands-on workshops, 4 tracks of writing and business panels, and 2 keynote speakers for writers of mystery and crime fiction. 2016 keynote speaker was C.J. Box. Also offers agent and editor appointments, and paid ms critiques. A full list of attending speakers and faculty is online. This event is put on by the local chapter of the Mystery Writers of America.

ACCOMMODATIONS Doubletree by Hilton in Deerfield Beach.

SOUTH CAROLINA WRITERS WORKSHOP

4840 Forest Dr., Suite 6B, PMB 189, Columbia SC 29206. **E-mail:** scwwliaison@gmail.com, scww2013@gmail.com. **Website:** www.myscww.org. Estab. 1991. Conference in October held at the Metropolitan Conference Center in Columbia, South Carolina. Held almost every year. Conference duration: 3 days. The conference features critique sessions, open mic readings, presentations from agents and editors, and more. The conference features more than 50 different workshops for writers to choose from, dealing with all subjects of writing craft, writing business, getting an agent, and more. Agents will be in attendance.

SOUTHEASTERN WRITERS ASSOCIATION—ANNUAL WRITERS WORKSHOP

E-mail: purple@southeasternwriters.org. **Website:** www.southeasternwriters.org. Estab. 1975. Event is held at Epworth-by-the-Sea, St. Simons Island, Georgia. Annual four-day workshop—open to all writers. 2016 dates: June 18-21. There are 3 free evaluation conferences with instructors that are included with tuition (minimum two-day registration). The workshop has writing contests with cash prizes. Ms deadline: May 15 (contests), May 25 (evaluations).

COSTS $445 for 4 days; lower prices for daily tuition. See website for final pricing.

ACCOMMODATIONS Lodging at Epworth and throughout St. Simons Island. Visit website for more information.

SPACE COAST WRITERS GUILD ANNUAL CONFERENCE

E-mail: stilley@scwg.org. **Website:** www.scwg.org/conference.asp. Annual conference held the last weekend of January along the east coast of central Florida, though the event is not necessarily held every year. Conference duration: 2 days. Average attendance: 150+. This conference is hosted in Florida and features a variety of presenters on all writing topics. Critiques are available for a price, and agents in attendance will take pitches from writers. Previous presenters have included Debra Dixon, Davis Bunn (writer), Ellen Pepus (agent), Jennifer Crusie, Chuck Sambuchino, Madeline Smoot, Mike Resnick, Christina York, Ben Bova, and Elizabeth Sinclair. Check the website for up-to-date information and future dates.

ACCOMMODATIONS The conference is hosted on a beachside hotel, with special room rates available.

☼ SURREY INTERNATIONAL WRITERS' CONFERENCE

SiWC, 151-10090 152 St., Suite 544, Surrey BC V3R 8X8 Canada. **E-mail:** kathychung@siwc.ca. **Website:**

www.siwc.ca. **Contact:** Kathy Chung, proposals contact and conference coordinator. Annual professional development writing conference outside Vancouver, Canada, held every fall. There are writing workshops geared toward beginner, intermediate, and advanced levels. The event has more than 70 workshops and panels, on all topics and genres, plus pre-conference master classes. Blue Pencil and agent/editor pitch sessions included. Different conference price packages available. Check the conference website for more information. This event has many literary agents in attendance taking pitches. Annual writing contest open to all.

TAOS SUMMER WRITERS' CONFERENCE

Department of English Language and Literature, MSC 03 2170, 1 University of New Mexico, Albuquerque NM 87131. **E-mail:** swarner@unm.edu. **Website:** taosconf.unm.edu. **Contact:** Sharon Oard Warner. Estab. 1999. Annual conference held in July. 2016 dates: July 24-31. Offers workshops and master classes on topics such as the novel, short stories, poetry, creative nonfiction, memoir, prose style, screenwriting, humor writing, literary translation, book proposal, the query letter, and revision. Participants may also schedule a consultation with a visiting agent/editor.

COSTS Weeklong workshop registration $700; weekend workshop registration $400; master classes cost between $1,350 and $1,625; publishing consultations are $175.

TEXAS WRITING RETREAT

Grimes County TX **E-mail:** paultcuclis@gmail.com. **Website:** www.texaswritingretreat.com. **Contact:** Paul Cuclis, coordinator. Estab. 2013. The Texas Writing Retreat is an intimate event with a limited number of attendees. Held on a private residence ranch an hour outside of Houston, it has an agent and editor in attendance who both teaches and takes pitches. All attendees get to pitch the attending agent. Meals and excursions and amenities included. This is a unique event that combines craft sessions, business sessions, time for writing, relaxation, and more. The retreat is not held every year. It's best to check the website and see if there is a retreat in any given year.

COSTS Costs vary per event. There are different pricing options for those staying onsite vs. commuters.

ACCOMMODATIONS Private ranch residence in Texas.

THRILLERFEST

P.O. Box 311, Eureka CA 95502. **E-mail:** infocentral@thrillerwriters.org. **Website:** www.thrillerfest. com. **Contact:** Kimberley Howe, executive director. Estab. 2006. Annual. 2016 dates: July 5-9 in Manhattan. Conference duration: 5 days. Average attendance: 1,000. "A great place to learn the craft of writing the thriller. Classes taught by best-selling authors." Speakers have included David Morrell, James Patterson, Sandra Brown, Ken Follett, Eric Van Lustbader, David Baldacci, Brad Meltzer, Steve Martini, R.L. Stine, Steve Berry, Kathleen Antrim, Douglas Preston, Gayle Lynds, Harlan Coben, Lee Child, Lisa Scottolini, Katherine Neville, Robin Cook, Andrew Gross, Kathy Reichs, Brad Thor, Clive Cussler, Donald Maass, M.J. Rose, and Al Zuckerman. Three days of the conference are CraftFest, where the focus is on the craft of writing, and 2 days are ThrillerFest, which showcase the author-fan relationship. Also featured: PitchFest—a unique event where authors can pitch their work face-to-face to 50 top literary agents. Lastly, there is the International Thriller Awards and Banquet.

COSTS Price will vary from $475-1,199, depending on which events are selected. Various package deals are available offering savings, and early bird pricing is offered beginning September of each year.

ACCOMMODATIONS Grand Hyatt in Manhattan.

TMCC WRITERS' CONFERENCE

Truckee Meadows Community College, 7000 Dandini Blvd., Reno NV 89512. (775)673-7111. **E-mail:** wdce@tmcc.edu. **Website:** wdce.tmcc.edu. Estab. 1991. Annual conference held in April. 2016 date: April 16. Average attendance: 150. Conference focuses on strengthening your fiction and nonfiction works, as well as how to pitch projects to agents and publishers. Site: Truckee Meadows Community College in Reno. "There is always an array of speakers and presenters with impressive literary credentials, including agents and editors." Speakers have included Chuck Sambuchino, Sheree Bykofsky, Andrea Brown, Dorothy Allison, Karen Joy Fowler, James D. Houston, James N. Frey, Gary Short, Jane Hirschfield, Dorrianne Laux, and Kim Addonizio. Literary agents are onsite to take pitches from writers.

ACCOMMODATIONS Contact the conference manager to learn about accommodation discounts.

ADDITIONAL INFORMATION "The conference is open to all writers, regardless of their level of experience. Brochures are available online and mailed in January. Send inquiries via e-mail."

UNICORN WRITERS CONFERENCE

P.O. Box 176, Redding CT 06876. (203)938-7405. **E-mail:** unicornwritersconference@gmail.com. **Website:** www.unicornwritersconference.com. **Contact:** Jan L. Kardys, chairman. Estab. 2010. This writers conference draws upon its close proximity to New York City and pulls in over 35 literary agents and 15 major editors to pitch each year. There are ms review sessions (40 pages equals 30 minutes with an agent/editor), query/ms review sessions, and 5 different workshops every hour. $325 cost includes all workshops and 3 meals.

COSTS $325 includes all workshops (5 every hour to select on the day of the conference), a gift bag, and 3 meals. Additional cost for ms reviews: $60.

ACCOMMODATIONS Held at Reid Castle, Purchase, New York. Directions available on event website.

UNIVERSITY OF NORTH DAKOTA WRITERS CONFERENCE

Department of English, 110 Merrifield Hall, 276 Centennial Dr., Stop 7209, Grand Forks ND 58202. (701)777-2393. **Fax:** (701)777-2373. **E-mail:** crystal.alberts@e-mail.und.edu. **Website:** und.edu/orgs/writers-conference. **Contact:** Crystal Alberts, director. Estab. 1970. Annual event of 3-5 days. 2016 dates: April 6-8. Offers panels, readings, and films focused around a specific theme. Almost all events take place in the UND Memorial Union, which has a variety of small rooms and a 1,000-seat main hall. Past speakers include Art Spiegelman, Truman Capote, Sir Salman Rushdie, Allen Ginsberg, Alice Walker, and Louise Erdrich.

COSTS All events are free and open to the public. Donations accepted.

ACCOMMODATIONS Accommodations available at area hotels. Information on overnight accommodations available on website.

ADDITIONAL INFORMATION Schedule and other information available on website.

UNIVERSITY OF WISCONSIN AT MADISON WRITERS INSTITUTE

21 N. Park St., Madison WI 53715-1218. (608)265-3972. **E-mail:** laurie.scheer@wisc.edu. **Website:** https://uwwritersinstitute.wisc.edu. Estab. 1990. Annual conference. 2016 dates: April 15-17. Conference on fiction and nonfiction held at the University of Wisconsin at Madison. Guest speakers are published authors, editors, and agents.

COSTS $125-260, depending on discounts and if you attend 1 day or multiple days.

UW-MADISON WRITERS' INSTITUTE

21 N. Park St., Room 7312, Madison WI 53715. (608)265-3972. **Fax:** (608)265-2475. **E-mail:** laurie.scheer@wisc.edu. **Website:** www.uwwritersinstitute.org. **Contact:** Laurie Scheer. Estab. 1989. Annual conference usually held in the spring. Site: Madison Concourse Hotel, downtown Madison, Wisconsin. Average attendance: 600. Conference speakers provide workshops and consultations. For information, send e-mail, visit website, call, or fax. Accepts inquiries by SASE, e-mail, phone, fax. Agents and editors participate in conference.

COSTS $180-330.

ACCOMMODATIONS Provides a list of area hotels or lodging options.

ADDITIONAL INFORMATION Sponsors contest.

WESTERN RESERVE WRITERS & FREELANCE CONFERENCE

7700 Clocktower Dr., Kirtland OH 44094. (440)525-7812. **E-mail:** deencr@aol.com. **Website:** www.deannaadams.com. **Contact:** Deanna Adams, director and conference coordinator. Estab. 1983. Annual. Last conference held September 26, 2015. Conference duration: 1 day or half-day. Average attendance: 120. "The Western Reserve Writers Conference is designed for all writers, aspiring and professional, and offer presentations in all genres—nonfiction, fiction, poetry, essays, and creative nonfiction. There are sessions on the business of writing, including Web writing and successful freelance writing." Site: Located in the main building of Lakeland Community College, the conference is just off the I-90 freeway. Included throughout the day are one-on-one editing consults, a Q&A panel, and author signings.

ADDITIONAL INFORMATION Brochures for the conferences are available by January (for spring conference) and July (for the fall event). Also accepts inquiries by e-mail and phone. Editors always attend the conferences. Private editing consultations are available, as well.

WILLAMETTE WRITERS CONFERENCE

2108 Buck St., West Linn OR 97068. (503)305-6729. **Fax:** (503)344-6174. **Website:** www.willamettewriters. com/wwcon. Estab. 1981. Annual conference held in August. Conference duration: 3 days. Average attendance: 600. "Willamette Writers is open to all writers, and we plan our conference accordingly. We offer workshops on all aspects of fiction, nonfiction, marketing, the creative process, screenwriting, and more. Also, we invite top-notch inspirational speakers for keynote addresses. We always include at least 1 agent or editor panel and offer a variety of topics of interest to writers." Agents will be speaking and available for meetings with attendees.

COSTS Pricing schedule available online.

ACCOMMODATIONS If necessary, arrangements can be made on an individual basis through the conference hotel. Special rates may be available.

ADDITIONAL INFORMATION Brochure/guidelines are available for a catalog-sized SASE.

WOMEN WRITING THE WEST

8547 E. Araphoe Rd., Box J-541, Greenwood Village CO 80112-1436. **E-mail:** conference@womenwrit ingthewest.org, pamelanowak@hotmail.com. **Website:** www.womenwritingthewest.org. 2016 conference dates: October 13-16; location: Santa Fe, New Mexico. "Women Writing the West is a nonprofit association of writers, editors, publishers, agents, booksellers, and other professionals writing and promoting the women's West. As such, these women write their stories of the American West in a way that illuminates them authentically. In addition, the organization provides support, encouragement, and inspiration to all women writing about any facet of the American West. Membership is open to all interested persons worldwide. Open to students. Members actively exchange ideas on a list e-bulletin board. WWW membership also allows the choice of participation in our marketing marvel, and the annual WWW Catalog of Authors' Books. An annual conference is held every fall. Our blog, Facebook, and ListServ publish current WWW activities. We also share market research and articles of interest pertaining to American West literature and member news. Sponsors annual WILLA Literary Award, which is given in several categories for outstanding literature featuring women's stories, set in the West. The winner of a WILLA receives a cash award and a trophy at the annual conference. Con-

test open to nonmembers. Annual conference held the third weekend in October. Covers research, writing techniques, multiple genres, marketing/promotion, and more. Agents and editors will be speaking and available for one-on-one meetings with attendees. Conference location changes each year."

COSTS See website. Discounts available for members, and for specific days only.

ACCOMMODATIONS See website for location and accommodation details.

WORDS & MUSIC

Words & Music, A Literary Feast in New Orleans, The Pirate's Alley Faulkner Society, Inc., 624 Pirate's Alley, New Orleans LA 70116. (504)586-1609. **E-mail:** faulkhouse@aol.com. **Website:** www.wordsand music.org. **Contact:** Rosemary James. Estab. 1997. Annual conference held in November. Conference duration: 5 days. Average attendance: 300. Presenters include authors, agents, editors, and publishers. Past speakers include agents Deborah Grosvenor, Judith Weber, Stuart Bernstein, Nat Sobel, Jeff Kleinman, Emma Sweeney, Liza Dawson, Brettne Bloom, Jennifer Weltz, and Michael Murphy; editors Sarah Crichton, Brenda Copeland, Andra Miller, Kristine Puopolo, Webster Younce, Ann Patty, Will Murphy, Jofie Ferrari-Adler, and Elizabeth Stein; critics Marie Arana, Jonathan Yardley, and Michael Dirda; fiction writers Adam Johnson, Julia Glass, Stewart O'Nan, Tom Franklin, Tom Piazza, Tea Obreht, Robert Goolrick, Oscar Hijuelos, Robert Olen Butler, Shirley Ann Grau, Mayra Montero, Ana Castillo, and Horacio Castellenos-Moya. Agents and editors critique mss in advance then meet with attendees one-on-one during the conference. A detailed schedule of master classes and workshops is available online.

COSTS See website for a costs and additional information on accommodations. Website will update closer to date of conference.

ACCOMMODATIONS Room block available at Hotel Monteleone and sister hotel, Bienville House in New Orleans.

ADDITIONAL INFORMATION Winners of 2016 William Faulkner Creative Writing Competition will be presented at Words & Music.

⊙ WRITE CANADA

The Word Guild, Suite 226, 245 King George Rd., Brantford Onatrio N3R 7N7 Canada. **E-mail:** write canada@thewordguild.com. **Website:** thewordguild.com/events/write-canada. Conference duration: 3 days. Annual conference in Ontario for writers who are Christian of all types and at all stages. Offers solid instruction, stimulating interaction, exciting challenges, and worshipful community.

ADDITIONAL INFORMATION Write Canada is the nation's largest Christian writers' conference held annually. Each year hundreds of writers, editors, authors, journalists, columnists, bloggers, poets, and playwrights gather to hone their craft at the three-day conference. Over the past 3 decades, Write Canada has successfully equipped writers and editors, beginner to professional, from all across North America.

WRITE ON THE SOUND

City of Edmonds Arts Commission, Frances Anderson Center, 700 Main St., Edmonds WA 98020. (425)771-0228. **E-mail:** wots@edmondswa.gov. **Website:** www.writeonthesound.com. Estab. 1985. Intimate, affordable annual conference focused on the craft of writing. Held the first weekend in October. 2016 dates: September 30 through October 2. Conference duration: 2.5 days. Average attendance: 300. Features 30 presenters, a literary contest, ms critiques, roundtable discussions, book signing reception, onsite bookstore, and opportunity to network with faculty and attendees. Edmonds is located just north of Seattle on the Puget Sound.

COSTS See website for complete information.

ADDITIONAL INFORMATION Schedule posted on website mid-June. Registration open by late July.

WRITERS@WORK WRITING RETREAT

P.O. Box 711191, Salt Lake City UT 84171-1191. (801)996-3313. **E-mail:** jennifer@writersatwork.org. **Website:** www.writersatwork.org. Estab. 1985. Annual conference held in June. (The 2016 conference was June 15-19.) Conference duration: 4 days. Average attendance: 45. Workshop topics include a focus on novel, advanced fiction, generative fiction, nonfiction, poetry, and young adult fiction. Afternoon sessions will include craft lectures, discussions, and directed interviews with authors and editors. In addition to the traditional, one-on-one ms consultations, there will be many opportunities to mingle informally with visiting writers and editors. Held at the Alta Lodge in Alta Lodge, Utah. Speakers have included Steve Almond, Bret

Lott, Shannon Hale, Emily Forland (Wendy Weil Agency), Julie Culver (Folio Literary Management), Chuck Adams (Algonquin Press), and Mark A. Taylor (Juniper Press).

COSTS $650-1,000, based on housing type and consultations.

ACCOMMODATIONS Onsite housing available. Additional lodging information is on the website.

WRITERS CONFERENCE AT OCEAN PARK

P.O. Box 172, Assonet ME 02702. (401)598-1424. **E-mail:** jbrosnan@jwu.edu. **Website:** www.oceanpark.org. Estab. 1941. Annual conference held in mid-August. Conference duration: 4 days. Average attendance: 50. "We try to present a balanced and eclectic conference. In addition to time and attention given to poetry, we also have children's literature, mystery writing, travel, fiction, nonfiction, journalism, and other issues of interest to writers. Our speakers are editors, writers, and other professionals. Our concentration is, by intention, a general view of writing to publish with supportive encouragement. We are located in Ocean Park, a small seashore village 14 miles south of Portland, Maine. Ours is a summer assembly center with many buildings from the Victorian age. The conference meets in Porter Hall, one of the assembly buildings which is listed in the National Register of Historic Places. Speakers have included Michael C. White (novelist/short story writer), Betsy Shool (poet), Suzanne Strempek Shea (novelist), John Perrault (poet), Anita Shreve (novelist), Dawn Potter (poet), Bruce Pratt (fiction writer), Amy McDonald (children's author), Sandell Morse (memoirist), Kate Chadbourne (singer/songwriter), Wesley McNair (poet and Maine faculty member), and others. We usually have about 8 guest presenters each year." Writers/editors will be speaking, leading workshops, and available for meetings with attendees. Workshops start at 8:30 a.m. on Tuesday and continue through Friday. Opening event is Monday at 4 p.m.

COSTS $200. The fee does not include housing or meals, which must be arranged separately.

ACCOMMODATIONS "An accommodations list is available. We are in a summer resort area where motels, guest houses, and restaurants abound."

ADDITIONAL INFORMATION 2016 marks the conference's 76th anniversary.

WRITER'S DIGEST CONFERENCES

F+W: A Content and eCommerce Company, 10151 Carver Rd., Suite 200, Blue Ash OH 45242. (877)436-7764. **E-mail:** writersdigestconference@fwmedia.com. **Website:** www.writersdigestconference.com. **Contact:** Taylor Sferra. Estab. 1995. The Writer's Digest conferences feature an amazing lineup of speakers to help writers with the craft and business of writing. Each calendar year typically features multiple conferences around the country. In 2016, the New York conference will be August 12-14 at the New York Hilton Midtown. The most popular feature of the east coast conference is the agent pitch slam, in which potential authors are given the ability to pitch their books directly to agents. For more details, see the website. There will be a 2016 west coast event in October 2016.

COSTS Cost varies by location and year. There are typically different pricing options for those who wish attend the pitch slam and those who just want to attend the conference education.

ACCOMMODATIONS A block of rooms at the event hotel are reserved for guests. See the travel page on the website for more information.

WRITERS IN PARADISE

Eckerd College, 4200 54th Ave. S, St. Petersburg FL 33711. (727)864-7994. **Fax:** (727)864-7575. **E-mail:** wip@eckerd.edu. **Website:** writersinparadise.eckerd.edu. Estab. 2005. Annual event held in January. Conference duration: 8 days. Average attendance: 84 maximum. Workshop. Offers college credit. "Writers in Paradise Conference offers workshop classes in fiction (novel and short story), poetry, and nonfiction. Working closely with our award-winning faculty, students will have stimulating opportunities to ask questions and learn valuable skills from fellow students and authors at the top of their form. Most importantly, the intimate size and secluded location of the Writers in Paradise experience allows you the time and opportunity to share your mss, critique one another's work, and discuss the craft of writing with experts and peers who can help guide you to the next level." Previous faculty includes Andre Dubus III (*House of Sand and Fog*), Michael Koryta (*So Cold the River*), Dennis Lehane (*The Given Day*), Laura Lippman (*I'd Know You Anywhere*), Seth Fishman (literary agent), Johnny Temple (Akashic Books), and more. Editors and agents attend the conference.

ADDITIONAL INFORMATION Application (December deadline) materials are required for prospective attendees.

WRITERS' LEAGUE OF TEXAS AGENTS & EDITORS CONFERENCE

Writers' League of Texas, 611 S. Congress Ave., Suite 200 A-3, Austin TX 78704. (512)499-8914. **E-mail:** conference@writersleague.org, jennifer@writersleague.org. **Website:** www.writersleague.org. **Contact:** Jennifer Ziegler, program director. Estab. 1982. Annual event held in June. For writers at every stage of their career, this standout conference includes panel discussions, genre-specific meetings, one-on-one consultations with top notch agents and editors, keynote speakers, and opportunities to network and connect.

COSTS Registration opens December 1 for members only at the early bird rate of $349. After January 5: $389 members / $449 nonmembers. After April 6: $429 members / $489 nonmembers. After June 5: $469 members / $509 nonmembers.

ADDITIONAL INFORMATION Contests and awards programs are offered separately. Brochures are available upon request.

WRITERS WEEKEND AT THE BEACH

P.O. Box 877, Ocean Park WA 98640. (360)665-4367. **E-mail:** director@opretreat.org. **Website:** www.opretreat.org/event/writers-weekend-at-the-beach. **Contact:** Brandon Scheer; Tracie Heskett. Estab. 1992. Annual conference held in March. Conference duration: 2 days. Average attendance: 45. A retreat for writers with an emphasis on poetry, fiction, and nonfiction. Held at the Ocean Park Methodist Retreat Center & Camp. Speakers have included Miralee Ferrell, Leslie Gould, Linda Clare, Birdie Etchison, Colette Tennant, Gail Denham, Patricia Rushford, and Marion Duckworth.

COSTS $200 for full registration before Feb. 15 and $215 after Feb. 15.

ACCOMMODATIONS Offers onsite overnight lodging.

WRITE-TO-PUBLISH CONFERENCE

WordPro Communication Services, 9118 W. Elmwood Dr., Suite 1G, Niles IL 60714-5820. (847)296-3964. **Fax:** (847)296-0754. **E-mail:** lin@writetopublish.com. **Website:** www.writetopublish.com. **Contact:** Lin Johnson, director. Estab. 1971. Annual. 2016

Conference dates: June 8-11. Average attendance: 200. Conference is focused for the Christian market and includes classes on writing for children. Writer workshops geared toward all levels. Open to students. Site: Wheaton College, Wheaton, IL (near Chicago).

COSTS Call or e-mail for more information.

ADDITIONAL INFORMATION Conference information available in January. For details, visit website, or e-mail brochure@writetopublish.com. Accepts inquiries by e-mail, fax, and phone.

WRITING AND ILLUSTRATING FOR YOUNG READERS CONFERENCE

1480 E. 9400 S, Sandy UT 84093. **E-mail:** staff@wifyr. com. **Website:** www.wifyr.com. Estab. 2000. Annual workshop. June 2016 dates: June 13-17. Conference duration: 5 days. Average attendance: 100+. Learn how to write, illustrate, and publish in the children's and young adult markets. Beginning and advanced writers and illustrators are tutored in a small-group workshop setting by published authors and artists and receive instruction from and network with editors, major publishing house representatives, and literary agents. Afternoon attendees get to hear practical writing and publishing tips from published authors, literary agents, and editors. Held at the Waterford School in Sandy, Utah. Speakers have included John Cusick, Stephen Fraser, Alyson Heller, and Ruth Katcher.

COSTS Costs available online.

ACCOMMODATIONS A block of rooms are available at the Best Western Cotton Tree Inn in Sandy, UT at a discounted rate. This rate is good as long as there are available rooms.

ADDITIONAL INFORMATION There is an online form to contact this event.

WYOMING WRITERS CONFERENCE

E-mail: president@wyowriters.org. **Website:** wyowriters.org. **Contact:** Chris Williams. This is a statewide writing conference for writers of Wyoming and neighboring states. 2016 conference dates: June 3-5, in Riverton, Wyoming. Each year, multiple published authors, editors, and literary agents are in attendance to meet with writers and take pitches. The location (city) of the conference varies from year to year.

LITERARY AGENT SPECIALTIES INDEX

CONTEMPORARY ISSUES

CRIME

DETECTIVE

MAINSTREAM

MIDDLE GRADE

SHORT STORY COLLECTIONS

SPORTS

SUPERNATURAL

SUSPENSE

THRILLER

URBAN FANTASY

WAR

WESTERNS

WOMEN'S

YOUNG ADULT

NONFICTION

AGRICULTURE

AMERICANA

ANIMALS

ANTHROPOLOGY

ARCHEOLOGY

ARCHITECTURE

BUSINESS

CULTURAL INTERESTS

CURRENT AFFAIRS

EDUCATION

ENVIRONMENT

ETHNIC

FILM

FOODS

HISTORY

AGENT NAME INDEX

Westberg, Phyllis (Harold Ober Associates) 223

Westwood, Bruce (Westwood Creative Artists, Ltd.) 257

Whalen, Kimberly (Trident Media Group) 250

White, Melissa (Folio Literary Management, LLC) 168

White, Trena (Transatlantic Literary Agency) 249

Williams, Mary (Robert Lecker Agency) 202

Willig, John (Literary Services, Inc.) 206

Wing, Eric (The Carolyn Jenks Agency) 194

Winick, Eugene H., Esq. (McIntosh & Otis, Inc.) 216

Winston, Lois (Ashley Grayson Literary Agency) 180

Wiseman, Caryn (Andrea Brown literary Agency, Inc.) 144

Witherell, Jenny (Inkwell Management, LLC) 192

Witherspoon, Kimberly (Inkwell Management, LLC) 192

Witte, Michelle (Mansion Street Literary Management) 210

Witthohn, Christine (Book Cents Literary Agency, LLC) 135

Wofford-Girand, Sally (Union Literary) 252

Wojcik, Tim (Levine Greenberg Rostan Literary Agency, Inc.) 203

Wolf, Kent D. (The Friedrich Agency) 174

Wolf, Kirsten (Wolf Literary Services, LLC) 258

Wolfson, Michelle (Wolfson Literary Agency) 258

Wood, Eleanor (Spectrum Literary Agency) 242

Wood, Laura (Fineprint Literary Management) 167

Woods, Monika (Inkwell Management, LLC) 192

Worrall, Anna (The Gernert Company) 177

Wyckoff, Joanne (Carol Mann Agency) 209

Wynne, Tara (Curtis Brown [AUST]

Pty Ltd) 143

Yarbrough, Lena (Inkwell Management, LLC) 192

Yarn, Jason (Jason Yarn Literary Agency) 260

Yoder, Wes (Ambassador Literary Agency & Speakers Bureau) 128

Yoon, Howard (Ross Yoon Agency) 234

Yorke, Laura (Carol Mann Agency) 209

Young, Cy (Hartline Literary Agency) 185

Young, Erin (Dystel & Goderich Literary Management) 161

Zacker, Marietta (Nancy Gallt Literary Agency) 175

Zahler, Karen Gantz (Karen Gantz Zahler Literary Management and Attorney at Law) 261

Zavala, Megan Close (Keller Media, Inc.) 195

Zimmerman, Helen (Helen Zimmerman Literary Agency) 261

Zuckerman, Albert (Writers House) 260